82627

Democratizing the Old Dominion

VIRGINIA AND THE

SECOND PARTY

SYSTEM

1824–1861

Democratizing
the Old Dominion

VIRGINIA AND THE
SECOND PARTY
SYSTEM

1824–1861

William G. Shade

University Press of Virginia

Charlottesville and London

The University Press of Virginia
Copyright © 1996 by the Rector and Visitors
of the University of Virginia

First published 1996

Frontispiece: County Election Number Two by George Caleb Bingham.
(Collection of Mr. and Mrs. Wilson Pile, Jr.)

♾ The paper used in this publication meets the minimum requirements
of the American National Standard for Information Sciences—Permanence
of Paper for Printed Library Materials, ANSI z39.48-1984.

Library of Congress Cataloging-in-Publication Data
Shade, William G.
    Democratizing the Old Dominion : Virginia and the second party
system, 1824–1861 / William G. Shade.
        p.   cm.
    Includes index.
    ISBN 0-8139-1654-2 (alk. paper)
    1. Virginia—Politics and government—1775–1865.   2. Regionalism—
Virginia—History—19th century.   3. Political parties—Virginia—
History—19th century.   I. Title.
F230.S53   1996
320.9755—DC20   96-2709
                                                                      CIP

Printed in the United States of America

For

the past

of William Stephen Shade

and

the future

of Aidan Thomas Newell

"a way a lone a last a loved a long the
riverrun, past Eve and Adam's . . ."

Contents

Contents

8
Political Development and Political Decay 262

Appendixes

Illustrations

Figures

Maps

Maps

Graph

Tables

Preface

*"The full experiment of government democratical, but
representative, was and still is reserved for us."*

Thomas Jefferson to I. H. Tiffany, 1816

IT IS NOT WITHOUT some trepidation that I refer to democracy in the title of this book about partisan politics in antebellum Virginia. As we come to the end of the twentieth century and of the second millennium A.D., scholars and social critics living under the world's oldest constitution have raised a collective cri de coeur concerning the state of democracy in America. An unusual number of such writers insist that the train has been derailed in the relatively recent past and somehow the cars must be righted and gotten back on track. The reasons given for the present predicament and the prescriptions for reform are as varied and various as those who have gathered to assess the damage.

It sometimes seems that the failure of American democracy, however defined, is so obvious that the country's leading intellectuals have put all else aside to focus on the issue. They are not alone in their concern for cultural fragmentation, rampant self-indulgence, social and economic injustice, and widespread political apathy and cynicism about our government and its leaders. The party's over and the polling booths are empty; the spirit of community is dead; civic virtue and civility are relics of the past; democracy has been betrayed by elites who practice politics by other means; and there is no one left to tell the people. There are those, of course, who insist that the problems with American democracy are of less recent vintage and not a few who contend that democracy has never existed and never could in a capitalist country marked by an extravagant commitment to "possessive individualism."

Recently one of the country's most consistently creative historians, Robert Wiebe, has joined the debate about democracy with his book *Self-Rule: A Cultural History of American Democracy* (Chicago, 1995), in which he assays some "sixty-odd studies" produced by philosophers, publicists, and social scientists since the 1960s and concludes that they have been "talking past each other," preaching their jeremiads only to the converted of "their own kind." Not surprisingly he finds most of these writers woefully in need of a historical understanding of the subject. While the thrust of *Self-Rule* deals with prescriptions—to break down hierarchies and disperse power—which are abstract and none too clear in their particulars, Wiebe's general comments about American democracy merit consideration and are directly relevant to this study.

Wiebe insists that historical democracy has involved a political process which in reality never can be fully realized and always "acquires a cluster of characteristics peculiar to time and place." After reciting a litany of what democracy is *not*, he settles on a "spare" definition:

> Its first principle is self-government. Hence it is necessarily political, and as it encompasses many people, it involves tallying judgments and choices in order to register popular decisions. Although opinion polls, group demands, and even individual market choices may have some role to play in the process, elections remain the crucial procedure . . . [but] voting is not enough. . . . To make political participation effective, citizens need the information and the possibilities for association that give them access to the political system, and they need government officials who respond to popular decisions. (8–9)

The relatively informed citizen framing opinions and voting in open elections is the central focus of democracy, but the process is incomplete if the actual governing bodies—legislatures, courts, and administrative apparatus—fail to respond reasonably to the popular will.

Wiebe neither forecloses the debate nor suggests a consensus, but he restates the case for legitimately describing antebellum American politics as democratic while acknowledging the limits of the process. Alexis de Tocqueville was only the most eminent of the swarm of nineteenth-century Europeans who crossed the Atlantic to witness for themselves democracy in action. Most commentators in the United States had little doubt that the democratic day had dawned and they were riding the wave of the future. The country's leading journal of opinion was called the *Democratic Review*. In the presidential election of 1840, both of the newly organized major parties used the words *democracy* or *democratic* as part of their official designation. The following year George Sidney Camp, a northern Whig, produced a commentary on Tocqueville called simply *Democracy*, and his publisher claimed that it was the first book ever designed expressly "to elucidate democratic *theory*." It was followed at the end of the decade with a far more penetrating analysis of *The Nature and Tendency of Free Institutions* by Frederick Grimké, the southern-born Ohio Supreme Court judge who was a Democrat in politics and brother of the famous abolitionists. Grimké justified slavery and Camp dismissed the "woman issue," but both emphasized the broad-based property holding and bourgeois values that placed American democracy in the vanguard of progress. They rejected Tocqueville's fears concerning tyranny of the majority, and exalted public opinion, celebrating man's capacity for self-government.

With its emphasis on elections, the political process, and the vitality of nineteenth-century democracy, Wiebe's approach has a certain traditional air about it. The Progressive historians who dominated professional history up through World War II had portrayed political progress as the "march" of American democracy associated with the stepwise expansion of popular participation in American politics and what they believed to be the constructive response of certain reform-minded politicians. The Consensus historians of midcentury challenged the Progressives' understanding of the dynamics of the process but measured progress in similar terms although they tended to emphasize the effectiveness of political parties dominated by pragmatic politicians who practiced the art of the possible. Rereading these writers and other midcentury theorists of American democracy whom Wiebe chastises, one is struck less by their Cold War chauvinism and conservative elitism than by their heady optimism about the American democracy. It is hard to imagine Richard Hofstadter posing his student Christopher Lasch's question, "Does Democracy Deserve to Survive?"

What follows is the study of the expansion of political participation in a slave state that came late to white manhood suffrage and the partisan response of a government generally committed to the maxim "That government governs best that governs least." It argues implicitly that mass political parties served as the agencies for aggregating the political emotions and interests of an array of social groupings in which individuals had multiple memberships and for articulating policies that could be evaluated both prospectively and retrospectively through regular elections. While the political agenda was hardly all inclusive and ignored some of today's social critics and historians' preferred items, it was widely voiced through an extensive and highly partisan public press, a broad circulation of political documents, and a rhetorical style that featured long and detailed speeches at endless public meetings. There were also extensive, easily available reports of legislative activities and debates in constitutional conventions. It was a society drenched in public information, most of which dealt with politics and religion—the two most popular group activities in antebellum America.

It is in part true, but also highly misleading, to say that I have been working on this project for twenty years. While my initial idea was to write about political culture in mid-nineteenth-century America and a stint as a visiting professor at the University of Virginia encouraged me to begin looking into the Old Dominion's antebellum politics, the present book bears little likeness to its early ancestors. In fact, its main arguments are quite different from those put forward in a paper presented at the 1982 meeting of the American Historical Association, and the style and organization are radically altered from the false start of four chapters written at the end of the decade. Thus there has been a great deal of pulling and hauling, reformulation and revision, and not a little new research on neglected nooks and crannies, that has led to this version of the book.

Any project that has taken as many twists and turns as this over such a long period of time leaves a trail of unpaid debts to friends and fellow scholars who in various ways sustained me through the process—sometimes unknowingly. To try and list them all would be an impossible task. But please humor my attempt knowing that some will be inadvertently slighted.

I have been employed by Lehigh University since 1966, and its office of research (under various names) has supported numerous forays below the Mason-Dixon Line to exploit the marvelous resources of the Library of Congress, the Library of Virginia, the Virginia Historical Society, and the University of Virginia Library. The Lehigh University libraries under the direction of Berry Richards have also graciously purchased materials and enabled me, with the assistance of Bill Finke, to obtain others through interlibrary loan. Steve Lichak and Elia Schoomer struggled with the maps and my patience.

A fellowship from the Virginia Center for the Humanities presided over by Rob Vaughan provided an office for eight months, access to the resources of the University of Virginia, and the intellectual companionship of David Wyatt and Ed Ayers. The Inter-University Consortium of Political and Social Research at the University of Michigan supplied most of the quantitative data used in the voting analysis, although crucial materials were also provided by my old friend Jean Friedman and by Ralph Wooster whom I have never met in person. Dick Holway at the University Press of Virginia endured.

While all of my colleagues in the history department at Lehigh have provided an exemplary environment in which to teach and work, Joe Dowling, Roger Simon, and Jim Saeger encouraged my work at specific points. Chris Daniels appeared at a crucial point to reinvigorate this project. A number of friends and colleagues—Ballard Campbell, Dan Crofts, Tom Jeffrey, Rick Matthews, and Janet Tucker—helped me with careful critical readings of parts or all of the manuscript and generally encouraged my efforts. Joel Silbey and Deborah Van Broekhoven both improved the manuscript in their readings for the press. Special thanks must go to Michael Holt whose extensive comments and repeated readings of the manuscript are responsible for its present form although he basically wanted a different book that someone else may yet write.

There is no way to thank my oldest and finest friends, Lew Gould and Ron Formisano, for the numerous ways in which they have contributed to this book and to my understanding of the American past and of history in general. It is impossible to put into words what their intellectual companionship and stead-fast support have meant to me over the years. The breadth of Lew's interests and his encyclopedic knowledge of American politics continue to amaze me. Although he has a personal publishing record that would be the envy of anyone in the profession, he has always found time to provide a critical reading by re-turn mail, flagging each and every instance of careless and unclear prose. Ron is a volcano of energy, opinion, and insight on practically every topic worth talk-ing about. His wicked commentary on too many versions of some of these chapters lightened the burden imposed by his always incisive criticism. Most of the ideas developed in this book grew out of our conversations over the years of our friendship

Finally, I must thank my most intimate friends, Lou, Alex, and Chris, who are not historians and who have had to put up with "dad lectures" in response to innocent questions and with a husband and father who too often treated them with "benign neglect." Lou has read every word several times over. More important, she has shared my life and provided encouragement, love, and joy beyond measure.

Introduction:
The Partisan Leader

URING THE presidential election campaign of 1835–36, the newborn southern Whigs made their opponent's previous record on slavery the central issue in the South. They forced Martin Van Buren, the vice president and Andrew Jackson's handpicked successor, to issue numerous disclaimers and clarifications and prompted the Democrats in Congress to embrace the gag rule limiting the discussion of antislavery petitions. This commitment to the peculiar institution constituted the Democratic Republican platform in the slave states where the New Yorker was challenged by the Tennessee senator and slaveholder Hugh Lawson White.[1]

The debate in the public press, particularly in Virginia, concentrated on slavery and produced one of the most remarkable campaign documents in American history, *The Partisan Leader*, a novel written by Nathaniel Beverley Tucker, the half brother of John Randolph of Roanoke and a professor of law at the College of William and Mary. Historians and literary scholars interested in this eccentric fire-eater's early commitment to secession have glossed over a delightful irony. Professor Tucker portrayed Van Buren primarily as a corrupt politician seeking a fourth term as president and a symbol of the new democratic order in which party politics held sway. The partisan hero of Tucker's romance was a guerrilla leader of Virginia's secessionist forces in a civil war against the Union over which Van Buren, the unprincipled partisan, presided.[2]

Judge Tucker had been an outspoken opponent of the Missouri Compromise when he served in that territory and later he supported South Carolina in the nullification crisis. The novel broadcast his extreme states' rights position and commitment to the proslavery ideology as well as his advocacy of a southern confederacy headed by his home state. During the 1830s and 1840s his regular contributions to the *Southern Literary Messenger* defending slavery and strict construction of the Constitution, and his proselytizing among his William and Mary students, enhanced his position as an exponent of views more popularly associated with John C. Calhoun and his South Carolina colleagues. Running through all of Tucker's lectures, including the capstone of his career delivered to the delegates at the Nashville Convention in 1850, was his hostility to political parties, universal suffrage, and the "meddling spirit of Democracy" that he argued undermined social order, corrupted civic virtue, and threatened the individual liberty and sanctity of private property. Tucker, an advocate of what William W. Freehling has termed "unlimited paternalism," lived just long enough to curse the constitution of 1851 that finally instituted the reforms that Thomas Jefferson had espoused seventy-five years earlier.[3]

Beverley Tucker's opposition to modern mass parties and political democracy represented a futile effort to sweep back the tide of change rising within the Old Dominion as he wrote. Van Buren's leading Virginia advocate in 1836 was Thomas Ritchie, the editor of the *Richmond Enquirer*, who had helped orchestrate the revival of the New York–Virginia alliance on which the Democratic Republican party was based. Ritchie had agreed with Van Buren that "we must always have party distinctions and the old ones are the best." The Union would be preserved by "the most natural and beneficial" combination "between the planters of the South and the plain Republicans of the North." Although the Virginian retained a certain Jeffersonian ambivalence toward his opponents, whose existence he seemed incapable of rationalizing, and preferred the traditional label "Republican" to the newer "Democracy," Ritchie lived to praise the constitution of 1851. His perspective on the politics of these years spread across the pages of the *Richmond Enquirer* has influenced most historians of the Age of Jackson. "Father" Ritchie had encouraged revision of the commonwealth's constitution and clearly believed that the party led by the heroes of the common man, Thomas Jefferson and Andrew Jackson, acted as the historical agent of democratic reform. At the time of his death in 1854 Ritchie's optimism seemed justified.[4]

Few historians would deny that Alexis de Tocqueville correctly described what he saw in America as true democracy, although it was a democracy exclusively of white men and it implied legal equality within this group rather than equality of condition among them. Above all else Thomas Jefferson emphasized broad participation and actual representation as its essential elements. In the mid-twentieth century, historians and political scientists commonly accepted this equality before the law as the essence of democracy in America and viewed the United States as the primary example of democracy in the modern world. Progress was written by the extension of these rights widening the circle of those included in the community of equals.[5]

Yet it always has seemed inappropriate to write about the politics of antebellum Virginia in these terms since even Herrenvolk democracy was imperfectly realized in the Old Dominion before 1851. When Tocqueville visited the United States in the 1830s, the commonwealth lagged behind the times, retaining property-based suffrage and a system of representation that incorporated a mixture of property and population. The Old Dominion was also a slave state—the largest in the Union—and one generally perceived to be in economic decline, existing on the profits of slave sales to the expanding states of the Cotton South.[6]

In the historical literature Virginia has seemed to be the sum of Thomas Jefferson minus an incredible number of eccentrics led by every historian's favorite, John Randolph, and followed in train by "decadent aristocrats" "favoring heart over head," and reliving scenes from *Ivanhoe*, jousting on the piedmont plain as the modern world passed them by. The Virginia Whigs, who surfaced in the wake of the nullification crisis and were dominated by tidewater conservatives and defenders of states' rights, fought with the national Whigs and died out with Virginia's last nineteenth-century president, John Tyler.[7]

Historians have been unable to focus their lenses clearly upon Jefferson's country. The period from his retirement to the secession crisis has gone practically unstudied except as the backdrop for biographies of sometimes powerful, generally flamboyant and idiosyncratic, but essentially second-rate men. This study addresses the main themes of the history of the commonwealth during these years and integrates them by relating each to party development and the advance of democracy. From this perspective Virginia's experience appears far more similar to that of its sister states than the historical literature has acknowledged.

Professional history in the United States emerged in the late nineteenth century and has continued to reflect many of the aspects of the so-called Progressive period. For the South in general and Virginia in particular, that era combined contrasting strains of traditional commitment and progressive change that tended to associate the "true" Virginia tradition with Jeffersonian insistence on the rights of the states and to equate democracy—and the Democratic party—with the dominance of local elites that gave to the politics of the Old Dominion in the early twentieth century a distinct eighteenth-century cultural cast. The Civil War drew a curtain across the commonwealth's history as though Woodrow Wilson's generation had established some sort of Un-Virginian Activities Committee to expunge evidences of any remotely Yankee-like behavior from the historical record. In this they gained the cooperation of their critics, whose own agendas determined that they would retain certain aspects of the traditionalists' new-made scenario.

This study draws back the curtain and portrays the commonwealth as less exceptional and more commonplace than either its hagiographers or critics have conceded. The Old Dominion typified the nation in that it was actually partitioned during the Civil War. While no state was a microcosm of the whole, Virginia's claims to representing mid-nineteenth-century America are much stronger than those of Massachusetts or Mississippi and superior to those of Pennsylvania, Tennessee, Illinois, or Missouri. The commonwealth resembled its neighbors in striking ways. Economic development proceeded along the lines fairly typical of the other states of the eastern seaboard.

Virginia's party system developed at the same rate, in most of the same ways, and to about the same degree as those in the other states of the Union. It was neither so hyperactive as that of New York nor nearly so comatose as that of South Carolina. The Whigs and Democrats of the Old Dominion stood for the same principles in both state and national politics as did the Democrats and Whigs in the other states and were similar in organization and social composition. Because of the development of a comparatively modern party system by the 1840s, Virginia's politics had become relatively democratic before the actual reform of the state's constitution in 1851.

The constitutional defects of the commonwealth that conflicted with Jefferson's personal sympathies are well known: essentially, subordinates of the patriarchy were disfranchised and the General Assembly was badly malapportioned. Slaves, minors, women, Indians, and quasi-free blacks could not vote although the phrase "white male" did not appear until 1830. The electorate was further limited by the freehold qualification that disfranchised over one-third of the white adult males. Representation of the electorate was skewed in favor of the slaveholding counties in the east since each county had two house seats without reference to either the size of its white population or the number of its eligible voters. But Virginia's constitution of 1776 had created an independent commonwealth that contained elements of a democratic polity. It had a bill of rights limiting arbitrary government, regular and free elections, and a functioning representative assembly that in fact governed the new state. The democratization process during these years involved the achievement of universal white manhood suffrage and a more equitable scheme of representing the expanded "political nation."[8]

Eventually the number of elective offices was increased. This had its greatest impact on local government. Before 1851 the self-perpetuating county courts—the government closest to the people—were the keystone of gentry domination of the political system. By the time it was written into law, however, this shift was mostly symbolic. Partisanship had come to determine these offices, and the property distribution among the members of the Virginia county courts in 1850 was almost exactly the same as that among legislators. Much the same can be said concerning the final tardy implementation of white manhood suffrage. Voter turnout jumped, but the percentage of increase was not nearly so impressive in the early 1850s as it had been in the late 1830s, when the new political parties organized to bring out a larger percentage of the traditional electorate than at any other time in the history of the Old Dominion. The constitutional reform of the elective system similarly produced little social change in the course of the decade before the Civil War. Rather it ratified a restructuring already well advanced.

The process involved the increased social democracy inherent in a leveling of status differences within the political sphere. Nineteenth-century democracy was associated with competitive, modern parties. In the Old Dominion they evolved slowly, emerging first with relatively limited scope and function but eventually facilitating broad participation of the electorate and an increased articulation of popular demands. The nature of the political elite changed, consequently, in two distinct ways. The social origins of the governors, legislators, and members of constitutional conventions came to resemble more closely those of the electorate, thus narrowing the social distance between voters and officeholders. At the same time the nature of representation changed as politicians competed for the voters' favor with promises to protect the people's interests and respond to their demands. Increasingly these new men, who so offended Beverley Tucker, pandered to the voters with populistic promises and mass media campaigns for office.

While Virginia may have lagged behind the new western states and failed to keep pace with some of the original thirteen rebellious provinces, the commonwealth was not only one of a confederation of democratic republics, but it also closely resembled the others in practically every other relevant way. European visitors surveying American democracy looked upon Virginia as a prime example of the phenomenon they came to damn or praise. The democratization of the Old Dominion coincided with the democratization of the new nation. The conditions occurring elsewhere that encouraged this advance generated change within the state at a pace only slightly less swift than in its most advanced neighbors.[9]

The constitutional rules of the game, such as winner-take-all presidential elections and single-member districts, determined that a series of two-party systems would emerge. As the social order hypothesized by republican ideologues failed to materialize, voluntary associations filled the functional void. These extraconstitutional structures provided a mechanism for the translation of the will of the majority expressed through periodic elections into the basis for legitimate government between elections without the necessity of separate referenda on each and every issue to arise "in the course of human events." A liberal capitalist society, in which classical civic virtue was in short supply, necessitated a new technology that performed the functions of the political socialization and recruitment while articulating and aggregating diverse interests.[10]

The Old Dominion was a huge and diverse state that during the period from the end of the War of 1812 through the mid-nineteenth century underwent the same dynamic economic and social development that characterized the country as a whole. While thousands of men born in Virginia moved west and at specific times even some of the wealthiest families suffered, the economic decline of the Old Dominion and the exceptionalism of Virginia have been grossly exaggerated. In the years following the depression of the early 1820s, social and economic development underlay the emergence of the second party system. By most standards the society of antebellum Virginia displayed the social and economic characteristics that accompanied the appearance of nineteenth-century democracy across the new nation. Its population grew rapidly; its economy both expanded and developed; its sundry people prospered and became more diverse as they became more numerous.

The republican ideology of the Revolution hostilely portrayed factions and parties as illegitimate conspiracies of self-interested parts acting against the general good of the people as a whole. The commonwealth ideal implied a consensus of communal interest in a homogeneous society. The Founding Fathers erected a "constitution against parties" with its separation of powers, division of functions, and cumbersome electoral rules. Yet Jefferson's generation remained ambivalent about parties just as classical republicanism was blended with, and eventually overwhelmed by, the burgeoning strains of their liberal individualism. Men like Madison seemed unable to decide if parties were a positive good or a necessary evil.[11]

The Jeffersonian generation used the word *party* loosely, and their descriptions did not denote the kind of institutions that would emerge in the 1830s. Most studies of parties have ignored the developmental dimension, paying little attention to differences of style, structure, and function of the successive party systems. The need for the aggregation and articulation of interests arose from the growing complexity of the society and the liberal, "pragmatic-bargaining" style long associated with American party politics replaced the republican, "absolute value" style of both the Federalists and Jeffersonians.[12]

The Democrats and Whigs expressed new patterns of behavior and emotional commitment. Each consisted of substructures populated by three classes of partisans: those who voted for the party's candidates; those who held office and actually governed; and the cadre who staffed the party organizations and managed their election campaigns. During the second party system the major parties thus conformed to the Key/Sorauf model of modern political parties. In reality these demarcations are by no means clear, nor are the categories mutually exclusive, but rather this tripartite conception permits students of party politics to focus upon one aspect of the structure at a time and to conceive of development in terms of the configuration of these elements.[13]

As the second party system emerged, the development of party organization and the penetration of partisan activity into all of the counties of the commonwealth prompted the expansion of popular participation. By the 1840s voter turnout came to include almost all of those eligible, and a sizable number of voters were involved in the activities of county committees. Although some critics of the "new political history" have decried its emphasis on electoral behavior, few would deny the centrality of voluntary popular participation to any definition of a democratic polity. Beyond that, however, the participants need to believe in the efficacy of their political activity. In Virginia the rise in voter turnout was directly connected to the parties' campaigns that involved increased organizational development and the exploitation of the new technologies of communication. By 1850 sixty-two political newspapers were being published in the state, and fifteen of them were dailies.[14]

Party development in the Old Dominion followed stages similar to those sketched in the other states of the Union. Both the nature of the institutions and their conflict over issues mirrored the behavioral patterns of Whigs and Democrats not only in the other southern states but also in those north of the Mason-Dixon Line as well. What happened reveals both the character and the limits of the democracy in Tocqueville's America. There were pockets of Adams support in Virginia in 1828, but the election that year was not very competitive, nor did it involve an exceptionally high turnout. Rapidly after 1836 counties gained a partisan coloring and voted very consistently for one side or the other. By 1840 the percentage of white adult males participating doubled, and two evenly matched parties fought for the vote in the Old Dominion.[15]

During the participant phase of this party period, voter turnout came close to being universal among eligible white men. In that sense it was an era of the common man. Men moved in and out of the electorate seemingly choosing when to vote and for which offices to vote as it suited them, but they consistently behaved in a partisan fashion. Most Virginians shared their fellow Americans' ambivalent faith that governmental authority and individual freedom could coexist. The price of liberty was eternal vigilance. Voting was a generally retrospective but positive act of control over their representatives by punishing them for their misdeeds. Yet in its minimalist way the Old Dominion was governed. Its General Assembly fought publicly every year for three dreary winter months about just what that might mean. Twice conventions gathered to reformulate the rules of the game and define anew the nature of limited government based on the sovereignty of the people.[16]

In early America the idea of representation evolved from widespread deference to the disinterested members of the social elite who supposedly knew how to blend the various demands for justice into the common good toward actual representation of local and group interests in the cosmopolitan legislative body where the equivalent of Adam Smith's invisible hand molded public virtue from the private vices of diverse interests. American democrats came to believe by the 1830s that their legislatures should reflect the political community and give legal sanction in some fashion to its multifocal desires through adherence to the will of the majority.[17]

Before 1851, Virginia's bicameral General Assembly constituted the government of the commonwealth, and its governors were little more than the executive officers of the legislature, often setting forth policy proposals in their messages but having little ability to see that they were implemented. Thus any consideration of the growth of democracy in the Old Dominion must look at the social background of the legislators who controlled the commonwealth and at what that government actually did. Who sat in the assembly? What sort of laws did it enact? Finally, whose interests were served by those laws?

The answer to these questions involves further investigation of the ways in which interests were represented in antebellum Virginia, a line of questioning that leads directly to the expanding role of political parties and, in fact, to their very invention as a vehicle for the aggregation of popular demands and the articulation of public policy. Along with the expansion of public participation came a shift in the social origins of the members of the Virginia assembly, and with these, clear changes in legislative behavior that characterized the second party system. The colonial assemblies were composed of the indigenous social and economic elites who eventually provided the leadership of the rebellion. The Revolution in Virginia left most of these men in power as the first-among-equals in an expanded and, consequently, more "common" elite, but the socio-economic profile of Virginia legislators changed greatly between Jefferson's death and midcentury. Most legislators owned slaves and typified the "ruling race," but few were planters, who owned twenty or more slaves. The assembly mirrored at least the "political nation" of common white men more nearly than ever before.[18]

Legislative parties developed first as a response to national issues and then expanded to encompass state issues such as money and banking in the depression years of the late 1830s and early 1840s. Voting behavior in the House of Delegates defined the different issue orientations of the Whigs and Democrats and the relationship between partisanship and policy. Not all issues engendered party disagreement, and the rank order of the issues in each party's policy agenda differed. Those roll calls that continued to elicit the greatest party unity were related to the maintenance of the party as an institution. In the late 1840s, with a general improvement in the economic environment, local demands for internal improvements increasingly overwhelmed the business of the assembly. Consequently, partisanship appears to have weakened, but on traditionally partisan questions there continued to be a sharp division between the Democrats and the Whigs. Internal improvements as a general policy issue separated the parties, but individual votes were at heart matters of local self-interest and the trading of favors, something that partisans accepted as a corollary of legitimate behavior in a system made up of inclusive parties and geographically defined constituencies.[19]

The second party system in the Old Dominion achieved a much higher degree of development than had its predecessor, if in fact the party fragments of the Jeffersonian era can be said to have formed a system at all. Both the Whigs and the Democrats wore the trappings of party: recognizable labels, party platforms, state and national nominating conventions, and an increasingly elaborate committee structure that reached down into the rural neighborhoods of the commonwealth. Each party generated a flood of printed propaganda, and legions of speakers brought the party message to every county in the state. Popular participation and electoral competition penetrated into and structured all elements of the political system.[20]

Policy was the product of compromise rather than the translation of party promises directly into legislation, because of the close balance between the parties in the legislature as well as in the electorate. Self-interest and/or constituent interests often conflicted with party programs. In contrast to their republican predecessors, these democratic politicians were more willing to claim publicly that they represented the self-interest of their constituents, although they associated this with the will of the majority. While it is difficult to explain exactly how all of the elements of the major party coalitions came to accept a common policy agenda, various forms of self-interest account for both the consistent cohesion and the intermittent deviation, as in the case of the soft money Democrats who broke with the party on banking legislation.[21]

Such clear partisan division within the General Assembly raises obvious questions concerning the connection between policy and public opinion since all definitions of representative democracy have implied some form of linkage between the legislators and the voters—some rational relationship between the party-in-the-legislature and the party-in-the-electorate. Contemporaries often described the parties as representing different elements of society. John Herbert Claiborne, the son of a Jacksonian congressman and himself a Democratic politician, expressed clearly in his reminiscences the conventional wisdom concerning the social basis of his opponents when he wrote: "The Whig Party . . . represented the conservative element of Virginia . . . the culture and the wealth of the State. It was the party of the cities and of the older and eastern sections . . .

the party of the low grounds on the big rivers, and the party of the old colonial mansions." To this he added that the "old Whigs," for whom he showed considerable sympathy, "knew each other by the instincts of gentlemen."[22]

Most often historians have relied on rationalist-activist models that emphasize the primacy of economic issues and correlate the behavior of legislators with the economic interests of their constituents. The historian of the Virginia Whigs described the conflict between the Jacksonians and their opponents as "in large part a class struggle" in which the "non-slaveholding Germans" of the Valley and the "small independent farmers" in the counties of the southwest typified the Democrats. Large slaveholders in the east and those nascent manufacturers involved in the production of salt, iron, and woolens in the west were the backbone of the Whig party. In sharp contrast, the historian of iron manufacturing in antebellum Virginia drew the conflict—at least within the confines of postbellum Virginia, which includes the southwest and most of the Valley— as one of "planters versus industrialists." She emphasized Whig strength in the cities and towns of the Old Dominion and the planter base of the eastern Democracy. Neither of these studies is sufficiently detailed to sustain their contradictory contentions. Further, both leave out large classes of voters—actually many more than they include—making impossible any attempt to connect the social groups supporting each of the parties and preventing as well any evaluation of the influence of the parties' coalitional structure on their policy orientations.[23]

Traditional generalizations have been based on indeterminate and often fragmentary discussions of the sectional divisions of the Old Dominion that require serious revision. The geographical pattern of Virginia voting during the second party system became far more complex than it had been in the Jeffersonian era. The spread of party competition into all of the regions and constituencies of the state differentiated the two periods of party politics as clearly as did the growth in voter participation.

Most inferences about Virginia voting behavior that continue to make their way into general studies are either factually inaccurate or so fragmentary that they sustain totally false impressions. Neither the Democrats nor the Whigs can be accurately described as "the party of the west" or, conversely, "the party of the tidewater." Regional subdivision yields some clusters of partisan concentration, but even these were few and scattered around the commonwealth. The Federalists were a "sectarian" party representing regional interests arrayed against the Republican center, but both the Democrats and the Whigs were "inclusive" parties composed of complex coalitions of various overlapping interests.[24]

Since neither party was exclusive, each contained elements with different marginal tendencies toward support and a different mix of conflicting components. The Whigs consistently prevailed in the towns and town-dominated counties—what historians with slight exaggeration have sometimes termed "urban/commercial" areas, which some recent historians have hypothesized were closely connected to "the market." The Democrats did better than their opponents in the tobacco-growing areas dominated by slaveholding planters. They were the party of the farmers and planters—large and small—while the Whigs appealed to those involved in nonagricultural pursuits regardless of wealth. These economic groups that disproportionately favored one party over the other describe the largest elements of each party's coalition, but other forms of group affiliation interacted with these economic influences.[25]

While the most detailed study of the Virginia Democratic Republicans insisted that ethnicity and religion did not influence voting, the analysis of both polling place "neighborhoods" and individual voters shows ethnoreligious factors to have been crucial determinants of partisan identification for a significant number of voters. The importance of neighborhoods clustered around churches with a community core of kinship networks can hardly be exaggerated. Men tended to participate in politics in groups rather than as individuals and statewide coalitions involved both denominational and ethnic cohesion.

The most visible ethnoreligious group, the traditional German Lutherans, were the most Democratic constituency in the Old Dominion, and within this group economic differences only modestly affected individual political behavior. Ethnicity, especially when reinforced by religion, was clearly more salient for members of some groups than others and produced greater political cohesion within these groups. Inevitably these groups overlapped and reinforced each other, and local context, the politics of one's friends and family, was the most important determinant of voting behavior in antebellum Virginia, just as it was elsewhere throughout the United States.[26]

Traditionally historians of Virginia have minimized the differences between the Whigs and Democrats and posited a shift in political culture from Jeffersonian liberalism to Calhounite conservatism. They have emphasized the evolution of the proslavery argument from the uneasy acceptance of slavery as a necessary evil to the comfortable embrace of the peculiar institution as a positive good and the transformation of the appeal to states' rights from a democratic assertion of the will of local majorities to a conservative protection of the sectional minority rights. These two were obviously linked. The minority to be protected was the southern slaveholders (and the many southern whites who aspired to their social position) whose rights were defined by state laws.[27]

One formulation of this argument insists that "the economic or social and cultural basis for who became Whigs and Democrats" was essentially irrelevant, because a shared commitment to racism and the peculiar institution ensured that "the politics of slavery" rather than "a politics defined by economics and finance" determined political behavior in the Old Dominion. "Slavery issues always occupied center stage" during presidential elections, and the Whigs and Democrats disagreed primarily on who best represented the interests of slaveholders and the rights of the southern states. While there is a great deal of evidence to sustain the view that both parties were proslavery, this evidence fails to support either the claim that other concerns were less important in determining political behavior or the assertion that the parties took the same position on the sundry slavery-related issues.[28]

The "peculiar institution" gave rise to a variety of policy questions, but ending slavery in the foreseeable future was never an option. At most, Virginians considered the viability of slavery within the commonwealth, entertaining the possibility of eliminating the institution west of the Blue Ridge while retaining it in the east where the majority of the population was black or suggesting the gradual sale of economically redundant slaves to the states farther south, a policy that Virginians claimed was based on the experience of New York and New Jersey. Closely connected but logically separate were questions concerning the position of free blacks in the Old Dominion and projects for their colonization, which some people joined with schemes for gradual emancipation but generally were designed to rid the commonwealth of its growing free black population.

The dominant response to slavery during the Jeffersonian era—at least among those who chose to discuss the matter publicly—focused upon questions of racial accommodation moderated by random outpourings of guilt. Those whose concern did not quickly subside channeled their energies into the colonization movement, which spread an umbrella broad enough to accommodate thoughts of gradual emancipation and the salvation of perpetual slavery. Following the uprising in Southampton County led by Nat Turner, the Virginia House of Delegates gave over one week to the traumatic debate on the propriety of considering the issue of emancipation. The "great debate" defined the limits of antislavery in the Old Dominion, and the roll-call votes in the house reflect the spectrum of acceptable opinion on the issues related to the peculiar institution. The lines of conflict were primarily sectional, with the center challenged by the periphery, but curious partisan overtones placed the majority of Republicans in the conservative camp and the ex-Federalists, National Republicans, and future Whigs among the reformers.[29]

In the course of the next two decades, the arguments that had been heard in the great debate were developed in the public press, and a new, more self-conscious defense of slavery emerged. While Virginians articulated nearly all of the elements of the proslavery ideology during the 1830s and 1840s, the most widely held views tied slavery to republicanism and the rights and liberties of whites, justifying its existence to an evangelical audience through reference to the Bible. The critics of slavery in the Old Dominion also basically emphasized the peculiar institution's effect on whites and usually insisted on the inefficiency of slavery and the superiority of free labor in the quest for economic progress. As a consequence, both parties played the politics of slavery, but those who questioned slavery and pictured its economic effects as detrimental to the development of the state tended to be Whigs. The Whigs held a much more ambivalent view of slavery than their Democratic opponents who increasingly associated themselves with the protection of the rights of white men to hold slave property.[30]

By the 1840s the defense of slavery had become so thoroughly entwined with states' rights that those asserting even the moderate Madisonian version of constitutional nationalism were considered in the minds of many Virginians to be abolitionists. Those making such charges were invariably Democrats, who repeatedly referred to theirs as the party of states' rights and wrote a commitment to the Doctrines of '98 into their party platform. Since they denied Madison's interpretation of his views and questioned Jefferson on the principles associated with the Northwest Ordinance, the advocates of southern rights clearly conflicted with the originators of the "Virginia ideas" although they shared corresponding conceptions of the Constitution and took a similar rhetorical stance.

These differences have led one constitutional historian to assert that there were two "very different, and even incompatible, strains of states' rights thought." The liberal democratic version associated with Jefferson "triumphed with the election of Andrew Jackson," who along with "many Virginians advocated states' rights to secure majority rule; [while] proslavery interests espoused the doctrine of states' rights to protect the interests of a minority . . . [and threatened] the continued existence of the Union." This interpretation takes constitutional arguments as seriously as did the men of the time — far more seriously than the Progressive historians who saw noneconomic arguments other than their own as "claptrap" — but it tends to overrate the support of Virginia advocates of states' rights (other than Jefferson) for democracy and underrates the importance of the slavery question for Virginians (including Jefferson) before the nullification controversy. The debate among the Virginia elite produced a revival of antifederalism among the advocates of states' rights that eventually made the interpretation of the Constitution an important distinction between the Democrats and the Whigs.[31]

Both arguments — that emphasizing the politics of slavery and that declaring the commonwealth to have been characterized by a democratic version of states' rights before 1832 — assume that Virginians were of one mind on the issue and that the party battle had the "hollow sound of a stage duel with tin swords." The contest between the Jacksonian Democrats and the Whigs, they argue, had ended by the early 1840s, and there was little continuity between

Jackson's supporters and the increasingly proslavery Democracy. Their Whigs appear only in the guise of Calhounites who were at best short-term, fretful allies and Tyler's "awkward squad." In fact, most Virginia Whigs stood for constitutional views similar to those of Madison and Marshall. As on most other political issues, they were in the camp of Henry Clay, who was by birth a Virginian and always campaigned vigorously in the Old Dominion. As mainstream Whigs of the upper South, two of their leaders, William B. Preston and Alexander H. H. Stuart, were rewarded with positions in the now forgotten cabinets of Zachary Taylor and Millard Fillmore.

The nullification crisis split the supporters of the Jackson administration in the General Assembly but failed to produce a new alignment of parties. While some of the advocates of nullification eventually did join the anti-Jackson coalition, most of those who supported states' rights and opposed Jackson's proclamation to South Carolina remained within Democratic ranks and, in fact, made up a majority of the party's leaders. The commonwealth's constitutional nationalists were concentrated in areas associated with the Whig party: the northwest, the northern piedmont, and the "urban/commercial" counties east of the Blue Ridge. While the only constitutional nationalists among the Jacksonians could be found in the west, most western Democrats defended strict construction. The two main elements of the party in the region—the traditionalist Germans and the southwestern farmers—embraced that position while the huge number of western Whigs could see their economic future written in the strokes of broad construction, supporting internal improvements at federal expense, a credit system, and tariff protection for their infant industries and home markets.

A persistent segment of the Virginia Whig party came from the Eastern Shore and portions of the tidewater north of the James, but the most outspoken states' rights Whigs in this region retained only a loose commitment to the party. They had kicked over the traces by the 1840s, becoming Democrats while a significant majority of the voters remained loyal Whigs voting for Henry Clay in 1844 and Zachary Taylor in 1848. Most of Virginia's Whig leaders in the 1830s and all of the party's spokesmen, newspapers, and congressmen in the 1840s took positions in federal affairs similar to those of the other Whigs of the upper South. The Democrats of the Old Dominion remained consistent advocates of strict construction and states' rights, prided themselves on adherence to the Doctrines of '98, and led the proslavery southern rights movement that is usually associated with the lower South. Symbolically, Senator James M. Mason read Calhoun's last speech to the Senate in 1850.

As a young man Mason had represented Frederick County in the constitutional convention of 1829–30, where he was a supporter of reform, and in 1832 he served as a Jackson elector. The senator's personal experience suggests a more complex relationship between states' rights sentiment and the support for democratic reform than implied in the various interpretations of the shift from Jeffersonian liberalism to Calhounite conservatism. Neither of these concepts usefully characterizes the contending parties in the conflict over constitutional reform within the commonwealth. Like slavery, reform did not describe a single issue, and neither of the parties can be equated with the basic elements of democratic change—either the equalization of representation or the expansion of the suffrage.

Historians usually have emphasized the importance of sectionalism in bringing about constitutional reform and have ignored partisan differences or subsumed them within an image of a liberal Democratic west and a conservative Whig east. The product of the convention in 1829–30 was distinctly disappointing to reformers since it only altered the scheme of representation slightly and expanded the suffrage modestly. Constitutional revision was basically a sectional issue that set the center against the periphery and thus poised the protoparties of the first party system against each other. Practically all the conservatives were Old Republicans who at the time supported Jackson as an opponent of the American System and defender of states' rights. The ex-Federalists and advocates of the Adams administration led the forces of reform. But party identification was too weak and discipline too lax to see this as little more than a coincidence of sectional conflict that focused on apportionment of the assembly. Constitutional reform had traditionally split the Republican majority along sectional lines.[32]

Modern parties first appeared during the next decade, and their effects were felt in the reform convention of 1850–51 that did make major changes, reapportioning the legislature and introducing universal white manhood suffrage. The influence of sectionalism remained to dictate the debate and compromise on representation. The introduction of popular election of a range of offices from governor to the justices of the county courts was as a source of some debate but provoked little formal opposition from either party. The expansion of the suffrage passed easily without partisan division. The effects of party took a different form, focusing upon those issues that divided Whigs and Democrats in the other states that rewrote their constitutions at the same time. The parties differed most sharply on questions concerning the legitimacy of government activity in various realms.

The Democrats favored limiting legislative action in all areas, most simply by mandating short, biennial sessions and more fundamentally by circumscribing the assembly's power to spend, tax, and pledge the state's credit to improvements projects. They particularly frowned upon the creation of banks of issue and what the Whigs called the credit system. The Whigs were quite willing to risk legislative activism in order to encourage economic development and to elevate the moral tone of the society. Constitutional reform in mid-nineteenth-century America was not a single issue that set the advocates of democracy against their conservative opponents but a cluster of issues on policy that sometimes followed and sometimes cut across party lines. In Virginia the issues related to representative democracy and political individualism—apportionment, suffrage, and popular election—were not partisan matters, while those concerning the powers of the state government were.

By 1852 the Old Dominion had come into line constitutionally with the other states and was behaving in a fashion that was democratic for the day. Of course, the commonwealth's huge black population—the largest in the country—was disfranchised, and white women neither had nor expected the vote although they clearly found ways to participate as second-class citizens. The combined effects of gerrymandering and single-member districts meant that both the Virginia General Assembly and the state's congressional delegation were heavily skewed in favor of what was a modest majority in the electorate. But the system was one from which its constituent elements demanded relatively little and one in which their desires—if not their needs—were fairly well represented. Given all of these defects, white male Virginians were surely more democratically governed in the 1850s than at any previous time and, most probably, better represented in their government than during the subsequent century and a half.[33]

✍ 1 ✍

Notes on the State of Virginia

I T IS ONE of the supreme ironies of American history that the home state of Thomas Jefferson retained its whiggish eighteenth-century political structure long after liberalism had triumphed elsewhere. Not until 1851 did Virginia extend the suffrage to all white men and allow them to choose their magistrates in place of the self-perpetuating oligarchies that traditionally controlled the county courts. The new state constitution brought the commonwealth belatedly into the nineteenth century, finally enacting most of the reforms suggested by Jefferson seventy-five years earlier at the time of the Revolution. The dawn of the new democracy in the Old Dominion represented not reverence for his radical politics but a concession to social and economic changes at odds with Jefferson's conservative vision of a homogeneous agrarian society.[1]

After fleeing the governor's chair in mid-1781, the thirty-eight-year-old author of the Declaration of Independence began work on what would be his first and only book. *Notes on the State of Virginia* consists of a series of answers to twenty-three "queries" posed by "a Foreigner of Distinction then residing among us"—the secretary of the French legation, the marquis de Barbé-Marbois. These chapters range in length from a paragraph to over fifty printed pages. Some of the comments are trivial; others express ideas that educated people associate with the Sage of Monticello: his concerns about slavery, his advocacy of the agricultural life, his distrust of manufactures and of the mobs of the cities. At the same time *Notes* presents Jefferson the empiricist, an acute if not dispassionate observer, whose commentaries on the geography, people, economy, and government of the Old Dominion in the early 1780s serve as both benchmark and a guide for future students of the state's history.[2]

At the time of the Revolution, the commonwealth was dominated by a relatively homogeneous planter elite who were landowners, slaveholders, Anglicans descended from English families that had migrated years previously, and related by the bonds of marriage and kinship. In a population of over half a million, including over three hundred thousand whites, the "One Hundred" richest

17

Virginians dominated the economy, society, and government of post-Revolutionary Virginia.

In the course of the next three-quarters of a century, this traditional order fragmented into a pluralistic society, and the politics of republican consensus gave way to a politics of liberal conflict rooted in a commitment to a democracy of white men in which slaveholders were a minority and planters a tiny elite, sectarianism dominated a vibrant religious life, and economic development produced a diversity of commercial activity. Nearly all of the state's farmers, however small, raised a portion of their crop to feed the expanding commercial market, and the nonagricultural sector of the economy rapidly increased. In all of this, the Old Dominion was swept by the same tides of change that surged over the other states of the new nation.

The antebellum period of Virginia history remains terra incognita, concealed by half-truths concerning political impotence and agricultural decline. Much of what has been written about the commonwealth during the decades following the demise of the Virginia Dynasty has focused far too narrowly on the fate of a desiccated planter aristocracy and the antics of a handful of romantic reactionaries who in the 1850s sought through secession "to roll back the Reformation in its political phase." In fact, antebellum Virginia was a sprawling, populous, diversified, even dynamic region-in-itself as different from Jefferson's "country" in the 1780s as it was from the England of Sir Walter Scott's imagination.[3]

Consequently, any study of the Old Dominion before the Civil War must begin with a reexamination of the state of Virginia and its people in the seventy-five years following the Revolution during which the forms and practices of democratic politics appeared. The social and economic changes witnessed during these years constituted the preconditions of democratic reform. They established an environment in which innovation could flourish and generated a level of social conflict that challenged the traditional constitutional order. Demographic diversity, economic development, and geographic and social mobility underlay the rise of political individualism and the democratization of the Old Dominion.

As the new nation began its existence under the Constitution, the Old Dominion loomed as the largest and most populous state in the Union with nearly three-quarters of a million people, approximately equal to Pennsylvania and New York combined. Aside from dominating the presidency in the first three decades of the Republic's existence, Virginia consistently controlled a disproportionate number of the seats in Congress. Gradually the commonwealth was overtaken, first by New York and then in turn by Pennsylvania and Ohio, and its political influence waned accordingly. But in 1850 Virginia was the fourth

Table 1.1. Virginia population, 1790–1850

	Population	Whites		Slaves		Free blacks	
		No.	%	No.	%	No.	%
1790	748,303	442,115	59.1	293,427	39.2	12,766	1.7
1820	1,065,139	603,087	56.6	425,153	39.9	36,889	3.5
1830	1,211,405	694,300	57.3	469,754	38.8	47,348	3.9
1840	1,239,797	740,858	59.8	449,087	36.2	49,852	4.0
1850	1,421,661	894,800	62.9	472,528	33.2	54,383	3.8

Source: Seventh Census of the United States . . . 1850 (Washington, D.C., 1853), 261. There are slight differences between the data in this compilation and those in the earlier volumes, but these do not change the percentages.

largest state in the Union and still a major factor in American politics. Over the course of these sixty years its population had grown at a relatively steady rate of slightly over 10 percent per decade, and until the Civil War the Old Dominion remained the largest slave state with the largest number of substantial slave-holders.[4]

Between 1790 and 1820 a huge number of slaves and their masters left Virginia for the states in the West. Although at first migration to Kentucky and Tennessee involved footloose whites of modest means, increasingly planters joined the mass migration. In the first two decades, they transported nearly seventy-five thousand slaves out of the Old Dominion, primarily to the new southwestern states. With the emergence of the professional slave trade, the number of black migrants multiplied. Over fifty thousand slaves were taken from the Chesapeake to the new states of Mississippi and Alabama during the decade between 1810 and 1820. Yet during these years the number of slaves in Virginia kept pace with the growth of the state's population, constituting two-fifths of the total.

Jefferson had worried that "this blot" was increasing faster than the white population. At the low point in 1820, whites made up only 56 percent of the Virginia population, and the state seemed headed for a black majority (table 1.1). The liberal manumission law of 1782, combined with the refusal to enforce later legislation to rid the commonwealth of their presence, caused the number of "free colored persons" to grow rapidly and their proportion of the population to jump from 1.7 percent in 1790 to 4.0 percent by 1840. The combination of an absolute decline of the number of slaves during the 1830s and an upsurge in the growth of the white population in the 1840s changed the racial equation by 1850 so that slaves constituted only a third of the commonwealth's population and whites just under two-thirds. Of these, approximately fifty-five thousand held slaves, and one-tenth of that group were planters—those who held more than twenty slaves.[5]

More important than the ratio of whites to blacks was the changing distribution of the two groups and the concentration of the peculiar institution nearly exclusively in the eastern half of the state. Between 1790 and 1860 the population of the area that would become West Virginia grew at three times the rate of the state as a whole. By 1840 the counties west of the Blue Ridge had more than doubled their population and contained a larger number of whites than did those in the eastern portion of the state. There blacks outnumbered whites. Half of the eastern population was enslaved, and quasi-free blacks made up an additional 5 percent.[6]

East of the Blue Ridge only in two counties—Accomack on the Eastern Shore and Patrick in the southwestern corner of the piedmont—did slaves make up less than 40 percent of the population. The largest concentration of slaves was in the sixteen Southside counties from Sussex to Halifax. Only one, Dinwiddie, had a free majority, and eleven were over 60 percent enslaved. African Americans outnumbered whites three-to-one in Nottoway County. The black belt in Virginia extended north in the piedmont above the James River and east into the tidewater, constituting twenty-one contiguous counties with slave majorities. In these areas and throughout the tidewater, anxieties about economic decline mixed with darker fears of "Africanization" and the attendant evils personified by Nat Turner's bloody insurrection in Southampton County in 1831.[7]

Thus, Virginia was actually two slave states. The eastern half of the commonwealth contained a slave society with proportions of African Americans similar to the states of the Cotton South. West of the Blue Ridge, there were few slaves and fewer planters; it was a diversifying agricultural society in which slaves formed a small minority of its labor force and over 85 percent of the population was white. In the east, slaves constituted a major form of property, and slavery bred a distinctly conservative attachment to the social order and, in many planters, a stubborn resistance to change.

This sharp division of the Old Dominion into a slave society east of the Blue Ridge and a society with slavery in the west has symbolized the role of intrastate sectionalism in the history of antebellum Virginia. Its effects have been reinforced in the minds of those looking back at this period through the smoke of the Civil War by the subsequent division of the Old Dominion with the creation of West Virginia in 1863. But such notions clearly existed earlier: the Blue Ridge bisected the state, and the federal census of 1840 reflected the contemporary conception of sectionalism by establishing an Eastern District and a Western District. The New York Democrat and essayist James K. Paulding com-

Life in eastern Virginia and western Virginia. From Henry Howe, *Historical Collections of Virginia* (Charleston, S.C., 1846).

mented that the westerners "call those east of the mountain *Tuckahoes*, and their country Old Virginia. They themselves are *Cohees*, and their country New Virginia." The etchings presented by Henry Howe in his 1846 history of the commonwealth similarly contrasted the images of eastern paternalistic planter life in the lowlands with the rugged individualism of the frontier farmer living in the western mountains.[8]

In fact, this simple dichotomy obscures the realities of regionalism in antebellum Virginia and denies the Old Dominion's geographic, social, and economic diversity. The constitution of 1830 divided the state politically into four regions: the tidewater, east of the fall line; the piedmont, constituting the area to the west, but east of the Blue Ridge; the Shenandoah Valley; and the trans-Allegheny. In 1835 Joseph Martin wrote in his gazetteer of the state, "These four sections are so distinctly marked in their features as to be recognized in the fundamental law of the State and must ever have import and political and moral effects."[9]

But even this fourfold division fails to capture the geographical, demographic, and economic complexity of the Old Dominion. For analytical purposes this discussion further subdivides the state into seven geographic regions of differing population (table 1.2), using the James River as a boundary between the northern and southern portions of the tidewater and the piedmont and the valleys of the Great Kanawha and Greenbrier rivers to define the northern and southern segments of the trans-Allegheny region. The lower portion of the Valley also is included here in the southwest (map 1.1).[10]

Table 1.2. Regional population, 1830–50

	1830	1840		1850			
	Total	Total	Whites	Total	Whites	Slaves	Free blacks
Lower tidewater	126,233	118,544	57,086	122,085	58,791	52,775	10,610
Upper tidewater	246,883	240,903	111,108	263,711	124,338	119,70	19,776
Southern piedmont	283,255	279,261	125,667	294,306	131,996	152,172	10,219
Northern piedmont	76,609	166,234	81,455	176,596	86,325	84.741	5,530
Valley	174,308	170,182	132,742	198,385	156,738	36,281	4,366
Southwest	98,164	116,384	102,418	146,883	127,354	16,293	1,255
Northwest	90,965	126,419	120,356	167,601	159,496	8,051	1,051

Source: Inter-University Consortium for Political and Social Research (ICPSR) data for 119 counties.

Ethnic variations among antebellum Virginians were far less noticeable than those of race, but nonetheless they divided the whites and affected their political behavior. Virginia was not the destination of a large number of nineteenth-century immigrants. Only 3 percent of the population in 1850 had been born in Europe; about half of these were Irish, and one-fourth Germans. Only a dozen counties had even modest concentrations of foreign-born, and within them immigrants generally settled in the cities and towns. Over one-third of the free workingmen in Richmond on the eve of the Civil War had been born abroad. Frederick Law Olmsted in 1852 noted "a considerable population of foreign origin, generally of the least valuable class; very dirty German Jews, especially, abound, and their characteristic shops (with their characteristic smells quite as bad as Cologne) are thickly set in the narrowest and meanest streets, which seem to be otherwise inhabited mainly by negroes." [11]

Smaller concentrations of foreign-born could be found in Lynchburg, Norfolk, Petersburg, Fredericksburg, and Alexandria, but nearly two-thirds of the foreign immigrants settled in the western half of the state where they could be found in the commercial towns along the turnpike from Staunton to Martinsburg and in Jefferson County on the Potomac. In the northwest they accounted for 7 percent of the population, crowded primarily into Wheeling and the other industrial towns of Ohio County.[12]

1.1. Sections of Virginia

Table 1.3. National origins of the white population, 1850 (in %)

	Lower tide-water	Upper tide-water	Northern pied-mont	Southern pied-mont	Valley	South-west	North-west
English	43	45	41	42	29	33	36
Scotch-Irish	19	22	19	21	27	28	31
Germans	12	22	21	12	31	21	9
Welsh	15	12	11	13	7	10	11
Irish	6	5	4	5	5	6	7
French	5	5	3	6	2	3	3

Source: R. Bennet Bean, *The Peopling of Virginia* (Boston, 1938). Bean combines Scots and Scotch-Irish. The northwest estimates are based on various secondary sources and the proportions of religious groups.

The most relevant ethnic differences in the Old Dominion, however, stretched back to earlier migrations before the Revolution. Throughout the seventeenth century the population of the colony, rich and poor, free or indentured, was predominately English with a small minority of Welsh who—like most of the English—came as servants. In the eighteenth century they and a smattering of French Huguenots, who had entered the colony following the revocation of the Edict of Nantes in 1685, drifted west from the tidewater into the piedmont. From 1750 to 1790 Germans and the Scotch-Irish from Pennsylvania surged south up the Valley of Virginia and washed over the Blue Ridge into the western piedmont.[13]

The census figures on foreign-born in 1850 thus fail to reflect the ethnic mosaic in the Old Dominion in the 1830s and 1840s. Moving west across the commonwealth, one found relatively fewer Englishmen and more Scotch-Irish and Germans, large numbers of whom still spoke their native tongue in an ancient accent (table 1.3). The older areas of the tidewater and the Southside had the largest proportion of men with English surnames. The small French population clustered in these counties intermarried early with the English. In the northern piedmont the English made up slightly less than half the white population, and Scots, Scotch-Irish, and Welsh together contributed about one-third; there was also a large German element—about one-fifth—but fewer French than in "Old Virginia."[14]

Everywhere west of the mountains there were fewer English, but the ethnic mix varied in the three western regions. Two-thirds of the Valley whites were either German or Scotch-Irish. The share of English and Welsh was lower than in any of the other regions of the state. The trans-Allegheny counties generally were heavily populated by the Scotch-Irish. Although a portion of the southwest was an extension of the Valley, the area generally had fewer Germans; outside of Montgomery and Wythe counties, Scotch-Irish and Welsh together made up a majority of the whites while those with English surnames constituted slightly over one-third of the inhabitants. In the northwest there was a more diverse population. Aside from the European immigrants, 16 percent of those living in the region had been born outside the commonwealth, primarily in Pennsylvania, Maryland, and New Jersey.[15]

The effects of ethnicity depended upon the interaction of national origin with religion, and antebellum Virginia was rent by sectarian controversy. The Reformation etched sharp lines of battle across Europe that spawned emigration to the British colonies and the new nation. Dissenters fled persecution. Conflicts between Catholics and Protestants, Anglicans and reformers, were transplanted in the New World. While denominationalism defined the shape of American Protestantism, the Great Revival at the end of the eighteenth century and the Second Great Awakening in the nineteenth century heightened sectarian tensions by creating both an increased commitment to the reformed Protestant consensus and a growing necessity to define denominational differences.[16]

Protestants dominated the Old Dominion, like the South generally. The census takers in 1850 found only seventeen Roman Catholic churches scattered about the state with approximately 15,000 communicants, a growing number of whom were Irish and German immigrants. All major cities had Roman Catholic churches; there were two in Norfolk, two in Richmond, one in Wheeling, and one in Alexandria. The 1850 census enumerated fourteen Protestant groups that had churches in Virginia. The two largest denominations were the Methodists and the Baptists, who together accounted for 70 percent of the churches in the state (table 1.4). The Presbyterians, however, owned 240 churches and the Episcopalians 173, and the buildings were larger than those of the Methodists and Baptists, increasing the importance of their congregations and making them relatively more influential than the membership data indicate, especially among the whites. There were also over one hundred "Free" churches whose facilities were shared by several sects. Each denomination had a distinct pattern of distribution throughout the Old Dominion and combined with national origin to create ethnic enclaves within the larger regions of the state.[17]

The Virginia Germans were not recent immigrants but the descendants of the Pennsylvania "Dutch" who had moved into the Valley during the eighteenth century. This group included Mennonites, Moravians, and Tunkers, but most were "church people," Lutheran or German Reformed. Many of these

Table 1.4. Church accommodations in Virginia, 1850

	Lower Tide-water	Upper Tide-water	Northern Pied-mont	Southern Pied-mont	Valley	South-west	North-west
Methodists	37,725	49,130	28,025	67,123	31,290	49,365	44,450
Black*	7,545	9,820	5,605	13,425			
Baptists	24,655	71,375	35,125	54,894	13,000	19,030	19,810
Black*	12,328	35,688	17,563	27,447			
Presbyterian	3,150	9,180	7,070	29,075	2,665	14,450	12,950
Episcopal	8,250	30,480	11,200	15,754	7,250	2,700	4,750
Lutheran	0	500	1,500	0	11,300	4,350	500
Union*	0	3,200	600	900	13,550	3,300	4,950
Total	79,635	174,815	103,270	176,396	111,490	92,995	89,385

Source: ILPSR data for 119 counties.

* The estimates of black Methodists are 20 percent of the total; black Baptists, 50 percent of the total; and Union totals are doubled because two congregations occupied the same church.

worshiped in the Union churches where two congregations used the same building on alternate Sundays. Basically the distribution of the German churches followed the distribution of German surnames. Six modest Mennonite churches, eight small Moravian congregations, and seven of the eight churches belonging to the pietistic sect called Tunkers could be found in the Valley. Eight of nine of the German Reformed churches, thirty-two of Virginia's fifty Lutheran churches, and half of the Union churches sustained the German communities of the Valley. Most of the other Lutheran congregations were in the southwest.

Early historians of West Virginia emphasized the importance of the Scotch-Irish and presumed that they all were Presbyterians, firmly devoted to "the cause of religious and political liberty" and "responsible for what little education the frontier people had." They descended from Ulstermen who had been persecuted by the Church of England and had fled in part because of this. By 1850, 45 percent of the Scotch-Irish Presbyterians in the state had settled east of the Blue Ridge where in the nineteenth century they assumed the role of the "intellectuals of Virginia Protestantism." They founded the *Virginia Religious Herald* in Lexington in 1804 and slightly later the *Virginia Evangelical and Literary Magazine* edited by John Holt Rice. Doctrinally they had drifted from strict, deterministic Calvinism to an Arminianism resembling Max Weber's "Protestant ethic." They insisted upon an educated clergy, establishing schools and colleges including Washington College in Lexington and Hampden-Sydney in

Prince Edward County where, according to the visiting free spirit Anne Royall, they manufactured puritanical "blue-skins wholesale and retail."[18]

The Presbyterians had constructed 10 percent of the churches, providing 12 percent of the accommodations listed in the 1850 census. In the Western District they were weakest in the northwest where their churches supplied only one-seventh of the seats, but in the Valley they constituted one-quarter of the churchgoers. Augusta County alone had thirteen Presbyterian churches, and Rockbridge had eleven. About one-sixth of the Protestants in the southwestern Virginia were Presbyterians. Washington County alone had eight churches.

The Southside harbored many more Presbyterians. These congregations originated with the surge of the Scotch-Irish east over the mountains as they moved south from Pennsylvania to the Carolina backcountry. Nearly two-thirds of the Presbyterians in the lower piedmont clustered in five contiguous counties stretching east from Bedford to Prince Edward and including Halifax on the North Carolina border to the south. Charlotte had eight Presbyterian churches, the largest number of that denomination's accommodations listed in the census of 1850, although its northern neighbor Prince Edward, with seven churches and two seminaries, was said to have more Presbyterians than "any other Co. in the state."[19]

There were very few Presbyterians in the piedmont north of the James River or in the tidewater where they were generally confined to the areas around Richmond, Norfolk, and Fredericksburg. Two-thirds of those in the northern piedmont lived in three counties: Albemarle, Fauquier, and Loudoun. Jefferson's home county had eight Presbyterian churches and 40 percent of all the Presbyterians in the region.

In contrast to the German denominations and the Scotch-Irish Presbyterians, the Episcopalians were primarily descendants of the original English settlers, and fully four-fifths of them could be found east of the Blue Ridge; half were located in the tidewater. During the colonial era the Church of England constituted the state church in the Old Dominion, supported by taxes and the returns from glebe lands and controlled in each county by a vestry made up of locally prominent men. The Revolution decimated the Anglicans in Virginia. Twenty-three of the ninety-five parishes that existed before the Revolution disappeared. Thirty-four were left without ministers as two-thirds of the clergy left the state in the course of the war.[20]

Even before the Revolution the Anglicans were being challenged by the growth of both Presbyterians and Baptists, who together claimed a majority of adherents by 1776. Within the fold of the "English Church" itself, revivalism spawned Methodism. The new group split free in 1784 and the parent denomination lapsed into what one historian termed "a sort of respectable torpor."

The legislature ended the compulsory support of the clergy in 1776, adopted Jefferson's Bill for Establishing Religious Freedom a decade later, and after a heated debate took over the old glebe lands from the church in 1799, completing the process of disestablishment. In the 1820s and 1830s, however, the Episcopalians were recovering lost ground under the leadership of Bishop William Meade, and by 1850 they owned just under 10 percent of the churches in the commonwealth.[21]

In 1790 at the time of the first census, when the Virginia population stood at three-quarters of a million, there were reportedly twenty thousand Baptists and eighteen thousand Methodists in the state. By 1830 each group had approximately doubled in size, but the Methodists gained new converts at a greater rate and as a result of revivals in the 1820s and 1830s surpassed all of their rivals, making up at least 40 percent and perhaps half of all the churchgoers in the Old Dominion by the mid-nineteenth century.

Nearly one-third of the churched in 1850 were Baptists, who concentrated more heavily east of the Blue Ridge, where they competed for people's souls primarily with the Methodists. In Halifax County in the southern piedmont on the North Carolina border, there were seventeen Methodist and twenty-one Baptist churches, but the northern piedmont and the upper tidewater also contained Baptist strongholds. Comparing the size of these two denominations with that of the Presbyterians and the Episcopalians is difficult because of their vastly greater appeal to the blacks. A contemporary human geographer estimated that one-fifth of the Virginia Methodists in 1835 were "colored" and half of the fifty-four thousand Baptists were "slaves."[22]

The Baptists were a doctrinally simple sect distrustful of the pretensions of education, the "intrigues of lawyers," the "frauds of priests," and government generally. They were congregational in polity and antinomian in spirit. But in contrast to their frontier image, the Virginia Baptists' greatest appeal was to the eastern planters and their slaves. The leading proponent of the biblical defense of slavery was a Baptist minister, Thornton Stringfellow, who owned seventy slaves and two thousand acres. In the tidewater the denomination accounted for two-fifths of the churched Christians. West of the Blue Ridge where most of the Baptists were white, the denomination served slightly fewer than one-fifth of the churchgoers.[23]

Methodists were not only more numerous than Baptists but also more evenly spread across the commonwealth. A majority of the white Methodists could be found east of the Blue Ridge, and the faith was particularly strong on the Southside, but the denomination was most popular in the trans-Allegheny region where Methodists ministered to a majority of all Protestants. In the southwestern counties of Wythe, Giles, and Greenbrier, they made up two-thirds of the religious population. One-fifth of all the Methodists in the southwestern counties were located in Wythe where they had twenty-one churches. A similar proportion of northwestern Methodists resided in a single county, Monongalia, and an additional twenty-five churches were located in two others, Lewis and Kanawha.[24]

While the sect retained its rigid structure of denominational governance, the Methodists increasingly turned to itinerant preachers with an emotional evangelical appeal and a simplified liturgy. The circuit rider and the camp meeting characterized the Methodists, who tended to find their most likely converts among those of English (and Welsh) descent who had fallen away from Anglican influence. Continental pietism gave to Methodism its moralistic emphasis on the individual sinner's sorrow over his state and a rebirth through the "second blessing" of sanctification that involved turning against the belief in predestination associated with the Calvinist tradition. God's grace was open to all; man had free will to accept or reject it. "Arminianism and Perfectionism became the denomination's most distinctive features."[25]

During the 1830s and 1840s all of the major denominations divided over questions of dogma and polity. Presbyterians split into advocates of the "New School" and followers of the "Old School" majority, reflecting differing responses to revivalism. In the 1830s the Baptists were in a turmoil over the Campbellite reformers and home missions. In the 1840s the Methodists split over slavery and matters of doctrine; the northwestern wing of the denomination played a role in the creation of West Virginia. These schisms in the state's most populous churches reflected the potential for religious conflict in what has often been viewed as a homogeneous Protestant population.[26]

As revivalists spread "Methodist measures" to the Baptists and the Presbyterians, competition for converts encouraged a sectarian spirit by exaggerating doctrinal distinctiveness and interdenominational tension within the Old Dominion became acute. The tenor of the religious debate was described on all sides as a state of "Holy War." Alexander Campbell attacked his fellow Baptists as "proscriptive, illiberal and unjust" and insisted that he would sooner send a sinner to a Muslim for salvation than to a Methodist circuit rider. At the same time his Presbyterian opponents called Campbell and his ilk, "the curse of the West—more destructive and more injurious . . . than avowed Infidelity itself."[27]

The important place of the Methodists in the denominational history of the Old Dominion highlights changes in the cultural context that encouraged democratic tendencies and affected Virginia politics in the antebellum years. Revivalism created an environment of religious populism that emphasized the individualism implicit in free will and at the same time the conformity to the strict moral code associated with Victorian America. Baptist John Leland was "self-reliant to an eccentric degree," distrusted wealth and authority, opposed the creeds and confessions of official Christianity, and lectured on the incompatibility of book learning and true morality. Although Alexander Campbell was a graduate of the University of Edinburgh and a fearsome foe of Leland's Baptists, he and his followers, the Disciples of Christ, reflected a similar religious populism that sought to "place laity and clergy on equal footing," rejected formalistic theology, and emphasized the individual's personal understanding of the Bible.[28]

Revivalism involved a dramatic turning away from Calvinist determinism toward the necessity of a strict moral code that implied an efficacious individual in a democracy of sinners. Preachers took on the role of the exhorter—the pitchman of the Word—rationalizing their enterprise in the most pragmatic fashion possible and judging their success by the number of sinners who voted for salvation. Presbyterian Charles G. Finney's widely circulated *Lectures on Revivals of Religion* constituted a handbook on the applied science of saving souls. Finney related his own work to that of his contemporaries who invented modern mass political parties.[29]

As religious controversy splintered society and elevated individual agency in the struggle for salvation, expansion of the economy and the multiplying forms of economic activity further fostered a pluralism of personal experience that encouraged the culture of political liberalism in the Old Dominion. Individuals were forced upon their own responsibility although they often desperately needed assistance from kin and community. While cooperation seemed essential to commercial success or even survival, agriculture in the Old Dominion fostered the fierce independence that Jefferson extolled. In contrast to the morbid picture drawn by the Old Dominion's "doomed aristocrats" and the later antislavery propagandists, Virginia agriculture during the antebellum era mirrored the economic fortunes of the American economy generally.[30]

The Old Dominion shared in the new nation's experience of social and economic mobility. Not only were a sizable number of freemen and slaves moving west from the troubled tidewater, but even the economically expanding areas of the commonwealth witnessed unprecedented geographic mobility. Persistence rates for the piedmont from 1810 to 1830 were low: two-thirds of those found there at the beginning of the War of 1812 had died or moved on by the time Andrew Jackson entered the White House. In Prince Edward County only 40 percent of the household heads in 1840 remained in the county ten years later. As elsewhere in nineteenth-century America, the persisters did fairly well, with the majority improving their economic position.[31]

The panic of 1819 ushered in a period of depression that hit portions of the Old Dominion particularly hard. Madison lamented in 1820 that "the remarkable down fall in prices of two of our great staples, breadstuffs and tobacco," brought "privations to every man's door." The low point was reached in 1823, and throughout the remainder of the decade there was a modest revival. During the 1830s prices increased; in 1835 and 1836 the index of all commodities in Virginia rose nearly 50 percent to the highest point of the antebellum era. The panic of 1837 dampened prices only slightly at first, but they fell rapidly as the depression set in. Midway through the 1840s, prices returned to about the 1830 level and remained steady for several years before taking off again in the boom of the 1850s. The transportation revolution created a national market, narrowing the gap between the prices at Richmond and Cincinnati and those in the ports of New York and New Orleans, and the fortunes of Virginia's farmers increasingly rose and fell with the nation's economy.[32]

Two things stand out: in the long run, prices of all products of Virginia agriculture rose and farmers prospered; in the short run, the Virginia farmer faced fluctuating prices for his produce from year to year; in fact, from month to month. He was the hostage of a market over which he had no control. For example, the average price per bushel of wheat was $.93 in 1834, down ten cents from the previous year but seventy cents below the decade high of $1.63 reached two years later. Wheat brought $.78 a bushel on the Richmond market in April 1834 but $1.02 for those who had it to sell in November. Antebellum agriculture constantly involved decisions about planting and marketing crops. Each year farmers had to choose the proper mix of crops to raise to maximize future profits and hedge against starvation.[33]

If Jefferson actually believed that "those who labor in the earth are the chosen people of God," he lived among them. Throughout the antebellum period the number of people going into agriculture grew, following the trend of the state's population. In the last federal census taken before Jefferson's death, Virginia ranked first among the states in the number of farmers, thirty thousand ahead of New York. Those in agriculture made up nine-tenths of the working population and one-fourth of the total population of the commonwealth, twice the proportion for Pennsylvania. Two decades later the 1840 census showed that the state had fallen to second behind New York in the number of people in agriculture, although the number of farmers had increased by about 15 percent.[34]

Yet in the 1840s as in Jefferson's time, the majority of those who labored in the earth of the Old Dominion were not the sturdy yeomen in whose breasts Jefferson believed God had implanted "substantial and genuine virtue," but African Americans whose natural allotment of virtue plagued the Sage of Monticello. In looking down from his little mountain, the author of the Declaration of Independence viewed hundreds of blacks slaving in his fields and those owned by his wealthy white neighbors. The portion of Albemarle County that

Jefferson surveyed daily with his telescope typified the eastern counties of Virginia in which half of the population was enslaved and over four-fifths of the gainfully employed worked in agriculture.[35]

The commonwealth's relative decline, as new areas were opened and the older states dramatically expanded their output, overshadowed the expansion of Virginia agriculture during these years and the fact that it was the most agriculturally diverse state in the country. Although reliable data for all the major crops are not available before 1839, the extant statistics suggest that the fruit of Virginia farms multiplied during each decade following 1819. The farmers of the Old Dominion enjoyed good years and bad along with those of the rest of the country and suffered from the same vagaries of the weather and the same pests and blights endured by their neighbors to the north and west. The mid-1830s were extremely good years with generally high prices and bountiful crops raised by a relatively stable population. At the end of the decade the Old Dominion stood first in tobacco production, marketing half again as much as Kentucky, which ranked second, and two and one-half times the amount grown in third-place Tennessee. The commonwealth was third in corn production behind Tennessee and Kentucky and fourth in wheat production behind Ohio, Pennsylvania, and New York. In the southeastern corner of the state, slaves even picked three and one-half million pounds of cotton in 1839.[36]

From the time of its colonial beginnings, Virginia was associated with the growth of tobacco. The land of the Old Dominion was suited to the weed. The "culture of tobacco" dictated the rhythms of planter-class life and justified the growth of slavery in the eighteenth century. By the War of 1812, the sandy soil of the tidewater was exhausted, and most of the efforts at agricultural reform were directed to reconstructing this area. Tobacco migrated to the piedmont where it was grown primarily in the Southside counties between the James and the North Carolina border.[37]

Exports remained stable for nearly a half century following the adoption of the Constitution. During the Era of Good Feelings, tobacco prices plummeted before stabilizing for a decade and a half. "Virtually all the period from about 1823 to 1834 was a discouraging time for tobacco planters," and there were numerous considerations of alternatives and calls for reform by men such as Edmund Ruffin, who produced striking results with the introduction of marl and lime, which reduced the acidity in the soil. In the 1830s tobacco's fortunes rose sharply before the bottom again dropped out of the market. After a series of bad years during the depression of the early 1840s, however, the tobacco business revived. In 1850 Virginia was by far the nation's leading tobacco producer and stood on the threshold of a decade of exceptional prosperity.[38]

The tendency of historians to emphasize the Old Dominion's leading staple crop has led to an obsession with the problems of these declining planters located primarily in a small number of eastern counties in the commonwealth. In fact, antebellum Virginia had a balanced and thriving agricultural economy. Before the 1850s the corn belt stretched across the upper South and Virginia raised over 10 percent of the nation's corn crop. Every farmer in the state raised some corn to feed his family and his livestock. It was heartier than wheat and gave a greater yield per acre. Cornpone, hominy grits, and hoecakes formed the basis of the common man's diet in Virginia, although farmers in the commonwealth undoubtedly provided their families a more varied fare than those farther south.[39]

Wheat was primarily a cash crop grown for the market. While it is usually thought of as a crop grown by free labor, wheat could be profitably raised with slave labor on large plantations; the crop required more land than tobacco, and production increased with the size of the slaveholding. Nearly all planters and two-thirds of the slaveless farmers raised at least a few bushels for the market. The greatest concentration of wheat production in the state was in the counties stretching north from Augusta in the Valley and in the northernmost counties in the piedmont. Although Virginia ranked fourth among the states in wheat production, the commonwealth's continuing competitiveness evinced the agricultural revival of the Old Dominion in the antebellum era.[40]

Virginia clearly held its own as the leading agricultural state in the South. The Old Dominion was not nearly so economically backward as ideologically motivated commentators like Frederick Law Olmsted argued. General farming could be found throughout the state. No area, county, or even plantation was devoted to a single crop. That would have involved what one historian calls "catastrophic risks." Wheat, corn, oats, and potatoes grew in every county of the state; farmers in all the counties raised cows, sheep, and pigs as well. The commonwealth had over ten million acres of improved farmland worth over $216 million, fourth among the states of the Union.[41]

There was, however, regional variation in the relative importance of crops and livestock. Tobacco was concentrated in the lower two-thirds of the piedmont and grown in only a quarter of the state's counties. Over four-fifths of the 1849 tobacco crop was raised the southern piedmont; 36 percent came from just four contiguous counties: Halifax, Mecklenburg, Pittsylvania, and Charlotte. Practically none was grown west of the Blue Ridge or in the tidewater. The piedmont was the most populous region in the state and the most agriculturally productive. The area above the James River led the state in the production of wheat, corn, oats, and white potatoes. It also led in the raising of swine and cattle. In Orange and Greene counties just north of Albemarle over 70 percent of the farms reporting in 1849 raised some wheat, corn, Irish potatoes, horses, cows, and pigs. They all produced butter as well. The primary difference between large and small farms was not specialization but the size of their surpluses produced for the market.[42]

The long-depressed tidewater had become by the 1840s a "meat and potatoes" area raising 40 percent of the state's pigs and nearly one-third of the cattle. Nearly half of the white potatoes and 70 percent of the sweet potatoes were grown in the tidewater counties. Farmers in the Norfolk area cultivated strawberries and watermelons as well as garden produce that was shipped to markets in Baltimore and Philadelphia and even as far north as Boston. The only cotton produced in Virginia came from the southeastern counties that also raised about one-third of the hay grown in the state for the urban markets of Richmond, Petersburg, and Norfolk.[43]

The Great Valley of Virginia yielded a variety of grains besides wheat: rye, barley, buckwheat, and, in lesser amounts, oats and corn. Its fertile soil produced exceptional yields, and its farmers raised more hay than any other region, a sizable number of cattle, and one-third of the state's butter. Pigs and sheep were concentrated in the northern counties. While there were few planters in the Valley, the area was dominated by large and notoriously well kept farms.

The trans-Allegheny followed a similar pattern—grains and hay; cows, pigs, and sheep—but the area was less well developed, and holdings of cleared land were generally smaller. The region, particularly the southwest, depended heavily on corn, buckwheat, and herding. Logan County on the Ohio River in the southern part of present-day West Virginia was the largest corn producer in the western half of the state; Harrison and Monongalia in the northwest were the leading livestock and grain counties. While less productive agriculturally than either the Valley or the piedmont, the northwest became increasingly involved in Virginia's antebellum industrial movement.[44]

During these years the number of Virginians employed in various pursuits other than agriculture increased dramatically, especially among the white male population that took part in the democratic changes of the era. While the federal census of 1840—the first that provided information on the society's occupational structure—confirms traditional wisdom that eight of ten Virginians worked on farms, it also shows that a large number of individuals were involved in other pursuits. The nonagricultural sector grew by 50 percent between 1820 and 1840. The area of "manufactures and trades" employed fifty-four thousand, while "commerce," the "learned professions and engineering," "navigation," and "mining" taken together occupied an additional fifteen thousand Virginians.[45]

At the time these were not exclusive categories. The manuscript schedule shows that the household of one of Prince Edward County's largest landholders, Abraham Venable, included eight people in agriculture, one in commerce, four in manufacturing, and one professional. Rural iron plantations showed great flexibility in their use of workers. At Buffalo Forge in Rockbridge County, "the forgemen were planting corn" in April and "at harvest time all hands were farmers." As Olmsted observed, "In harvest time most of the rural mechanics closed their shops and hired out to the farmers for a dollar a day. . . . At other than harvest time, the poor white people who had no trade, would sometimes work for farmers by the job; not often any agricultural labour, but at getting rails or shingles, or clearing land." At the other end of the economic scale, the political elite included a large number of lawyer-planters who symbolized the mingling of census categories.[46]

The 1840 employment figures were reported by household and included women, children, and slaves, but the census of 1850 listed the occupations of 226,875 free men—nearly all the white adult men in the census—employed in 280 different job classifications from "agents" to "woolen manufacturers," providing an occupational profile of Virginia's white adult males. Nonagricultural employment played a much larger role than previous historians have acknowledged. Those who described themselves as "farmers" or "planters" made up only 48 percent of the total, fewer than half of the free men in Virginia in 1850. Over one-fifth of those listed described themselves as "laborers," exclusive of the significant number of artisans—carpenters, smiths, wheelwrights, and millers—listed separately and specifically designated "not agricultural" although some surely worked seasonally on farms. Even in agricultural counties the percentage of nonagriculturally employed white men was much higher than generally portrayed. In the western piedmont counties of Orange and Greene, which had no sizable towns or manufacturing concerns, farmers made up only 42 percent of the free male workers over fifteen. Some of the additional quarter of the free male population in these counties listed as "laborers" worked on farms during a part of the year, and there and elsewhere many of those in the category "law, medicine, and divinity" were also planters, but nearly half of the white adult males were not planters, farmers, or farm laborers.[47]

Virginia's antebellum "industrial movement" of these years began with the growing bituminous coal trade. Until 1828 Virginia had led Pennsylvania in coal exports, and in the 1840s the state was the nation's third leading coal producer. In the two decades preceding 1842, the mines in the Richmond Coal Basin, west of the capital in the piedmont, exported two million tons of coal. Three out of every five Virginians in the coal industry worked there. Henrico County with over one million bushels of coal and Chesterfield with just under a million were the leading producers east of the Blue Ridge. Eventually the coal industry emerged as "the economic backbone of the Alleghenies." By 1840 western mines far outstripped eastern production; 70 percent of the state's coal came from the Western District. Ohio County mined over a million bushels, and

Kanawha County alone produced six times that, accounting for three-fifths of the state's bituminous coal. All eight of the coal-producing counties in the western part of the state were in the northern half of the trans-Allegheny region.[48]

In 1850 the Old Dominion ranked third among the states in the production of pig iron, fourth in iron castings, and fifth in wrought iron with a total of 122 establishments. The Western District outproduced the Eastern, and both iron and coal were relatively more important to the economy west of the Blue Ridge. These counties had only 35 percent of the state's population but employed 70 percent of the state's ironworkers. Ohio and Monongalia counties were the leading western producers, although there were bloomeries, forges, and rolling mills throughout the Valley as well. Brunswick County in the southern piedmont produced the largest tonnage of cast iron in the state, and Buckingham and Nelson counties in the western piedmont and Spotsylvania County in the east had sizable furnaces. Henrico County was the commonwealth's leading producer of bar iron, employing more people in ironwork than any other county, and the most important iron producer in the antebellum South, the Tredegar Iron Works, was located in the city of Richmond.[49]

Two of Virginia's leading antebellum industries, flour milling and tobacco manufacturing, involved processing the commonwealth's major commercial crops. Flour mills, like sawmills and gristmills which served local needs, could be found in practically every county of the Old Dominion. Flour was one of the state's major exports, and Richmond became a major antebellum milling and distribution center. Alexandria, Petersburg, Fredericksburg, and Norfolk were also involved in the flour trade. Mills that produced for the markets of the northeastern cities and Latin America stretched west from Richmond into the central piedmont along the James River–Kanawha Canal. In 1840 the seventy-five thousand barrels of flour milled in Henrico made it the second most productive county in the eastern half of the state. Loudoun County in the northern piedmont on the Maryland border produced ninety thousand barrels exported through Alexandria and Baltimore. Elsewhere in the eastern half of the state, only Albemarle produced over fifty thousand barrels.[50]

The Western District closely challenged the eastern counties, milling nearly half of the state's flour in 1840. Jefferson County at the northern end of the Valley on the Maryland border exceeded Henrico and approached its eastern neighbor Loudoun. Four contiguous counties in the Valley around Jefferson accounted for almost half of the Western District's total output. The production of Brooke and Ohio counties, in that little finger of Virginia that poked above the Mason-Dixon Line, helped to make Wheeling an important flour-trading center that shipped hundreds of thousands of barrels to the lower South and the West Indies.[51]

The Old Dominion led the nation in tobacco manufacturing. Virginia's factories, which primarily produced chewing tobacco, underwent their greatest expansion between the 1830s and the Civil War. By 1840 Virginia produced over 40 percent of the national output, three times that manufactured in New York, and purchased two-thirds of the crop of the Old Dominion. Tobacco factories employed more men, women, and children than any other form of manufacturing. The number of hands jumped from three thousand in 1840 to over five thousand in 1850.[52]

The city of Richmond rapidly became the most important tobacco-manufacturing center in the world. The census reported almost one thousand employees in fifteen factories, probably an underestimation since the city directories of 1845 and 1850 listed thirty-one and forty-three tobacco factories, respectively. Richmond factories accounted for about one-third of the capital invested in tobacco manufacturing in the commonwealth in 1840. Lynchburg, Petersburg, and Danville were also major tobacco-manufacturing cities. There were also a large number of factories in the Southside from Prince Edward County to Patrick County, but these small country works gave way to the city factories in the 1850s.[53]

Richmond was not only the political capital of Virginia but also the commonwealth's economic center. Even Olmsted praised the city, looking to it for a renaissance of the Old Dominion. The city's waterpower and easy access to raw materials gave Richmond the potential to be a major manufacturing city. In the late 1840s both Virginia boosters and foreign travelers believed that Richmond might become "the Manchester or Birmingham of America." After visiting the state, Daniel Webster told an Andover, Massachusetts, crowd in 1843: "In Wheeling, Petersburg, Richmond, Lynchburg and Kanawha County, there are more than $11,000,000 employed in the leading manufactures of the place. There are besides cotton manufactories, blast furnaces, and foundries, in many counties. Virginia has every element and every advantage for manufacturing."[54]

Jefferson, who was no town booster, combined apology with confidence in asserting that towns in Virginia in his day were most "properly . . . villages or hamlets." Certainly the common image of antebellum Virginia is one of uninterrupted rural sprawl. On his ride from Washington to Richmond, Olmsted observed that "not more than a third of the country . . . is cleared; the rest mainly pine forrest." In 1840 Virginia, the largest and most populous state in the South, ranked third behind Maryland and Louisiana in "urban population." Yet residents of relatively large cities made up 6 percent of the Old Dominion's population, and Virginia's town element was growing faster than its population generally. In the federal census of 1840, the state's three largest cities had over ten thousand people each, and four other towns had at least six thousand inhabitants. Further, two-thirds of the town dwellers were white, and only one-quarter were slaves. Like other aspects of demographic differentiation and economic development, small-scale urbanization influenced the democratization of the Old Dominion.[55]

The 1850 census listed thirty-four "cities and towns," but the actual number was probably closer to one hundred. Townspeople touched to some degree by bourgeois culture constituted over 10 percent of Virginia's population. About half of these "urbanites" lived in the seven largest cities listed. The smallest of these, Lynchburg, had just over eight thousand people; Richmond, the largest, had grown close to thirty thousand. An even larger number of Virginians lived in the thirty towns that ranged in size from Fredericksburg in the east that had slightly over five thousand residents to Charleston in Kanawha County with a population of one thousand. Finally, another fourteen thousand Virginians lived in the sixty villages and towns with populations under one thousand whose interests were tied to the surrounding agricultural hinterland.[56]

Slavery was a fixture in Virginia's easterm cities, but urban slavery represented an anomaly for both contemporaries and subsequent historians. Richmond's population was 55 percent white and 74 percent free at a time when less than half of the population east of the Blue Ridge was white and only a bare majority free. Only three of the towns and cities listed in the census of 1850 had black majorities, and two of these—Danville and Charlottesville—were relatively small, with fifteen hundred and two thousand people, respectively. Petersburg stood out because of its huge free black population that made up one-fifth of the city. Lynchburg had a modest white majority and a large slave population, 42 percent of the total. Norfolk and Fredericksburg were over three-fifths white, while Alexandria actually had more free blacks than slaves, and three-quarters of its people were white.[57]

Cities and towns were not evenly distributed across the commonwealth (map 1.2). Those with populations over one thousand could be found in only one-fifth of the Virginia counties. Four were clustered in the southeast corner of the state around Norfolk, including Hampton on the north bank of the James, the only town in the traditional tidewater area. Petersburg, Richmond, and Fredericksburg lay along the fall line separating the tidewater and the piedmont. Lynchburg was one hundred miles west of Richmond on the James River in the foothills of the Blue Ridge. The only towns truly in the Southside were Farmville west of Petersburg on the Appomattox River and Danville on the Dan River along the North Carolina border. There were four towns along with Fredericksburg in the northern piedmont and a similar number in the northwest. Ritchieton was in Ohio County near Wheeling, while Parkersburg and Mason were farther south on the Ohio River, and Charleston grew up at the confluence of the Elk River and the Great Kanawha. The region with the largest number of

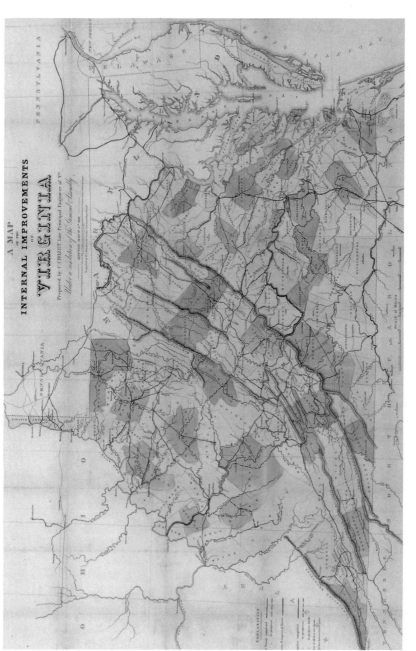

1.2. Internal improvements and towns, 1848. (Courtesy of the Virginia Historical Society)

small towns was the Valley where there were ten with over a thousand people; Winchester, the largest, had about four thousand inhabitants.[58]

These rapidly growing cities and towns were centers of manufacturing, commerce, and politics in the counties and the various regions of the state. They served as the nodes of the system of communication. Not only were practically all those employed in manufacturing and commerce in 1840 townspeople, but also the professional elite were concentrated in the towns. For example, in the census Norfolk Borough accounted for only half of Norfolk County's population but had nine-tenths of those in the category of "learned professions and engineers." Lynchburg with only a third of Campbell County's people had three-fourths of the doctors, lawyers, clergymen, and teachers. Planter-lawyers who chose to go into politics often opened offices in the small towns, and many moved to them while continuing to maintain their economic ties to the countryside. Even medium-sized towns established libraries, lyceums, and institutes like the Franklin Society at Lexington (population 1,743) where a famous debate over the Reverend Henry Ruffner's scheme for gradual emancipation occurred in 1847. Many of Virginia's towns produced newspapers such as the *Lexington Gazette*, the *Warrenton Jeffersonian*, and the *Charlottesville Advocate* to compete with the thriving religious press and the better-known partisan papers of larger cities. There were fifty-one Virginia newspapers in 1840. Thomas Ritchie's *Enquirer* and the *Richmond Whig* edited by John Hampden Pleasants appeared daily and had national reputations.[59]

The bourgeois context sustained social and political perspectives at variance with those of the planter aristocracy. Historian Clement Eaton concluded from his analysis of town life in the antebellum South that "the spirit of feverish money making and of business enterprise that was emerging in the southern cities brought their inhabitants closer to the sense of values of the Yankees than to the ideal of the agrarian gentry." The town fathers, such as those of Danville in Pittsylvania County and Farmville in Prince Edward, could combine their agricultural interests with a desire to promote banks and railroads, but Virginia's planters and yeomen farmers, for the most part, followed the dictates and prejudices of Jefferson that accepted commercial expansion as the handmaiden of agriculture while rejecting economic development that implied urbanization and industrialization.[60]

Money constituted the lifeblood of bourgeois commercialism, and the credit system spread slowly across the Old Dominion during these years as banks appeared in the major cities and towns. The ebb and flow of commodity prices reflected the fortunes of Virginia's banks. Although Jefferson grumbled about banks and paper speculators most of his life, he and those Virginians who shared his prejudices grudgingly accepted the expansion of Republican-controlled institutions. Their development in the Old Dominion was characterized by a conservative policy establishing a few large mother banks that spawned branches in satellite cities. The state legislature chartered the Bank of Virginia in 1804 and provided for Republican domination of its board. After the charter of the First Bank of the United States expired in 1811, the assembly extended the Bank of Virginia's capital and established a second mother bank, the Farmers Bank of Virginia, with headquarters in Richmond and branches in Lynchburg and Winchester.

Petitions flowed into the legislature after the War of 1812, and several extralegal private banks popped up in the northern piedmont and west of the Blue Ridge, leading the Federalist advocate of economic development, Charles Fenton Mercer, to present a bill to increase the capital of the existing institutions and create an additional fifteen branches to meet the obvious need. Although the hesitant legislature rejected Mercer's expansive proposal, the dominant planter element moved to mollify western demands for credit facilities by creating the Bank of the Valley of Virginia in Winchester and the Northwestern Bank of Virginia in Wheeling on the model of the Bank of Virginia. These banks had the power to create branches and were quasi-public in that the state subscribed two-fifths of their stock. The new Second Bank of the United States also opened offices in Richmond and Norfolk, further expanding the credit system in the state.[61]

Although the population of western Virginia grew at a much faster rate than that in the eastern half of the state, the sectional disparity in credit facilities continued to exist until the mid-1830s. During these years the banks first curtailed business during the depression following the panic of 1819 and then gradually expanded in the course of the 1820s. The price of stock in the two leading banks hit bottom in 1822, but it recovered as business brightened. The value of shares in the Bank of Virginia doubled, and the pressure for more banks increased as the economy improved. The bank got permission to increase its capital, as did the Bank of the Valley that opened a new branch at Harpers Ferry, and in 1834 the Merchants and Mechanics Bank was established at Wheeling.

Jackson's veto and subsequent removal of the government deposits from the Bank of the United States heightened the pressure on the Virginia legislature to expand the credit system. At first the assembly dragged its feet, in 1836 defeating a broad proposal to double bank capital in the state. A year later, however, two months before the onset of the panic of 1837, a new general banking law liberalized the system by opening up banking to those who complied with a prescribed set of regulations. The same legislature established the Exchange Bank of Virginia in Norfolk with branches in Richmond, Petersburg, and Clarksville and further increased the capital of the older banks, allowing them to open seven new branches. The commonwealth was to purchase most of this stock with its share of the surplus revenue from the federal government after the national debt was extinguished in 1832. Before this massive program could go into effect, the panic hit, and the next few years saw periodic suspensions and a constant struggle in the assembly between the hard money Democrats and the Whig champions of the credit system.[62]

In 1839 the assembly chartered the Bank of Kanawha in the hope of providing small loans in the west. During the depression circulation, deposits, and discounts all declined as the banks curtailed their operations. The revival of business brought a slow increase in discounts and deposits back to the prepanic levels of the mid-1830s. There were no bank failures in Virginia, and total capital in the state actually expanded by about 50 percent between 1838 and 1842. To answer the increased demand for more banks as the economy grew, the Virginia legislature joined those of most of the other states in authorizing free banking in 1851. Within three years thirteen new banks had been established: four in the northwest, four in the Valley, four in the northern piedmont, and one at Lynchburg.[63]

The economic development of antebellum Virginia, like that of the other states of the Union at the time, depended upon transportation and communication as much as money and credit. The lines of transportation heightened the economic differentiation of the Old Dominion's dominant regions. Commercial towns failed to develop in the tidewater, because "the so-called rivers were really arms of the sea, permitting the ocean-going craft of colonial times to sail in freely to the individual wharves of a thousand planters." Being graced by the environment, the lowland Virginians were suspicious of the attempts of those less lucky to use the powers of the state to their advantage. Sectional and local rivalries over state aid to internal improvements were important in every state in the Union. By the Civil War the state and local governments of the Old Dominion had invested $55 million. Yet it was a grudgingly financed and often ill-planned use of resources primarily focused upon the central connection of the James and the Ohio rivers via the Great Kanawha. Virginia was a distant third among the states of the Union in canal mileage; even after alternative technologies became available, the commonwealth's designated company stuck stubbornly to the idea of "slack water navigation."[64]

Following the extensive report of a committee chaired by Mercer, who had just made his proposal for an expansion of banking facilities, the assembly had created a Fund for Internal Improvement and a Board of Public Works in 1816. The fund absorbed the state's stock in the Bank of Virginia and the Farmers Bank, and the assembly agreed to subscribe two-fifths of approved future projects. As Mercer told Congress several years later, public involvement was designed to provide "modest insurance against loss" and "to elicit the subscription of individual wealth to use." By 1851 the board had become involved in construction of three thousand miles of turnpikes and nearly nine hundred miles of "the most capacious and substantially constructed canals in the Union" as well as ten plank roads and twelve bridges. A year after founding the board, the assembly passed the general turnpike law that outlined the board's relation to new companies. Fifteen years later when the assembly reorganized the James River and Kanawha Canal Company, it increased the ratio of the state's subscription of turnpike stock. The system grew greatly in the 1830s in response to western demand, beginning with the incorporation of the Northwestern Turnpike Road in 1831 and culminating in the fight over the general improvements bill in 1838. Although the advocates of improvement lost on this legislation, they were able to establish the Valley Turnpike, the Staunton and Parkersville Turnpike, and the Southwestern Turnpike, which brought extensive economic benefit to the western half of the state, especially the Valley region.[65]

While never funding the proposal properly, the state government adhered to the idea of a central connection via the James and Kanawha rivers through a series of reorganizations of the canal company. The Board of Public Works intended to improve the two rivers with canals around falls and other obstructions and join them with a turnpike over the Appalachian barrier although the company's 1835 charter did leave open the possibility of the use of "rail roads" along the route to the west. The focus of the company with its eastern eyes was to connect Richmond to Buchannon, approximately two hundred miles west of the capital in the foothills of the Blue Ridge.[66]

With state and local aid, railroads were also being built or at least being chartered. County and city governments were willing to use local taxes to buy the securities of companies they believed would improve their own economic positions. Of these, the Staunton and Potomac chartered in 1831 was the first, and subsequently other companies built small segments of track and began operation piecemeal. Although Virginia's expenditures were not used as effectively as they might have been and did not represent a large per capita commitment to internal improvements, the commonwealth was doing reasonably well. In 1850 Virginia was seventh in the country in miles of track laid or under construction, just behind Massachusetts.[67]

Between the War of 1812 and midcentury, the distribution of Virginia's white population shifted dramatically with the development of the piedmont and the multiplying counties west of the Blue Ridge while the economy of the Old Dominion both expanded and diversified. With the exception of the years of national depression from 1839 to 1843, the Old Dominion experienced a generally high level of economic growth little different from the other states of the Union. The three decades after Jefferson's death were characterized by agricultural revival rather than decline. The Virginia State Agricultural Society, like the

Virginia State Historical Society that appeared at the same time, was born not of pessimism but of a faith in the future of the Old Dominion.[68]

The effects of economic change were not uniform across the common-wealth, and the regions within the state assumed contrasting socioeconomic characteristics. The tidewater, which has too often served to typify the Old Do-minion, had been hard hit by the depression of the early 1820s. Old Virginia suf-fered from soil exhaustion and the migration of its "planters, small farmers, and negro slaves to the West and Southwest." Much to the distress of its consump-tive poets, various romantics, and general naysayers of doom, the patient recov-ered. Market forces dictated agricultural reform and diversification. Between the 1830s and the 1850s, the value of land in the region increased by $20 million.

The main results of migration and reform were an increase in the propor-tion of both slaveholders and landowners and a diminution in the size of hold-ings. Once the home of the Lees and Washingtons, Westmoreland County in the Northern Neck between the Rappahannock and the Potomac had a black majority that included over one thousand "free colored" people and thirty-five hundred slaves. Of the white family heads, 70 percent owned slaves and a slightly larger proportion were landholders, but only about one in eight was a planter. On the Eastern Shore whites made up two-fifths of the population of Northampton County; three-quarters of the white families owned their own farms, and nearly all possessed slaves although only a handful held over twenty.

South of the James River in the area around Norfolk where about four-fifths of the families owned slaves, there were also very few planters. Three-quarters of the whites owned land, and two-thirds of the landless were tenants. Throughout the tidewater counties reported black majorities with a large "free colored" element, relatively few landless whites, and a sizable proportion of white families, generally over 70 percent, who owned slaves. There were, how-ever, few planters. As part of the movement for agricultural reform, "land re-duction was expected to encourage intensive farming, diversification and sci-entific methods."[69]

Outside its major cities Old Virginia was cut off from the corruptions of the modern world. The industrial movement hardly touched the tidewater. Al-though the region was ringed by Fredericksburg, Richmond, Petersburg, and Norfolk, which served as markets for its produce, the rural counties had no cities and very few towns. Transportation other than along the major rivers lan-guished. The region remained the most English in the Old Dominion. Most churchgoers were Methodists, but the Episcopalians' resurgence made them more numerous in the tidewater than in any part of the state. Populated by a sizable number of poverty-stricken quasi-free blacks and old families who owned too many slaves, the region was the heartland of decadent paternalism.[70]

The piedmont plateau that stretched from the fall line to the Blue Ridge emerged during these years as the most populous region of Virginia and dictated much of the character of the Old Dominion. Its southeastern half was the center of plantation agriculture and the peculiar institution—the most typically "southern" section of the state. Slaves outnumbered the whites in these counties, which included eleven of the twelve in which slaves made up over 60 percent of the population. There were twice as many plantations in the piedmont as in the tidewater.

From the mid-1820s until the Civil War, the region's economic prognosis steadily improved. The southeastern two-thirds of the piedmont produced nearly all of the tobacco grown in the state; its northern counties were nationally important producers of wheat. Grain "farms" were larger than tobacco "plantations," and the northern piedmont was the only Virginia region where the majority of holdings were over two hundred acres.[71]

In Amelia County in the center of the piedmont west of Richmond, south of the James River, nine-tenths of the family heads owned land; 85 percent held slaves, and one-third of them were planters with twenty or more. Although Amelia represented an extreme case, in most of these counties two-thirds to three-quarters of the white families held slaves; only about a third of the householders were landless, and at least half of these were tenants. Roughly one-quarter of the slaveholders had a sufficient number of bondsmen to be designated planters. There was generally a high correlation between the number of acres and the number of slaves held, but there was a group of white family heads who owned slaves but no land, renting out their chattel or using them to work leased land.[72]

The piedmont's ethnic and religious makeup was mixed although the largest single group was the English. The Scotch-Irish, Scots, and Welsh accounted for 35 percent of those living in the area, and north of the James River, there were a number of Germans. In the northern piedmont the Methodists predominated as they did everywhere in the state, but in this section they were followed in importance by the Baptists and the Episcopalians. On the Southside there were proportionally even more Methodists among the whites—half the population—while the Presbyterians ranked second, claiming about one-fifth of the whites.[73]

The Great Valley of Virginia west of the Blue Ridge stood in stark contrast to the lower piedmont. The region included the South Branch of the Potomac and the headwaters of the James as well as the Shenandoah and its tributaries. Its major towns like Staunton and Winchester grew up along the Valley Turnpike at the points where it was crossed by east/west routes, but the area was dotted with numerous smaller towns as well. The Valley had the highest percentage of nonagricultural workers of the four major regions in the state in 1840. Yet it was a predominately agricultural area with extremely rich soil that made it Virginia's prime wheat-growing area.

Of course, the relative absence of the peculiar institution posed the most striking difference between the Valley and the piedmont. While half of the people in the piedmont were enslaved, four-fifths of those living in the Valley were free. There were, consequently, far fewer slaveholders. Even in Bath County where slightly over one-quarter of the whites owned slaves, only 4 percent held twenty or more. Farmers in the Valley also had smaller landholdings. The average farmer in Augusta County worked 228 acres while in Pittsylvania, a Southside county with roughly the same population as Augusta, he owned 361 acres. A further comparison of these two counties highlights the contrast between the Valley and the piedmont. While roughly the same proportion of householders owned land, almost twice as many of the Pittsylvania farms were over 500 acres, but a much larger proportion of the acres on the smaller farms in Augusta were cleared for cultivation. The Valley county also had twice as many towns and half as many farmers.[74]

The picture of economic diversity in the Valley was matched by the region's ethnic and religious makeup. The English portion of the population was counterbalanced by the Scotch-Irish and the Germans. They accounted for over 70 percent of the settlers of both Shenandoah and Rockingham. Although they were hardly abolitionists, the Germans were less likely to be slaveholders than the English and Scotch-Irish. Clannishness and cultural conflict between the two dominant ethnic groups were commonplace. In Winchester in the northern part of the Valley, "on Sunday afternoons the opposing religious processions of the Irish [Scotch-Irish] and the Dutch [Germans] started little wars that frequently resulted in bloody noses."[75]

This ethnic mixture guaranteed a different religious complexion as well. Although Methodists were the largest denomination in the Valley, there were as many white Presbyterians as white Methodists, and the collective German religious groups—the Lutherans being the largest—outnumbered both. There were also significant numbers of white Baptists and Episcopalians. Again one may contrast Augusta with Pittsylvania. Forty-four of the fifty churches in the eastern county were Baptist or Methodist, and the others were either Episcopalian or Presbyterian. Augusta's forty-one churches served nine different denominations—even the Roman Catholics, Tunkers, Moravians, and Mennonites all had at least one place of worship. Obviously the Valley was far more cosmopolitan than the Southside.[76]

In the trans-Allegheny region there was a striking difference between the northern and southern portions that would lead to the creation of the state of West Virginia. The southwest had proportionally more farmers and agricultural laborers than any of the other areas of the state, but the land was mountainous and large portions lay undeveloped. Over 90 percent of the heads of families in Floyd were farmers, and two-thirds owned their own land, but southwestern farms were small and relatively poor. They grew very little wheat and emphasized corn and livestock production. These counties also had the highest ratio of home manufactures to population in the commonwealth. The region had no towns with over one thousand inhabitants, and transportation was primitive.[77]

Despite the number of independent farmers, the southwest was hardly a yeoman's utopia. Its most populous counties had much larger landless white populations than those in either the Valley or the northwest and a higher portion of tenants. The area had by far the highest rate of illiteracy for white adults in the commonwealth, half again that for the northwest. It also had twice as many slaves as the northwest and a surprising number of slaveholders among the white adult males who could vote. In Washington County, the most populous county in the southwest, one-quarter of the landed families owned slaves. At the same time a majority of the county's household heads listed in the 1850 census were landless. Even in Tazewell, where there were a larger number of landowners, over one-fifth of the farmers held slaves.[78]

The northwest was wealthier, much more economically diversified, and ethnically more cosmopolitan. The two trans-Allegheny subregions had only a modestly different ethnic and religious breakdown among the native Virginians, but only three-quarters of the population of the northwest had been born in Virginia. Twenty thousand had come from the states to the north and eight thousand from foreign countries. Of the southwesterners, in contrast, 94 percent were natives of the commonwealth, and there were few foreigners. Those born outside the Old Dominion came from the slave states to the south and west.

The farmers of the northwest were more market oriented than their fellows in the southwestern counties. The northern area had more towns, better transportation, and a much more diversified economy. A far larger proportion of the population of the northwest worked at nonagricultural jobs. The region had three times as much capital and four times as many industrial employees as the southwest. By the 1830s Wheeling had flour mills, glass factories, distilleries, textile factories, paper mills, and sawmills. Along the Kanawha were coal mines, forges and foundries, and saltworks. Most of the area's modest number of slaves were involved in these industries, consequently there were practically no planters in the northwest.[79]

The American Revolution brought relatively little change in the social order of the Old Dominion and the Jeffersonian era constituted a stable period of planter hegemony. The commonwealth contained an aristocratic society composed of gentlemen freeholders presided over by landed gentry committed to conservative republicanism. At the apex of the this elite stood the "One Hundred" richest families who translated their social position into political power. The average member of this group owned three thousand acres in his premier plantation, and most had several such holdings. Eighty-five percent were primarily planters, and the average member of the "One Hundred" owned eighty slaves, a similar number of cattle, and two dozen horses. Generally their economic interests extended beyond their agricultural holdings into the mercantile and commercial world. Nearly all were extensive land speculators.[80]

In the nineteenth century one of the main changes in the commonwealth involved the decline of this superrich segment as the rural society of the eighteenth century became more pluralistic and atomized. For the most part the "decline thesis" dealt with the sad experience of this small segment of Virginia society. As they lost the myriad mercantile sources of sustenance, they had to rely increasingly on the production of tobacco to maintain their vast estates. Plagued by soil exhaustion, they watched their neighbors and children migrate west, leaving their tired tobacco lands to the eldest son to continue the family line while encouraging their daughters to marry well and their younger sons to find lucrative careers in the professions. By the Civil War most of their descendants were neither slaveholders nor particularly wealthy. Only about half of the grandsons of the great planting families and one-quarter of their great-grandsons were still planters. Most had moved away, many to urban areas where one-fourth were shopkeepers and artisans.[81]

By the mid-nineteenth century the pinnacle of Virginia society included a segment of survivors from the eighteenth century's richest "One Hundred," and they were not so wealthy as their ancestors, although two-thirds still qualified as planters, and 7 percent owned over one hundred slaves. These men were joined in the new antebellum elite by descendants of eighteenth-century families of lesser wealth who had persisted in their home counties, expanding their holdings, and by highly mobile new men who accumulated their fortunes as they moved from county to county in the commonwealth seeking the main chance. This antebellum economic elite included fewer planters and more men who made their wealth outside of agriculture than had their predecessors. Of course, most were still planters, but even in the rural counties they made up a smaller proportion of the new elite.

In urban counties like Henrico, Fairfax, Spotsylvania, and Norfolk, nearly two-fifths of these men were professionals, merchants, and manufacturers. Eighty-five percent of the new elite held slaves, but the average holding was down from 162 in the 1780s to 33; of over eight hundred of the commonwealth's wealthiest men in 1860, only four owned more slaves than the 1788 elite averaged. Virginia's growth in population and wealth from 1800 to 1840 and the diversification of its economy offered an opportunity for a new pluralistic elite to take the place of the monolithic planter class associated with the Golden Age of the Old Dominion.[82]

The antebellum movement away from an aristocratic republic of gentlemen freeholders toward Herrenvolk democracy focused on the rights and privileges of the white men who after 1851 constituted the political nation of the Old Dominion. The white majority lived west of the Blue Ridge and made up a larger proportion of the population in those counties than in the east. Most were Methodist, Baptist, and Presbyterian evangelicals. While the largest single ethnic group was the English, a majority of white Virginians had come from England's "celtic fringe"—Ireland, Scotland, and Wales—and nearly one-fifth were Germans. In 1850 most had been born in the state, but there was a great deal of both geographic and social mobility.[83]

The Old Dominion was a slave state, and in 1850 about one-third of the families owned slaves. Over half of the slaveholders owned fewer than five blacks, and the proportion of slaveholders in the society was falling. The majority of white men living in the Old Dominion at midcentury differed little from those in the rest of the nation. Approximately two-thirds were landholders. Only about half were planters or farmers. Although most of the rest were tied in one way or another to the state's agricultural base, the size of the nonagricultural element among these potential voters is striking given the usual perception of the Old Dominion. The proportion of farmers in antebellum Virginia's free male population was not only much lower than that found in most of the southern states but also lower than that in the majority of northern states, including Virginia's larger western neighbor, Ohio.[84]

All of these social and economic changes that beset the commonwealth during the "age of the common man" from the end of the War of 1812 to the middle of the nineteenth century were occurring throughout the Union; they were, in fact, the kinds of shifts in the socioeconomic environment and the mentalité of the relevant groups that bred political individualism and the expansion of democracy everywhere. Historian Kathleen Bruce has argued that "the industrial movement quietly progressed in the little cities of the commonwealth where it generated business notions and promoted the accumulation of capital." She might have added notions of political individualism and liberal democracy that triumphed finally in the constitution of 1851. That the Old Dominion lagged behind its sister states is a testimony to the tenacity of the eastern conservative element who continued to exploit the prerogatives granted to them by the constitution of 1776, their uniquely powerful hold on local power, and the republican ideology of the American Revolution to which all Virginians claimed fidelity.[85]

๛ 2 ๛

The Constitution of Virginia

G EORGE MASON and the other delegates who gathered in Williamsburg
to declare the colony's independence from the crown in the early summer of 1776 designed the Virginia Declaration of Rights and the constitution of the commonwealth to serve the ends of the republican ideology that
animated the American Revolution. Except for the changes made in relation to
the executive branch, the new constitution retained the colonial frame of government that had functioned—more closely than any other colony—in line
with the Country ideal. The new document stripped away the powers of governor and his council and made the legislature, in true republican fashion, the
government of the Old Dominion. Its members chose the executive and in
principle regulated the makeup of the county courts, although the latter remained, in fact, self-perpetuating bodies.[1]

Virginia's new General Assembly was bicameral. A twenty-four-member
senate was elected in a scheme of rotation that retired six men every year. Members of the House of Delegates were elected annually; each county chose two,
and the incorporated towns, one apiece. Local government was left to the
county courts, which with their local juries upheld Virginia's common law and
guaranteed gentry control. Suffrage was limited to the gentlemen freeholders
who had held the privilege during the colonial era.

Ownership of land served as the source of a citizen's independence and as
the "evidence of permanent common interest with and attachment to the community" that determined the right to vote. "Dependence," wrote Jefferson,
"begets subservience and venality, suffocates the germ of virtue and prepares fit
tools for the designs of ambition." Except for "Ministers of the Gospel," all
freeholders could serve in the General Assembly, although the senators had to
be twenty-five years of age. Frequent elections assured a government "fresh
from the people," while brief sessions and modest pay guaranteed republican
simplicity. Well into the nineteenth century, as the other states of the Union

The Virginia constitutional convention of 1829–30. (Courtesy of the Virginia
Historical Society)

adopted more democratic frames of government, the commonwealth of Virginia continued to operate under its republican charter.[2]

In "Query XIII" of his *Notes on the State of Virginia*, Jefferson wrote respectfully of Mason's work but pointedly noted that the constitution "was formed when we were new and inexperienced in the science of government" and went on to suggest major revisions. He had been disappointed at not being able to be present to take part in the writing of the document and miffed by the convention's dismissal of his own draft that he had forwarded to Edmund Pendleton. Jefferson believed that the Virginia constitution paid insufficient attention to the separation of powers. The fact that the state senate and the House of Delegates hardly differed in their makeup failed to provide the "proper complication of principles . . . which alone can compensate the evils arising from dissensions in the legislative branch."

Reflecting on his own unhappy tenure as governor, Jefferson worried that the constitution created an "*elective despotism*" by consolidating "all the powers of government, legislative, executive, and judiciary" in the hands of the assembly. He differed most clearly with Mason and the conservatives, however, on the questions of suffrage and representation, which would remain at the center of the constitutional debate in the Old Dominion for the next seventy-five years.[3]

Most of Jefferson's fellow Virginians shared the belief that all political history consisted of the ongoing conflict rooted in human nature between liberty and authority, freedom and power. They agreed with the English publicist Thomas Gordon, who stated, "What is good for the People is bad for their governors; and what is good for the governors, is pernicious to the People." These conservative republicans posed a rigid distinction between government and society, the magistrates and the people, that in eighteenth-century England was embodied in the conflict between the Country and the Court.[4]

From their reading of history and their understanding of human nature, the Revolutionary republicans were well aware that such governments had proved fragile in the past and relied upon the moral quality of the people. Ancient republics traditionally had been subverted by invasion from without and corruption from within. In particular, these eighteenth-century Virginians imbibed the Country's fear of faction and hostility to parties. They contrasted the expression of partial interests in the form of factions with the maintenance of civic virtue and independent judgment; they rejected the liberal politics of conflict and sought consensus. The ideal republican government represented the interest of its virtuous and independent citizens by circumscribing the power of their magistrates and thus ensuring strict accountability.

These general views dictated that the debate over the suffrage provisions of the constitution would revolve around the amount and kind of property that would assure personal independence and a stake in society. Mason had proposed a somewhat higher amount of landed estate be required of voters than the convention accepted. Jefferson resisted universal suffrage but proposed that the qualification be even lower. A town lot or twenty-five acres of land in the countryside and the payment of local taxes for the previous two years should be sufficient to permit men to select members of the house. He also sought to add two more radical amendments suggesting that the franchise be extended to members of the militia as well as taxpayers and that the state create freeholders by giving sufficient land to deserving heads of households.[5]

Mason had expressed the traditional view that the members of the assembly should be "men . . . of independent Circumstances and principles." Jefferson certainly did not want to encourage the "low politician" who would curry the favor of the electors or become "dependent on them," but he told Edmund Pendleton that he saw no need for candidates to "possess distinguished property" since "his observations" had failed to convince him that integrity was a "characteristic of wealth." But Jefferson worried more about the scheme of representation in the new constitution than either its suffrage provisions or the qualifications for officeholding. In contrast to the views of Mason and the other delegates in 1776, he argued that giving each county representatives in the house was unfair; instead "the number of representatives" should be proportional "to the number of qualified voters."[6]

James Madison agreed with his friend on the need for revision of the constitution of 1776, but his position stood closer in spirit to Mason's than to Jefferson's and foreshadowed the moderate position he would take in the convention of 1829–30. In the 1780s he pushed for reform of the state constitution and legal system, advocating a six-year term for the state senators to guarantee against "the infirmities of popular governments" and general elections to undermine the "spirit of *locality*." He also sought a "middle way" on property qualification and representation in which property determined who voted for the senate. Finally, Madison feared that choice of the governor by the legislature encouraged "faction intrigue and corruption," and thus, he favored popular election of the executive.[7]

The liberal Madison, however, was too radical for the Virginians of his day. Twice during the 1780s Madison's attempts to get the assembly to consider calling a convention to revise the 1776 document were overwhelmingly rejected by those who agreed with Mason that it was best to leave well enough alone. Thus, the commonwealth's conservative republicans rejected the arguments on constitutional revision of both Jefferson, whose ideas have been treated by historians as synonymous with Virginia Republicanism, and Madison, the key figure in the formation of the Jeffersonian Republican party.

The assembly modestly extended the suffrage when it set the election laws in 1785 by defining freeholders as either white males holding fifty acres of land or townsmen who could claim an estate worth over £50. Although the provision was seldom enforced, the law also provided for compulsory voting. Conservative republicanism remained inviolate; the county courts guaranteed the continuation of a social order rooted in the idea of a stable community led by the planter class.[8]

In Old Virginia a man's worth was measured in terms of his property, and "property" meant slaves as well as land. Slavery was thus related directly to taxation and consequently became central to the debates about constitutional revision. As Jefferson agonized over the proper form that democratic republicanism would take in the Old Dominion, he was drawn back constantly to the fearful presence of the peculiar institution. "I tremble for my country when I reflect that God is just," he wrote in his *Notes*. "His justice cannot sleep forever." Jefferson saw clearly the effect of slavery on the slaveholder: "The whole commerce between master and slave is a perpetual exercise of despotism on the one part, and degrading submissions on the other. Our children see this. . . . The parent storms, the child looks on, catches the lineaments of wrath, puts on the same airs in the circle of smaller slaves, gives a loose to his worst passions, and thus nursed, educated, and daily exercised in tyranny, cannot but be stamped by it with odious peculiarities. The man must be a prodigy who can retain his manners and morals un-depraved by such circumstances." The future president's understanding of the conflict between slavery and democracy reflected the moral tension within the political culture of antebellum Virginia and the new nation as a whole.[9]

For the next half century the question of constitutional revision would be debated by Virginians endlessly repeating the basic arguments aired in 1776 by the constitution's author, Mason, and by its most severe critic, Jefferson. The central focus of the debate involved the extent of the franchise and the basis of representation in the lower house of the legislature and thus mirrored similar debates in all of the states of the Union. The demands for constitutional change generally included efforts to reform the judicial systems of the states as well, and in Virginia reform of the county courts threatened the dominance of the society by the conservative local planter elites. Further, each of these matters—suffrage, representation, and the courts—was intimately connected to the maintenance of slavery in the Old Dominion, and consequently the whole range of interests related to slavery were woven into the debate over the democratic reform.

Almost solely because of the demographic distribution of slaves and slaveholding in Virginia, the conflict of interests in this debate followed a sectional pattern that set the Revolutionary republican center against the emerging periphery which led the movement for democratic change. While Thomas Jefferson personally put forth a radical position that was not written into the commonwealth's fundamental law until a quarter century after his death, his name has been associated with those who dominated Virginia politics in the formative period and used by historians to describe the era of American political history when he was active in the federal government as secretary of state, vice president, and president. It would be too much to say that Jefferson was a prophet without honor in his own time and in his own "country," his term for the portion of Virginia from which he came. But on these matters the Sage of Monticello did not represent the views of the dominant Revolutionary center that ruled the Old Dominion during his lifetime and is known as the Jeffersonian Republican party.

While the number of slaveholders grew relatively in the first two decades of the nineteenth century, planters and their families remained a small minority. The landed gentry clung to the reins of power in Virginia, relying on the essentially conservative Country ideology to maintain control of the institutions that most intimately affected their lives and well-being. They spoke a rhetoric of localism and community control that demanded deference from not only slaves, women, and children but also countless white men and defended their own individual liberty against the corrupt authority of government at a distance, London, Philadelphia, New York, and eventually even the District of Columbia, part of which they had ceded to the new "foreign" government created by the Constitution.

In the wake of the panic of 1819 and the Missouri debate, the conservative components of Virginia's political culture reasserted themselves in a vigorous defense of states' rights, strict construction, and slave property that tended to set the Revolutionary "center" against the emerging "periphery." The modernizing, urban, and urbane influence that the center/periphery dichotomy implies, however, was inverted in the Old Dominion. The political power of the planter aristocracy predominated in the rural slaveholding tidewater and the southeastern piedmont the area known as Old Virginia. Encircling the city of Richmond, the commonwealth's "center" was economically stagnant and populated by old white families descended from the early migration of the English, Welsh, and French, surrounded by a growing black majority that made the region demographically and socially similar to the lower South. It was the breeding ground of conservative paternalism. The periphery extended in an arc from Norfolk to the Eastern Shore across to the Northern Neck, along the Potomac, and down the Ohio to the mouth of the Big Sandy River, encompassing all of the counties west of the Blue Ridge. This zone of transition was economically dynamic, ethnically and religiously varied, and socially fluid. These peripheral areas and the Old Dominion's few cities welcomed political and economic change.[10]

Mired in a sluggish agricultural economy that needed diversification and reform, the leading spokesmen of the conservative center seem to have been overcome in the 1820s with a sense of impending doom expressed in romantic histories and the genre of plantation novels typified by George Tucker's *The Valley of the Shenandoah*, John Pendleton Kennedy's *Swallow Barn*, and Beverley Tucker's *George Balcombe*. William Wirt's biography of Patrick Henry extolled the virtue and patriotism of the leaders of the Revolution, in contrast to the low character of the politicians of his own day. The present seemed unbearably grim: "Virginia—poor Virginia furnishes a spectacle at present which is enough to make the heart of her real Friends sick to the very core."[11]

Writing to Dabney Carr at the end of the decade, Wirt expressed the general disgust with politics and parties that characterized the political culture of the eastern planter elite: "I have an utter distaste to politics. I hate from my heart all these vile intrigues and cabals. . . . I hate all the quarrelling, lying and slandering, and the hot blood and feverish contentions which, now-a-days, at least seem inseparable from political life. . . . I have not the pride of Coriolanus, but I shall never stoop to ask for office. I have always disapproved, upon principle, this business of canvassing. . . . Party is high and hot here, it is a Moloch to which I will never sacrifice." This distaste for the liberal politics of conflict and partisan contention appeared most clearly in Beverley Tucker's novel *The Partisan Leader*, in which it was combined with the siege mentality of the Southside squirearchy to depict a future civil war to rid Virginia of the tyranny and corruption inherent in the sixteen-year reign of the man who came to epitomize the party politician, Martin Van Buren.[12]

Even Jefferson was hardly optimistic about his country's future after the War of 1812. Nearing death, the Sage embraced the states' rights Radicals in his denunciation of consolidation. Jefferson complimented Judge Spencer Roane on his "Hampden" letters and supported him in his struggle against the centralizing tendencies of the Marshall Court. When young William Fitzhugh Gordon asked the former president's advice on the proper response to the threats to the Constitution posed by the incoming Adams administration, the elder statesman replied, "It is but too evident that the branches of our foreign department of government, executive, judiciary, and legislative are in combination to usurp the powers of the domestic branch also reserved to the States, and consolidate themselves into a single government without limitation of powers."[13]

On the matters concerning the rights of the states, Jefferson clearly joined with the conservative center and differed with his friend Madison's moderately nationalist views, but this agreement on federal matters has obscured the sharp conflict between Jefferson and the majority of Virginia's "Jeffersonian Republicans" on the necessity to reform the commonwealth's constitution. On this matter Jefferson was more radical than Madison and Madison more radical than the majority of Virginia's political elite. While Jefferson's position changed very little over the years, that of the conservatives hardened in the 1820s; "the frustrations felt by the gentry in the wake of Old Virginia's decline had united the lowland squirearchy in an all-out defense of the status quo."[14] The debates over constitutional reform offer a glimpse of the political cultures of the reactionary center and democratic periphery. In the constitutional convention of 1829–30, former senator John Randolph, speaking for the commonwealth's conservatives, portrayed the democratic Jefferson as a visionary fool: "We are not struck down by the authority of Mr. Jefferson. Sir, if there be any point in which the authority of Mr. Jefferson might be considered valid, it is in the mechanism of a plough." The references to "Virginia ideas" and "the Principles of '98" that formed the bedrock of the political culture of the center strayed from Madison's meaning and embraced the more extreme Antifederalist doctrines of John Taylor of Caroline and Judge Spencer Roane. Strict construction and states' rights degenerated into a defensive posture that combined a nostalgic allegiance to the political status quo and the rights of slaveholders with a distrust of democracy and party politics that verged on the paranoid. The political order of Old Virginia became the prescription of the center to maintain traditional authority.[15]

From its inception the Virginia constitution of 1776 came under criticism, and periodically the assembly considered the possibility of reform. As western population grew, the basis of representation increasingly became the primary issue. Initially the approach to reform was to seek redress through traditional prayers to the legislature from county meetings. Petitions from Frederick County in 1796 and the southwestern piedmont counties of Patrick and Pittsylvania a decade later argued that the assembly appeared "afraid to trust the people." The conservatives who controlled the legislature rejected these and other petitions on the grounds that any revision of the constitution would promote instability and anarchy by setting the Old Dominion "adrift on a sea of uncertainty."[16]

Throughout the 1790s and up through the War of 1812, the loosely knit Republican interest, rooted in the southeastern slaveholding gentry of Old Virginia, controlled the commonwealth and resisted any attempts at reform of the original constitution or the traditional legal system. Denouncing foreign tyrants and outside agitators, the Virginia Republicans conceived of local government as the bulwark of their liberties. The eastern conservative gentry who made up the Revolutionary center came to view change of any kind as the enemy of their independence. After Madison's attempts to force reform in the 1780s, petitions from the western piedmont and beyond the Blue Ridge drifted into Richmond intermittently, calling on the assembly to convene a convention to consider constitutional revision to reapportion the House of Delegates.

The Republicans had huge majorities in both houses and at any time could have revised the constitution in line with Jefferson's wishes. The question of revision came up repeatedly and was one of the few state issues considered by the assembly. Ten times between 1801 and 1813 reformers introduced resolutions to call a convention; twice the proposal was passed by the House of Delegates only to be quashed by the conservative eastern planters in the state senate. Because the practical problems involved the creation of new counties and reapportionment of legislative seats, the conflict was basically sectional and revolved around interest rather than ideology to a greater degree than either side wished to acknowledge. A frustrated Madison had earlier written his father concerning reform of the courts, "The difficulty of suiting [legislation] to every palate, & the many latent objections of a selfish & private nature which will shelter themselves under some plausible objections of a public nature to which every innovation is liable render the event extremely uncertain."[17]

With the return of peace in 1815, liberal democratic demands for reform confidently reasserted themselves in the expanding periphery. The cries for change came most often from the western piedmont and the Valley, but these reformers had allies along the Potomac in the northern piedmont as well. In Norfolk and Richmond artisanal republicanism flourished among the mechanics and small manufacturers. In June 1815 reformers gathered in Harrisonburg to protest "the inhibitions to the elective franchise" and issued an address on July 4 appealing appropriately to the Declaration of Independence, the Virginia Bill of Rights, and the heritage of the Revolution.[18]

Echoing Jefferson, the delegates insisted that along with the men recently "coerced into military service," all of those who paid taxes deserved "a voice in the election of the Legislators by whom those taxes are imposed." "The existing system is a tyrannical, and anti-republican destruction of the inherent and inalienable rights of man." Taxation without representation was "the grand political heresy for which the men of 1776 declared the independence of the United States." To right this injustice and bring the commonwealth back to its true principles, the address urged the counties to petition the assembly to call "a CONVENTION of the PEOPLE."[19]

The western counties responded, sending batches of petitions to the assembly. When the house again narrowly defeated the plan in the session of 1815–16, the reformers looked to the device of a counterconvention or informal gathering to memorialize the assembly for a formal constitutional convention. Jefferson contributed to the cause a long letter to westerner Samuel Kercheval in which he repeated his earlier position and clearly outlined the issues as he saw them: "The sum of these amendments is, 1. General Suffrage. 2. Equal Representation in the legislature. 3. An executive chosen by the people. 4. Judges elective or removable. 5. Justices, jurors, and sheriffs elective. 6. Ward divisions. And 7. Periodical amendments of the Constitution."[20]

Actually this list implies a broader suffrage than Jefferson intended and included two of Jefferson's pet projects that had not been part of his earlier scheme. For some time he had wished to reform the county courts and hoped to institute a system of wards based on a New England model to create democracy at the grass roots. Jefferson conceived of a hierarchy of ascending republics for the new nation. He wrote Joseph C. Cabell earlier that year, "The elementary republics of the wards, the county republics, the States republics, and the republic of the Union, would form a gradation of authorities, standing each on the basis of law, holding every one its delegated share of powers and constituting truly a system of fundamental balances and checks for the government." At the base was the "ward-republic" that would be governed by elected magistrates.[21]

Such radical ideas found little support in the Old Dominion, particularly among eastern planter Republicans. Even some of the "reformers" agreed with the outspoken Chapman Johnson, who urged equalization of the representation but opposed expansion of the electorate. Jefferson's friend Archibald Stuart, from the western piedmont, worried about the landless voters owning no part of the country: "Experience has taught us how even free holders who are in a State of Dependence may be influenced to commit foolish acts what then might we expect if the Idle, the vicious and the worthless are to have an agency in carrying on our government." [22]

Most of the critics of the old constitution, however, advocated the elimination of the freehold requirement as well as reapportionment of the legislature. During the summer of 1816, a number of counties held mass meetings to demand a convention. A gathering of eleven western counties met in early August in Winchester, and then later in the month an even larger convention of reformers met at Staunton with representatives from thirty-five counties. They produced a memorial that focused upon a call for a constitutional convention and clearly stood for discarding the freehold suffrage requirement and equalizing representation. The issue that united the reformers was the demand for the convention itself, not the specifics of constitutional revision. Their attempts to bring about change forced them to rely on methods that were traditional in their outward appearance but were inherently populist and contributed to altering the entire governing process. [23]

The *Richmond Enquirer* covered these activities, and its editor Thomas Ritchie spoke for moderate eastern Republicans in urging at least some reform, if only to retain the loyalty of the counties in the Valley and the southwest. He feared that anti-Republican elements might use the issue to rally support against eastern domination of the government of the commonwealth. To thwart radical reform and divide the periphery, a few eastern Republicans joined with the Federalists and the westerners in the assembly to respond to demands from the Valley for banks and internal improvements. They also passed a bill that revised apportionment of the state senate—which had consistently blocked reform— by doubling the number of representatives from west of the Blue Ridge and decreasing the number from the east. But fearing that it might go beyond the modest changes proposed and undermine the power of the gentry, eastern Republicans refused to call a convention. [24]

In the short run these actions quieted western demands, but both constitutional reform and economic development continued to depend upon eastern sufferance. The depression triggered by the panic of 1819 severely affected eastern Virginia, undermining earlier promises and encouraging the reassertion of planter conservatism. In the mid-1820s the constitutional question became enmeshed in state politics and the struggle against the Richmond Junto's continued control of the Old Dominion that involved both sectional animosities and personal politics. In defending the interests of his father, Republican senator James Pleasants, the editor of the *Lynchburg Virginian*, John Hampden Pleasants, joined other opposition editors from the outlying towns to put Ritchie and the Old Republicans on the defensive. Employing traditional republican demonology, they created the image of a corrupt "Court faction," picturing it as an "all powerful club," the Richmond "Junta" whose influence insinuated itself into all aspects of state politics, including the conservative center's resistance to constitutional revision.[25]

As economic conditions improved, the growing desire for government aid in the expansion of credit and construction of internal improvements continued to meet resistance from conservative easterners in the House of Delegates. At the same time the census of 1820 revealed the extent of western growth. Demands for constitutional reform resurfaced in the form of both petitions and mass meetings that now took place in towns and counties in the east. While generally they memorialized the legislature, some of these meetings declared that a constitutional convention could be convened by the people without legislative approval.

Accomack County on the Eastern Shore and several counties in the northern piedmont became hotbeds of reform sentiment, joining the westerners who continued to agitate for a convention. The reformers flooded the assembly with petitions and seemed to be winning the fight among the people, but the conservatives who dominated the legislature continued to prevent change by branding their opponents as dangerous radicals. The issue came before the assembly in the 1823–24 session, and when the legislature refused to provide for a referendum on the issue, reformers opened polls in a number of counties to allow the voters to register their opinion on the matter.[26]

At the time of the election, the *Enquirer* opened its pages to a vigorous debate on the propriety of reform, even though as the voice of Virginia's Republican party, it clearly opposed calling a new convention. On the other hand, the *Richmond Constitutional Whig* complained about minority rule by an odious "landed aristocracy." Once again Jefferson encouraged reform, this time in a letter to the editor of the *Whig* that was later published in the *Enquirer*. Jefferson stood on the familiar ground of a half century, insisting that the constitution of 1776 abridged the natural rights of the people in both its restrictions on suffrage and its malapportionment of representation. The former president failed to see the justice of allowing "every citizen of Warwick as much weight in government as . . . twenty-two equal citizens of Loudoun" or "refusing to all but freeholders any participation in the natural right of self-government." Surely those who served in the militia in the late war and those who paid taxes deserved the vote. The constitution as it stood was unrepublican and "an usurpation of the minority over the majority."[27]

Eventually another counterconvention met in Staunton in August 1825, asserting the necessity of a statewide convention that would produce a constitution with apportionment based on the white population and the extension of the suffrage to all white adult males. The reformers contrasted the "white basis" of representation with both the "black basis" that prevailed and the proposed "federal numbers" that would include three-fifths of the slaves in the formula determining apportionment of house seats, either of which left control of the commonwealth in the hands of "the slave owning eastern aristocracy."

Charles Fenton Mercer, Philip Doddridge, John R. Cooke, and Thomas Jefferson Randolph presented various resolutions from their counties—Loudoun, Brooke, Frederick, and Albemarle—demanding the desired constitutional changes. Reformers bombarded the assembly in Richmond with over fifty petitions, and twenty-eight counties passed referenda instructing their representatives to support the call for a new convention. Pleasants, who had become editor of the *Richmond Constitutional Whig*, joined the reformers in condemning "the aristocratic tendency of the existing constitution" and "the rottenness of our state institutions."[28]

On the whole, the reformers' demands were relatively moderate, short of Jefferson's more sweeping program of reform. They agreed with him on representation and on the reorganization of the executive through the abolition of the council. They also wanted to provide for future amendment of the constitution and to expand the electorate without embracing universal suffrage. Mercer hurried to assure the easterners that they desired no changes that would "impair the Independence of the judiciary" and, without specifically mentioning slavery, insisted that they were "opposed to any interference with the rights of property." The memorial to the General Assembly was deferential and carefully worded, emphasizing that the reformers' primary desire was to bring the issue of a convention before the voters of Virginia at the next election.[29]

Smarting from the opposition's attack and troubled about the implications of reform for the continued existence of slavery and the traditional order of Old Virginia, Thomas Ritchie, the editor of the *Enquirer*, equivocated and turned his readers' attention to the mess in Washington: the "corrupt bargain" between Adams and Clay. Two leading Republicans, Senator Littleton Waller Tazewell and future senator Benjamin Watkins Leigh, led the conservative resistance to constitutional revision. Leigh bitterly denounced both the members of the Staunton convention and Jefferson for preaching anarchy and disunion, at odds with "true Republican principles." He associated the reformers with both the Old Federalists and the advocates of Clay's American System, insisting that they opposed states' rights and local government exemplified by the county courts.[30]

As the main conservative spokesman, Leigh clearly represented the majority of the Old Dominion's Republicans, who viewed the call for a convention as a part of a general scheme of legal revision and economic development. The Republican leadership chose to cast their arguments in terms of states' rights and strict construction—"the true Principles of '98"—and appealed to the unwritten constitution that had evolved from before the Revolution and that was upheld and interpreted by the judges and the juries of the country courts. While Jefferson sometimes agreed with the Old Republicans in opposition to national consolidation and the expansive doctrines of the Marshall Court, they agreed with none of his democratic ideas on constitutional and legal reform.[31]

In the assembly Leigh was aided by the young Northampton County lawyer Abel Parker Upshur, who candidly confessed that his motive in resisting reform was the protection of the peculiar institution. Upshur told his friend Francis Walker Gilmer that it was "the principal object" of men like Mercer and "the politicians of his school to induce a gradual abolition of slavery." Mercer had been a Federalist and was a prominent congressional supporter of both economic nationalism and the American Colonization Society. Thus, Upshur and other Republicans managed to unite federal and state issues in a fashion that connected the western demand for constitutional revision to the congressional assault on the Doctrines of '98.[32]

In a series of essays in the *Enquirer* written under the pseudonym "Mason of '76," Leigh laid out the classic conservative argument. Change was both dangerous and unnecessary; the old constitution had served the commonwealth well. For a half century it provided the necessary basis for the stability and order that ensured Virginia's primacy in the new nation. Only by remaining true to its principles could the Old Dominion continue to maintain its moral leadership. Leigh further insinuated that the recent agitation was a Federalist plot, a new "Hartford Convention," directed at the rights of the states. He declared that its desperate leaders were willing even to give "the right of suffrage to free negroes" to regain control of the commonwealth.[33]

Mercer replied to Leigh's "Mason" letters. Doddridge attacked the eastern elite in both the press and the House of Delegates. "One of the People of Virginia" wrote to the *National Intelligencer* in Washington, D.C., assailing the constitution's "oligarchic form" and noting that "there is little doubt that a few men in Virginia give direction to all important measures. . . . These may be called the *Junta of Virginia.*" Although the advocates of change kept up their consistent calls for a convention, the conservative Republican leadership continued to hold off the reform coalition for two more years.[34]

In the House of Delegates the votes on allowing a referendum were extremely close—generally a matter of four or five out of over two hundred delegates—and consistently divided along clear sectional lines. The reformers included most of the western members, regardless of their position on national issues, and a majority of the easterners who supported the Adams administration. A small group of eastern Republicans were moving toward the view that moderate reform was politically expedient, but in the session of 1826–27 they still supported their section.

On July 4, 1827, a meeting at Wheeling supporting the reelection of John Quincy Adams toasted the liberation of South America, Ireland, and Greece and expressed the hope that the Old Dominion, "although degraded and fallen," might be restored by reform to "her former glory and importance among her sister states." Letters from "non-Freeholders" and "Mechanics" derided the Republican governor, William Branch Giles, and other "aristocratical politicians of the east" as "turbulent demagogues . . . forever croaking about liberty and state rights" while violating "every principle of democracy, and trampling "under their feet the very bill of rights that gave to the state her political existence." [35]

The spring 1827 elections for Congress and the assembly had featured the usual high number of uncontested seats, but in some areas the reformers again adopted the strategy of opening a poll on the convention question. These counties were proconvention, and in them most of the candidates took the same position on this informal referendum. The strategy had some effect in that the new House of Delegates included enough eastern Republicans—roughly a dozen—who now switched and voted for a bill, subsequently accepted by the senate, asking the freeholders to choose between a "Convention" or "No Convention." [36]

Virginia's freeholders favored a convention by a majority of slightly over five thousand votes out of nearly forty thousand cast at the April election of 1828. The result reflected the sharp sectional split on the subject, but the eastern counties that had participated in the movement for reform such as Accomack, Fairfax, Fauquier, and Loudoun cast nearly unanimous votes in favor of calling a convention. Since almost the same number of voters participated in the referendum and the presidential election that fall, it appears that there was an inverse relationship between those favoring reform of the state constitution and those voting for Jackson. [37]

In fact, however, the two elections were quite distinct events and bore practically no relationship to each other. The similarity in turnout figures for the state as a whole masks large fluctuations from county to county. In Albemarle, Jefferson's home county, 600 voters turned out to give Jackson a heavy majority, but only 264 went to the polls in the spring, and a majority of them opposed a convention. Adams received his largest number of votes in Loudoun County, 525 of the 754 votes cast; in April, that county's freeholders had voted 934 to 2 in favor of a convention.

Any systematic correlation would be confounded by the sectional pattern of the vote. In the west heavily Jacksonian areas like the German counties of the Valley and "Little Tennessee" in the southwest favored reform. Washington

County, which gave 97 percent of its vote to Jackson, had voted 670 to 6 for a convention. But anti-Jackson counties in the Valley and the northwest also overwhelmingly demanded change. Berkeley County gave Adams 63 percent of its vote and supported for a convention 362 to 5; Ohio polled 56 percent for Adams and 517 to 9 in favor of a convention. In each of these cases, the turnout in the spring was significantly different from the turnout in the fall.

In the eastern half of the commonwealth, numerous counties provide clear examples of Jackson voters who opposed reform, but there were also a few counties that voted for Adams and opposed calling a constitutional convention. At the *Enquirer* the conservative Claiborne Gooch differed with the moderate Ritchie, and consequently the "voice of Virginia Republicanism" equivocated on constitutional revision. When the paper spoke of "Jackson and reform," it meant reinstituting republican principles in the federal government; no one equated support for the Old Hero with expanded suffrage or fair apportionment of the legislature. It was the supporters of President Adams who emphasized the issue. The leading advocates of changing the Virginia constitution were all vocal supporters of the incumbent administration. Led by Doddridge, they also supported choosing the delegates to the convention on the basis of white population, while Ritchie and William Fitzhugh Gordon pushed the compromise of four delegates from each of the commonwealth's senatorial districts.[38]

The assembly, unsure of its authority and deadlocked over a scheme of organization, finally compromised on a conservative plan based on senatorial districts and called a convention that met in Richmond in 1829. Since there were no residency requirements for its members, this gathering featured more major national figures than any other state constitutional convention in American history. Madison, Monroe, Marshall, Giles, Randolph, and Tyler were all present. The Committee on the Judiciary was headed by the most notable man ever to serve as chief justice of the Supreme Court. That on the executive was chaired by the man called the Father of the Constitution of the United States. Counting those who had held or would hold the offices, there were three presidents, seven senators, fifteen congressmen, and four governors. The remainder were sitting judges or members of the Virginia assembly. Three-quarters of the body had read the law and been admitted to the bar. It was a truly illustrious panel, dominated by the leading Republicans of the Old Dominion.

Not only was representation slanted toward eastern planter power, but the mode of election produced a body that was distinctly wealthier and more conservative than the House of Delegates at the time. The result maintained the political structure of Old Virginia. On practically every issue the reformers lost, and the new constitution, while modestly increasing the electorate to include leaseholders and male household heads and granting a larger number of seats to the Valley, reaffirmed the status quo.

The debates prove the eastern conservatives, the giants of the "Great Generation," to have been reactionaries in the extreme. At the same time, the reformers from the western counties were hardly the "demented French Jacobins" portrayed by their opponents. Nor were they abolitionists, or precapitalist yeomen resisting the expansion of the market, but rather representatives of an emerging periphery, hostile to the planter gentry of the east that dominated the government in Richmond and turned a deaf ear to their constituents' economic and political desires.[39]

The reformers prided themselves on their adherence to true republicanism and appealed to both Jefferson—"the father of our political church"—and the principles enshrined in Mason's Declaration of Rights. Reformer John Cooke, a Winchester lawyer, declared that the delegates must look "to the white population . . . to *the people*" for legitimate authority, "not to the wealthy, not to overgrown sectional interests, not to the supposed rights of the counties." In response to Leigh's taunts, he insisted that change was necessary to rid the commonwealth of "*aristocratic privilege*" and firmly establish a government that would "derive its power *from* the people and be responsible *to* the people." Philip Doddridge put the reform position plainly: "The effort we are making is one, the object of which, is to reform our constitution, on our own principles, and to give practical effect to those declared in the Bill of Rights. What we contemplate is not a revolution. The Government is an elective Republic and we mean to leave it so." He was tired of "listening to Burke on the French Revolution" and being "incessantly lectured like schoolboys about the Republics of Greece, Sparta, Lacedaemon, Rome, and Carthage. In our sense of the term, in the Virginia sense of it, neither of these was a Republic."[40]

Doddridge was right. The spokesmen of the conservative center took a decidedly Burkean stance attacking the "wild abstractions" and "metaphysical subtleties" put forth by the advocates of reform and denying the existence of natural rights. "Government is a practical thing, and *that* Government is best which is best in its practical results. There is no end to speculative systems. The world has been full of them, from Plato, down through Harrington and Moore. . . . Experience is the best guide." Yet after spending most of its time debating the relative merits of a "mixed basis" of representation—that is, some combination of property and population—or a white basis, the convention followed neither argument and compromised upon a conservative plan that claimed no intellectual rationale at all.[41]

That the constitution had existed for half a century became a most un-Jeffersonian argument for retaining it. In line with the wishes of his constituents from the Eastern Shore who were truck farmers and fishermen, Upshur voted to reform some aspects of the old constitution, but he believed that it had worked well and that to call for majority rule was to invite anarchy. The planters seemed truly terrified of the "demented French Jacobins" and "the peasantry of the west." An extreme hostility to change dominated the conservative center. With his usual rhetorical flair, Randolph spoke of "this *maggot* of innovation" in the debate over the power to amend the new constitution. In the midst of his defense of freehold suffrage, Philip N. Nicholas, a banker himself, attacked the holders of stocks and bonds on the grounds that "a man may transfer this kind of property in a few moments, taking his seat on the stage, or embark on the steamboat and be out of the State in one day carrying all he possesses." To Nicholas and other eastern conservatives, that "attachment to the community . . . and common, permanent interest" spoken of in the Declaration of Rights was "only to be found in a lasting ownership of the soil."[42]

The convention briefly considered Jefferson's suggestions of an elective executive and reformed judiciary, but the major debates were over the basis of representation and the extension of the suffrage. These two issues were joined in the attempt to define "the people"—in English terms, "the political nation." Against the tenor of his own conservative opinions, John Marshall introduced the petition of the nonfreeholders of the city of Richmond that argued: "Virtue, [and] intelligence, are not among the products of the soil. Attachment to property, often a sordid sentiment, is not to be confounded with the sacred flame of patriots." These representatives of the petite bourgeoisie denied that they posed a danger to property since they aspired to accumulate it.[43]

Suffrage reform, however, was less important than the "basis question," since westerners of all classes resented eastern control of the government in Richmond, while easterners clearly distrusted the emerging western majority whose representatives in the convention owned a good deal of land but few slaves. Upshur adamantly insisted that there "is a majority in *interest* as well as a majority in number." "Those who have the greatest stake in the Government . . . [should] have the greatest share of power in the administration of it." With Randolph and Leigh, he rejected Lockean liberalism and openly ridiculed Jefferson's commitment to majority rule. Since "Persons and *property*" constituted the essential "elements of society," a mixed basis of representation provided the only truly republican solution to the question. He foresaw impending doom in the western demands, which he associated with the worst excesses of the French Revolution: "Take away all protection from property, and our next business is to cut each other's throats."[44]

The Republicans in the convention continued to portray parties as the product of "aristocracy" and the work of "crafty demagogues" in conflict with the best interests of the commonwealth. Antipartyism constituted a major tenet in the Country ideology, and the opposition to factions and self-interested parties permeated the Virginia elite in the Jeffersonian era. The word *party* appeared in several different contexts in the debates. Marshall, for example, talked about the "state of parties" in which the advocates of a white basis confronted those insisting upon a mixed basis. Upshur was startled by the organization of "the reform party." But basically the easterners were quite unwilling to believe that the political process could work in their favor if the majority with no interest in their peculiar institution was allowed to rule.[45]

Nicholas's outburst against stockjobbers included an attack upon party politics: "Place power in the hands of those who have none, or a very trivial stake in the community, and you expose the poor and dependent to the influence and seductions of wealth. The extreme rich and the extreme poor, if not natural allies, will become so in fact." Thus were constituted the "aristocratic" parties that would replace the rule of independent gentlemen. Leigh dismissed the idea that universal suffrage would result in truly popular elections. To him it would be a matter of corruption by either the caucus or the convention in which he found little difference.[46]

The reformers pointed out that Virginia was one of the last states to deny suffrage to all white, adult males, but the conservatives held firm and even made light of the fact. To the young and abusive Leigh, manhood suffrage was but another of those plagues that descended from the North like the Hessian fly. He mocked Jefferson as a "dreamer" whose ideas only meant the "eventual despotism" of "lazy and drunken men." He preferred the traditional argument that based the vote upon a stake in society, supporting what the modern political theorist C. B. Macpherson has termed "possessive individualism": only those who owned themselves could stand independently above the threat of bribery. The slaves of the eastern portion of Virginia, Leigh said, simply filled "the place of the peasantry of Europe" and differed little from "the peasantry or day-labourers" of the North. "In every civilized country under the sun, some there must be who labour for their daily bread, either by contract with, or subjection to others, or for themselves." Surely no one believed that the landless and day laborers should participate in politics any more than the slaves. Political activity at all levels should be restricted to men of substance and sufficient leisure to assure independent judgment. Those obliged "to depend upon their daily labor for daily subsistence" never had entered into political affairs, and the convention should not contemplate inviting them to do so.[47]

Despite its emphasis on freeholders, ultimately the opposition to reform boiled down to a defense of states' rights and slavery. In fact, the conservatives in the convention charged that the demands for reform constituted an attack upon the rights of the states, because the changes posed a threat to slavery. The opponents of change constantly portrayed themselves as defenders of property but rejected the arguments of the workingmen who said they aspired to own property and the westerners who assured them that they already held great tracts of land, because to the easterners "property" was an euphemism for slave

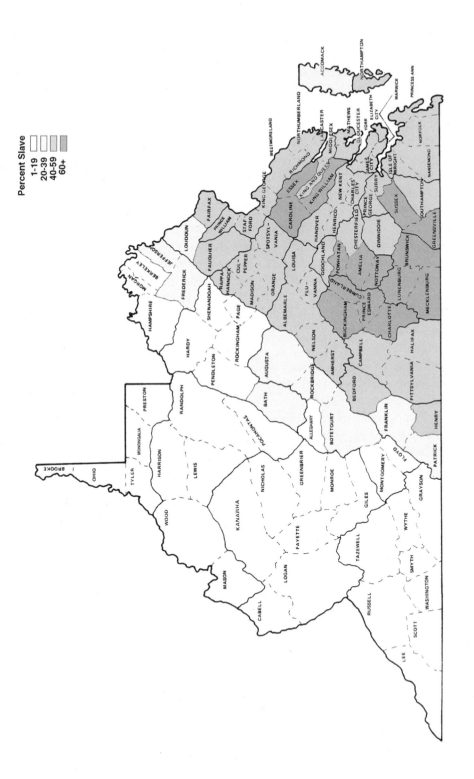

Percent Slave
1-19
20-39
40-59
60+

chattel (map 2.1). This meant not simply owning one or two slaves as servants or even a few whose de facto position was little different than that of the hired hands on western farms. "Property" in slaves implied substantial holdings and a stake in a slave society. In a similar fashion the repeated references to states' rights—the contemporary usage was most often "state-rights"—served also as an indirect defense of the peculiar institution by a planter class that cared little for local democracy.

As Upshur put it, the "Eastern divisions of the State" had a "peculiar . . . and great, and important, and leading interest" in slavery. Randolph plainly stated that he spoke for "the great tobacco-growing and slave-holding interest." While the reformers avoided explicitly attacking the institution and insisted that the continuance of slavery depended upon the support of the nonslave-holders, the conservatives chained their cause to the proslavery argument. They refused to trust their fate as slaveholders to the growing body of westerners who would soon outnumber them. If representation was "established on the basis of white population," Randolph warned, "in less than twenty years you would have a Bill brought into the House of Burgesses for the emancipation of every slave in Virginia. . . . I would lief trust the fanatics of Free-Masons Hall London . . . as the Fanatics of Virginia."[48]

Like so many antidemocratic arguments presented in the Old South, the exaggerated scenarios of gloom and doom repetitiously painted by planter conservatives depended upon dubious projections of future behavior from tangentially related population trends. There is no doubt that Virginia society was changing between 1810 and 1830, but this reactionary rhetoric represented a distortion of the actual threat that the eastern gentry faced. For all the voluminous debate, it is almost inconceivable that the reformers had a chance of seriously changing the social order even though they did come close to carrying the day for their limited objectives. The conservatives had stacked the convention, and their speeches were designed to bring the weak of heart into line. As Chapman Johnson told his fellow delegates, "We are engaged . . . in a contest for power—disguise it as you will—call it a discussion of the rights of man, natural or social . . . still . . . all our metaphysical reasoning and our practical rules, all our scholastic learning and political wisdom are but arms employed in a contest.[49]

The divisions on the most important roll calls were extremely close, decided by only a few votes. Initially both the white basis and the extension of suffrage fell only two votes shy of passage; the popular election of the governor was defeated only on reconsideration. But in the end there were simply more conservatives than reformers. Among the few who broke ranks on one of the major issues, there were still more moderate conservatives than moderate reformers. The ninety-six delegates divided into four blocs that voted together consistently on the substantive roll calls cast in the convention. There were forty-two conservatives. While including the largest number of delegates, this bloc did not constitute a majority. Thirty-nine reformers made up the second largest group in the convention, roughly two-fifths of the delegates. There were nine moderate conservatives, who voted against change on most issues, and six moderate reformers.[50]

Just how reactionary the conservative delegates were can be seen in the fact that Upshur, whose rhetoric sustained the status quo in the debate on the basis issue, and Gordon, who proposed the final "practicable" solution to the dilemma of representation, voted with Madison and the moderate conservatives. For their part, the reformers were hardly the radicals Randolph and other reactionaries depicted. They refused to press their demands as far as Jefferson had gone in the 1780s. Nearly half of them voted against an attempt to alter the county courts that served as the central element of squirearchal rule, and when westerner Lewis Summers proposed consideration of Jefferson's democratic ward system of local government, the committee dismissed the motion without serious discussion.

The document produced was antediluvian, even in terms of its own times. While it modestly extended the republican idea of a stake in society to include householders, the Virginia constitution of 1830 represented a triumph of traditionalism that strengthened gentry rule through its recognition of the primacy of the county courts. Virginians continued to reject the politics of conflict inherent in political individualism—the political equivalent of Adam Smith's "invisible hand"—and to reiterate conservative republican principles of representation designed to govern a homogeneous agrarian society. The Old Dominion's leading Jeffersonian Republicans unanimously rejected constitutional reform, although Madison to his credit tried to play a conciliatory role and encourage compromise before caving in to pressure from the conservative majority.[51]

The behavior of the delegates clearly reflected the split between the center and the periphery that had characterized Virginia's politics during the Age of Jefferson. All nineteen of the delegates from the trans-Allegheny region voted for revision of both the suffrage and apportionment, and thirty-one of the thirty-nine reformers came from the western half of the state. Four other westerners from the Valley were moderate reformers. Only one delegate representing a county west of the Blue Ridge voted as a moderate conservative, Chapman Johnson, who owned a plantation in Augusta County in the Valley but practiced law and lived in Richmond at the time of the convention. Although he opposed extension of the suffrage, he is best known for his outspoken stand in favor of the white basis and thus is usually described as a reformer.[52]

Just as there were no conservatives west of the Blue Ridge, only eight of the reformers represented the eastern counties. They came from four counties in the

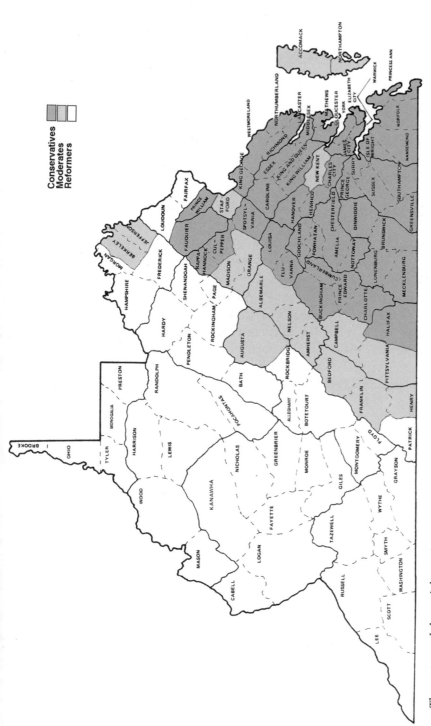

Conservatives
Moderates
Reformers

2.2. The center and the periphery, 1830

southwestern part of the piedmont and from two—Loudoun and Fairfax—in the north along the Potomac. Thirty-two of thirty-six tidewater delegates were conservatives. One, John B. Clopton of New Kent County northeast of Richmond, voted with the moderate conservatives from the Eastern Shore. The majority of members from the piedmont also opposed change. Ten were conservatives from the southeastern counties. Four others, including Gordon and Madison, were moderate conservatives who represented the western piedmont, a band of counties directly east of the Blue Ridge that formed a buffer zone between Doddridge's New West and Randolph's Old Virginia—between the rising periphery and the economically stagnant center (map 2.2).

Even the representatives of the "commercial" areas of the east around Norfolk and Richmond and the pro-Adams counties of the Northern Neck along the Potomac opposed reform. At the time of the convention, much of the piedmont was new country and economically thriving. The Valley too was prospering in contrast to the image put forth by Tucker in his romance written in the depths of the postwar depression. The west was growing, and this expansion, along with its quite different patterns of social volatility, represented the future that the conservatives isolated in Old Virginia found so abhorrent. Just as stagnation produced reaction, expansion bred reform. All of the delegates from the counties that had lost white population during the previous decade resisted change in representation, while those easterners favoring the white basis came from dynamic areas characterized by extreme population growth and economic diversity.

The western reformers repeatedly assured the eastern planters that their property would be safe. Slavery was spreading in the west; many of the most influential men in the section had a personal interest in the peculiar institution. But the patterns of slaveholding in the west differed markedly from those in the east, and there was a clear correlation between slaveholding and the way delegates voted (table 2.1). Six of the seven slaveless delegates were western reform-

Table 2.1. Slaveholding and voting blocs in the 1829–30 constitutional convention

	Slaves				
	None	1–9	10–19	20–49	50+
Conservatives	1	6	7	17	13
Moderate conservatives	0	0	1	6	2
Moderate reformers	0	1	3	2	0
Reformers	6	16	7	7	1
Total	7	23	18	32	16

ers. The only eastern nonslaveholder was the twenty-three-year-old chronicler of the convention, Hugh Blair Grigsby, who replaced reformer Robert B. Taylor when Taylor resigned rather than follow the instructions from his Norfolk constituents. Grigsby, a protégé of Tazewell, posed no such "treason to the East" and voted the conservative line.[53]

Over 90 percent of the delegates from counties west of the Blue Ridge owned slaves, but only eight were planters. The largest holding was that of Gordon Cloyd of Montgomery County in the southwest, who used his fifty-three slaves as cowboys on his 3,000-acre ranch. In sharp contrast, 70 percent of the eastern delegates were planters, and fifteen owned over fifty slaves. One-fourth of the eastern delegates and nearly one-third of the conservatives were among the richest people in the United States, hardly typical even of planter society. The average conservative owned over three thousand acres in the county he represented, and most had extensive holdings elsewhere. Descendants of the first families of Virginia, the eastern conservatives epitomized the traditional elite increasingly threatened by the parvenu planters and professionals who would come to dominate the Old Dominion by midcentury.[54]

The contrast between the tremendously wealthy and the men of more moderate means stands out sharply when one looks at the relationship between slaveholding and the four voting blocs in the convention. The reformers were far less wealthy and clearly less committed to the peculiar institution than the conservatives. Thirty of the forty-four conservatives were planters who held over twenty taxable slaves; thirteen owned over fifty. Eight of the nine moderate conservatives were also planters; four of the six moderate reformers held fewer than twenty slaves. A majority of the reformers who did own slaves held fewer than ten. Only one-fifth of the proponents of democratic change could be called planters. Four of the six moderate reformers held fewer than twenty slaves; eight of the nine moderate conservatives were planters. Thus, there was a practically perfect correlation between slaveholding and opposition to democracy.

The conservatives also represented an earlier day. Among the men who held federal office or served in the assembly, clear differences stand out that tie the opponents of reform to the old order. Members of the convention who participated in the second party system came almost equally from the ranks of conservatives and reformers, but four times as many conservatives as reformers had been associated with the first party system and the heyday of the Virginia Dynasty—and all except Marshall were prominent Jeffersonian Republicans. Among those who were important in both periods, the leading conservatives— Upshur, Barbour, Tyler, Leigh, and Tazewell—were also Jeffersonian Republicans more at home in the old world than the new.[55]

Eastern delegates differed from the westerners in other related ways. Not only were four-fifths of the conservatives planters or planter-lawyers, but also

Table 2.2. Occupation and voting blocs in the 1829–30 constitutional convention

	Planters	Lawyers*	Farmers	Others
Conservatives	33	8 [25]	1	0
Moderate conservatives	9	0 [5]	0	0
Moderate reformers	3	1 [5]	2	0
Reformers	10	8 [16]	7	14
Total	55	25 [51]	10	14

*The numbers in the brackets include all lawyers, while those outside the brackets include those who were only or primarily lawyers. Two men with 18 and 19 slaves and large landholding are classified as planters.

a similar proportion of the planters were conservatives (table 2.2). All of the remaining conservatives were eastern lawyers connected to the planter elite. Yet lawyers also constituted the largest single occupational group among the reformers. Ten planters and eight farmers (including three slaveholders) were reformers, as well as all fourteen delegates who followed nonagricultural pursuits other than the law. The occupational diversity and emerging bourgeois nature of the reformers stand out.[56]

Related differences can be seen in the contrasting religious backgrounds of the conservative and reform delegates. Essentially, Episcopalians opposed reform while the evangelical denominations favored it. Four-fifths of the delegates whose religious affiliation is known were either Episcopalians or Presbyterians, and these two groups lined up on opposite sides. Eighty-four percent of the former were conservatives; 80 percent of the latter denomination were reformers. Nine of the eleven Methodist and Baptist evangelicals, led by Alexander Campbell, the founder of the Disciples of Christ, as well as three Lutherans and a Mennonite voted with the Presbyterians for reform. The two Quakers in the convention were conservative planters owning sixteen and twenty-two slaves, respectively.[57]

Reformers and conservatives differed in ethnic background as well. Again the homogeneity of the conservatives stood in contrast to the heterogeneity of the reformers. Over 80 percent of the tidewater delegates were of English origin, and the remainder were the descendants of seventeenth-century French Huguenots who had intermarried with the English. The piedmont produced delegates almost as uniformly English as those from the tidewater. Only one-third of the western delegates, however, were of English stock. The Germans of the Valley, although they were split along religious lines on other matters, joined the Scots and Scotch-Irish in support of reform. The latter predominated among the Valley and upper Potomac delegates and made up two-thirds of the members from the trans-Allegheny. Occupation and education, religion and ethnicity all correlated highly with the division between conservatives and reformers and defined the differences between the center and the periphery.

The forces of reform were led by a man whom Europeans such as Tocqueville would have thought the typical American of his time. Young Grigsby said of Philip Doddridge that he was "busy as a bee and dirty as a hog." He epitomized the culture of the periphery, having "none of the bland and polished manner belonging to the South. . . . He speaks in a broad Scotch Irish dialect although he is an excellent scholar & a man of extensive and profound research." Born in Pennsylvania, he had moved west to Virginia where he established himself as a small-town lawyer and politician who made a reputation as an advocate of public education. Doddridge was a Methodist and owned two slaves in 1830. In the assembly he had fought in favor of organizing the convention on the white basis and was the leading democratic voice in the debates.[58]

The reformers led by Doddridge tried to block the ratification of the new constitution at the polls in 1830. The trans-Allegheny counties sent to the polls one-third of those Virginians who responded to the issue and registered strong opposition to the measure, but elsewhere the election interested far fewer voters than the presidential election of 1828. The new constitution passed by a comfortable margin. Historians have emphasized the strong vote of the tidewater, but ratification was the product of the nearly unanimous vote in the piedmont and the two-to-one majority it received in the Valley. Both the Valley, the heartland of demands for reapportionment, and the piedmont, the center of planter power, gained from the arbitrary changes in the size and distribution of the representatives to the assembly at the expense of the languishing tidewater.[59]

The most vocal opposition came from National Republicans and opponents of Jackson in the trans-Allegheny region who hoped that if the constitution was defeated, a new convention would be called. During the convention the Wheeling Town Meeting—its very name indicative of the most unsouthern nature of the area above the Mason-Dixon Line that spawned the likes of Doddridge—had called upon the representatives of the "freemen of Virginia" to withdraw from the convention, insisting that "the assertion that the free laborers of the West, are, in every sense, on a level with the slaves of the east or the peasantry of Europe is as false in fact, as it is ungracious and illiberal." The vociferously anti-Jackson *Wheeling Gazette* opposed ratification.[60]

The subsequent political careers of the members of the convention reinforce the impression derived from the debates that those who stood with the Democratic party during the course of the second party system were more likely to have been reactionaries than reformers in 1830. The outspoken Doddridge, who died in 1832, had been a Federalist who later supported Adams and Clay against Jackson. Fifteen of the twenty-one reformers who lived beyond

1838 and can be identified became Whigs. Of the twenty-two conservatives whose later political affiliation is known, sixteen supported the Democrats Van Buren and Polk. Five of the six conservatives who joined the "Opposition" were Tylerites, and two of them, Gordon and Tazewell, were "State-Rights Democrats" who merely cooperated with the Whigs in the mid-1830s. The only one who stayed with the Whig party in the 1840s was Chapman Johnson, who in 1830 eloquently advocated the white basis of representation.[61]

Not only did most of the conservatives become Democrats, but they were among the most powerful men in the party. The reactionaries who voted with John Randolph included Philip P. Barbour, whom Jackson elevated to the Supreme Court in 1836, and later congressional Democrats George Dromgoole, William O. Goode, John Jones, George Loyall, and John Y. Mason. In the mid-1840s the Jacksonians made Jones the Speaker of the House, and Mason held two positions in Polk's cabinet. On the other hand, James Murray Mason, grandson of the author of the constitution of 1776, was the only reformer to become a Democratic leader of national prominence. He was elected to Congress for one term as a supporter of the Van Buren administration in 1837. Ten years later he was elevated to the Senate where he became a prominent spokesman of the Calhounite proslavery element of the Democratic party.[62]

The Virginia constitution of 1830 was a conservative document that brought little change. It was a product of the conflict between the traditional center and the reform-minded periphery that had characterized the political battles of the Jeffersonian era in the Old Dominion. The Republican reactionaries who wrote it were struggling to save as much of the skeletal structure of the old order as they could. It strengthened the county courts and enhanced the power of the piedmont planters. A constricted electorate ratified the new constitution. In this process sectional interest rather than ideology determined the outcome as the piedmont conservatives courted the moderates of the Valley at the expense of the northwest. There were few "fanatics for democracy" in the Old Dominion. A majority of white Virginians in 1830, however, were eager to embrace Herrenvolk democracy, but the eastern slaveholding gentry, jealous of the authority that seemed to be slipping from their grasp, stacked the deck and continued to resist the democratic trend of nineteenth-century America.

Most historians have followed political theorists in assuming that democratic changes in the constitutional and legal structure of the states generally preceded the development of mass political parties. In dealing with the expansion of liberal democracy in nineteenth-century America, they have emphasized that the shift in suffrage requirements from "property to democracy," the popular election of state officials, and the equalization of representation within the states predated the appearance of the Democrats and the Whigs. In the Old

Dominion, however, constitutional changes in the rules of the game lagged behind party development. Virginia followed an independent course that reflected the impact of the larger political environment in which the commonwealth evolved. As in the other states, the organizational developments associated with mass political parties emerged to produce democratic change in the form of increased political participation and pressures upon the government of the Old Dominion to respond to the demands of the new interest groups that had been generated by social and economic change.[63]

The division between the center and periphery that had dominated the politics of the Old Dominion in the heyday of the Richmond Junto and dictated the outcome of the convention of 1829–30 gave way to modern party politics that could be seen in the workings of the Reform Convention twenty years later. This shift has been obscured both by historians' exclusive focus on representation and suffrage and by their desire to portray democratic change as the product of either sectionalism or class conflict crudely reflected in the party battle. Neither position has satisfactorily explained change that was more complex in its nature and was generated in the hothouse of pluralistic politics. Appropriately, it was the "new men" of the middle reaches of comfortable white society whose names are hardly known in Virginia today who brought the nineteenth century's idea of democracy to the Old Dominion. They acted in response to the social and economic changes sweeping over the Old Dominion in the nineteenth century, casting aside the conservative republic of the Fathers and demanding that the government serve their needs.

⌒ 3 ⌒

A Candid State of Parties

I N HIS FIRST inaugural Thomas Jefferson greeted Congress with a warning against both foreign influence and the spirit of faction. To this he added his famous plea for national harmony and an end to partisan controversy: "We are all Republicans, we are all Federalists." Although the Virginian gave voice to the idea that parties were "necessary to induce each to watch and relate to the people the proceedings of the other," he did so as an aside in the midst of a diatribe against the "cunning of Hamilton," the spirit of state-based parties, and the potential of secession. Jefferson never conceived of permanent party conflict as part of a republican government. This ambiguity can be found in the perceptions of party held by most of Virginia's planter elite.[1]

Eighteenth-century Virginia could have served as a model of the social order envisioned by the Country ideologues who so influenced Revolutionary republicanism. The planter aristocracy of the Old Dominion constituted a single broad, homogeneous interest that rose in rebellion against the crown. Few of the internal conflicts that accompanied the Revolution in the other colonies distracted Virginia's planter elite from focusing upon the confrontation between the House of Burgesses and the imperial government. In none of the rebellious colonies was the appeal of classical republicanism so widespread.[2]

With this ideological commitment came conceptions of "faction" and "party" that Viscount Bolingbroke and educated eighteenth-century Virginians often conflated: "Party is a political evil . . . faction is the worst of all parties." Virginia republicans extolled the commonweal and perceived any partial, special interest as a corrupting influence. Their central moral imperative—civic virtue—implied the suppression of self-interest in favor of the greater good of the community. Conflict of interests disrupted the social fabric and opened the way for corruption and chaos. While republicanism offered a useful justification for a peripheral uprising against central authority, the Country ideology left little room for the idea of a legitimate opposition.[3]

The planter republicans of the Old Dominion tended to view the political

John Tyler. (Courtesy of the
Library of Congress)

Benjamin Watkins Leigh.
(Courtesy of the Virginia
Historical Society)

William Cabell Rives. (Courtesy of the Library of Congress)

Thomas Ritchie. (Courtesy of the Virginia Historical Society)

John Hampden Pleasants.
(Courtesy of the Virginia
Historical Society)

James Murray Mason. (Courtesy of
the Library of Congress)

Alexander Hugh Holmes Stuart.
From Alexander F. Robertson,
*Alexander Hugh Holmes Stuart,
1807–1901: A Biography*
(Richmond, 1925).

world through Manichaean lenses. Jefferson brooded about "an aristocracy founded on banking institutions and moneyed incorporations under the guise and cloak of their favored branches of manufactures, commerce and navigation, riding in victory over the plundered ploughman and beggared yeomanry." James Madison argued anonymously against Hamilton's program, portraying a conflict between an "anti-republican party," led by the "monied" interests who took "advantage of all prejudices, local, political and occupational," in pursuit of their selfish ends, and the true "republican party" that represented the "mass of the people." John Taylor of Caroline, the "philosopher of Jeffersonian democracy," put forth the purest Virginia formulation of the Country conception, mounting an attack on the "paper system" of securities and banknotes as artificial wealth that produced a real dissimilarity of interest among the "several states" and gave rise to "a spirit of bigotry."[4]

This "Jeffersonian persuasion" endured longer in the Old Dominion than in any other state in the Union. The late coming and limited extent of constitutional reform in Virginia sustained deferential politics and militated against the development of modern political parties. The constitutional limitations on the franchise, the small number of elected officials, and gentry domination of the county courts made unnecessary the aggregation of diverse interests. During the existence of the Virginia Dynasty, the conservative political culture of the state retarded party development. Yet modern parties evolved in the Old Dominion through stages similar to those that appeared in the other states.[5]

The undeveloped first party system that emerged in the 1790s and lasted through the War of 1812 typified the political era extending from the Revolution into the 1830s during which the political culture distrusted parties and popular involvement. Organization was sporadic and lacked continuity; participation fluctuated wildly and rarely included even half of the eligible voters; and candidates reflected the continuing power of deference to one's social superiors. The Jacksonian interlude of slightly over a decade when the Hero of New Orleans played a central role in national politics represented a transitional phase leading into another long political era during which the transformed political culture came to accept, even revel in, the politics of conflict and an affirmation of party affiliation as an essential element of American democracy. This era witnessed the birth of modern mass political parties that relied upon complex organization to penetrate all aspects of the political system and to produce the highest levels of popular participation in American history, presenting to the world the fearsome promise of political liberalism.[6]

The second party system straddled these two political eras. The political alignments that characterized its formative phase in Virginia proved highly unstable through the mid-1830s. Participation in presidential elections increased, but primarily this involved voters previously socialized into the political system who now voted in the quadrennial fall presidential elections as well as the yearly spring elections to choose members of the General Assembly. Political organization began to shift from the traditional elite connections rooted in kinship and commercial interests, involving face-to-face relationships of prominent men, to the instrumental institutional structures and cadre of a more common origin that typify modern political parties.

The presidential election of 1840 symbolized a new stage of institutional development in which parties more deeply penetrated the electoral system and generated a greater degree of citizen participation than ever before in the history of the commonwealth. By the mid-nineteenth century over one-third of the white adult males took part in party organizations as members of county committees, and nearly all of those eligible voted in both federal and state elections. The Democrats and the Whigs were novel institutions that contributed to the democratization of Virginia's politics by performing the classic functions of democratic parties in a pluralistic society, particularly encouraging communal cooperation in the political system and mobilizing the electorate.

Well into the nineteenth century personal relationships among prominent men dominated the political process in Virginia. While identifiable factions advocating contrasting federal agendas emerged in the 1790s, and a frenzy of organizational activity accompanied the "Revolution of 1800," rudimentary party structures appeared only intermittently, and popular participation remained low and sporadic, bounded by its colonial parameters. Little in the way of modern electoral machinery existed, and for most of the Jeffersonian era, the Old Dominion registered the lowest turnouts in the new nation. Even the Federalist revival that followed the Embargo and peaked in the partisan excitement of 1812 brought to the polls fewer than one-fifth of the white adult males. Turnout fell to 6 percent in 1816, and in 1820 only four thousand Virginians voted to return the incumbent James Monroe.[7]

The initial attempts to fashion party machinery in the commonwealth came in response to the Federalist challenge in the late 1790s. An assembly of the congressional "Republicans" who opposed the Adams administration caucused and set up a standing committee to coordinate the activities of the county committees. Several years later Judge Spencer Roane took the lead in establishing the *Richmond Enquirer* and installed his cousin from Essex County, Thomas Ritchie, as its editor. Every four years a State Central Committee of Correspondence was chosen—including Ritchie—and this organization served to bring together the representatives of locally powerful elites in the interest of party unity and continuity. After the War of 1812, Roane mounted his successful campaign to restore strict construction as the touchstone of republican purity and to resist consolidation in all of its nefarious forms. By returning to republican ideological orthodoxy, the Richmond Junto sought to revive Virginia's reputation among the states and reestablish its moral leadership of the new nation.[8]

The Junto's urban base of operations and its affiliation with Virginia's conservative banking system belie the fact that the clique epitomized the traditional system of planter elite domination, but these men embraced the conservative commercial agrarianism associated with John Taylor of Caroline and Jefferson that was more antimercantilist than liberal. The essence of Junto ideology, however, lay in the states' rights philosophy expressed in the Doctrines of '98 as interpreted by Antifederalists like Roane rather than either Jefferson or Madison, whose reputations slowly receded in Republican circles as the *Enquirer* became the voice of Virginia particularism.[9]

Family influence defined the Junto. All of the members bore some filial relation to one another and to the great families of Virginia. This "connection" involved the Nicholas brothers, the Campbell brothers, the Brockenbrough brothers, the Roanes, and the Munfords, father and son. Spencer Roane, Thomas Ritchie, and the Brockenbroughs were all cousins. William Brockenbrough and Andrew Stevenson married sisters. as did Ritchie and Richard Parker, who in doing so became sons-in-law of party stalwart, Richmond mayor, and postmaster Dr. William Foushee. The Junto thus maintained the traditional familial mode of organization of the commonwealth's government. These were men of substance and education who knew instinctively that they had been raised to rule.[10]

The Richmond Junto formed the nucleus of the Republican center and, consequently, became the primary target of politicians of the periphery. The idea that a "Richmond Party," "Junta," or "Junto" existed grew out of charges that appeared in the pro-Calhoun *Washington Republican* in 1823. These letters were later published as a pamphlet and circulated by several papers most particularly the pro-Adams *Lynchburg Virginian*, edited in part by John Hampden Pleasants and serving the interests of his father, Senator James Pleasants. In 1824 young Pleasants became editor of the *Richmond Whig* and remained the constant critic of the Junto and Ritchie until his death two decades later in a duel with one of Ritchie's sons.[11]

The Junto's importance lay in its being the only organization in early Virginia politics outside the frame of government and in its control over the weak mechanisms of the Republican interest in the state. Essentially this small clique of men—no more than twenty—held what power there was at a time when there was little to command. The Richmond Junto's successes relied upon elite consensus, and its many failures derived from the arrogance of the well-connected but extremely independent, not to say eccentric, gentlemen-of-means who made up Virginia's planter elite.

The presidential election of 1824 and the role of the Richmond Junto in it typified the traditional politics of the commonwealth in the Jeffersonian era. Five potential candidates associated with the administrations of both Madison and Monroe emerged. The *Enquirer* came out rather early in support of the secretary of the treasury, William H. Crawford, who had been born in the Old Dominion, and a caucus of two-thirds of the commonwealth's assemblymen overwhelmingly endorsed the Georgian. After the congressional caucus nominated him as the Republican candidate, Ritchie, who had favored Roane, anointed Crawford as the embodiment of the Doctrines of '98 and heir to Jefferson. Yet the response of the eastern planter elite to the various contenders remained distinctly personal, giving no hint of future partisan alignments. Ritchie's associate at the *Enquirer*, Claiborne W. Gooch, promoted Clay as vice president; the senior editor and most of the eastern gentry looked upon John Quincy Adams as their second choice. Nearly all the Virginia elite rejected General Jackson, whom young John Tyler described as a "mere soldier." Not only did Virginia's Old Republican electors stick with Crawford after he had a stroke in May, but distrusting Calhoun's nationalism, they also unanimously cast their second ballots for one of their own kind, Nathaniel Macon of North Carolina.[12]

Crawford received 56 percent of the Virginia popular vote, but few bothered to go to the polls, and most counties went heavily for either Crawford or one of the other candidates; there were very few counties in which two candidates competed. The center supported the caucus candidate while the disorganized periphery rejected the dictation of the Junto (map 3.1). Three-quarters of Crawford's votes came from the planter-dominated region east of the Blue Ridge where he carried fifty-seven of the sixty-five counties. Adams and Jackson split the disaffected anticaucus vote. Adams won the borough of Norfolk and sixteen counties. Jackson carried four southwestern counties, Lee, Russell, Scott, and Tazewell, and did well in Washington, but the general made his strongest showing in the German counties of the Valley and ran surprisingly well in the southern piedmont where he garnered one-fifth of his vote—twice what he got in the southwest.[13]

John Quincy Adams had retained the support of the Crawfordites until his first annual message, in which he associated himself with Clay's American System, caused these Old Republicans to turn against the administration. They agreed with John Tyler that the address constituted "a direct insult upon Virginia," confirming their distrust and sectional anxiety engendered by his appointment of Clay as secretary of state and Rufus King as ambassador to England. An angry Jefferson assailed the tendency toward "consolidation." Ritchie and the Old Republicans heaped ridicule upon the president as the opposition in Congress gathered steam with the support of leading Virginians. John Randolph's acerbic "Blifil and Black George" speech, alluding to Fielding's *Tom Jones* and accusing the coalition of Adams and Clay of corruption, led to a duel

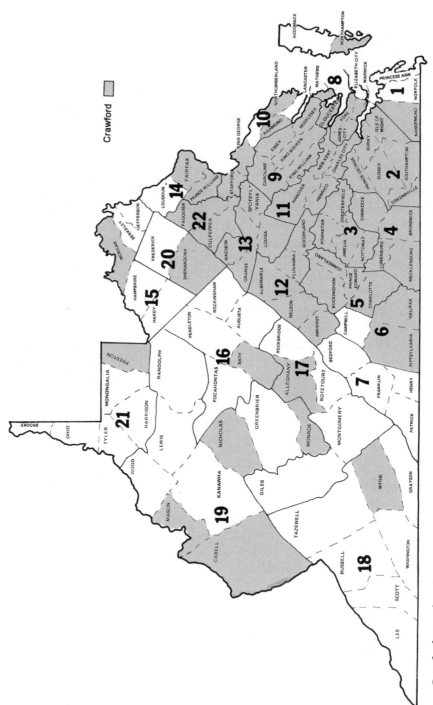

Crawford

3.1. Crawford counties, 1824

between the Virginia senator and the secretary of state. On nearly every issue to come before Congress, the supporters of Calhoun, Crawford, and Jackson joined to frustrate the Adams administration and resist all aspects of the American System: bankruptcy legislation, land policy, internal improvements, colonization, and, of course, the protective tariff. In the process this anti-Adams coalition settled upon Andrew Jackson, whom they had previously declared unfit, as their candidate for the presidency in 1828 on a platform stressing his commitment to "Virginia ideas" and the general's vow to return the federal government to republican purity.[14]

The crucial figure in the organization of the emerging Jackson party was New York senator Martin Van Buren, whose strategy of drawing "old party lines" around the ideals of states' rights and strict construction depended upon rekindling the New York–Virginia alliance—joining "the planters of the South and the plain Republicans of the North." Ritchie and the Virginia supporters of Crawford thus played a crucial role in forming the modern Democratic party, but they retained a traditional conception of partisanship that reflected Jefferson's ambivalent views and emphasized their role as the defenders of republicanism. Governor William Branch Giles encouraged the Virginia assembly to reaffirm the Doctrines of '98 and denounce the administration's association with the American System. "Father" Ritchie wrapped Jackson in the mantle of Jefferson, portraying the Old Hero as a "politician of the Richmond school."[15]

With the aid of Vice President Calhoun, Van Buren knit together the "Jackson party" in Congress. He called those favorable to Jackson to a caucus that established a Washington-based Central Committee to raise money and coordinate the activities of corresponding committees in the states. Van Buren toured the South in 1827 to unite the various capital cliques and cement ties between the Albany Regency, the Richmond Junto, and the Nashville Junto in Tennessee. The New Yorker knew that as a northerner he had to convince his planter allies of his commitment to the Doctrines of '98 and assure them that the plain Republicans of the North represented no threat to the South's peculiar institution. Ritchie's *Enquirer* formed an essential link in the chain of papers that laid down the states' rights line of the new party.[16]

As the 1828 campaign unfolded, Ritchie denied the charges of Jackson's complicity in the Burr Conspiracy and defended his personal character against the condemnation of his execution of militiamen put forth in the "Coffin Handbill," but the main thrust of the Jackson campaign reasserted the general's adherence to Virginia ideas and constitutional purity. To the editor of the *Enquirer*, the country faced a constitutional crisis. Governor Giles denounced Adams as "in no sense a Republican either in theory or in practice." The Virginia state committee encouraged the organization of local Jackson rallies; the pro-Jackson press included appeals to both the Germans and the Scotch-Irish, emphasizing the association of John Adams with the Alien and Sedition Acts. In October the Jackson Central Committee of Virginia issued an address attacking the president's latitudinarian constitutional views and expansive economic policy. Simultaneously the *Enquirer* printed a letter charging the administration with sacrificing the West Indian trade that became, along with the tariff, a leading economic issue for eastern Virginians, who blamed their economic malaise on the "wild Am. System designed to enrich the manufacturers and capitalists of the North at the expense of the planters."[17]

As Jackson's forces mounted their assault on the administration, its defenders, led by Secretary of State Henry Clay, gathered their supporters in Congress, established a Central Committee in Washington, and erected their own network of newspapers that included the anti-Junto editors Richard Toler of the *Lynchburg Virginian* and Pleasants of the *Richmond Whig*. Mixing old and new methods, they established committees of correspondence and held meetings in the northwest, portions of the Valley, and the eastern commercial counties to choose delegates to their state convention. Large gatherings at Wheeling, Staunton, Lynchburg, Norfolk, and Richmond during October and November urged the reelection of the president. Eventually two hundred delegates attended the Convention of National Republicans at Richmond and unanimously endorsed Adams and Pennsylvanian Richard Rush. They selected a slate of electors that included former presidents Madison and Monroe and issued an address attacking General Jackson. Like its rivals, the Adams party created a state central committee to help organize county committees and to communicate with the congressional steering committee that included several Virginians, as well as Secretary of the Navy Samuel Southard of New Jersey, who visited his favorite watering holes in the Old Dominion to drum up support for the president.[18]

The administration papers, which had been critical of the "hungry" office seekers who raised Jackson's banner, carried on the anti-Junto fight attacking aristocratic pretense and relating the questions of constitutional reform to the "caucus" nomination of Jackson by an assembly that did not truly represent the people of the state. Nearly all the known advocates of reapportioning the state and expanding the suffrage favored Adams. Reformers dominated the National Republican convention: Archibald Stuart presided, Chapman Johnson wrote its address, and they and Lewis Summers served as electors. Philip Doddridge, Samuel McDowell Moore, Charles Fenton Mercer, and Jesse Burton Harrison all played major roles in the campaign to reelect Adams.[19]

The convention's anti-Jackson address, however, concentrated on the general's lack of qualifications for civil office and endorsed the constitutionality of a protective tariff, specifically associating the party's position with that of Madison while attacking Governor Giles. It argued that the main difference between

Adams and Jackson involved a question of character. The anti-Jackson press denied that the campaign signaled a return to "the ancient state of parties" and pointed out that all of the Jefferson electors of 1800 except Giles now favored President Adams. The *Whig* associated the "caucus Military Ticket" of Jackson and Calhoun with the "madness" of nullification while the *Virginian* argued that the "Peoples Ticket" of Adams and Rush championed the ideals and practical policies of Madison.[20]

The competition generated by these organizational efforts and the focus provided by two such contrasting candidates led to an unprecedented outpouring of voters across the commonwealth. During the reign of the Virginia Dynasty, voters in the Old Dominion showed little interest in presidential elections, but the Adams administration alienated large numbers of Virginians who now voted against the New Englander, his "corrupt bargain" with Clay, and the American System. From the Revolution into the 1820s, participation in the political nation of Virginia hardly ever exceeded one-third of the white adult men. The contest between Jackson and Adams brought 28 percent of these men to the polls, exceeding the turnout of 1800 and any other presidential election although it remained below the figures for congressional and county elections. More voters went to the polls in the eastern half of the state than in the west, where a smaller proportion of the white adult males were freeholders and relatively little organization existed to encourage participation. The hostility to the Adams administration that grew out of a mix of ideology, economic interests, and sectional animosity activated men who normally voted in the spring elections to return to the polls in the fall of 1828.[21]

Jackson assumed Crawford's role as the candidate of Virginia's Republican center, and he made a particularly strong showing on the Southside. Ironically, the Old Hero did better east of the Blue Ridge than in the west, and in the Valley he was more popular with the Germans than with the Scotch-Irish. The trans-Allegheny contained both the most pro-Jackson and the most anti-Jackson subregions: in the southwest he received over 80 percent of the vote, and in the northwest he gained less than 60 percent. All in all, Jackson was popular throughout the state, but his election represented a victory for the eastern planter regime and the particularist philosophy associated with the Richmond Junto as articulated in the pages of the *Enquirer*.

Virginia's Old Republicans believed that because they had shifted into Jackson's camp at some cost to their ideological purity, they deserved a leading role in his administration, but it never materialized. Most had never liked or trusted the general and found him only preferable to the New England Puritan. John Tyler thought that the parties in Washington displayed "the want of some convenient cement to bind them together" and that the new president "cannot be considered as standing at the head of a *party*, for in truth he has none." Yet Andrew Jackson proved himself an effective party leader and a consistent Jeffersonian Republican. His administration emphasized strict construction and states' rights in his public positions on internal improvements, Indian policy, the Supreme Court, and the Bank of the United States, although the spoils system and the Old Hero's patronage policy generally alienated many of the commonwealth's conservatives, who thought Jackson showed insufficient respect for the Old Dominion's primacy of place within both the Union and the Jacksonian coalition.[22]

In 1832 the malcontents representing the old Republican order had little choice; they focused briefly on the movement to put Philip P. Barbour on the Jackson ticket as vice president but acquiesced when Van Buren was selected. Most Virginia freeholders voted as they had four years previously. Partly because of the provisions of the new constitution, participation increased, and Jackson's share of the Virginia vote jumped to nearly 80 percent. The Old Hero once again ran relatively better in the east among the aristocratic planters than with the yeomen west of the Blue Ridge, but both his total vote and his percentage of the vote increased throughout the state. Clay carried only the cities of Richmond and Norfolk and eight peripheral counties: Norfolk and Princess Anne in the lower tidewater; Lancaster, King George, Loudoun, Jefferson, and Berkeley along the Potomac; and Ohio County, which included the town of Wheeling. The National Republican candidate did best in the northwest, which had the highest increase in turnout, but even there Jackson won handily.

The 1832 election represented Ritchie's finest hour. The abortive attempt to run Barbour with Jackson fizzled, and Virginia's twenty-three electoral votes went to Van Buren for vice president. The New York–Virginia alliance was sound. At the opening of the legislative session, William C. Rives, a protégé of Jefferson and Madison who had served Jackson as ambassador to France, was elected to the United States Senate practically by acclamation after satisfying the particularists of his ideological purity. If the election was a referendum on the American System as Ritchie attempted to define it, Virginia's voters soundly rejected Clay's formula in favor of the Doctrines of '98. Republicanism was triumphant, and the Old Dominion had asserted its moral and political leadership. While private discontent with aspects of the general's first administration had arisen among Old Republicans who doubted his doctrinal purity and personal competence, Jackson seemed more powerful in the Old Dominion than Jefferson had been after his victory in 1800, and his annual message in early December, expressing his commitment to Virginia ideas, pleased Ritchie tremendously.[23]

The Virginia political system, however, had not changed greatly. Turnout increased, but still two-thirds of the white adult males did not participate in the presidential elections. Most of those who did also went to the polls in the spring when members of the assembly were elected and congressmen were chosen on the odd years. But these elections like the vote on ratification of the new constitution in 1830, divided the state sectionally and witnessed few intracounty contests involving conflicts over issues. Politics was personal and dominated by the county courts. Members of the Richmond Junto controlled the Jackson Central Committee and issued its addresses over their names. Ritchie's *Enquirer* continued to lay down the Republican party line that emphasized commitment to principles rather than men and assured voters that Jackson and Van Buren adhered to states' rights and strict construction. Yet a torrent of new issues disrupted Republican harmony during Jackson's second term. By the end of the decade, the second party system matured and thoroughly reshaped Virginia's political universe.

The volatile constitutional controversy over nullification that split the political elite into the State-Rights and Unionist parties in the legislature had little impact on the behavior of Virginia voters in either the elections for the assembly or the congressional contests in 1833 in which the National Republicans gained two seats in the west. Not until the following year, when the focus had shifted from nullification to Jackson's removal of the federal deposits from the Bank of the United States, did the name "Whig" or "Wig" appear as a partisan designation in the politics of the Old Dominion.[24]

The Jacksonian press concentrated on the Bank War in the assembly election of 1834, portraying their opponents as neo-Federalists who threatened the reign of Republicanism. The "monster" Bank gave substance to the traditional constitutional questions originally laid out by Jefferson in his 1791 letter to Washington on Alexander Hamilton's proposal for a Bank of the United States and repeated in the arguments of the particularists, Roane and Taylor, in the early 1820s when the issue came before the Supreme Court. Ritchie's Jeffersonian conception of party could be seen in his emphasis on the "piebald" nature of the coalition opposing Jackson and the Junto. The contrasting constitutional views of the nullifiers and the National Republicans proved the Whigs' factious nature as an unprincipled coalition of self-interested groups.[25]

Ritchie's reporting reflected the disarray among the various leaders of the opposition that was in fact an unstable coalition focused on the single practical issue of censuring the president for overstepping his constitutional authority. In 1834, however, the Whigs captured control of the Virginia assembly and set about dismantling the Jacksonians' hold on the Virginia government, taking the official printing from Ritchie, removing Peter Daniel from the governor's council, and coming within two votes of ending the long tenure of Linn Banks as Speaker of the House of Delegates. The anti-Jackson coalition of Calhounites and National Republicans then proceeded to instruct the state's senators to vote

to restore the federal deposits. After Rives resigned rather than obey their instructions, they chose Old Republican Benjamin Watkins Leigh to replace him
in the Senate. A new partisan era had dawned in the Old Dominion.

From 1834 to 1838 each yearly election produced new permutations and com-
binations, refashioning electoral behavior as old-style local leaders were forced
to take public positions on national issues. The presidential election of 1836
typified the transitional nature of the mid-1830s. In the Old Dominion the politics of slavery dominated the campaign from the beginning and produced a
marked difference between the support given Jackson and that retained by Van
Buren. While the general had won over three-fourths of the votes cast, his
hand-picked successor received only 56 percent of an enlarged electorate
(table 3.1). Turnout had increased, and the distribution of the vote changed
dramatically. The New Yorker did less well across the state, but his showing was
particularly poor in the eastern half of the commonwealth. The Democratic
vote declined most precipitously in the areas with the most slaves—the tidewater and the lower piedmont—where Van Buren ran behind the 1835 Democratic candidates for Congress as well as Jackson in 1832.[26]

The transitional nature of the mid-1830s can be seen in the changing distribution of the vote from one election to the next.

The pattern of Van Buren's support correlated only slightly with Jackson's
(table 3.2). More indicative of the fickle nature of the Virginia voters at the time,
the statewide returns from the congressional election of 1835 do not correlate
closely with those from either the 1832 or the 1836 presidential elections. The
pattern of voting for the House of Delegates also shifted from year to year in the
mid-1830s. After losing control of the legislature in 1834, the Jacksonians re-
bounded strongly in 1835, registering a net gain of fourteen seats to win a com-

Table 3.1. Regional variation in the Democratic percentage of the presidential
vote, 1828–52

	1828	1832	1836	1840	1844	1848	1852
Tidewater	66	75	45	45	50	49	54
Piedmont	81	85	59	51	53	51	57
Valley	64	73	65	58	60	58	62
Trans-Allegheny	70	76	64	51	54	49	54
Virginia	70	78	56	51	53	51	56

Source: ICPSR data for 119 counties.

Table 3.2. Interelection correlations of the Democratic vote in presidential elections, 1828–52

	1832	1836	1840	1844	1848	1852
1828	.85	.57	.41	.50	.47	.42
1832		.59	.48	.55	.53	.48
1836			.82	.78	.73	.67
1840				.90	.91	.89
1844					.94	.90
1848						.94

fortable majority. Although the Democrats retained their majority the following year, twenty-four seats changed hands. Similar fluctuation characterized the congressional returns.

Turnout reached a new level in spring 1835, and most elections took on the outward appearance of two-party contests. Nearly all the candidates could be identified by party. The Democratic Republicans ousted five of the eight Whigs who had won as National Republicans two years earlier and lost only one of their own congressional seats. The sweeping victory involved winning individual constituencies by narrower margins than Jackson had obtained in 1832 and close competition in nearly every district. While the Democrats controlled three-quarters of the seats in the Virginia congressional delegation (table 3.3), they won only 56 percent of the votes cast. The elections of 1833 and 1835 each produced ten new congressmen; only four of the sixty men who represented the commonwealth at the time sat continuously from 1831 to 1837.[27]

The panic of 1837 broke upon the nation in May after Virginia's assembly and congressional elections. Although economic conditions stabilized and then briefly improved, the country slid into a major depression that lasted until the mid-1840s. The crisis heightened the saliency of questions concerning money and banking as each of the emerging parties constructed its own interpretation of the nation's economic ills and provided partisan prescriptions to heal the stricken patient. The Democratic administration bore the distinct disadvantage of both being in office and having taken explicit pride in its destructive war upon the Bank of the United States. The logic of the situation forced the Democrats into an antibank stance. Van Buren blamed the banks for the crisis and told Congress that the people too often looked to government to solve their problems.

Table 3.3. Partisan affiliation of congressmen, 1829–53

	Party	
Congress	Jackson/Democratic	Opposition/Whig
21st (1829–31)	18	6
22d	18	6
23d	16	8
24th	16	5
25th	15	7
26th (1839–41)	14	9
27th	12	10
28th	11	6
29th	15	1
30th	10	6
31st (1849–51)	14	2
32d	14	2

Sources: *Biographical Directory of the American Congress 1774–1927* (Washington, D.C., 1928); Stanley Parsons, William H. Beach, and Dan Herrmann, *United States Congressional Districts, 1788–1841* (Westport, Conn., 1978), 280–85, 368–73.

Note: Jackson/Democrats includes those labeled Republican, Democrat, Jackson Democrat, State Rights Democrat, and Independent—in the case of Hunter in 1841. Opposition/Whigs includes Federalists, National Republicans, Whigs, and, in 1843, two Tyler Whigs.

As the policy of the Jackson administration had unfolded in the years after the Bank veto, some of the president's Virginia supporters proved unwilling to accept its less orthodox elements. They continuously opposed efforts to recharter the Chestnut Street "monster" but resisted both the high-handed removal of the deposits and the corruption inherent in establishing the new "pet" banks. In the debate over governmental regulation of those banks, the Virginians generally advocated a very conservative approach to specie reserves and the issuing of small notes. Virginia Calhounite William F. Gordon even suggested that the federal government sever itself entirely from the banking system.[28]

In mid-1837 William C. Rives, now back in the Senate, and a small group of congressmen set up the *Daily Madisonian* in Washington, D.C., hoping to influence the legislation in the upcoming special session called by Van Buren. In its first number a "Conservative Manifesto" advocated a "well regulated mixed currency," supported the government's use of state banks, and attacked the hard money "Jacobins." Rives, its author, was a traditional Republican who worshiped Madison and looked constantly to retrenchment through the elimination of small notes and the establishment of conservative ratios of specie to both circulation and deposits. But he showed little patience with the extreme antibank views of Missouri's Senator Benton or the New York Loco-Focos who challenged his position within the Republican party.[29]

Van Buren's message to the special session blamed the banks for the financial collapse and suggested the establishment of an Independent Treasury system in order to protect the federal funds. The president's message underscored his commitment to both laissez-faire and states' rights. The *Democratic Review* insisted that the administration was "friendly to banks" and advocated neither "a purely metallic currency" nor "the destruction of credit," but in Congress and the press, Democrats increasingly attacked banks and called for a "divorce of bank and state." Along with Rives, Virginia congressmen James Garland, George W. Hopkins, and James M. Mason, who had all previously supported Jackson, resisted the administration on this matter and joined the "Conservative Revolt."[30]

The bank issue had already entered into Virginia state politics by the time Congress met in the fall of 1837. Following the suspension of specie payments in May, the new governor, David Campbell, called a special session of the assembly. A friend of Ritchie and an old Junto affiliate, Campbell asked the legislature to provide temporary relief for the banks so as not to disrupt the normal marketing of the wheat and tobacco crops. The Democratic legislators generally preferred to steer a moderate course, holding off resumption for six months and making state banknotes acceptable for all debts in the interim. The majority of the party, however, signaled its distrust of paper money in voting against the small-note bill pushed through by a coalition of Whigs and Democratic "softs."[31]

The issue tore the Junto apart. Governor Campbell allied himself with Rives and warned against the control of the party by Benton and the Loco-Focos, but he and Rives underrated the appeal of the administration's proposal. Not only Peter Daniel and Richard Parker but also John Roane and Ritchie's banker-cousin John Brockenbrough favored an Independent Treasury, and the Democrats in the assembly proposed a set of resolutions endorsing Van Buren's policy. They were joined by the Calhounites, who were slowly returning to the Democracy, while the Conservatives voted with the Whigs.

The Whigs benefited at the polls from the economic discontent. Virginia voters rejected both the Van Buren administration and its allies in Richmond. The fight in Congress over the Independent Treasury and the Democrats' attempt in the assembly to place limitations on the state banks consumed the partisan press. Ritchie struggled to find a workable compromise, but essentially he and the majority of Virginia Democrats embraced the administration proposal and saw Rives, Governor Campbell, and the small coterie of Conservatives as overly pro-bank—Whigs in disguise.[32]

The success of the Whigs in 1838 was most pronounced in the piedmont, but they gained across the board. Nearly half of the counties in which the Whigs won new seats lay west of the Blue Ridge. Economically distressed voters turned against the Democrats, but the shift to the Whigs was no more common in wealthy counties than in poor ones. The following year national issues dominated the spring elections, and both parties relied on county vigilance committees to draw a huge number of the voters directly into the campaign. Party labels had become routine. The Democrats called upon the Virginia voters to close party ranks and rally around the Republican banner. Support for the Independent Treasury gave immediate economic meaning to the continuing constitutional debate over strict construction. The voters had a choice: "Bank or no Bank? a latitudenous construction of the Constitution according to the school of Hamilton, Adams, and Webster, or Republican doctrines of Virginia of '98–99."[33]

In Virginia the Democratic Republicans' response to these questions was not a matter of proper economic policy but of constitutional fidelity. The *Enquirer* turned the history of the party struggle back to 1789 and proclaimed the Democrats heirs of the principles of Jefferson's opinion on the constitutionality of the first Bank as well as the Virginia and Kentucky resolutions. According to Ritchie, the Whigs, like their Federalist forebears, favored a "latitudenous construction of the Constitution" and the Alien and Sedition Acts. The Democratic editor called upon the Virginia voters to defeat the corrupt, pro-Bank policies of Rives and his friends and put a stop to federal aid to internal improvements in any form. "To arms then freemen—to arms ye State Rights men."[34]

But the Whigs won control of the assembly and gained eight seats in the Virginia delegation to Congress. The independent Calhounite Robert M. T. Hunter and the Conservatives Garland and Hopkins stood apart from the administration as well. Van Buren could count on only ten Virginians in the fight over economic policy. A frustrated Ritchie was ready to sign up Hunter and trade Garland to the Whigs. While the fight over the Independent Treasury did draw some entrepreneurial Democrats into Whig ranks, it also brought Hunter and the Calhounites back into the Democratic party where they were eventually joined by some Conservatives like Mason who were also strong advocates of states' rights. Their constitutional views ultimately proved more important than their position on economic policy. In the 1840s Hunter and Mason emerged as the dominant voices in the Virginia Democracy.[35]

Turnout in 1839 increased slightly in the tidewater and the west but declined in the piedmont and the Valley. The fears fostered by the worsening economic situation had their greatest impact—and the Whigs made their greatest gains—in the northern piedmont and west of the Blue Ridge. For all of Ritchie's praise of "Little Tennessee" and subsequent historians' belief that hard money politics had a strong appeal in areas loosely tied to the market, the southwestern farmers turned out in unprecedented numbers and the Democratic majority in the area plummeted from 76 to 53 percent—the largest drop of any of Virginia's subregions. Only among the planters of the Southside did the Democrats retain a convincing majority.[36]

The spring elections of 1839 and 1840 affirmed the new electoral alignment that had appeared in 1838, but it was the Log Cabin campaign that truly signaled the coming-of-age of the second party system in the commonwealth. The sedate elitist politics of Jeffersonian Virginia managed by the Richmond Junto and the gentry in the county courts gave way to Walt Whitman's noisy democrat "yop" and party drill. Party organization appeared in its modern garb; the campaign's merchandising style celebrated populist politics, and the common people participated in record numbers and in unprecedented ways. Over half of the white adult males—four-fifths of those eligible to vote—went to the polls. While the population of Virginia held constant between 1830 and 1840, the number of voters doubled. This represented a huge jump from 1836, caused by the entrance of nearly thirty thousand new participants into the political system of the Old Dominion.

For the first time in Virginia history more men voted in a fall presidential election than in the spring assembly elections. Van Buren barely held off the Whig challenge, winning the state by a whisker. He did better in the western counties than in the east, but historians have exaggerated the sectional split: 49 percent of the Van Buren vote came from counties east of the Blue Ridge (map 3.2). What stood out startlingly in the 1840 returns was not a sectional division of sentiments but the competitive balance in all of the subregions and in most of the counties of the state. Party identification appeared in its modern form for the first time, revealing a shift in the political culture that sanctioned the legitimacy of party strife.

Both the unprecedented level of voter response and the heightened interest in the presidential election reflected the new politics. The *United States Magazine and Democratic Review* expressed shock at the Whig campaign, and its frustrated editor complained, "We have taught them how to conquer us!" The Democrats had won with a popular general; "why then might not the name of General Harrison 'tickle the ears of the groundlings' with the same charm as the old hero of New Orleans?" The Democrats had used symbols like the hickory

3-2. Whig counties, 1840

Whig ▨

tree, and now it was log cabins, cider barrels, and coonskins that roused "the hurrah of popular enthusiasm." The Whig managers had avoided "all public exposition of their principles, of the views and intentions which they would bring with them into power." Rather, they offered only criticism of the Van Buren administration "of a mere partisan character" and relied upon the re-sources of a "large and wealthy party . . . in playing off before the ignorant mass . . . a great variety of silly mummeries calculated for the presumed level of their capacity." Worst of all, they had "out Heroded Herod" by appropriating "the name to which they ascribe our popular strength," calling themselves the "*Democratic* Whigs."[37]

Across the country two modern national parties competed effectively for the first time in American history. Voters flocked to the polls. Participation in 1840 increased by over 40 percent; four-fifths of the nation's white adult males took part in the 1840 election. Although various elements of the electoral orga-nization had existed previously, two effective modern machines emerged to mount the Log Cabin campaign. The Democratic Whig National Convention at Harrisburg in early December 1839 was the first to choose a party's presidential candidate from among possible contenders and the first to form a ticket care-fully designed to balance the contending elements of the party coalition.

Under the leadership of Thurlow Weed and Thaddeus Stevens, the Whigs carried modern party management a step beyond the Sly Fox himself. They es-tablished an executive committee to direct the campaign led by congressmen who typified the new generation: Thomas Corwin of Ohio, Truman Smith of Connecticut, and the representative from Richmond, John Minor Botts. They became responsible for raising money from a wide variety of sources and circu-lating handbills, pamphlets, speeches, and political sermons using a master mailing list provided by party leaders. Much of the Whigs' propaganda was vapid, and some of it salacious, like Pennsylvania congressman Charles Ogle's speech that Democrats called "The Omnibus of Lies" depicting the regal splen-dor of the Van Buren White House or deceased Tennessee congressman David Crockett's scathing *Life of Martin Van Buren* that had been written for the 1836 election. A larger number of campaign biographies, both authorized and unau-thorized, appeared than ever before.[38]

While voters may well have been confused by the variety of claims and sometime wanton disregard for the truth in press reporting, they did not lack for information in 1840. The number of newspapers in the country had ex-panded greatly during the 1830s with the introduction of new printing technol-ogy. Most of the popular press was unabashedly partisan, with editors playing a crucial role as party leaders. They reported on "Monster" rallies and parades "leading to, from, and swirling around" the candidates' "stump" speeches that lasted as long as three or four hours, in which they presented detailed analyses of economic policy amid the ritual chastisement of their opponents' veracity and virtue. These new forms characterized the Log Cabin campaign and foretold the nature of the new populist politics.

Party luminaries in greater numbers than ever before toured the country offering long and detailed indictments of their opponents. Candidate William Henry Harrison himself made twenty-three such speeches. After Virginia senator Rives declared for Harrison, he was added to the circuit and spoke out against the Van Buren administration's monetary policy in the North as well as the South. For his part, Daniel Webster traveled south and in Richmond tried to moderate sectional tensions by praising the commonwealth's Revolutionary heritage and assuring the planters that they had nothing to fear concerning federal interference with slavery. More popular than great orators were the stable of Whig workingmen like the "Learned Blacksmith" Elihu Burritt and Henry Wilson "the Natick Cobbler." The most energetic, John W. Bear, the "Buckeye Blacksmith," made 331 speeches in eight states. Even the reticent vice-presidential candidate John Tyler was drawn into a number of uncomfortable public appearances in which he generally responded to questions about the tariff and banking by insisting that he agreed with General Harrison and Senator Clay.[39]

The campaign's merchandising style involved parades, great balls rolled from town to town, the raising of 250-foot flagpoles, and the construction of 50-foot-square log cabins. For all the ballyhoo and misrepresentation of which each party complained, it was nearly impossible for voters to avoid the contrasting partisan interpretations of the nation's economic ills and the glittering generalities of each party's policies. The Democrats' position was clearer than that of the Whigs, because they were the party in power, and they had written the first American party platform. Designed primarily to secure the return of the prodigal Calhounites by emphasizing states' rights and strict construction, it consisted of nine resolutions declaring that the federal government was one of limited powers and could not "commence or carry on" internal improvements, assume the debts of the states, pass protective tariffs, spend money excessively, "charter a national bank," interfere with slavery, or "abridge the present privilege of becoming a citizen." "Thou shalt not" was written over the Democratic door. The one positive resolution called for an Independent Treasury—"the separation of the moneys of the government from banking institutions, is indispensable from the safety of the funds of the government, and the rights of the people."[40]

Basically the Whigs took the offensive and charged that their opponents— "the party"—had undermined the Republic by corrupting the Constitution. The Independent Treasury would dangerously unite the purse and the sword in the hands of the executive, and this subversion of the Constitution would be furthered by the secretary of war's proposal to federalize the militia. Whig party symbolism portrayed Harrison—"part soldier; part farmer"—as Cincinnatus, standing above corrupt faction and striving to return the government to the people and reinstate the Congress to its proper role that had been usurped first by King Andrew and now by Van Buren, the new pretender to the throne. The Whigs advocated a more positive economic program designed to maintain the credit system and to foster industry.

Within this context the party's most effective speaker, Senator Clay, put forth the Whigs' response to the laissez-faire economic policy etched out in their opponents' platform. After telling his rapt audience at Taylorsville, near where he was born in Hanover County, Virginia, that "the Whigs of 1840 stand where the Republicans of 1798 stood, and where the Whigs of the Revolution were battling for liberty, for the people, for free institutions, against power, against corruption, against executive encroachments, against monarchy," Clay devoted the majority of his two-hour speech to a detailed discussion of Whig policies. He advocated restricting the powers of the president with a single term and limiting executive veto, appointment, and dismissal as well as "control over the Treasury of the United States." "Candor and truth require me to say that, in my judgement, whilst banks continue to exist in the country, the service of a bank of the United States cannot be safely dispensed with."[41]

The candidate, Harrison, also made the Whig position clear in his speeches. At Dayton, Ohio, the general associated himself with "the principles of Jefferson" and attacked the "violence of party spirit." Responding to his own rhetorical question, "Are you in favor of paper money?" Harrison replied, "I am in favor of the credit system . . . because I am a democrat." He desired a "safe" and "correct" banking system. In a somewhat convoluted fashion he expressed his support for a national bank, if Congress chose such a course, noting to the audience's applause that Madison had approved the Second Bank's charter.[42]

After gaining control of the government with Harrison's victory, the Whigs quickly moved to overthrow the policies of the Van Buren administration by repealing the Independent Treasury law and instituting a broad positive program that Clay and the other Whigs had laid out in the campaign. This constituted a new-model American System joining a bankruptcy act, the distribution of the proceeds from land sales to encourage education and internal improvements, a national bank in some form, and a modestly protective tariff. Resolutions on these policies along with questions of stay laws, new commercial taxes, and state banks dominated the legislative agenda as well.[43]

The Virginia Democrats chose to fight the revival of the American System on traditional particularist grounds and to depict the party's position in familiar constitutional and moral terms. Almost daily the Democratic press referred to the "Principles of '98," and the Central Committee circulated Madison's *Report of 1800* as a campaign document. Various addresses attacking the "extremes of Federalism" and appealing to the "friends of State Rights" called for "retrenchment and reform." The Democrats wished to return to the Independent Treasury and warned that the Whigs would bring back the "monster Bank" and "saddle the South with a tariff." The Whig policy of distribution "would destroy the constitutional balance of power between the Federal and the State Governments," while the bankruptcy law "impaired the obligation of contracts" and corrupted the morals of the people. "Rally under the States' Rights flag, the consecrated banner of '99 and as it conducted us *then* to victory and to the Civic Revolution of 1800, so will it guide and lead us on to victory now."[44]

The Whigs had done extremely well in the Virginia congressional elections of 1841 with party regulars winning four new seats from their opponents, so that for the only time during the life of the second party system, the Virginia delegation was split equally between the Democrats and the Whigs. Because of its stagnant population growth, however, the commonwealth lost six seats in Congress following the census of 1840. The assembly's redistricting ensured seven seats in the new, smaller delegation for the Democrats and three for the Whigs including Henry A. Wise's Eastern Shore district and tipped the scales in the Democrats' direction in the other districts by submerging centers of Whig power in a sea of contiguous Democratic constituencies. Consequently, the general shift away from the Whigs in 1843 brought a crushing victory for the Democrats in the Old Dominion as they took ten of the fourteen seats and won 54 percent of the popular vote. Two others went to Tyler Whigs—Wise and Thomas W. Gilmer—who ran now as Democrats against regular Whig opponents. There was a low turnout even in competitive areas, and four Democrats faced no opposition at all. By Ritchie's count eleven "Republicans," three Whigs, and one "Wise" made up the new delegation.[45]

In 1844 both parties nominated slaveholders as their presidential candidates, thus blunting the direct impact of the slavery issue. The question of Texas annexation led southerners including the Virginians to block the renomination of Van Buren and to put forward James K. Polk of Tennessee, who campaigned on a traditionally Jacksonian program proclaiming a new Democratic order that included "the re-annexation of Texas and the re-occupation of Oregon." In contrast to 1840, both parties put forth platforms that defined the issues along the lines that had emerged in the 1830s. The Whig candidate Henry Clay campaigned aggressively for the policies associated with his name and in vain argued against his opponents' belligerent stance on the Texas issue.[46]

The results in the Old Dominion maintained the basic paradigm of the second party system. The turnout remained high, and the Democrats increased their portion of the vote slightly, but the configuration of the returns continued unchanged from 1840. The elections were highly correlated. No one region or subregion was responsible for the statewide Democratic gain. Polk was slightly more popular everywhere than Van Buren. The Texas issue had disrupted the New York–Virginia alliance and turned the commonwealth's Democrats against Van Buren's candidacy, but it was not solely responsible for Polk's margin of victory. His proportion of the Virginia vote was almost exactly that received by the Democratic congressional candidates in 1843 before the annexation of Texas became an issue.

The Democrats' momentum from the presidential campaign carried over into the Virginia state elections of 1845, as they regained control of the legislature and took all but one of the commonwealth's congressional seats. The Whig debacle resulted primarily from the redistricting and the falloff of Whig votes in the districts where victory seemed impossible. It would be premature, however, to read into this "great victory" the death knell of the Whig party. The election occurred in an environment structured by two highly competitive and well-organized parties in which a small surge to the Democrats gave them narrow victories in closely contested districts. Such elections are decided at the margins. Editors from both parties made insistent pleas to their followers to vote and often reported elections won by a few votes to show the voters the importance of their personal participation.

There was a normal Democratic majority in the Old Dominion during the duration of the second party system, but it was so small and competition existed in so many constituencies that the Whigs consistently threatened to take control of the House of Delegates. In the 1840s, if Whigs or Democrats found their party nominee distasteful, they generally stayed home rather than vote for the lesser evil put forth by the odious opposition. The seemingly huge swing to the Democrats in 1845 resulted from many small shifts across the board. Whigs lost exactly the same number of seats in the east as they did in the west, and close competition characterized the counties that changed hands. Two examples must suffice. The Whig candidate for the assembly won the seat from Caroline County in 1844 by 13 votes. Five months later Polk carried the county with 467 votes to Clay's 399. Then in the spring of 1845, a Democrat recaptured the house seat by a margin of 63 votes out of 951 cast. Similarly, in neighboring Hanover County the Whig candidate won the house seat in 1844 by a narrow margin of 58 votes out of 1,136. In the fall slightly fewer voters (1,040) gave the county to Clay by 76 votes. But then four months later the county voters sent a Democrat to Richmond with a narrow 532-to-517 victory. Obviously, in some counties assembly elections still drew more voters than presidential elections. There were small fluctuations in turnout but few shifts from one party to the other. The closely correlated elections of 1844 and 1845, however, demonstrate the strength of the second party system and the degree to which it had penetrated the politics of the Old Dominion.

The election of Polk eventually led to the Mexican War, which proved to be less popular in Virginia than the annexation of Texas that precipitated it. In the closely contested spring elections of 1847, the Whigs bounced back, regaining six of the Old Dominion's fifteen seats in the House of Representatives and improving their position in the assembly. Again a shift in a small number of votes was responsible for the seemingly radical result. In fact, the underlying pattern of voter response in the Old Dominion remained remarkably stable, and in 1848 the commonwealth witnessed another election maintaining the second party system even though the slavery issue reentered the political debate in a way that caused a Democratic surge, sapping Whig strength without greatly altering the basic configuration of electoral behavior in the Old Dominion.

The divisive new form this issue took involved not abolition but the handling of slavery in the territory taken in the Mexican War. In August 1846 a Pennsylvania Democrat, David Wilmot, introduced an amendment to the bill authorizing appropriations for the prosecution of the war against Mexico. The Wilmot Proviso that would have prohibited the extension of slavery into any newly acquired area passed the House but was held up in the Senate at the close of the session. When it was revived by the New York Democrats and again passed by the House in 1847, Calhoun put forth a set of resolutions outlining the new doctrine of "an equality of rights" in the territories that denied Congress's power to restrict slavery. The Virginia assembly almost immediately attacked Wilmot's proviso, endorsed Calhoun's position, and elected to the Senate two strong supporters of southern rights, James M. Mason and Robert M. T. Hunter.[47]

The politics of slavery seemed to favor the Whigs, who ran a Virginia-born slaveholder, General Zachary Taylor, against the Democrats' venerable Lewis Cass of Michigan. The northerner, however, had married into a prominent western Virginia family and with his "Nicholson letter" supporting popular sovereignty satisfied the leading Virginia Calhounites.At the Democratic national convention, the delegation from the Old Dominion, dominated by advocates of southern rights, solidly supported Cass and hoped to see Southside planter John Y. Mason, who had served in the cabinets of both Tyler and Polk, selected for the second spot on the ticket. When Mason's chances faded, the Virginians quickly lined up behind William O. Butler of Kentucky. The only excitement in the convention came when William Loundes Yancey and the Alabamians tried to get a more specific defense of southern rights into the platform and then eventually bolted. But the Virginians stood with the regulars and endorsed the platform that repeated the pledges of 1844 and congratulated Polk and the Democracy on the acquisition of Texas and the successful prosecution of the war.[48]

The Whigs, much to the disgust of Clay and one of his leading supporters in the Old Dominion, John Minor Botts, tried to win over wavering Democrats by portraying Taylor as a war hero and a "no party" man. Taylor's nomination in Virginia had been put forward in a legislative caucus in December and then pushed through at the state party convention in February 1848 by a group headed by William B. Preston. Botts struggled to get the Virginia Whigs to send an uninstructed delegation, but the Taylor forces stampeded the delegates by spreading the rumor that Clay's home state, Kentucky, had gone for the general. The powerful *Lynchburg Virginian* attacked the Taylorites' duplicity and challenged the authenticity of the "Allison letter" in which Taylor declared his Whiggism. The archpartisan Botts could hardly defect to the Democrats.[49]

But all in all, the 1848 presidential election in Virginia set traditional Whigs against traditional Democrats squabbling over traditional issues and playing the traditional politics of slavery. This time the Whigs ran a slaveholder for president and the Democrats put forth a northerner. As a result turnout declined significantly, and the Democrats again squeaked by with a bare majority of the state's vote—almost exactly what Van Buren had received in 1840. The Democratic turnout fell particularly in the eastern half of the state where the planter elite refused to support Cass, but the distribution of the vote correlated highly with the two previous elections.

The disaffected Clay supporters like Botts also refused to go to the polls. The "no party" strategy hurt the Whigs in Virginia. Taylor did relatively better than Clay in both the northern tidewater and the northern piedmont, but he actually received fewer votes than Clay in both areas. In the northwest the Whig vote remained the same as it had been. Unhappy Democrats who stayed at home caused Taylor's proportion of the vote to be higher than Clay's, but the only area in which the Whigs actually gained votes was the traditionally Democratic southwest. There Cass held on with a mere 51 percent majority. In 1847 the southwest had sent a Whig, Andrew Fulton, to Congress, but such Whig successes in the region were contingent on low Democratic turnouts. Two stable partisan blocs continuously opposed one another in election after election during the decade following 1838. The fluctuating results were produced not by a movement of independent voters from one party to the other in response to new policy positions or the popularity of individual candidates, but by the decisions of partisans whether to vote or not in specific elections.

In part because the proviso appeared at first to be a mischievous attempt of the New York politicos to use sectional hostility in their intramural political games, its impact was delayed in Virginia until the spring congressional elections in 1849 when slavery emerged as the "Question of the Day" and the shift toward the Democrats occurred. These contests for congressional seats and control of the legislature were preceded by Calhoun's Southern Address, the debate in Congress on Virginian William B. Preston's compromise proposal on slavery in the territories and a fight in the General Assembly over the resolutions reaffirming opposition to the proviso and attacking the personal liberty laws that had been passed by the northern states.[50]

The elections involved the startling shift of a small but significant group of Whigs to the Democrats and the Democracy's total commitment to the defense of slavery and southern rights. The *Enquirer* embraced Calhoun and attacked Old Jacksonian moderates like Thomas Hart Benton. The *Enquirer's* editors—Ritchie's sons—chastised their opponents as "Free Soilers"—"Whigs of the rankest Federal School"—whose "latitudenous construction of the Constitution gives almost unlimited power to the federal Government—and leads them naturally to concede the power of excluding the Southern States from the new territories."[51]

The presidential election of 1852 saw the further development of the institutional structures associated with modern political parties in an attempt to provide national coherence. Both the Whigs and the Democrats met in convention to nominate their candidates and write platforms that represented the compromises necessary to attain party unity. Both parties had to paper over factional infighting and in some fashion endorse the Compromise of 1850, although sectionalism clearly plagued the Whigs more than the Democrats. Each created a National Committee to coordinate the campaign but also designed to be permanent and maintain institutional continuity between presidential elections. The Whigs ran the Virginia-born war hero Winfield Scott with the well-known North Carolina nationalist William A. Graham on a platform reasserting the traditional Whig economic program against Democratic dark horse Franklin Pierce of New Hampshire and the rotund Alabama senator William R. King.[52]

Virginia Democrats were pleased with the ticket and set out not only to mobilize those who had abstained in the 1848 election but also to bring into the party as many of the new voters enfranchised by the constitution of 1851 as possible. The party's platform emphasized state's rights and strict construction, referring explicitly once again to the Virginia and Kentucky resolutions and Madison's *Report*, repeated the traditional economic positions of the Democracy, attacked the abolitionists and upheld the president's veto power. The Democrats congratulated themselves and "the American people on the results of the war, which so manifestly justified the policy and conduct of the Democratic party." But economic recovery blunted the point of Polk's policies, and the party's constitutional stance became increasingly connected to the defense of southern rights in the minds of the majority of Virginians. If anything, these traditional guideposts of the Jeffersonian faith now posed a clearer choice between the Democracy and the Whigs than they had during the depression years.[53]

As the *Enquirer* and the other Democratic papers across the commonwealth focused upon the politics of slavery, their party's traditional states' rights stance gave it a distinct advantage over the Whigs. The result was foreordained. Pierce swept the South and gained a greater portion of Virginia's votes than any candidate since Van Buren in 1836. Pierce's popularity presented a clear contrast to Cass's poor showing in 1848. The election witnessed a new high level of voter turnout in Virginia, and the Democrats gained from three to six percentage points in each of the state's subregions. This Democratic surge was first evident in the congressional elections of 1849, in which the Democrats won fourteen of Virginia's fifteen seats. The question of slavery in the territories produced the swing to the party of southern rights that caused some eastern Whigs to change their allegiance and gave the Democracy greater appeal to new voters entering the electorate.[54]

The Democratic sweep of 1852 did not bode well for the Whigs, who had come close to winning the state's first popular gubernatorial election in 1851, when the western reformer George Summers lost narrowly to future Confederate general Joseph Johnson. The distribution of the vote continued to follow the basic outlines etched in the late 1830s, but only 44 percent of the newly expanded electorate had voted for Winfield Scott—down five points from 1848—and in the expanded House of Delegates the Whigs retained an even smaller proportion (two-fifths) of the seats. The Democrats could count upon the Old Dominion in presidential elections, and the congressional delegation would become entirely Democratic in 1853 when longtime Whig C. J. Faulkner defected to the Democrats. Yet the dying Whigs cast a dark shadow on the 1850s; a very sizable minority of Virginia voters rejected the Democracy and despised "the Chivalry" who dedicated the party of Jefferson and Jackson to the maintenance of southern rights.

The second party system in the Old Dominion evolved through two stages representing different levels of development. Jackson and the conflicts associated with him dominated the first. The second featured the close competition of two relatively modern parties that deeply penetrated the state's political system. In two of Andrew Jackson's three campaigns for the presidency, he ran essentially without competition and garnered three-quarters of the commonwealth's popular vote. The Democrats managed to win all of the presidential elections in Virginia during the years of the second party system, but of the five contests between 1836 and 1852, all were reasonably competitive, and three were extremely close. None of Jackson's successors could command more than 56 percent of the vote.

Participation in presidential elections in the Old Dominion followed the national trend during these years. Jackson's election in 1828 brought out a large number of new voters, but they were mainly men who had voted in state elections at the time. The changes in the rules of the game that led to universal white manhood suffrage had their greatest effect in the growth of the national electorate between 1836 and 1840. The size of the commonwealth's electorate— even without significant democratic reform—grew substantially. In every presidential election after 1820, when a mere 3 percent of the state's white adult males cast their votes for the unopposed incumbent James Monroe, the number of Virginians going to the polls in presidential elections went up.

Although there was a slight increase following the enactment of the new constitution in 1830 and a sizable jump after the introduction of universal white manhood suffrage in 1851, the largest leap forward came between 1836 and 1840 at a time when there was no change in legal requirements or electoral procedures. During these three decades there was only one dip, a relatively modest decline in 1848. Even in that year nearly two and one-half times as many people participated as had twenty years earlier. The increase in voters between 1848 and the more democratic election of 1852 was larger than the entire Virginia electorate that had "poured out" to give Jackson his victory in 1828.

The turnout of Virginia voters in the various other elections that took place

Table 3.4. Regional variation in the percentage of white adult males voting in presidential elections, 1828–52

	1828	1832	1836	1840	1844	1848	1852
Upper tidewater	23	25	31	53	52	45	58
Lower tidewater	36	35	34	64	62	58	85
Northern piedmont	39	39	44	61	68	60	86
Southern piedmont	28	34	43	57	61	53	67
Valley	28	36	38	60	62	57	84
Northwest	26	34	35	53	51	45	72
Southwest	25	26	33	52	51	44	57
Virginia	28	31	35	55	54	47	63

Sources: The figures for the state are from J. R. Pole, *Political Representation in England and the Origins of the American Republic* (London, 1966), 562; the regional averages are from the ICPSR data.

during these years followed the same general pattern, showing a gradual increase in participation (table 3.4). Initially, assembly and congressional elections drew more voters than presidential elections. After a period when they tended to draw the same number of voters, for several years the increase in the spring elections exceeded that in the fall. Then in the 1840s, although the turnout in the state races remained relatively high, it lagged consistently behind that for the national elections. When suffrage was extended to all white men and the governorship was made elective in the 1850s, turnout in state elections reached its highest antebellum level.

The growth in the Virginia electorate during these years was primarily due to the politicization of eligible voters rather than constitutional change. In this calculating and individualistic society, common men came to believe that their participation at the polls counted. The proportion of white adult males voting in presidential elections jumped dramatically between 1824 and 1828, and then over the next two presidential elections it moved up more modestly from 28 to 35 percent. Presidential politics increasingly interested Virginians. The number of the state's voters who went to the polls in the spring and returned to vote in the fall grew (graph 3.1).

The Log Cabin campaign produced an entirely new level of citizen interest that brought out four-fifths of the state's eligible voters. Certainly that year the epidemic of democracy spread to the Old Dominion from the surrounding states where turnouts ranged from 78 to 90 percent of the white adult males. Non-Virginians visited the commonwealth to court the voters and assure them that the fate of the nation rested in their hands. Webster's speech to the Richmond ladies was but one part of the Whigs' general appeal to women, manipulating the bourgeois symbols of domesticity and civility.[55]

The excitement associated with that campaign throughout the country rolled across the commonwealth. In preparation both parties dramatically altered their popular appeals and significantly cranked up their electoral machines, mobilizing new voters in record numbers. Turnout jumped by twenty points—a 60 percent increase! Approximately thirty thousand men who had never before cast a vote for any office materialized to choose between Tip and Van. Four years later nearly all of them returned to the polls when 55 percent of the state's white adult males gave a narrow victory to Polk over Clay in a similarly exciting and well-organized contest.

The cross pressures on voters generated by the Whig selection of a military hero and slaveholder as their candidate caused many Democrats to stay at home in 1848, and turnout declined. But both the return of old voters and an infusion of new ones created by constitutional reform produced a new high in 1852. After years of having one of the lowest rates of participation in the country, the Old Dominion produced turnouts comparable to those of Vermont, Maine,

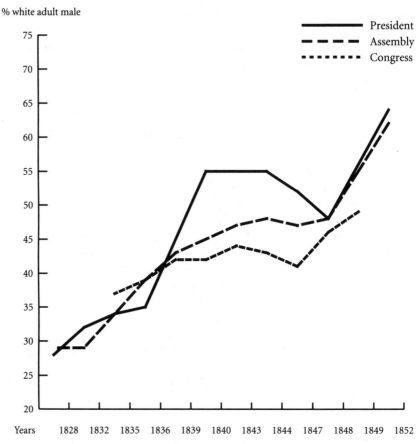

% white adult male

Graph 3.1. Voter turnout in Virginia, 1828–52

Illinois, Kentucky, and Mississippi and well ahead of Massachusetts and eleven other states.[56]

The media hype of the Log Cabin campaign added to the electorate a new group of voters who came out only for presidential elections. Turnout for legislative and congressional elections generally remained below that in the nationally charged contests, but the two converged in the course of the 1840s. While turnout fell in the presidential election of 1848, it equaled almost precisely that of the spring election. The same veteran Whigs and Democrats returned to the polls in 1849. Over half of Virginia's white adult males voted in all of the elections in the two years before the liberalization of the franchise. The presidential returns reveal the general trend but conceal the slow, inexorable growth of popular participation in the Old Dominion.

Then in 1851 the lowering of the suffrage requirements brought another new element—the nonlandholders—into the state's electorate. Although they would fuel the record turnout of white men in the 1850s, the newly enfranchised were less likely to vote than the previous participants of the 1840s. Ironically, when both the participation rate and the total vote increased following the introduction of universal white manhood suffrage, the portion of the eligibles who went to the polls actually declined. The new voters, who were more likely to be poor, socially marginal, and illiterate, were less apt to vote than the previously enfranchised freeholders. Under the new constitution the regional variation in turnout emerged more clearly.

Captivated by the concept of "Jacksonian democracy," historians have overestimated and misconstrued the importance of the presidential election of 1828 in relation to the entrance of the common man into the American electorate. The expansion of electoral participation stretched over three decades in the Old Dominion. Between the 1820s and the 1850s, two revisions of the state's constitution enlarged the size of the commonwealth's political nation. The immediate increase in the first instance was relatively small; obviously other factors explain the growth of political participation in the quarter century before 1850. There were few quantum leaps from one year to the next, although between the spring and the fall of 1840, a 22 percent jump in the electorate resulted from the activities associated with the presidential campaign that gained momentum during the summer.

The main explanation for this gradual expansion in the number of Virginia voters was the influence of the environment in which their political participation took place. The rising tide of democracy lifted the commonwealth's ark from the quagmire of constitutional conservatism that had dominated the old Jeffersonian order. Yet Virginians did not simply mimic the political behavior of their more democratic neighbors. Rather, they experienced the same social and economic pressures that promoted political participation in the other states. For good or ill, the citizens of the commonwealth exhibited most of the typical characteristics ascribed to Americans of their day by foreign and domestic observers who connected these traits of national character to the development of democracy.[57]

An increasing sense of the common man's capacity to control both himself and his environment underlay the emergence of the widespread affirmation of the individual's ability to make a difference. Again and again, editors and politicians told the "plain folk" that their votes mattered and that government should reflect their will. Heady stuff! Participation became an expression of self-esteem. Through the early 1830s slaveholders were relatively more likely to vote than nonslaveholders, but the new voters at the end of the decade came disproportionately from the latter group. Even after a sizable proportion of the nonslaveholding property owners joined the planters in the political arena, however, the wealthy planters were still more likely to go to the polls than the poor, and turnout correlated with literacy as well as wealth.[58]

The grasping, self-absorbed American individualist described by Tocqueville was also paradoxically conformist. "Huddling alone together," Virginians notoriously embraced kin and community. Voting and political participation in the commonwealth constituted communal activities. As more men entered the electorate in groups, they did so increasingly as partisans. Virginia voters also chose to participate in an election-specific fashion. The decisions to go to the polls in the spring and the fall were separate acts, although they were gradually fused by partisan loyalty.

Not only did the size of the electorate expand dramatically in the late 1830s, but also the pattern of the vote within the state shifted. There was, for example, a fairly close relationship between the distribution of the Jackson vote in 1828 and that in 1832, but Van Buren's election was hardly related to either of Jackson's. A clear geographic reshuffling of the support for the two candidates occurred between 1832 and 1836. They simply did not draw voters from the same areas, although clearly some overlap existed. After 1838 a new pattern of electoral behavior stabilized. There was a closer correlation between the partisan distribution of the vote in the elections of 1852 and 1840 than between those in Jackson's two victories four years apart.

The emergence of partisan stability during these years varied regionally. From Jackson's first victory in 1828 through the election of Pierce, only thirteen Virginia counties remained stable in their partisan allegiance. Eight were Jackson/Democratic, and five were National Republican/Whig. The election of 1836 brought stability to forty-four more counties. These were divided nearly equally in terms of their partisan affiliation. In other words, the Whigs and the Democrats developed at the same rate. Four years later in 1840, with the addition of forty more counties, the mature phase of the second party system arrived in the Old Dominion, and the vast majority of Virginia's constituencies reached a state of stable two-party conflict. Finally, the addition of seven counties to the list in 1844 meant that partisan stability characterized 90 percent of the commonwealth.[59]

The basically stable nature of the second party system did not preclude short-term surface fluctuation from election to election. Movement in the Democratic percentages was a surface phenomenon that derived its importance from the "rules of the game": single-member districts and the way in which they were drawn. Although the Whigs generally held no more than one-third of the commonwealth's congressional seats, the average Democratic majority for congressional elections from 1835 to 1851 was 53 percent. Their largest victory was 56 percent in 1835! Those who held power during these years depended upon very slim statewide majorities. Elections were won by minuscule margins. When things were going the Democrats' way in the presidential election of 1844, the party gained control of only thirteen formerly Whig counties while losing five previously Democratic counties to their opponents.

In 1848 when the center of gravity shifted back toward the Whigs, the Democrats lost control of twenty counties but also gained nine. Only a small percentage of voters responded to the immediate conditions of each election. Spotsylvania County in the northern piedmont, which had turnouts ranging from seven hundred to nine hundred voters between 1840 and 1848, registered margins of victory of ten, four, and eight votes in these three presidential elections. Even in the debacle of 1852, the Democrats gained control in only twenty counties that the Whigs had dominated and even lost one of their own to their hapless opponents. The Whigs prevailed in forty-seven counties, a larger number than they had controlled in 1836.[60]

Between the 1820s and the 1850s, Virginia developed a coherent, fairly modern, and relatively democratic two-party system that evolved through two stages. Jackson's campaigns in 1828 and 1832 brought a new level of organization and a good deal more popular excitement than any previous presidential election in the Old Dominion. After 1834 a semblance of party organization appeared in the legislature, candidates began to associate themselves with party labels that were related to national politics, and voter participation slowly edged up, encouraged by the emerging party organizations and a highly partisan press.

With the election of 1840, Virginia entered an era of high turnouts and stable partisanship. This two-party period in which Whigs and Democrats competed at all levels of the political system lasted into the 1850s and structured Virginians' responses to both national and state politics. The issues of the 1840s were related to those associated with Jackson and his presidency, but party structures and voter response signaled an entirely new phase in the politics of the Old Dominion that involved unprecedented participation of the state's white male population. At the same time a new degree of partisanship entered into the process of governing of the Old Dominion.

∞ 4 ∞

Out of the Nature of Things

THOMAS JEFFERSON most often characterized partisan political divisions in psychological terms confounding political opinions and moral characteristics. Two years before he died, Jefferson told Henry Lee that party conflict in all societies involved those men who despised and distrusted the people and those who cherished them and had confidence in their judgment: "Call them therefore liberals and serviles, Jacobins and Ultras, Whigs and Tories, republicans and federalists, they are the same parties still and pursue the same object. The last appellation of aristocrats and democrats is the true one expressing the essence of all." [1]

In the midst of the partisan strife over the Jay Treaty, Jefferson informed his Italian friend Philip Mazzei that "the whole landed interest" was Republican, but "an Anglican monarchical aristocratical party" composed mainly of officeholders and "Americans trading on British capital, speculators and holders in banks and public funds," had "sprung up" to oppose true political principles. He implied that economic roles determined men's public character by perverting their moral sense. "I join in your reprobation of our merchants, priests and lawyers for their adherence to England and monarchy in preference to their own country and its constitution," he wrote a New England correspondent. He spoke invidiously of "bankers" as well but saved his most stinging reproach for the masses of urban workingmen whose "degeneracy . . . is a canker which . . . eats at the heart of a republic." [2]

Along with his generation, Jefferson associated virtue and independence with the possession of land and agricultural labor. "Corruption of morals in the mass of cultivators is a phenomenon of which no age nor nation has furnished an example." Of course, while he decried the effects of slavery on the slaveholder, he meant by "agriculturalists" the planters rather than the slaves who actually worked in the earth of Monticello and his neighbors' estates. The essence of Jeffersonian agrarianism was metaphorical rather than empirical. [3]

In contrast, James Madison consistently struck a more sociological stance. In the tenth number of *The Federalist,* Madison formulated his theory of class: "The most common and durable source of factions has been the various and unequal distribution of property. Those who hold and those who are without property have ever formed distinct interests in society. Those who are creditors and those who are debtors, fall under like discrimination. A landed interest, a manufacturing interest, a mercantile interest, a moneyed interest, with many lesser interests, grow up of necessity in civilized nations, and divide into different classes, activated by different sentiments and views." Madison also talked of occupational interests—"husbandmen, merchants, . . . manufacturers"—as well as sectional affiliations and adherence to different religious sects and to particular political leaders, but in essence the conflict of interests involved the "owners of different kinds of property &c., &c." Each tries to protect his property and his ability to acquire property, and "the great art of politicians"—the essence of good government—"lies in making them checks and balances of each other."[4]

Yet when Madison took up his partisan pen in opposition to Hamilton and the Federalists, his analysis differed little from that of Jefferson. Here he hewed rather closely to the verities of republican morality, insisting that men of monarchist tendencies aimed at consolidation and corruption. He tended to divide the world between those who believed "mankind incapable of governing themselves" and those who retained a faith in mankind and hated "hereditary power"—those opposing republican government and those favoring it.[5]

This ambivalent mixture of moralism and political sociology in the discussion of the conflict of interests marked the political culture of the Old Dominion throughout the early national and antebellum eras. Only tentatively did the acceptance of a politics of conflict allow the analysis of the interest group basis of the evolving party system. The protoparties of the Jeffersonian era remained elite coalitions of geographically rooted elements directed by men of influence tenuously tied to a network of connections. They contested each other's legitimacy and were electorally exclusive or sectarian, representing homogeneous, regionally isolated interests.

During the life of the first party system, the electorate clustered in specific geographic patterns that resembled the partisan distribution of legislators. Federalists continued to be strongest in the counties that had favored the Constitution; most Antifederalist areas became Republican. The Jeffersonians were the party of the center while the Federalists represented the periphery. Partisan controversy did not extend beyond the assembly, and voters tended to make choices between elite candidates on the basis of personal characteristics that would assure the best representation of the constituency's interest on which there was usually some consensus supported by the contending candidates. The

Jeffersonian Republicans drew votes from all economic groups and most areas of the Old Dominion. Federalism's appeal was limited to certain constituencies whose voters believed their interests were endangered by the Republican consensus.[6]

The Federalists showed some strength in the upper tidewater but in general represented the peripheral counties spreading from the Eastern Shore, along the Potomac, and west of the Blue Ridge in the Shenandoah, Kanawha, and Ohio valleys. The town vote during the Jeffersonian era was consistently more Federalist than that of the rural areas, and in 1800 John Adams also managed to capture half the votes in Virginia's two emerging cities, Richmond and Norfolk. In the east the Republicans controlled most of the tidewater counties and were invincible in the central and southern piedmont. The strongest Republican regions contained counties dominated by the tobacco culture. The Jeffersonians in the Old Dominion were the party of the planter gentry and represented the interests of the eastern conservatives.

Beyond the Blue Ridge, Jefferson's followers constituted large majorities only in Shenandoah and Rockbridge counties in the Valley and in the southwest, but few of the party's leaders came from these areas. The pattern can be seen clearly in the geographic distribution of the popular vote in presidential elections and of the partisan affiliation of congressmen who served the Old Dominion (table 4.1). In both cases electoral conflict was limited to certain constituencies, and most often the Republican candidate won easily. Most congressional elections during the first party system featured contests between supporters of the Virginia Dynasty, rather than between local Federalist and Republican candidates. The opposition consistently controlled a few constituencies in which candidates differed little over public policy. Some presidential electors, even in the most partisan election of the era, refused to reveal their preferences.

Table 4.1. Partisan affiliation of congressmen and senators, 1801–25

Section	Republican No.	Federalist No.	% Republican
Tidewater	22	5	82
Piedmont	41	2	95
Valley	8	9	47
Trans-Allegheny	10	4	71
Total	81	20	80

Source: Daniel P. Jordan, *Political Leadership in Jefferson's Virginia* (Charlottesville, Va., 1983), 62, 227–29.

In the east three of the tidewater Federalists came from the Eastern Shore, and the only two from the piedmont lived in Loudoun County on the Potomac. Western Federalists represented the northern counties in the Valley and the northwest. The Federalist opposition was rooted in the same peripheral areas that desired the Constitution in 1788 and would support John Quincy Adams in the 1820s. These constituencies were distinctly less wealthy than those carried by the Republicans. Fifteen of the twenty-two most Republican counties ranked in the wealthiest quarter of the commonwealth's counties.

A strong correlation between slaveholding and Republicanism also existed. Nearly four-fifths of the Republican congressmen represented districts dominated by the planter elite, and one-quarter came from the Southside. The heartland of Republicanism in Virginia included nearly all the counties that were more than 60 percent black. The party's strength thus centered in Old Virginia and the maturing planter areas of the piedmont, and as the proportion of whites who owned slaves grew, so did the support for the Republicans. The most rapidly growing areas in the western part of the state where there were few slaves generally sent Federalists.[7]

As the party of the periphery, the Federalists also showed relatively less appeal to the old-stock English and relatively greater strength among the culturally marginal Scotch-Irish. As a consequence Federalist counties contained twice as many Presbyterians as Republican counties. Within the western half of the commonwealth, however, the Germans in the Valley voted Republican, as did the ethnically diverse southwestern herders and subsistence farmers. The Republican counties had more Baptists in them, reflecting the Republican strength in the areas with the most slaves. The Republican and Federalist voters shared ethnoreligions profiles similar to the leaders of their parties and reflected the demographic segregation of the society. Electoral conflict in the Old Dominion never conformed to Jefferson's Republican model, and only to a limited degree did it fit that of the liberal pluralist Madison.[8]

As the second party system emerged, the clear-cut separation of the Republican center and the peripheral areas of opposition gave way to two-party competition in most of the counties of the commonwealth. Certain areas consistently favored one party or the other, but close competition characterized the electoral contests between the Whigs and the Democrats both in the state as a whole and in its diverse constituencies. A politics primarily rooted in regional differences was transformed into one involving intraregional interest group conflicts. As the society became more complex, the coalitional nature of the parties in the electorate reflected this social and economic diversity, and both the Whigs and the Democrats became inclusive (or comprehensive) parties with support drawn from overlapping interest groups spread evenly across the commonwealth.

4.1. Vote of congressional districts in the presidential election, 1840

By 1840 both the Whigs and the Democrats were well organized throughout the Old Dominion. Both parties had county committees and state committees. Virginia's congressmen and senators participated in national party structures and even campaigned in other states. These electoral machines were designed to bring out the vote, and that year they did so in an impressive fashion when nearly four-fifths of those eligible went to the polls. As parties slowly penetrated into the society, one of their primary functions became the aggregation of interests to give legitimacy to majoritarian, democratic decisions. Virginia government, beginning in the 1830s, became both more democratic and more modern than it had been during the preceding half century.

The new order, of course, did not completely erase the old, and the effects of regionalism remained, since representation continued to be decided on the basis of geographically described districts rather than through class, religion, or ethnic groups (map 4.1). Five of the commonwealth's fourteen eastern congressional districts had clear Democratic majorities: the Second, Third, Fourth, Fifth, and Thirteenth. These districts encompassed the Southside and the central portion of the northern piedmont. Thus, the eastern Democrats were concentrated in the area of the Republican center, which most strongly resisted democratic reform. If contiguous counties that were also strongly Democratic (such as Halifax from the Sixth and Louisa from the Twelfth) are added to these congressional districts, the dominance of the Democrats in the eastern tobacco region that had been traditionally the citadel of planter Republicanism is clear.[9]

In contrast, while Whigs controlled the area around the city of Richmond and down the James peninsula, their strength in the eastern half of the commonwealth was found primarily in the northern and western piedmont. Five of the congressional districts east of the Blue Ridge—the Seventh, Eighth, Eleventh, Twelfth, and Fourteenth—produced clear Whig majorities. The party controlled, with only two exceptions, the entire belt of counties extending south from Loudoun and Fairfax on the banks of the Potomac, along the eastern slope of the Blue Ridge, to the North Carolina border. One-third of the eastern Virginia Whigs lived in the Fourteenth, Twelfth, and Seventh districts, while only half as many Whigs came from the other area of Whig strength—districts Eight, including the Eastern Shore and some of the upper tidewater, and Eleven, around Richmond.[10]

The Eighth District, which is often used to illustrate the eastern and tidewater affiliation of the party, registered the greatest Whig majorities in the state, but the number of Whigs in the area was relatively small, and their representatives were notoriously eccentric. While four of the five mainland counties of District Eight as well as King George, Westmoreland, Richmond, and Lancaster counties in District Ten along the Potomac produced sizable Whig majorities, these eight counties polled less than 5 percent of the vote cast for Harrison east of the Blue Ridge, contributing together about the same number of Whig votes as Norfolk County (including Norfolk Borough), and fewer than either Henrico County (including the city of Richmond) or Loudoun, in the northern piedmont, the premier Whig county in the commonwealth.[11]

The Whigs had exceptional strength west of the Blue Ridge where they competed on an equal footing with the Democrats. Six of the seven western congressional districts contained more Whigs than the Eighth, and two of these were strongly and consistently Whig: the Seventeenth and the Nineteenth. The former comprised the southern part of the Valley and included Augusta County, second only to Loudoun in the size of its Whig electorate and yielding more Whigs than the eight banner counties of the tidewater added together. The most Whiggish congressional district in the west, however, the Nineteenth, encompassed the Kanawha Valley counties—Greenbrier, Nicholas, and Kanawha—and contained one thousand more Whig voters than the most heavily Whig district in the east. These westerners, rather than the "awkward squad" of the tidewater, typified Virginia's Whigs.

The vote in the counties west of the Blue Ridge slightly favored the Democrats and allowed Van Buren to squeak by in 1840, but the area contained only a few more Democrats (and slightly fewer Whigs) than the east. Two western districts had heavy Democratic majorities, the Sixteenth and the Eighteenth. The margin in these two constituencies was larger than in any of the other congressional districts in the commonwealth. The Eighteenth District, which covered most of the southwest, gave Van Buren 62 percent in 1840 and contained exactly the kind of inhospitable, hardscrabble backwater venues that historians have associated with the Jacksonians, but the area also included a sizable number of German-Americans. Adding Giles and Logan, the contiguous strongly Democratic counties to the north in the Nineteenth District, these ten southwestern counties contained 9.5 percent of those Virginians who voted for Martin Van Buren in 1840.[12]

The Sixteenth District, in the heart of the Valley, gave three-quarters of its vote to the Democrats. The district was composed of wealthy agricultural counties, but its most distinctive characteristic was its huge German population that mixed cultural autonomy with commercial farming. Shenandoah, Page, and Rockingham were three of the top five Democratic counties in the state, giving respectively 92, 92, and 85 percent of their vote to Van Buren. The Sixteenth also contained more Democrats than any other congressional district in the state, in fact, more than twice as many as the most populous eastern district. If there was a typical western Democrat, he was a German farmer in the Valley.[13]

Outside the heavily German localities, Whigs could be found everywhere throughout western Virginia. Although Democratic, the Twentieth and the

Table 4.2. Partisan affiliation of congressmen and senators, 1837–53

	Democrats	Whigs	Democratic % of seats	Democratic % of popular vote
Tidewater	30	19	61	53
Piedmont	48	28	63	50
Valley	24	5	83	59
Trans-Allegheny	29	10	74	52

Source: *Biographical Directory of the American Congress*. The table is based on the seats won for each Congress, not the individuals. Some men were counted more than once, sometimes for different parties. The Democratic percentage of the popular vote is the mean of the Democratic presidential vote in the region in the elections from 1840 to 1852.

Twenty-first districts in the northwest had huge Whig minorities. They ranked third and fourth among the commonwealth's twenty-one congressional districts in the number of Harrison voters. Ohio County, which included Wheeling, gave three-fourths of its votes to the Old General and produced the fifth largest Whig vote of all the counties of the state, behind Loudoun, Augusta, Norfolk, and Henrico. Monongalia County in the Twenty-first District and Harrison County in the Twentieth contained the second and third largest numbers of Democratic voters, behind Rockingham and just ahead of Shenandoah. Clearly, simple sectional generalizations about the geographical bases of the second party system in the Old Dominion must be carefully avoided (table 4.2). Both the Democrats and the Whigs had penetrated into nearly every county, and the party coalitions became sociologically more complex than they had been in Jefferson's day.

Those who lived in the cities and towns of the Old Dominion were more inclined toward the cosmopolitan party of Clay and Adams than were their rural neighbors. At least until 1852 Virginia's townspeople—of high station and low—flocked to the Whigs. Although the Richmond Junto dominated the protoparty politics of early years of the nineteenth century and the *Richmond Enquirer* spoke as the voice of the American Democracy through the antebellum period, the capital's voters were heavily anti-Jackson and pro-Whig in their partisan orientation. They backed Adams in 1828 and Clay in 1832. Even during the debacle of 1852, Richmond remained in the Whig column. Not only did the voters of Richmond, Petersburg, Norfolk, and Wheeling strongly support the Whigs, but so did those in the smaller trading centers as distant from each other as Fredericksburg at the falls of the Rappahannock River, Lynchburg in the western piedmont, and Charleston on the Great Kanawha in modern West Virginia.

The census of 1850 listed thirty-four "cities and towns" in the common-wealth, from tiny West Liberty in Ohio County with two hundred inhabitants to the city of Richmond with nearly thirty thousand. Twenty-seven towns had over one thousand inhabitants, and of these, twenty-one turned in consistent Whig majorities. The Democrats could control only six towns, three of which clustered together in Whig-oriented Jefferson County where support of the Democratic party was closely related to politics and patronage at the federal armory. Eighteen of the nineteen cities and towns with white populations over one thousand were Whig.[14]

This "urban" electorate made up only 10 percent of the voters of the Old Dominion, but nearly one-third of all Virginians lived in the counties that encompassed these cities and towns and shared their general political orientation. Twenty counties had the same partisan persuasion as the towns located within them. Two Whig towns, Fredericksburg and Winchester, were located in Democratic counties, and one, Petersburg, was in an evenly balanced county that fluctuated between the parties from election to election during the 1840s. In general, the towns gave larger Whig votes than the outlying polling places, even in those counties that shared their political orientation.

These town-influenced counties had a higher proportion of people in nonagricultural occupations, especially among the white adult males, and a relatively large proportion of Scots and Scotch-Irish. Two-fifths of the Presbyterian churches in the commonwealth were in these counties. They were also the home of nearly all of the foreign-born who migrated to the Old Dominion and a large number of those who had been born in other states. Finally, the towns and town-oriented counties had relatively more schoolchildren and fewer illiterate adults than the average for the state. Clearly these cosmopolitan and commercial areas of the Old Dominion sustained a bourgeois environment far more conducive to Whigs than Democrats.[15]

The Democrats had a definite edge in the rural regions. Polk gained three-fourths of his support there and won over 60 percent of the voters from counties without significant towns. A majority of the Whigs, however, could be found in these rural counties as well. As party development collapsed the crude geographical distinctions between center and periphery, the effects of congregation and family—the politics of friends and neighbors—remained to structure electoral behavior in the Old Dominion and provide the basis of the new parties whose faithful followers trooped to the polls in record numbers.

Electoral competition came to characterize each of the commonwealth's major regions and subregions. In the 1840s over 90 percent of the counties witnessed stable two-party contests in legislative, congressional, and presidential elections. At the lowest level of aggregation, the polling place, Virginians cast their votes in a consistently partisan fashion and in reference to their basic social relations defined by both economic orientation and ethnoreligious adherence, which interacted in a truly Weberian fashion.

Partisan equilibrium came to the tidewater in 1836, but it is nearly impossible to generalize about the group basis of the region's politics. The six congressional districts in the region split their presidential vote in 1840. The region included the urban Whig enclaves of Norfolk, Petersburg, Richmond, Fredericksburg, and Alexandria and the consistently Whig Eastern Shore. But these constituencies do not fit the stereotype of the declining and decadent region ravaged by soil exhaustion and the westward movement of both the tobacco culture and the flower of Old Virginia's youth. Actually, without its towns and Eastern Shore counties, the tidewater had a Democratic majority even in 1840 at the height of Whigs' strength in the state.

The urban/rural split defined the main differences between Whigs and Democrats in the tidewater. Whigs were more likely to have nonagricultural occupations and to be involved in manufacturing as both owners and workers, while Democratic voting correlated with slave ownership (table 4.3). Slave owners did not always control the finest soils; the rural lower tidewater was more Democratic than the counties north of the James River. Illiteracy—which plagued the region, in which one-fifth of the white adults could not read or

Table 4.3. Correlations between the Democratic presidential vote in the tidewater and several socioeconomic variables

	1832	1840	1844
1828 Jackson vote	+.67	+.16	+.33
Scotch-Irish	−.20	−.15	−.11
Germans	−.17	−.07	−.19
Welsh	+.22	−.03	−.09
Baptists	−.13	−.13	−.18
Episcopalians	−.02	−.41	−.42
Methodists	+.24	+.21	+.25
Farmers	+.27	−.20	+.02
Farm value	−.19	−.27	−.28
Slaves, 1840	+.28	+.12	+.12
Illiteracy, 1840	+.19	+.12	+.23

write—correlated with the Democratic vote, although the party's leaders in the rural tidewater came from the slaveholding elite that traced its roots to the first families of Virginia.

Ethnic and religious differences affected tidewater voters, who were less homogeneous than sometimes supposed. Although men of English ancestry dominated everywhere in the tidewater, there was a correlation between their relative strength and Democratic prevalence. The proportion of people with French surnames closely correlated with the Democratic vote. While less significant numerically, the Scots and Scotch-Irish were more likely to be Whigs. There was also a strong relationship between Whig voting and the percentage of Episcopalians in a county and a somewhat weaker relationship between the Baptists and the Whigs. Methodist accommodations correlated with Democratic votes. These factors interacted with the urban/rural split. Fairfax, Hanover, Henrico, New Kent, Norfolk, and Spotsylvania, which were influenced by their towns, all had Scots and Scotch-Irish communities, and five of the six contained Presbyterian churches. Half of the accommodations for Presbyterians in the entire tidewater region were in Henrico and Norfolk counties. Twenty-three of the rural tidewater counties had no Presbyterian churches. In these counties Democratic Methodists clashed with Whig Baptists, and political differences tended to follow denominational lines.[16]

In the central part of the northern tidewater lay King William, the region's most Democratic county north of the James (map 4.2). Yet it was bounded on the south by strongly Whig New Kent County and on the north and the east by the moderately Democratic King and Queen County. None of these three upper tidewater counties was poor, and each had a sizable number of slaves. Democratic King William was clearly the richest. In 1840 it ranked thirteenth in taxable wealth and seventh in slaveholding for the entire state. Slaves made up nearly 70 percent of King William's population. Whiggish New Kent ranked forty-fourth among the counties of the Old Dominion in taxes per capita and twenty-fourth in the proportion of its population enslaved, just one rank below moderately Democratic King and Queen in each case.

New Kent, the smallest of these counties with a population half that of King and Queen, outproduced its northern neighbors in both bushels of oats and tons of hay and did relatively well raising livestock, horses particularly but also cattle, sheep, and poultry. The county also produced nearly three times as much wool as King and Queen and slightly more per capita than King William. New Kent was contiguous to Henrico County and aside from poultry grew large crops of both Irish potatoes and sweet potatoes for the Richmond market. Economically and politically the county was completely within the orbit of the capital.[17]

These three counties lay in the most English portion of the state, but they differed in their ethnic and religious makeup. Democratic King William County

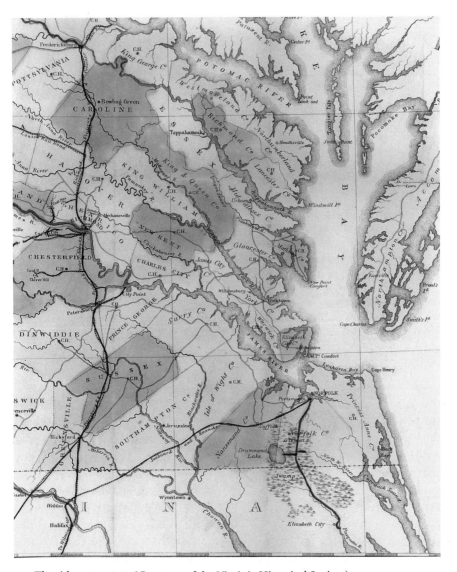

4.2. The tidewater, 1848. (Courtesy of the Virginia Historical Society)

contained an English majority and one of the largest concentrations with French forebears in the state. In contrast, Whig New Kent had an English minority, and Scots made up over 40 percent of the county's white inhabitants. King and Queen, moderately Democratic, had an English majority but a sizable minority of Scots and Welsh.

There were also differences in the religious patterns of these three northern tidewater counties. The most Democratic, King William, had the fewest churches.

Four of its nine were Free, or shared, churches, and a similar number were Baptist; the Methodists had "a large and excellent house of public worship." Joseph Martin wrote in 1835, "The Baptists are the most numerous sect, of whom the Reformers constitute the larger portion." In discussing the Free churches, he added, "These . . . are for the most part used by the Baptists, but free to all denominations." King and Queen County had eighteen churches, eleven of which were Baptist. Martin believed the Baptists to be the prevailing religious group in the 1830s, but there were also six Methodist congregations and a substantial Episcopalian church. Whig New Kent had ten churches although they were smaller and less wealthy than those of its Democratic neighbors. Six of the county's churches were Methodist; in fact, New Kent had the largest proportion of Methodists among the three. It also had an Episcopal church, and the courthouse was open for public worship. In these three counties the number and location of Baptist churches correlated with the Democratic majorities, and Methodist accommodations accompanied concentrations of Whigs.[18]

A more detailed examination of moderately Democratic King and Queen reinforces this view. A fairly wealthy county by Virginia standards, its population declined between 1830 and 1850, and slaves made up about 60 percent of its inhabitants. Martin described its soil as "once barren" but noted that the use of marl had revived the county's agricultural fortunes in the 1830s. King and Queen exemplified the rural tidewater.

The returns from the outlying polling places conflicted sharply with the vote at King and Queen Court House in the center of the county. Shackleford's store in the southeast and St. Stephens Church in the northwest were both on the main road through the county, and cross roads joined these two small towns to the neighboring counties. In 1844 James K. Polk received 67 percent of the vote at the Court House and 57 percent at St. Stephens Church, which gave the county comfortably to the Democrats by a larger margin than in either 1840 or 1848. The voters at Shackleford's, however, cast 62 percent of their votes for Clay.

The religious orientation of the neighborhoods around the polling places correlated closely with the political preference of the voters. The church communities, composed of kinship connections, formed the focus of the political communities. The strongly Democratic area around King and Queen Court House was a Baptist enclave. Two-thirds of the churches near St. Stephens Church were also Baptist. Methodists, however, dominated the southeastern segment of the county, having consecrated four-fifths of the churches around Shackleford's where nearly two-thirds of the voters were Whigs. There was a Christian meetinghouse near St. Stephens Church and a Presbyterian church near Shackleford's that affected the outcome, but more important, the Methodists at the southern end of the county were Scots, as were many of those in neighboring New Kent.

The rural lower tidewater land was less fertile and the counties outside the commercial orbit of Norfolk generally poorer than those north of the James. The importance of "neighborhoods" and "influentials" within the region can be clearly seen in Southampton County, which split its vote somewhat like King and Queen but where the denominations lined up differently. The site of the Nat Turner rebellion, Southampton was one of the counties in the Old Dominion that had a sharp intracounty political division. The lower county southwest of the Nottoway River, St. Lukes Parish, was strongly Democratic, while the eastern upper half of the county—traditionally in Nottoway Parish—was Whig. During these years when the county divided almost equally in both presidential and legislative elections, St. Lukes gave four-fifths of its votes to the Democrats and Nottoway nearly two-thirds of its to the Whigs. There was a larger proportion of men in nonagricultural employment among white household heads than for the state's population as a whole. Approximately 20 percent were professionals, merchants, and artisans. Both of the portions of the county were primarily agricultural, but the number of nonfarmers was greater in the Whig-dominated upper region. Harrison and Clay ran relatively well with these voters while Van Buren and Polk did slightly better among the county's farmers.[19]

Yet employment did not distinguish the county's sections and voters so clearly as did slaveholding. Half of Southampton's household heads owned slaves. Slaveholders made up 55 percent of this group in St. Lukes but only 45 percent in the larger upper portion of the county, Nottoway Parish. Not only were there relatively more slaveholders in the western half of the county, but also those living there had larger holdings. Two-thirds of the county's planters lived in the Democratic area of Southampton; three-fifths of the nonslaveholders resided in the Whig portion. The 1840 poll books reveal that 62 percent of the planters and 56 percent of those who owned slaves voted for Van Buren. Three-fifths of the nonslaveholders supported Harrison.

Landholding was similarly skewed. The Democrats were clearly the party of the planters in Southampton. Thirty-five percent of the farms in the upper county were under one hundred acres, and only 6 percent contained over five hundred acres. In the Democratic lower portion, over three times as many of the farmers owned over five hundred acres, and only 15 percent worked small holdings under one hundred acres. In the southwestern part of the county, nearly nine hundred bales of cotton were grown, and a large majority of the Southampton County cotton planters voted for the Democrats.

Within the county the political effects of religion were subtle but extremely important. Hebron—the "Old Church"—and Vicks below the river in St. Lukes Parish had been Episcopalian but were respectively Baptist and Methodist by the 1840s. South Quay near the only polling place above the river with a significant Democratic vote was Old School Baptist, but the other Democratic polling places were near Methodist churches that dominated that portion of Southampton County. The Whiggish upper county, however, was mixed, with only Indian Spring Methodist Church and Nottoway Chapel, which was used by the Methodists, but six of the county's Baptist churches, two Christian and two Presbyterian churches, and Black Creek Friends Meeting. The Baptist church at Black Creek honored its history of antislavery commitment by supporting the Whigs.

Most Quakers and Presbyterians found in the poll books were Whigs, and a majority of the Baptists also favored Harrison and Clay. On the other hand, the Campbellite Christians (or Disciples of Christ), a schismatic Scotch-Irish group, were Democrats, while the Methodists provided the basis of support for Van Buren and his party.

In Old Virginia—the tidewater and the southeastern portion of the piedmont into which the tobacco culture had spread in the eighteenth century—the English with an intermingling of Welsh represented the dominant ethnic strain, making up two-thirds of the population outside the town-oriented counties. These people descended from the seventeenth-century migrants, whose elite forebears had stamped their stylistic imprint on the society to such a degree that they dictated much of the cultural style that later visitors and historians have portrayed as truly "Virginian." Following the revocation of the Edict of Nantes and the dispersion of the Huguenots, a small but important French element entered the colony and fairly quickly intermarried with the dominant English, bequeathing French surnames to a portion of the tidewater elite families.[20]

Cavalier society, one of ranks and deference, defined Old Virginia through the Revolutionary era and continued to dominate in the heady days of the Virginia Dynasty. Not only the political elite but also the freeholders were predominately Englishmen and Anglicans until the Revolution. The Baptists gained a foothold first in the peripheral areas but eventually conquered the center and contested with the Methodists, whose greatest success was among the former adherents of the Church of England, especially in the two decades after 1790. It was not until the 1830s that the Episcopal Church reemerged in the Old Dominion, and then as an evangelical faith.

In the late eighteenth and early nineteenth centuries, the white poor were driven out of these counties. The proportion of slaveholding families actually grew, and a relatively large segment of the household heads owned property and could vote. Rather rapidly the wealth differential among the various denominations disappeared. The cultural norms of the Cavaliers, including their ambivalence toward work and their emphasis on conviviality and honor, permeated the society. They treated Republicanism as the reflection of their self-interest and Virginia as their own land. These true Virginians did not perceive themselves as an ethnic group but as the spokesmen of the center whose cultural prejudices represented the first principles of civilized society.

In fact, they were able to believe that politics was about adherence to true principles and remained innocent of the taint of self-interest underlying their behavior. Nowhere else in the commonwealth was such eccentric individualism tolerated in the name of liberty. Nowhere was the hegemony of gentry values so fully realized. There was no large disenfranchised white population in their rural counties to rise up in protest once the evangelicals had carried the day. The extension of the vote to upstanding tenant householders gave to these Englishmen the full extent of freedom. They voted for the gentry not out of hat-in-hand deference but with a sense of being part of a liberal society made only more free by the existence of slavery. Threatened only by the growing free colored population in their midst and the possible contagion of the less pure among themselves, they voted for their substantial friends and neighbors who promised to protect their liberties—what their fathers called their rights as Englishmen.

Economic pressures pushed these Anglo-Virginians west into the first frontier of the Old Dominion, the piedmont that stretched from the fall line in the east to the Blue Ridge and in the nineteenth century included the prime tobacco lands and some of the commonwealth's richest wheat-producing counties. Its northernmost counties—Loudoun, Fairfax, Fauquier, Culpeper, and Prince William—made up "one of the most important regions of general farming in the South." With the exception of the counties along the Potomac River, the region had been strongly for Jackson in both 1828 and 1832, but in the late 1830s the second party system came together in the piedmont, and the partisan division in this predominately agricultural region remained extremely stable into the 1850s.[21]

Politically the region divided into the Democratic southeastern triangle and the Whig-dominated western strip of counties from the North Carolina border to the Potomac. In the former the dominant commercial crop was tobacco, while the latter tended to the cultivation of wheat. The northernmost counties and those in the western piedmont, stretching southwest from Albemarle County along the east slope of the Blue Ridge, went heavily for Harrison and Clay. The east central and the Southside counties cast sizable majorities for Van Buren and Polk. Here in the heart of the black belt, the proportion of slaves in the population continued to increase into the 1850s while it fell in the state as a whole. Slaveholding and the proportion of the labor force in agriculture strongly correlated with Democratic voting. The planter-dominated counties of the tobacco region constituted the citadel of the Democracy of eastern Virginia (map 4.3).[22]

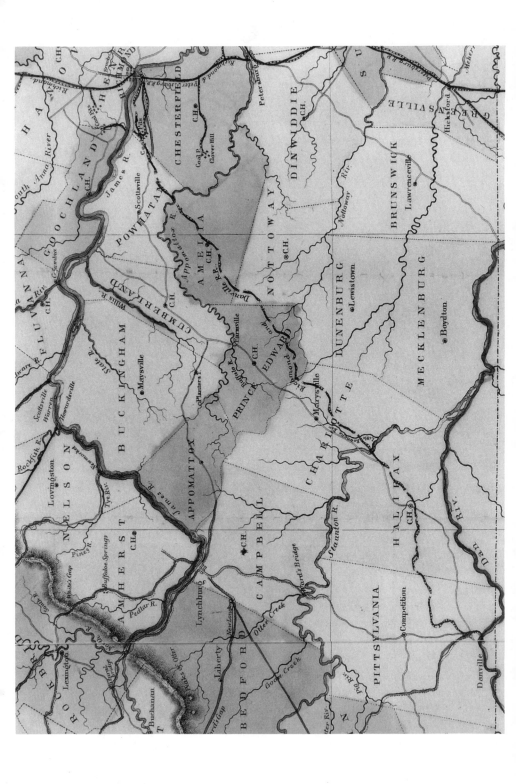

Halifax County, on the North Carolina border, produced nearly six and one-half million pounds of tobacco, over one-tenth of the output of the Old Dominion. Its neighbors, Mecklenburg to the east and Pittsylvania County to the west, were, respectively, second and third among Virginia's tobacco production. Together these three lower piedmont counties harvested 28 percent of the state's crop in 1850. Each of the three also produced large amounts of corn and oats and to a lesser degree a second staple, wheat, and grew relatively large crops of vegetables like sweet potatoes for local, primarily slave, consumption. Halifax produced the greatest amount of home-manufactured goods in the state by far, but Pittsylvania was third, and Mecklenburg fifth. As an earlier French visitor to Virginia remarked, "There are no lords, but each is sovereign on his own plantation." The gentry held a tighter rein on this region than any other in the Old Dominion. These counties of the central Southside typified the tobacco region economically; Halifax and Mecklenburg helped make it the most Democratic area of eastern Virginia. Pittsylvania, however, consistently returned Whigs to the assembly and stood stoutly by Harrison, Clay, and Taylor before faltering in 1852.[23]

Slaves made up approximately three-fifths of the population of Halifax. More than half of Halifax's white families held slaves, and the county was dominated by the planters, who possessed slightly more than half of the land in the county. While one-third of the slave owners had fewer than five slaves, and the median holding was ten, one in eight of the families owned over twenty slaves. Twenty percent of the families maintained more than five hundred acres. In many ways Halifax represented a typical southern slaveholding county committed to a major staple crop, including a majority of slaveholders among its white families, made up of large farms, and dominated by a sizable and wealthy but self-contained planter elite — the natural habitat of the "ruling race."[24]

In neighboring Pittsylvania County two-thirds of the household heads owned land. Four-fifths of the farmers held over one hundred acres, and one-fifth had large plantations of over five hundred acres. This Whig county closely mirrored its Democratic neighbor, but only half of the county's population was enslaved, and Pittsylvania's slave owners had smaller holdings than those in Halifax. The county was more diverse economically than its neighbors, containing one of the few real towns on the Southside, Danville, and a nonagricultural laboring population that worked in the tobacco factories clustered around the town.[25]

In these three counties the only Whig district, the southern half of Pittsylvania that included Danville, differed greatly from the other districts in its relatively high proportion of nonagricultural workers and small slave population. The most Democratic area in the three counties was upper Mecklenburg, where slaves accounted for two-thirds of the population and over nine-tenths of the workforce was in agriculture. Nearly one-third of the white adults in the heavily Democratic northern portions of these tobacco counties could neither read nor write; illiteracy and Democratic voting were correlated.

There were also clear differences in religious affiliation between the Whigs and Democrats in these Southside tobacco counties. In Pittsylvania, Danville—which gave two-thirds of its votes to Clay—had the only Presbyterian churches in the county, and Mount Airy in the center of the county had an Episcopalian church, but the Democratic northern portion of the county was carpeted with Baptists and Methodists. Voters at the Halifax County courthouse—the polling place for the developing small town of South Boston—gave the Democrats two-thirds of their votes, but the smaller outlying polling places cast between 76 and 98 percent of their ballots for Polk. Those polling places with Democratic majorities lower than the county average—Catawba and Republican Grove—had Presbyterian churches in the vicinity; those in which the Democratic majority exceeded 90 percent contained only Baptists.[26]

In his 1835 gazetteer Joseph Martin noted that Mecklenburg was dominated by Methodists who maintained twenty-six churches in the county in the mid-1830s while Baptists had fifteen. Both groups were spread rather evenly around the county. The Presbyterian and the Episcopalian churches, as elsewhere in the Old Dominion, were situated in towns. In Mecklenburg County the Southside Presbyterians were stronger supporters of the Whigs than were the Episcopalians. Martin listed one Episcopalian church in Christianville, a polling place that gave 87 percent of its votes to Polk. The Whigs did better in both elections where there were Presbyterians. The county seat, Boydton, which gave Harrison 45 percent of its vote in 1840, had a Presbyterian church, a Methodist church, and Randolph-Macon College, founded by the Methodist Episcopal Church.[27]

The striking political disparity between these three counties primarily reflected their cultural dissimilarity. The majority of the voters in both Mecklenburg and Halifax had English surnames. Scotch-Irish made up only 16 percent of the population of Mecklenburg County and just under 20 percent in Halifax. In both these Democratic counties, moreover, Welsh were nearly as numerous as Scotch-Irish. Pittsylvania, with the third largest Whig population in the eastern half of the commonwealth, had a quite different ethnic composition. Families with English and Welsh names constituted about half the population and the Germans slightly over 10 percent, but 40 percent were Scotch-Irish who had migrated down the Valley in the late eighteenth century and crossed the Blue Ridge, entering the region from the north and west.

In the mature phase of the second party system, ethnic conflict both between and within the descendants of primarily seventeenth-century migrants and those who came in the eighteenth century coincided more clearly with the cleavage between the parties throughout the piedmont. The Scots and Scotch-Irish sustained the Whigs, while the Germans and the Welsh were most often Democrats. The English split their allegiance.

The importance of ethnicity is equally clear in the northern piedmont. A cluster of contiguous counties—Madison, Orange, Greene, and Albemarle counties: Jefferson's "country"—that lay in the eastern foothills of the Blue Ridge clearly exhibited these ethnoreligious conflicts. While topographically quite similar, these four northern piedmont counties differed extremely in their political sentiments. Albemarle was consistently and safely Whig, the keystone of Whig control of the Twelfth Congressional District. In contrast, Madison gave nine-tenths of its votes to the Democracy, and Greene was nearly as Democratic. They were the first and third most Democratic counties in eastern Virginia, providing the basis for the Democratic domination of the Thirteenth Congressional District. Orange County fell politically as well as physically between Albemarle and Madison but was far less Democratic than rural Greene, which had been carved from it in the 1830s.

The western part of the piedmont in which these counties lay differed from the tobacco region to the south and east. The Whigs controlled most of the set

Table 4.4. Correlations between the Democratic presidential vote in the piedmont and several socioeconomic variables

	1832	1840	1844
1828 Jackson vote	+.96	+.56	+.59
English	−.05	−.29	−.27
Scotch-Irish	−.40	−.38	−.33
Germans	−.03	+.42	+.37
Welsh	+.30	+.36	+.36
Foreign born	−.49	−.42	−.40
Lutherans	+.12	+.40	+.52
Episcopalians	−.26	−.14	−.05
Slaves, 1840	+.44	+.37	+.23
Manufacturing capital	−.28	−.27	−.26
Slaves, 1850	+.51	+.39	+.30

of counties running along the eastern slope of the Blue Ridge. The towns of the piedmont—Danville, Lynchburg, Charlottesville, and Leesburg—were all bastions of Whiggery. The indicators of manufacturing activity—capital invested and people employed—were also positively related to support for the Whigs. As elsewhere the level of adult illiteracy correlated with the Democratic vote (table 4.4).

The rural regions of the northern and western piedmont were more Democratic than the town-influenced areas, but they had a higher proportion of Whigs than the tobacco-growing areas. While general farming and smaller holdings of slaves as well as fewer slaveholders distinguished the Whig counties in the western piedmont, Harrison, Clay, and Taylor also did extremely well in the wheat-producing portions of the piedmont. Here the plantations were large wheat farms—generally larger than the tobacco plantations—and land was more valuable than south of the James.

Albemarle County displayed most of the characteristics associated with Whig areas and was much more commercially centered than its three Democratic northern neighbors. The county extended from the Blue Ridge thirty miles east to Gordonsville (in Orange County) and south to the James River. It was bisected by the main road from Staunton in the Valley to the capital at Richmond that ran through the bustling little market town of Charlottesville. Albemarle's population approximately equaled that of the other three combined, but these counties were not very different economically. Albemarle was the wealthiest, but neither Orange nor Madison was poor. Greene was the poorest on every scale and the least commercial. The people in these counties tended to produce the same basic crops and run similar livestock. In terms of horses, cows, pigs, chickens, wheat, and corn, the counties were relatively equal. Albemarle vastly outproduced the others only in tobacco. The Whig citadel ranked modestly higher in taxes per capita than Democratic Madison County, but had relatively fewer slaves and a much lower proportion of its population in agriculture.

Ethnicity clearly affected political preference in these piedmont counties. Madison differed dramatically in its demographic makeup from Albemarle. The former had four times as many Germans as the latter, and they constituted a majority of the population of the county, which was contiguous to the heavily Democratic German counties in the Valley. Albemarle County was distinguished by its large Scotch-Irish population and modest number of Germans. Its western neighbor was Augusta, the bastion of Whiggery and Scotch-Irish Presbyterianism in the Valley.

Religion interacted with ethnicity in structuring the political battle in the heart of the commonwealth. Martin wrote at length about the religious condition of Madison County, which at the time had fifteen churches, six regular ministers, and "a number of itinerant preachers principally of the Methodist persuasion." At Madison Court House there were "2 houses of public worship of which one belongs to the Episcopalians, and the other is free for all denominations, (of which the principal part are Baptists, Methodists, Episcopalians, Presbyterians, and Lutherans.)" Although there were clearly a sizable number of Lutherans, he reported that the most numerous group in the heavily German county was the Baptists. Cosmopolitan Albemarle had forty-four churches according to the 1850 census. Although thirteen were Methodist, a nearly equal number were Baptist, and six were Free, serving both denominations. Albemarle differed from its neighbors primarily because it had five Episcopal and eight Presbyterian churches. In this portion of the central piedmont, Methodists and Lutherans usually voted for Democrats while Episcopalians and, more particularly, Presbyterians preferred the Whigs. Most Scotch-Irish were Whigs; Germans were Democrats.[28]

Albemarle County illustrates the complexity of intracounty politics in a partisan era (map 4.4). Jefferson's respected and liberal grandson Thomas Jefferson Randolph represented the county in the assembly during the 1830s as a Jacksonian Democrat, but Albemarle was consistently in the Whig column in the presidential elections during these years. The county went strongly for Harrison, who received nearly three-quarters of the votes cast at the courthouse in Charlottesville. The polling place at White Hall, northwest of Charlottesville, was also solidly Whig in 1840 and remained so throughout the decade. Stony Point, a small polling place north of Charlottesville, was generally Whig, but its vote was closely balanced during the 1840s. In contrast, Democrats dominated the southern half of the county. Two-thirds of the voters at Craig's Store in the southwest and at Porter's—the closest polling place to the James River, not far from Scottsville—favored Van Buren in 1840 and Democrats throughout the decade.[29]

Each half of the county had about the same population. In the census of 1840, the upper segment contained slightly fewer slaves while the southern half of the county had a higher proportion of people in agriculture. Sixty percent of those employed in commerce, manufacturing, and the learned professions lived in the Whig sector that included Charlottesville and the University of Virginia. Although there were small Baptist, Disciples of Christ, and Methodist congregations in the town, Presbyterians and Episcopalians prevailed. Nearly half of churches in the more Democratic southern portion of the county were Methodist, and more than a third Baptist or Free. There were only two Presbyterian churches near Porter's and the Cross Roads Episcopalian Church near the polling place at Craig's Store. Scottsville, a market town on the James River, with a Presbyterian, a Methodist, and a Free church, was a small Whig outpost. While

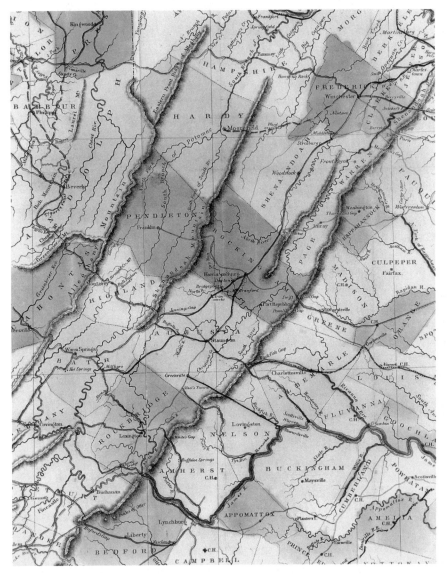

4.4. The Valley and the western piedmont, 1848. (Courtesy of the Virginia Historical Society)

it appears that a few Baptists and some Methodists in Albemarle were Whigs, nearly all of the former and a majority of the latter backed Van Buren and Polk. Presbyterians and, to a slightly lesser degree, Episcopalians voted Whig.[30]

While the difference in partisan preference between Orange and Greene counties in part reinforces the impression drawn from this comparison of

Madison and Albemarle counties concerning ethnic conflict, the importance of economic differences stands out among the English and the Welsh, who had relatively little sense of ethnic identity. The Germans in both counties voted for the Democratic candidates, and Greene's ethnic makeup indicates that its sizable Welsh population did so as well. Religiously both counties were quite similar, but the Methodists were Democrats and the Baptists split. Significantly, there was a large Episcopal church near Orange Court House, the most Whiggish polling place in the county.

At the same time the economic environment affected the political split. Orange was a commercially developing county and distinctly more diverse than Greene, which was something of an economic backwater. The small courthouse town, now called simply Orange, lay on the route between Charlottesville and Fredericksburg and "contained ten of the twenty-one general stores [in the two counties] and virtually all specialized shops were located there." The county had a much larger slave population than Greene, and its farms were more valuable. Whites made up only two-fifths of the population of Orange, but 60 percent of Greene's. While both were agricultural counties with nine-tenths of their labor force in farming, the portion of Orange's adult white male population employed outside agriculture was much larger than Greene's. The Democratic county was more homogeneous, rural, and agricultural and less market oriented than the increasingly middle-class Orange, which gave Van Buren a slim four-vote victory in 1840 and went for Taylor in 1848.[31]

One of the distinctive characteristics of the Whig counties of the western piedmont was the presence of Presbyterian churches, which were found most often in the wake of Scotch-Irish settlement. As this eighteenth-century element migrated south from Pennsylvania, they turned east through the Blue Ridge at the Staunton River and Maggoty's Gap and then pushed south into North Carolina. Six counties in the region contained half of all the Presbyterians in the piedmont; in five of those, Scotch-Irish made up at least 30 percent of the population. Although it is often difficult to isolate distinctive cultural traits that marked the Scotch-Irish, the extreme importance of kinship stands without question. Marriages cemented the commitment to clan among this peripatetic ethnoreligious group, and women served as the stabilizing element of communal attachment. This tended to strengthen collective identity and set apart the Scotch-Irish of the Valley and western piedmont as a self-conscious group to a far greater extent than the descendants of the seventeenth-century migrants, who saw themselves as Virginians.[32]

The counties with sizable numbers of Scotch-Irish Presbyterians had relatively high levels of literacy in the mid-nineteenth century, and the group provided leadership in the push for educational reform. From the eighteenth century when they established academies and colleges throughout the backcountry, the

Presbyterians had advocated an educated clergy and laity. Although the Presbyterians lagged behind the Methodists and Baptists in their embrace of revivalism, they eventually copied the tactics of those denominations and in the 1820s and 1830s encouraged enthusiasm. The Reformed version of Calvinism stressed the relationship between religious reformation, social uplift, and economic prosperity that underlay middle-class morality and the Protestant ethic in the heart of the Old Dominion.[33]

While there is hardly a perfect correlation between Whiggery and Scotch-Irish Presbyterianism, they clearly coincided. In the upper piedmont three strongly Whig counties—Albemarle, Fauquier, and Loudoun—contained two-thirds of the Presbyterians in that region. The western Whig portion of the area below the James River contained three-fourths of the lower piedmont's Scotch-Irish Presbyterians, while the Democratic eastern half—the true Southside—was heavily English and Welsh in family origins and overwhelmingly Baptist and Methodist.

The close correlation between the Scotch-Irish and the Whigs emerged most clearly west of the Blue Ridge in the Great Valley of Virginia where the Old

Table 4.5. Correlations between the Democratic presidential vote in the Valley and several socioeconomic variables

	1832	1840	1844
1828 Jackson vote	+.93	+.87	+.85
Scotch-Irish	−.66	−.82	−.81
German	+.40	+.54	+.55
English	−.33	−.21	−.27
Foreign born	−.76	−.58	−.53
Presbyterian	−.34	−.36	−.43
Lutheran	+.50	+.67	+.68
Episcopalian	−.82	−.43	−.47
Baptist	+.44	+.49	+.50
Methodist	−.36	−.20	−.17
Slaves, 1850	−.41	−.18	−.26
Farm value, 1850	−.61	−.16	−.22
Illiteracy, 1850	+.43	+.36	+.43

Dominion's two major outsider ethnic groups—the Scotch-Irish and the Germans—directly confronted each other (table 4.5). The central Valley contained Augusta County—the premier western Whig constituency—and several other Whig bastions along the Potomac, but Democrats controlled a majority of the Valley counties and the allegiance of a sound majority of the region's voters in the presidential elections of the 1840s. The most Democratic Virginia congressional district, the Sixteenth, held the center of the Valley and included Rockingham, Shenandoah, and Page counties where nearly nine-tenths of the voters were Democrats. The distribution of support for Jackson in 1828 and 1832 was much more similar to that for the Democrats in the 1840s than in either the piedmont or the tidewater.

Valley towns—Lexington, Staunton, Winchester, and Charles Town—with the notable exception of heavily German Harrisonburg, were Whig citadels. The Whigs also did well in areas with newspapers while rural areas with high rates of illiteracy went Democratic. But in this region, unlike both the tidewater and the piedmont, the proportion of the labor force in agriculture was unrelated to a county's partisan preference, and slaveholding correlated modestly with Whig voting. There were relatively few slaveholders in these counties, and the Germans notoriously avoided the peculiar institution. Finally, in the Valley Whig majorities correlated with farm value, and the Democrats did well in the mountains of Allegheny County, although the western counties of the Valley generally were not nearly so Democratic as the German counties. Hardy County voted strongly Whig and later became part of West Virginia.

Ethnic and religious differences, however, proved to be much more important in determining the political preferences of these counties than any other factors. Nowhere in the Old Dominion were the cultural contrast between Whigs and Democrats more sharply drawn than in the Valley where they were reinforced by religion and language. The main fault lines of party differentiation ran between the communities of Germans and those of the Scotch-Irish, all of whom migrated down the Valley at about the same time in the mid-eighteenth century. The most tightly knit group were the Germans who were Lutherans and who were nearly all Democrats, but the fairly large number of Germans in this area who had become Baptists voted Democratic as well. The Scotch-Irish Presbyterians, portraying a distinct ethnoreligious response, were overwhelmingly Whig.[34]

The prosperous and populous counties of Rockingham, Augusta, and Rockbridge lay in the heart of the Valley of Virginia in a line along the west slope of the Blue Ridge (see map 4.4). Economically these three counties were quite similar, yet they represented distinctly different political postures. The northern most of the three, Rockingham, voted strongly—nearly unanimously—Democratic, while Augusta, its immediate neighbor to the south, went Whig by only a slightly smaller margin. Rockbridge, south of Augusta, was moderately Whig.

Of the three Augusta was the wealthiest and Rockbridge the poorest, although the latter had the largest number of slaves per capita in 1840. The 1850 census reported that one-fourth of Rockbridge's population and one-fifth of Augusta's were enslaved, but blacks made up only one-eighth of Rockingham's inhabitants. Four-fifths of Rockingham County's workforce was in agriculture; the other fifth was in manufacturing. Augusta had a slightly larger manufacturing element, and in Rockbridge one-quarter of those employed worked in the mills and forges. Augusta differed slightly from its neighbors. The county enjoyed greater growth between 1840 and 1850 than they did, and its county seat, Staunton, was a thriving commercial center, but none of the three counties was stagnant. By the end of the decade they were all doing extremely well.

There were other economic differences between these three Valley counties that went beyond wealth and slaves. Even though they raised the same products, one county harvested a few more bushels of wheat, another a bit more corn, and the third reared a few more hogs and a few less horses. But moderately Whig Rockbridge stood out against its northern neighbors in harboring certain economic oddities. It produced a modest tobacco crop, the third largest west of the Blue Ridge, but more important, the county was a manufacturing center. Rockbridge milled a good deal more grain than most of the counties of the state and was a major iron producer. Rockbridge had a balanced economy, and when the canal finally reached the county in 1852, its economic prospects further brightened. Though real, these economic differences between the counties were so modest that they fail to explain the counties' political differences, particularly the diametric opposition of Augusta and Rockingham at the polls.

These three Valley counties differed radically in their ethnic composition. On the one hand, Rockingham was one of the most German counties in the Old Dominion: three-fourths of its people were of German origin. Many continued to speak the language, and during the constitutional convention of 1850–51 there were demands that the proceedings be published in German as well as English. Scotch-Irish comprised fewer than 10 percent of Rockingham's population. In stark contrast, Germans accounted for only one-sixth of the inhabitants of Augusta County, where three-fifths of the voters were Scotch-Irish. Rockbridge included a significant Scotch-Irish community, but the English and Welsh together formed slightly over 40 percent of the population, and Germans contributed an additional 20 percent.

The largest of the three counties, Augusta, was religiously diverse. In 1850 its forty-six churches were spread across the ecclesiastical horizon and even included a number of small German sects: Tunkers, Moravians, and Mennonites.

There were, however, nine Methodist and thirteen Presbyterian churches. The latter denomination had the largest churches in Augusta, and accounting for 35 percent of the religious accommodations in the county. While Rockingham did have among its thirty churches both Methodist and Presbyterian houses of worship, it had seven Baptist churches and, even more importantly, eleven Lutheran churches. These two counties represent a classic confrontation of church-based ethnic communities.[35]

Whig Rockbridge, the smallest of the three counties, had only eighteen churches, but eleven of those were Presbyterian and five Methodist. One of the histories of Rockbridge County reports at least ten other churches, and there were probably greater numbers of Methodists, Baptists, and Episcopalians than revealed in the census. Comparing church location and the polling places in Rockbridge demonstrates that most Presbyterians were Whigs as were the majority of the Episcopalians. Both groups tended to cluster around the Whig towns of Lexington, Buena Vista, Glasgow, and Brownsburg. In contrast to other parts of the state, the Methodists in Rockbridge seem to have been strongly Democratic, particularly in small outlying polling places like Collierstown. The Baptists and Lutherans were staunch Democrats.[36]

Rockingham County was so overwhelmingly Democratic that the party's majorities varied little across the county, ranging from 97 percent in the Plains-Linville area which made up the northern half of the county, to 78 percent in the central district area that included the town of Harrisonburg. Internal economic differences within Rockingham had only modest political effect. The relationship between churches and polling places in Rockingham indicates that the German Baptists, the Brethren (German Methodists), and the Lutherans fell solidly in the Democratic camp. Only the small number of Episcopalians and Presbyterians in and around Harrisonburg favored the Whigs.[37]

The Germans of the Valley were the descendants of eighteenth-century migrants and had little in common with the mid-nineteenth-century German immigrants who clustered in the cities. They were good farmers who occupied fertile land and produced abundant crops for the market; Rockingham was the leading wheat-growing county in the Old Dominion. At the same time these "Dutchmen" were notoriously conservative and culturally aloof, preferring to settle near other German-Americans and to build their communities around Lutheran churches and German-language schools. George W. Featherstonhaugh, who journeyed through the Valley in the early 1840s, described them as "plodding frugal persons, who hoard their profits in hard money and entertain a great dislike for bank paper and still a greater to the payment of taxes."[38]

Churches were not only spiritual but also educational and social centers of the community, and few Germans moved beyond their influence. The Old World heritage remained strong, with the hex signs decorating their red-and-white bank barns reflecting a legacy of folk belief in witchcraft and the occult. In some autonomous communities of Shenandoah County, German speakers continued to produce "in their homes and in their numerous small shops and factories nearly everything that was necessary to their welfare and comfort," but the growing impact of the market-based economy hastened the pace of cultural assimilation, and by the 1840s "the episode of bilingual politics" in the Valley had come to an end.

Such ethnoreligious differences between the Whigs and Democrats of the Old Dominion could also be found in the northernmost tier of counties in the Valley that made up the Fifteenth Congressional District. The district split evenly between the parties during this period. Jefferson County on the Potomac, up against the western slope of the Blue Ridge, consistently favored the Whigs. Jefferson contained the economic, ethnic, and religious diversity associated with the commercial counties of neighboring Maryland. Five towns in Jefferson were listed in the 1850 census; Charles Town even had a bank.

Farmers and agricultural laborers made up only 62 percent of the county's workforce, but about half of the white men held nonagricultural jobs. Just under a third of the population was black, and the majority of them were slaves. Jefferson's population also represented an ethnic amalgam of English, Scotch-Irish, and Germans, along with both Roman Catholic Irish and a "Yankee" element that had migrated from the North to work in the armory at Harpers Ferry. The Methodists, who had six churches of their own and also dominated the three Union churches, constituted the largest single religious group, but there were also four Presbyterian (one of which was German) and three Episcopalian churches. There were also two other German churches (one Reformed and one Lutheran), one Baptist church, and a large Roman Catholic church at Harpers Ferry.[39]

From the early 1830s into the 1850s, voter response was relatively stable in the county. Jefferson remained a moderately Whig county, but it included significant islands of Democrats. The area around Harpers Ferry was politically divided and religiously diverse. Smithfield on the western border of the county was one of the few Virginia towns that went consistently and strongly Democratic. There was a Presbyterian church in the area, but Martin emphasized in his gazetteer that the Methodists were particularly "strong" in that portion of the county. They had their own church there and also predominated in the Union church that was open to all evangelicals.

Charles Town in the center of the county and Shepardstown in the north on the Maryland border were consistently Whig and controlled by Presbyterians and Episcopalians. Shepardstown, the strongest Whig polling place in the county, had three German churches as well as Trinity Episcopal. Of the former, one was a large Presbyterian church, and the others were German Reformed

Table 4.6. Correlations between the Democratic presidential vote in the trans-Allegheny and several socioeconomic variables

	1832	1840	1844
1828 Jackson vote	+.92	+.61	+.62
Presbyterians	−.50	−.15	−.27
Methodists	+.31	+.20	+.33
Foreign born	−.36	−.28	−.25
Taxes, 1840	−.27	−.24	−.41
Slaves, 1840	−.44	−.12	−.23
Slaves, 1850	+.27	−.02	−.08
Farm value, 1850	−.44	−.12	−.23
Illiteracy, 1840	+.45	+.41	+.46

and Lutheran. The latter two differed over the question of the use of the German language. The Reformed Germans, who resembled the Presbyterians theologically, "anglicized more rapidly than any other [German] group." Although all three congregations cooperated in the Jefferson Sabbath School Union, the county Germans split politically. The Presbyterians and the Reformed favored the Whigs (as in neighboring Loudoun County). Those who were rural, Lutheran, and German-speaking voted for the Democrats.[40]

While the importance of such ethnoreligious conflict was relatively greater in the Valley than any other part of the Old Dominion, it also permeated the politics of the trans-Allegheny region that included both the northwestern counties that make up the bulk of present-day West Virginia and those counties of the southwest that avidly supported secession and the Confederacy. The entire region's vote was secure for Jackson except in Ohio County, which extended above the Mason-Dixon Line in the northwest corner of the state, and in the central counties along the Great Kanawha River. These areas often sent National Republicans to Congress. After the second party system stabilized in the 1840s, the trans-Allegheny was the most volatile and least cohesive region in the Old Dominion, with an expanding population made up of nearly as many Whigs as Democrats.

Population growth, economic change, and demographic diversity characterized the counties of the northwest. The city of Wheeling and the boomtown Charleston on the Kanawha in the center of the region anchored the western

Whigs. The social basis of voting behavior in this part of Virginia varied little from that in western Pennsylvania or in Ohio's southeastern counties on the western bank of the Ohio River. The proportion of people involved in mining, commerce, and manufacturing correlated highly with Whig voting and the handful of trans-Allegheny towns supported the Whigs.[41]

The southwest was the most rural region in the state. There were two and one-half times as many slaves in the Democratic southwest as in the more Whiggish northwest, but there were also other differences. The proportion of white adults who could not read or write was exceptionally high in the southwest. Larger portions of both Scotch-Irish and of Americans born in Pennsylvania, Maryland, and New Jersey lived in the Whiggish segment of the west. Methodist influence increased the Democratic vote throughout the region, while the presence of Presbyterians determined the degree of Whig success (table 4.6). There were twice as many Germans in the strongly Democratic area; those in the southwest tended to be Lutherans, while the northwest had only one Lutheran church.[42]

Mountainous Lewis County on the west fork of the Monongahela River in the heart of northwestern Virginia generally gave the Democrats two-thirds of its votes and fit the traditional portrait of a frontier Democratic outpost. Ninety-five percent of its people were farmers or farm laborers, and only a handful were slaves. Lewis County was economically underdeveloped and relatively poor, its people woefully unschooled. Only one-fourth of its acreage had been improved by 1850; it ranked in the poorest decile of the commonwealth's counties; and nearly 30 percent of its white adults could neither read nor write. While it produced hay, rye, and wheat for the market, the size of its corn crop, the number of swine slaughtered, the amount of flax grown, and the value of home manufactures indicate that a large number of its farm families lived close to subsistence. The county's two towns, Weston, where the turnpike from Staunton to Parkersburg crossed the West Fork, and Buchannon, sixteen miles to the east, were not big enough to be listed in the 1850 census (map 4.5).[43]

Democrats dominated the more populous western two-thirds of the county where the party's portion of the vote ranged from 60 percent in the town of Weston to 100 percent at the polling place at Beall's Mills. Within this western Democratic stronghold, however, ethnoreligious differences defined neighborhoods that exhibited contrasting political preferences. German and Irish laborers recently had migrated to the county to build the turnpike and settled the western and southern parts of the county where a town named Ireland still exists. As a result there was a United Brethren church at Freeman's Creek, and the Roman Catholics had a church at Indian Fork near Beall's Mills and a chapel in Weston. In Lewis County these Irish Catholics, Germans of all

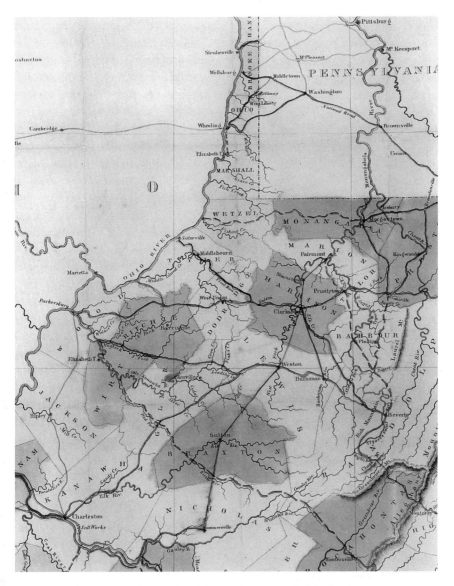

4.5. The northwest, 1848. (Courtesy of the Virginia Historical Society)

denominations, and most of Methodists regardless of ethnic background were Democrats.

In contrast, the polling place in the town of Buchannon, on the Staunton-Parkersburg turnpike in the eastern portion of Lewis County, recorded a Whig majority. According to Martin, "an industrious and enterprising people who have emigrated from the New England States within the last 15 years" occupied this tract, which also included the small town of French Creek. Between them these small Whig towns had two Presbyterian churches, four Temperance societies, three Tract societies, two Bible societies, and a common school system.[44]

Kanawha County, in the center of Virginia's northwestern region, vied with Ohio County during these years as the premier Whig constituency in the trans-Allegheny territory. It differed in almost every way from Lewis, its northern neighbor. The county was deeply involved in the antebellum industrial movement. Half of all the slaves in the Northwest were in Kanawha County where their owners used them in the saltworks, the forges, and the mines as well as in small-scale agriculture. A visitor who had approached from the east noted that "the dense dark columns of smoke which ascend from the salt furnaces announce the busy bustling scene which livens the highway to the village of Charleston," which by 1850 had a population of over one thousand.[45]

The county's works supplied salt for the entire Ohio Valley, and some of its sizable number of slaves worked in nonagricultural pursuits, making the Whig stronghold sui generis. In 1840 one-fifth of the labor force was employed in mining, manufacturing, and navigation. Over 400 men were producing salt, and another 127 were working in the county's grist and saw mills. These activities involved the largest investment of capital in manufacturing west of the Blue Ridge. Small farmers made up most of Kanawha's population, but the county produced relatively few agricultural commodities, basically potatoes, corn, "peas and beans," and slaughtered meat. Kanawha's farmers fed the "home market" created by the county's dominant nonagricultural sector.[46]

Kanawha was the largest of the band of strongly Whig counties stretching from Greenbrier west along the Great Kanawha to Mason on the Ohio River. Whig dominance in the county was so great that the Democrats had trouble even finding candidates to run. The party consistently won 70 percent of the county's vote and four-fifths of Charleston's. The county was divided nearly equally between the Methodists, Baptists, Presbyterians, and Episcopalians. The latter two denominations had larger and wealthier churches and controlled the area along the Great Kanawha River that included Charleston. Most white Baptists and the majority of the Methodists congregated in the outlying agricultural areas, where the latter tended to vote heavily for the Democrats. Tiny Pocatalico north of the city actually turned in a Democratic majority; its only church was antimission Baptist. When Boone County was created out of a rural northern segment of Kanawha, two-thirds of its voters were Democrats, and five of its six churches were Methodist. The ambiance of the northwest had more in common with western Pennsylvania than any part of eastern Virginia and contrasted sharply with the contiguous counties in the southwestern corner of the state that at this time was one of the most Democratic areas of the Old Dominion.[47]

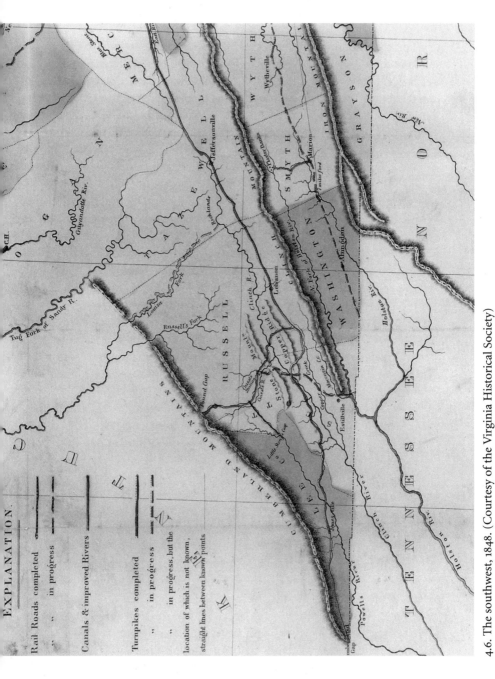

4.6. The southwest, 1848. (Courtesy of the Virginia Historical Society)

The eight counties, called "Little Tennessee" by Thomas Ritchie, cast two-thirds of their votes for Polk in 1844. In its center were the contiguous counties of Tazewell, Smyth, and Washington. All three were Democratic in various degrees. Polk received 86 percent of the vote in Tazewell, 66 percent in Washington, and 57 percent in Smyth. Ritchie worried about the latter as the only "doubtful" county in the region, and in 1848 this outlying fortress fell to General Taylor. Whigs also gained steadily in the prosperous and more cosmopolitan Washington, but rural Tazewell's Democratic vote never dropped below 70 percent.

In 1840 the population of Washington County was slightly larger than those of Smyth and Tazewell combined. Tazewell grew rapidly during the 1840s and by 1850 had nearly ten thousand inhabitants, two thousand more than Smyth. Smyth, however, was the wealthiest of the three by a modest margin. All had small numbers of slaves: 15 percent of Washington's population, 13 percent of Smyth's, and 11 percent of Tazewell's. Washington led the three counties in the production of wheat, oats, wool, and hay, but in each case, the much smaller Smyth produced about the same amount of these cash crops. Smyth County also listed nearly one-fifth of its labor force in nonagricultural pursuits; 15 percent were in manufacturing alone. It was the most diversified and economically dynamic of these three southwestern counties and the least committed to the Democracy (map 4.6).

Tazewell was clearly less developed than its neighbors. Nearly everyone farmed, but only a little over 25 percent of the county's acreage had been improved. Tazewell's agriculture also differed a good deal from that in the other two southwestern counties. Herding was much more important; the county reported more cattle and swine than the larger Washington County. Tazewell also led in the production of both sweet and Irish potatoes and in the value of home manufactures and grew nearly as much flax as Washington. Clearly this was a county with minimal market orientation in which the "social economy" predominated.[48]

Tazewell County would seem to fit the stereotype of an overwhelmingly Democratic, predominately white, self-sufficient county outside the market orbit, cut off by Clinch Mountain from "Rich Valley" that ran through Washington and Smyth counties to the south and west. It was, however, hardly a yeoman's paradise; a majority of the household heads were landless, propertyless, and, consequently, voteless before 1851. One-third of the resident landholders owned slaves. In the easternmost corner of the county, at Burkes Garden, resident gentry like the Floyd family and their kinsman by marriage George Frederick Holmes, the well-known defender of slavery and inventor of sociology, lived in slightly shabby seignorial splendor with a large number of white agricultural laborers under indenture for up to ten years. The situation generated a deferential response from those who worked for them, whose homes they owned, and who were bound to them by perpetual debt, encouraging the planter paternalism exalted by Holmes and his circle of mountain masters.[49]

The county also differed from neighboring Smyth in its ethnic and religious makeup. Of the three counties, Tazewell had by far the most English and Welsh and the fewest Scotch-Irish. Germans made up approximately 20 percent of the population in each of these three counties, helping to account for the Democratic dominance in the area. According to the 1850 census, Tazewell's fifteen churches were all Methodist. Methodists were everywhere, and everywhere they were Democrats, but so were the Baptists in this environment. Near Slate, an outlying polling place northwest of Tazewell Court House that all of its votes to Polk in 1844, there were two Baptist churches. A cluster of Presbyterians at Cove Creek near Jeffersonville accounted for the more respectable Whig minorities at the two polling places in that end of the county.[50]

Smyth County, Tazewell's southern neighbor, contained a higher proportion of Scotch-Irish and a heterogeneous collection of churches: five Methodist, two Baptist, one Presbyterian, one Lutheran, and three Union churches that served Methodists, Baptists, Presbyterians, and Lutherans. Chatham Hill and Broadford, near the Tazewell border, on the North Fork of the Holston River in a mountainous area drew voters from the "Poor Valley" and were dominated by the Democrats. Marion, however, a small town of about four hundred on the Middle Fork of the Holston, surrounded by the best farmland in Smyth County, polled the largest proportion of Whig votes in the county.

The "neighborhoods" within Smyth differed ethnically and religiously as well as economically. The early migration into the area had been dominated by Scotch-Irish Presbyterians who with the German Lutherans settled the Middle Fork area, but by 1850 Methodists had become the most numerous element, with churches in or near Chilhowie in the west, at Saltville and Chatham Hill along the northern border, and in Marion. Methodists also met at Union churches at Chatham Hill and Sugar Grove. Although they had a church in Marion, the Baptists were spread out in an arc from St. Clair Bottom along the Washington and Tazewell borders to Chatham Hill and at the Union churches there and at Sugar Grove. The Presbyterians who had failed to follow the stream of their kinsmen east congregated around Marion, although some worshiped at the previously mentioned Union churches. Others shared the Union church at Atkins with the Lutherans, who also had a church at Pleasant Hill near Groseclose and used the Union church at Chatham Hill. In Smyth County and the southwest generally, the Methodists and the German Lutherans, who in Smyth spilled over from Wythe County to the north, were Democrats. Scotch-Irish Presbyterians, as elsewhere across the commonwealth, tended to be Whigs.[51]

James Madison insisted that disparity in the ownership of property provided the most likely source of partisanship, and antebellum Virginia contained clear fault lines related to the ownership of both land and slaves. White society in Virginia was divided fundamentally between those who owned land and those who did not. Among landholders another sharp division came between those who owned slaves and those who did not, since even small-holders were distinctly wealthier than nonslaveholders. Finally, slaveholders were divided between the many with five or fewer slaves and the few in the planter class with twenty or more. While these lines were blurred by leaseholders who made a decent living as commercial farmers, the significant number of slaveholders who owned only one slave, and those who owned slaves but no land, the potential for class conflict existed, particularly between the planters on the one end of the scale and the landless at the other.

But during the era of the second party system in Virginia, these divisions in property holding did not define the difference between Whigs and Democrats. Both parties constructed inclusive coalitions of diverse overlapping interests whose allegiance each held in varying degrees. These interest groups were defined by occupation, religious affiliation, and ethnicity. Each of the parties contained a different combination of these identifiable interests, and their distinctive mix gave to the parties their electoral character.

The relationship between partisan preference and landholding varied from county to county. Because of the constitutional restrictions on suffrage, Madison's division between the property holders and the landless did not affect electoral behavior. In the planter precincts the Democrats tended to own the larger holdings, yet on the whole Whigs owned slightly better land. The distribution of landholding within each of the parties was strikingly similar. Most of the voters in both parties in Caroline County owned over one hundred acres. While the Whigs had a slight majority among voters with over five hundred acres, one-quarter of the Democrats and 30 percent of the Whigs fell into this group. In Southampton over two-thirds of the largest landholders were Democrats, while a majority of those without taxable land were Whigs. Yet there was practically no difference at all in Prince Edward where the distribution of both the size and value of landholdings was almost the same for both groups. Democrats were more likely to be large planters with over one thousand acres, while Whigs were much more likely than Democrats to own town lots. Taken together, the evidence from available poll books indicates that there were modest differences between the amount of land owned by Whigs and Democrats.[52]

The Democrats were the "planter party" only in a very limited sense. Planters and their families constituted a tiny proportion of the electorate. The Democrats held the allegiance of the majority of this group and predominated in counties where planters dominated the political process. The party of Jack-

Table 4.7. Individual level correlation between party affiliation and slaveholding in five counties, 1840

	Whigs		Democrats		%
Slaves	No.	%	No.	%	Democratic
None	419	37.4	485	37.7	54
1–9	475	42.4	539	41.9	53
10–19	134	11.9	148	11.5	52
20+	93	8.3	113	8.8	55
Total	1,121		1,285		53

N = 2,406 voters

Source: The poll books, census, and tax records of Alleghany, Caroline, Mason, Prince Edward, and Southampton counties.

son, Van Buren, and Polk did particularly well among the tobacco gentry in the conservative southeastern counties. Wheat planters who held more land and fewer slaves and controlled the western and northern part of the piedmont where planters made up a smaller proportion of the voters tended to be Whigs. These differences were relatively small, and many planters grew both crops.

The political affiliation of large slaveholders varied from county to county. Southampton County in the lower tidewater was evenly divided between the parties, but nearly two-thirds of its planters were Democrats. In moderately Democratic Caroline County, which lay across the fall line and was half in the upper piedmont, two-thirds of the planters were Whigs. Farther west in the piedmont south of the James River in the heart of the tobacco country, Prince Edward County gave 57 percent of its vote to Van Buren; 55 percent of the planters were Democrats. Thus, a majority of the 204 planters in these three counties were Democrats, but planters were not much more loyal to the party than the other citizens of these counties.[53]

A direct interest in the peculiar institution had little influence on the choice of party. Neither the Democrats nor the Whigs were the slaveholder party. The proportion of nonslaveholders voting for the Democrats was only slightly larger than that voting Whig, and this also varied from county to county. In strongly Democratic Allegheny County, in the mountainous southwestern corner of the Valley, a larger proportion of Whigs than Democrats owned slaves, but a majority of the slaveowners were Democrats. The Democrats were significantly younger than the Whigs, and thus, this difference in slave ownership disappears when age is controlled. In Caroline County 39 percent of the Democrats but

Table 4.8. Occupational characteristics of Whig and Democratic households in Prince Edward County, 1840

Household occupations	Whigs		Democrats		% Democratic
	No.	%	No.	%	
Predominately agriculture	64	27	113	36	64
Agricultural/manufacturing	59	24	111	35	65
Predominately manufacturing	30	12	31	10	51
Manufacturing	37	15	21	7	36
Manufacturing/commercial	26	11	17	5	40
Professional	25	10	20	6	44
Total	241		313		56

N = 554 households

Source: William G. Shade, "Society and Politics in Antebellum Virginia's Southside," *Journal of Southern History* 53 (1987): 181. The first five categories represent the household economy and its relative balance in terms of occupations listed in the Sixth U.S. Census, 1840, Prince Edward County. The sixth category is made up of those households headed by a professional. If one returns the professionals to the proper household category, the relationship remains strong and significant at the .001 level. The occupational categories in the 1840 census were: mining, agriculture, commerce, manufactures and trades, navigation, and learned professions.

only 33 percent of the Whigs were nonslaveholders. The pattern in Southampton again contrasts with that in Caroline. There 57 percent of the nonslaveholders supported Harrison; while two-thirds of the Democrats owned slaves, only 55 percent of the Whigs did. Higher proportions of both the slaveless and planters were Democrats in Prince Edward, although those without slaves made up only 12 percent of the county's Democrats. The poll books of five counties spread across the commonwealth that contained nearly 2,500 Whigs and Democrats reveal a similar distribution of slave ownership within the two parties. Both the planters and the nonslaveholders were slightly more Democratic than the group as a whole, but these differences are insignificant as predictors of partisan affiliation (table 4.7).

The differences in occupation and economic orientation stand out as the most important economic contrast between the Whigs and the Democrats. The majority of members of both parties in the counties examined were farmers, but in county after county they made up a much smaller proportion of the Whig voters. In Caroline County, where over nine-tenths of the workforce was in agriculture producing tobacco, wheat, corn, and oats, 80 percent of the Democrats but only 73 percent of the Whigs listed themselves in the census as farmers. In Prince Edward 70 percent of the Democrats but only half of the

Whigs were primarily farmers or planters. Nearly two-thirds of the household heads involved in manufacturing voted Whig (table 4.8). In general, three-fifths of the county's voters involved in manufacturing, commerce, and the professions were Whigs. The differential in the rural and Democratic Allegheny County was like that in Caroline, while in Whig Mason County on the Ohio River, 89 percent of Democrats but only 79 percent of the Whigs were exclusively in agriculture. Put differently, 68 percent of the manufacturing, commercial, and professional voters in the Old Dominion were Whigs. In that they captured a heavy proportion of those outside of agriculture as well as a large majority of the town voters, the Whigs in the Old Dominion were the party of the bourgeoisie.

But occupation was not the only difference between the major parties during the second party system. In Virginia as well as elsewhere, ethnicity and religion—especially when they overlapped and reinforced each other—created politically relevant interest groups with contradictory cultural outlooks that exerted an independent influence on voting behavior in antebellum Virginia. In a large number of constituencies, the conflict between Democrats and Whigs pitted German Lutherans against Scotch-Irish Presbyterians. Presbyterianism appealed to other ethnic elements in the commonwealth, and in general there was a tendency for Presbyterians to favor the Whigs. A few Germans and some

Table 4.9. Religious affiliation and occupation of Prince Edward County voters, 1840

	Religion							
	Presbyterian		Baptist		Methodist		Unknown	
Party	No.	%	No.	%	No.	%	No.	%
Predominately agricultural								
Whigs	21	42	20	43	4	29	77	33
Democrats	29	58	27	57	10	71	156	67
Total	50		47		14		233	
$N = 344$								
Predominately manufacturing								
Whigs	26	59	8	44	0	0	83	63
Democrats	18	41	10	56	12	100	49	37
Total	44		18		12		132	
$N = 206$								

Source: Shade, "Society and Politics," 189.

Scotch-Irish responded to the evangelical ministrations of Methodist circuit riders and Baptist farmer-preachers, although these groups and the revived Episcopalians had their strongest appeal to the older ethnic elements, the English and the Welsh. Almost everywhere in the Old Dominion the Methodists were strongly Democratic.

The poll book data from both Prince Edward and Southampton counties reinforce the impression that Methodists overwhelmingly favored the Democrats, but local conditions obviously affected the political response of various denominations. The Baptists leaned in different directions in these two constituencies. In Southampton practically all of the known Methodists supported Van Buren and Polk, while a majority of the Baptists along with the small group of Quakers voted for Harrison and Clay. Prince Edward Baptists tended to be slightly more Democratic than county voters as a whole, but the known Presbyterians were more Whiggish. Antimission Baptists were Democrats; New School Presbyterians, Whigs. Twenty-eight of thirty Prince Edward Methodists and all of the known Disciples of Christ were Democrats.

Household economic orientation modified the relationship between religious affiliation and political behavior, but it generally reinforced the primacy of church congregations in determining the outcome of the process. Occupation had no effect among the Baptists and only a modest one for the Methodists in Prince Edward (table 4.9). Democrats made up the same proportion of those Baptists who were farmers and those who were not. The denomination divided politically in exactly the same fashion as the county. Nearly three-quarters of the Methodist farmers and planters were Democrats, but all the Methodists connected with manufacturing voted for Van Buren. In sharp contrast, the Presbyterians involved in nonagricultural pursuits were heavily Whig, while those who were farmers and planters supported the Democrats to about the same degree as Prince Edward voters generally.

The idea that friends and neighbors determined local divisions in southern politics is a broadly accepted notion. The corollary that the precise form in which such groupings related to partisan discourse was heavily affected by the local context is similarly unexceptional—in fact, obvious. Partisan divisions within neighborhoods often followed the fault lines of sectarian controversy. In some counties Baptists confronted Methodists; in others, they made uneasy alliances when faced by an even less familiar foe. Taken together these local conflicts affected the nature of the Whig and Democratic coalitions in significant ways.

These neighborhood animosities and associations provided the basis for the larger connections from church to denomination, from county committee to the national party. Methodists, who had the largest white following in Virginia, were predominately Democrats, while the second largest denomination, the Baptists, split. Similarly, Episcopalians and Presbyterians fought or held their peace depending upon the relative importance of other available forms of allegiance or contrary sources of conflict, but the Episcopalians usually tilted toward the Whigs, and the third largest denomination in the commonwealth, the Presbyterians, consistently supported the Whigs. On the other hand, the fifth largest denomination in the Old Dominion, the Lutherans, was the most cohesive, and nearly all its followers were Democrats.

The role of church communities in affecting voting was primarily social rather than doctrinal. Congregations formed a crucial tie to kith and kin. In Prince Edward, among twenty-one "families" of household heads with the same surname sampled from the census, 78 percent were voters. Regardless of partisan preference, these "families" were tightly knit in the way they voted. Two-thirds were highly cohesive, and only one "family" split its vote more or less evenly. Nearly 40 percent of all the Prince Edward voters belonged to forty "families" with more than four voters in the poll books. Although this group includes commonplace names of unrelated individuals scattered about the county, three-fifths of these "families" had between 75 and 100 percent cohesion.

Of the sixty such "families" in Mason County in the far west, three-fourths had similar high cohesion. The German names particularly stand out in their commitment to the Democrats. Twenty voters in the county named Raush voted in either 1840 or 1844. All of their votes were cast at Adam Fisher's store, and all twenty were Democrats. At the same polling place, six Zirkles and five Yeagers were also Democrats; half of Polk's votes came from men with German names. The county was Whig, and twenty-seven of its nominal "families" were Whig. None of these had identifiably German names; for instance, twelve of the thirteen voters named Lewis were Whigs. But most of the Democratic "families" also had English names—from Cooper to Waugh. Those with Scotch-Irish names could be found on both sides, but most such "families" in this western county were Whigs.

Kin represent the distilled essence of ethnicity, and travelers through the South such as Timothy Flint and Frederick Law Olmsted noted the existence of what they called "racial traits" among the whites. Extended networks of kin linked party leaders in many counties (see Appendix 1). This was reinforced by the limited marital choices in the rural society of antebellum Virginia where marriage to various forms of cousins was commonplace among whites and sisters of one family often married brothers of another. Occupation mattered, religion mattered, but ethnicity was crucial in Prince Edward County. The early settlers of Prince Edward County came from the tidewater and were predominately English mixed with a smaller element of Welsh. This group also had families descendant from the French Huguenots who from the beginning intermarried with the English and the Welsh. Scotch-Irish strangers had moved in

Table 4.10. Ethnic background of Whig and Democratic voters in Prince Edward County, 1840

	Whigs		Democrats		% Democratic
	No.	%	No.	%	
English	136	55	210	63	61
Welsh	32	13	44	13	58
German	7	3	9	3	56
French	26	10	26	8	50
Scotch-Irish	48	19	34	10	41
Total	249		333		57

Source: Shade, "Society and Politics," 191. This has been slightly reorganized to separate the Welsh and Scotch-Irish.

from the west in the latter half of the eighteenth century. They were interlopers but also frugal and industrious seekers after the main chance.[54]

The English and the Scotch-Irish stood on opposite sides of the Prince Edward political fence. Three-fifths of the English voters in the county were Democrats, while a similar proportion of the Scotch-Irish were Whigs. Ethnicity had less effect among the other voters (table 4.10). The Welsh sided with the English and the Democrats. Those with French surnames made up fewer than one-tenth of the voters; they split between the parties almost equally, with only a slight leaning toward the Whigs. Few clearly German names appear; many like Miller, Smith, and Rice may have been Anglicized. This small German element favored the Democrats. Clearly ethnicity was less salient for these small scattered individuals forced by circumstance to assimilate, but the county's major ethnoreligious groups channeled their cultural conflict into the party battle.

Traditional sectional divisions are meaningless in explaining the contrasting social bases of party allegiances. Neither the Democrats nor the Whigs could be called the western party or the party of the tidewater. Smaller geographical divisions help isolate the tendencies of groups defined by types of economic behavior, but these do not explain the vast majority of those affiliated with either party and are particularly resistant to an understanding of intraregional distinctions. Within counties where economic differences in style and orientation as well as wealth and occupation were minimal, neighborhoods were at political sword's point.

These coalitions of overlapping interest groups joined in comprehensive modern parties to sustain the conflicts over economic and social policies that animated governmental behavior in antebellum Virginia. On the major questions concerning slavery and states' rights, party cohesion was strained by the pressures of intrastate sectional interests that arose from the distribution of the slave population. Nonetheless, the Whigs and Democrats did present general positions on these issues, although their support was less cohesive and partisan differences were more subtle than on other matters.

Partisan differences rooted in group responses to the new individualistic market society generated by the revolutions in production, transportation, and communication were highly correlated with cultural aspects that these neighborhoods shared with those similarly defined in their ethnic and denominational affiliation across the commonwealth. The historical experiences of these ethnoreligious groups nurtured psychological orientations toward change that dictated the individual's reaction to the new order of post-Tocquevillian America expressed in the social and economic changes sweeping over the Old Dominion. Virginia's Whigs came disproportionately from those social and economic groups that were more attuned than their opponents to the emerging set of human relationships that characterized nineteenth-century liberal capitalist society. The socioeconomic coalition that made up Old Dominion's Democratic party sustained men more comfortable with their traditional place in the simpler agrarian republic of their fathers. These partisan persuasions directed the behavior of the Old Dominion's political leaders as they struggled to respond to the expanding demands of the commonwealth's diverse interests.[55]

◡◠ 5 ◡◠

One Hundred and
Seventy-Three Despots

EVER FEARFUL of the dangers of consolidation, Thomas Jefferson conceived of the first Virginia Declaration of Rights and constitution as a check on the tyranny of the "kingly office." He proposed severe limits on executive power while vesting most of the governmental vigor in the legislature; the center of the new government should be an annually elected lower house that would choose both the upper house and the "Administrator." But after his unhappy and unsuccessful experience as governor, the future president complained that the constitution of the commonwealth dangerously concentrated "legislative, executive and judiciary" authority in the assembly, and he sought to curb the legislature's power. To this end he adopted the idea of representing wealth in one house and persons in the other to gain the benefits of "a proper complication of principle." [1]

The essence of Jeffersonian republicanism was limited government: "It is better to keep the wolf out of the fold than trust to drawing his teeth and talons after he shall have entered." In general he wished a new constitution "to bind up the several branches of government by certain laws which when they transgress their acts shall become nullities." While Jefferson embraced no easy ideological commitment to laissez-faire, he envisioned the new government functioning within narrowly circumscribed bounds, believing with most republicans that authority itself threatened liberty.[2]

James Madison's apprehension about representative government followed entirely different lines. While he prized stability, Madison also accepted—to a far greater degree that his Albemarle friend—the need for "energy" in government and consequently a certain efficiency in its administration. Representative government would avoid the classical problem of direct democracy degenerating into mob rule. The 1780s posed the immediate problem of how to remedy "vicious legislation," often as unjust as it was unwise, poorly drawn by the inexperienced legislators. Madison's commentary reflected his own successful career as a legislator and applied as well to the legislatures created by the new

158

state constitutions. Since the legislators would be "called for the most part from pursuits of a private nature, continued in appointment for a short time," they would be required to learn the arts of republican governance by practicing them.[3]

Madison understood the tension that existed between the tendency toward oligarchy and the practical need for experienced legislators. "A few members as happens in all such assemblies, will possess superior talents; will, by frequent re-elections, become members of long standing; will be thoroughly masters of the public business, and perhaps not unwilling to avail themselves of those advantages." While opening the possibility of corruption, this principle promised to provide political stability, committing "the bulk of the members" to the maintenance of a just society. Although he believed in annual elections as a check on corruption, Madison held out the hope that in the course of their legislative service, incumbents would gain a combination of patriotism and wisdom.[4]

The differing fears of Virginia's two greatest statesmen frame the continuing set of problems faced by those who would initiate representative republics. Ironically the optimist, Jefferson, proposed a government so limited that it could hardly govern at all, fueling future antigovernmental designs and an essentially negative liberalism. The pessimist, Madison, perhaps remembered most for his aphorism "If men were angels no government would be necessary," counseled the utopian belief that legislators would learn by doing and acquire civic responsibility while governing, a slim reed indeed upon which to build a faith in positive liberal government.

From 1776 to 1851 the constitutional standing of the Virginia General Assembly remained basically unaltered. The government of the commonwealth, however, changed dramatically in two important ways that reflected the political development of the United States during its first seventy-five years of existence. The social origins of the people in power shifted to encompass a more sizable segment of the middle stratum that represented the growing complexity of the commonwealth's economy and society. Eighteenth-century Virginia had been a society dominated by great planters; in the antebellum era they gave way to a combination of lesser planters, substantial farmers, and a rising bourgeoisie among whom lawyers made up the largest element. While the Revolutionary elite were truly independent gentlemen just as the colonial elite had been, the emerging democratic elite numbered in their ranks a new breed of professional politicians whose adherence to partisanship contrasted sharply with the disavowals of their predecessors.

The second major change affecting the assembly was the rather sudden appearance in the 1830s of two relatively modern parties in the legislature, organizing the behavior of its members and determining the nature of its policy agenda. The party system of Federalists and Republicans had penetrated into the activities of the Virginia assembly but was distinctly limited in scope and sporadic in its effects. Initially the Democrats and Whigs focused on resolutions and elections relating to federal affairs, but within a decade legislative parties came into conflict on a range of economic and social issues concerning the government of the commonwealth itself. While partisanship never completely controlled legislative activities, and local demands actually increased, party conflict became the dominant force shaping public policy.

During the life of the second party system, a set of salient issues clearly and publicly defined the difference between Democrats and Whigs to a degree unknown in the era of Republicans and Federalists. These issues became mingled with the parties' responses to slavery and states' rights in establishing their political character as well as their positions on public policy.

The number of assembly seats held by each party during these years more closely resembled the true partisan division of Virginia voters than did the coloring of the congressional delegation from the Old Dominion, even though the assemblymen were slightly more Democratic than the state's electorate as a whole. The state's House of Delegates thus functioned as a far better representative of the partisan perspectives and ideological outlooks of Virginia voters than did the commonwealth's congressional delegation in Washington. Ironically that meant that a sizable minority of Virginians consistently opposed the extreme states' rights position associated with the "Doctrines of '98" and embraced the limited nationalism of the Whigs. As a respectable minority during these years, the Whigs held a consistent proportion of the state's electorate and legislative seats. Virginia's Whigs were much more popular than historians have previously acknowledged and similar in outlook to their fellow Whigs throughout in the country.[5]

The constitution of 1776 created a classical republic of gentlemen freeholders who were generally loath to embrace democracy as they understood the term. The new Virginia House of Delegates showed a relatively high rate of turnover in its first thirty years. In the decade following the Stamp Act crisis, fewer than one-third of the burgesses had been new members. During each legislative session of the 1780s, however, new members made up slightly over half of the Old Dominion's legislature. With the exception of the volatile year of 1797 at the end of the decade, the 1790s brought stability that lasted throughout the Jeffersonian era, during which three-fifths of the legislators retained their seats from one year to the next.

Large planters dominated in the new government of the Old Dominion, and the power of the gentry receded at only a glacial pace. The Revolution had brought minor changes opening up some opportunity for men of the middling sort, but members of the assembly during the Jeffersonian era came from the aristocracy of the new Republic, well educated and wealthy. Half, in fact, bore the names of the families that had ruled the Old Dominion since the late seventeenth century. Nearly all shared Anglo-American origins; three-fourths were raised in the established church. The number of slaveless legislators grew modestly during the 1790s, but such men comprised fewer than one in ten of the members and played an even smaller role in actually governing the commonwealth. The small core of legislative leaders who were repeatedly returned included the wealthiest planters in the assembly.[6]

Throughout the Republican era there were high rates of absenteeism and little organization—in fact, very little system at all. Few roll calls were taken in the early years; factions gathered around dynamic individuals, but these blocs never included a majority of the members. Patrick Henry, the supposed leader of the "debtor-oriented faction," missed over half of the recorded roll calls on economic issues in the late 1780s. The Virginia vote on ratification was very close, and Madison carried the day for the new Constitution only with the promise of future amendments—"a few additional guards in favor of the Rights of the States and of the People." The clearest contrast between Federalists and Antifederalists in the Old Dominion was that the young Federalists represented the periphery and the older Antifederalists the traditionalist center.[7]

Most Virginia legislators in the 1790s retained the Revolutionary conception of the representative as a man of independent ways as well as independent means. The majority were "men of little faith," suspicious of the proposed new government and antifederal at heart. The General Assembly selected two prominent opponents of the Constitution, Richard Henry Lee and William Grayson, as the first United States senators from the commonwealth. Madison had to struggle against his Antifederalist friend James Monroe for a seat in the first Congress where he emerged as its most important member and eventually as the leader of the Republican interest later in the decade.[8]

At the same time that Congress divided over foreign affairs during the early 1790s, factions appeared in the Virginia General Assembly closely associated with either the Washington administration or the Republican opposition in Congress. While the former Federalist Madison was the acknowledged leader of the opposition in the Congress, a majority of the Republicans in the assembly had been Antifederalists, and the division represented a continuation of the geographically based conflict of the 1780s and the fight over ratification. In the mid-1790s the debate over the Jay Treaty dictated a new degree of partisan organization. Slightly more than half of those who served in the four sessions from 1793 to 1796 either consistently supported or opposed Federalist policies. The divisions on national issues carried over into economic matters with the Republicans favoring reduction of taxes and postponement of the collection of debts.[9]

Table 5.1. Region and partisan affiliation in the General Assembly, 1788–96

	1788–92			1793–96		
	Fed.	Anti.	Ind.	Fed.	Anti.	Ind.
Northern Neck	10	12	1	13	4	2
Middle tidewater	7	16	2	15	12	3
Piedmont	4	11	0	6	19	3
Southside	7	37	0	2	52	3
West	22	18	1	37	15	9
Urban	1	0	1	2	0	0

Source: Norman K. Risjord and Gordon DenBoer, "The Emergence of Political Parties in Virginia, 1782–1800," *Journal of American History* 60 (1974): 980.

Significantly more Republicans could be identified in the earlier sessions, but cohesive legislative parties were emerging, and while the Federalists remained a minority, they gained strength, holding 42 percent of the seats that could be identified with either faction. The planter region of the tidewater and southeastern piedmont, characterized by expanded tobacco production and the growing presence of the peculiar institution, commanded the Republican center (table 5.1). Federalist strength lay in the peripheral areas from the Eastern Shore up the Northern Neck between the Rappahannock and the Potomac to the Blue Ridge that shifted to the production of cereal grains for the markets in the West Indies and southern Europe. Washington's supporters were also strong in the Shenandoah Valley, in the counties along the Ohio River, and in the valley of the Great Kanawha. Finally, there were nests of "urban" Federalists in Norfolk, Richmond, and Alexandria.

During the administration of John Adams, party lines in Congress became more tightly drawn and affected a wider variety of issues than at any time while Washington occupied the presidency. The sessions of the Virginia assembly at the end of the 1790s also featured a greater influence of party than found earlier in the decade. Eighty percent of the members responded consistently in a partisan fashion. The 1797 election for the Virginia House of Delegates showed an assertion of Federalist strength that was part of a Federalist revival throughout the South as public opinion turned against the French, but in the Old Dominion three-fifths of the legislators were Republicans. The legislative resolutions of 1798, attacking the Alien and Sedition Acts were supported by 60 percent of the members who voted.[10]

The Virginia General Assembly continued to send former Antifederalists to the Senate throughout the 1790s, but the gubernatorial elections had no relation to federal questions until 1799 when the former ambassador to France, James Monroe, was elected over Federalist James Breckinridge. Partisanship further affected the selection of the Speaker and the state printer. The Republicans even moved to deprive Adams of the electoral vote he had received in 1796 by eliminating the district system and mandating the choice of electors in 1800 on a general ticket. The majority abolished oral voting and established a system that led to the circulation of printed ballots by the central committee of local leaders.[11]

Both parties were forced to organize for 1800. The advocates of the Adams administration printed a list of electors for the "American Republican Ticket" and put forth an address to the voters appealing to the spirit of Washington. Momentarily the trappings of a modern party system appeared in the Old Dominion. Relatively well organized parties contested the presidential election and produced the largest turnout of voters in the commonwealth until Andrew Jackson faced the younger Adams a quarter century later. The division of voters in 1800 reflected the factional conflict in the assembly, although Jefferson seems to have been more popular than his party with the voters of the Old Dominion.[12]

The conservative planter elite that long controlled the assembly hardly left their continued dominance to chance. They structured the government in every way possible to withstand any democratic threats. The scheme of representation discriminated against the western half of the state from the beginning. Republicans pushed through the general ticket law to control presidential elections by maximizing the impact of Virginia's electoral vote and explicitly gerrymandered the state after the censuses of 1800 and 1810 to exclude the slightest whiff of "aristocratic" Federalist influence in the name of "democracy" and to increase the number of Virginia Republicans in Washington.[13]

In the first two decades of the nineteenth century, the only clear distinction between the Republicans and the Federalists in Virginia involved their attitudes on foreign policy and the conflict between the Anglophiles and the "Friends of France." Modern party structures were absent from the scene. In the assembly the speakership of the house was generally uncontested, other legislative officers were unanimously elected, and committee memberships were assigned randomly. Neither the majority nor the opposition held regular caucuses or designated party whips to organize roll-call responses. The votes in the House of Delegates showed extremely low cohesion, especially among the Republicans. Partisans clustered together only on the few votes directly related to the parties themselves; the conflict between Federalists and Republicans had no relation to matters of state policy. Issues such as slavery, internal improvements, education, taxation, and public morals drew ad hoc support and opposition but were not matters of party interest.[14]

Few legislators, including even the stalwarts of the Richmond Junto, perceived politics as a profession. Sessions were short, and most men served only one term. Partisanship played a relatively unimportant role in either elections or the business of the assembly. As in the other states of the new nation, "parties" remained mere rudiments, traditional "connections," arising out of the locally powerful courts and networks of important families that structured state legislative activity during the Jeffersonian era. Members positioned themselves with either the Federalists or the Republicans on matters relating to foreign affairs, but these designations rarely affected decisions on domestic policy and local matters in which the periphery challenged the dominant center.

Rooted in the county courts, the Republicans were also less favorable to judicial reform than the Federalists. Had those legislators who were Republicans on foreign policy and federal affairs acted as a party, they could have secured Jefferson's democratic reforms at any time they chose. Rather, most Virginia Republicans showed no desire to change the constitution of 1776 in any fashion. The division on calling a new constitutional convention in these early sessions portended that pattern. Thirteen roll calls were taken on the issue between 1801 and 1816. In each case the Senate, which was malapportioned heavily in favor of the east and overwhelmingly Republican, blocked reform.[15]

On matters concerning economic development, the opposition always took the lead, demanding internal improvements and credit facilities similar to those being created in other states. Both before and after the War of 1812, Charles Fenton Mercer, from Loudoun County in the northern piedmont, pushed establishing a state system of internal improvements. Essentially the Federalists, who included relatively more westerners than their opponents, were enthusiastic and the Republicans restrained or opposed. For the tidewater planters, that government governed best that governed not at all. Finally enough piedmont Republicans came over to Mercer's side to establish the Board of Public Works and initiate a modest program of canal and road building, although most of the money went into the James River and Kanawha canal project that most benefited the central and western piedmont.[16]

While they had warmly supported the creation of the Bank of Virginia, the Federalist minority also agitated for additional banks in the western piedmont and the Valley, but the conservative Jeffersonians—who controlled the Bank of Virginia—pushed through a stringent law prohibiting all private notes and limiting the payment of state taxes to either specie or the notes of the two state banks. In 1816 they blocked a bill introduced by Mercer to "establish sundry Banks," but two years later as part of the attempt to mollify western demands for constitutional reform, a slim majority of the Republicans voted with most of the Federalists to charter the Bank of the Valley of Virginia and the Northwestern Bank of Virginia, with headquarters in Winchester and Wheeling, respectively.[17]

Although their response to these economic issues reflected the geographic basis of electoral support, the Federalist minority in the assembly also compiled a more clearly liberal record than the Republicans on social questions such as slavery and popular education. When it came to matters relating to race, neither party can properly termed antislavery, much less problack, but the Federalist minority were more humane than the dominant Jeffersonian Republicans. While legislation restraining the slaves' right of assembly and allowing blacks to sell liquor displayed this tendency, the provision of 1805 that required manumitted slaves to leave the Old Dominion within one year after gaining their freedom clearly revealed partisan differences. Two-thirds of the Republicans in the house favored this law, while three-fourths of the Federalists voted against it as overly harsh.[18]

On education the Federalists followed a more consistent reform line than either Jefferson or the Republicans in the legislature. Jefferson met strong opposition in his own party to his pet project—the establishment of the University of Virginia—but the former president himself resisted common school reform when he believed that it would interfere with the establishment of "his university" in Charlottesville. The eastern Republicans opposed spending their tax dollars on either proposal. Jefferson found himself forced to rely on Federalist votes and the aid of Mercer, but when Mercer proposed a state-funded public education scheme that stressed primary schools and audaciously suggested that the university be located in the Valley, Jefferson snarled against such dangerous "consolidation."[19]

In the years immediately following the Treaty of Ghent, Mercer gained a reputation as one of the South's leading advocates of popular education. He was more interested in general education at state expense than was Jefferson and proposed a comprehensive state-supported system of primary and secondary schools throughout the commonwealth that included the establishment of four colleges and the university. Mercer received the nearly unanimous backing of his Federalist friends and was able to convince enough Republicans to push an education bill through the house only to see it blocked by the Republican-dominated senate. Then during the 1820s the rough-hewed western reformer Philip Doddridge joined Mercer in pushing the demand for public education. On social, economic, and political questions, the Republican center of the Old Dominion strongly resisted reform pushed by the representatives of the periphery led by the Federalists and National Republicans.[20]

Elections to the assembly in the 1820s were conducted in personal terms not dissimilar from those of Washington's day. Individual characteristics and reputation were highly valued; local connections, rather than orientation toward specific state or national issues, were of utmost importance. Under these conditions the relatively small group of influential men in the capital known as the

Richmond Junto exercised inordinate power in the affairs of the Old Dominion from early in the nineteenth century until the 1830s. Nominations for the assembly were informal. Often "a number of his friends of both political parties" would "open a poll" for a candidate on election day. While there were no party designations, many candidates bore titles such as "Judge" and "Capt." referring to positions in local government and in the militia. There was little sign of formal campaigning for legislative office, and it continued to be "more important to win the favor of the few who already had power than to court the multitude with demagogic arts." [21]

At the end of the decade, the public press still paid practically no attention at all to the spring elections for seats in the assembly or even the congressional elections held at the same time. These were distinctly local matters spoken of in the plural. No connection was indicated between the exciting presidential canvass of 1828 and the spring elections that followed it. The returns for the 1829 legislative elections are fairly complete and illustrate the situation. While the turnout equaled that in Jackson's sweeping victory, the two elections were treated in the press as separate, unrelated events. There were no party labels. Two candidates stood unopposed in four of the seventy-two counties whose returns were reported in the *Richmond Enquirer*; in another twenty there were three men battling for two seats. In sixteen counties five or more candidates ran and received a reasonable number of votes. One-third of the counties reported returns that might indicate potential contests in which four candidates ran for two places, but in these, the distribution of the vote was erratic. Only in three counties—Wood, Randolph, and Montgomery—did the returns resemble those of a two-party contest. [22]

The few changes wrought by the new constitution of 1830 had no immediate effect in the early 1830s, and elections continued to be conducted as in the previous decade. Constitutional reform, slavery, and nullification played no role in the contests for legislative seats, where the politics of deference continued to hold sway. During March and early April 1832, following the great debate over slavery in the House of Delegates, the *Enquirer* discussed the upcoming presidential election. But when Ritchie's paper began reporting the returns for assembly seats on April 10, it did so without fanfare and listed the candidates without any partisan designations or any indication that the candidates were divided on public issues. Nullification was mentioned occasionally in reports from South Carolina but played no role in the election of 1832 and did not divide the contesting legislative candidates in most of the counties the following year. [23]

Contemporaries spoke and wrote of "conservative" and "reform" parties in the 1829–30 convention, an "abolition party" in the House of Delegates in 1832, and a "State-Rights party" the following year during the nullification crisis, but nothing resembling modern institutions, nor even legislative factions loosely connected to the presidential politics, existed before the appearance of the Whigs in the assembly elections of 1834 when the Bank War intruded into Virginia politics in the form of a debate over the election and instruction of the commonwealth's two United States senators.

After a six-month fight within his administration, Jackson forced the secretary of the treasury to withdraw the federal deposits from the Bank of the United States. For most Virginians, Jackson's actions represented an arrogant abuse of executive power and posed a matter of essentially constitutional, rather than economic, policy. Governor John Floyd, who disliked and distrusted the president in any case, condemned Jackson's policy. At the urging of Calhounite Thomas W. Gilmer of Albemarle, the assembly responded with resolutions attacking both the president's "unauthorized . . . and dangerous use of executive power" and the constitutionality of the Bank. The anti-Jackson majority then went on to instruct Virginia's senators to vote for restoration, to elect former senator Littleton Waller Tazewell as governor, and to send the conservative Old Republican Benjamin Watkins Leigh to the Senate in place of Jacksonian William C. Rives.[24]

Actually, the series of roll calls in 1833–34 related to this set of issues show much less party cohesion than this scenario suggests. Fewer than one-third of the legislators voted for both Tazewell and Leigh, the supposed party candidates. In the race for governor, Tazewell was challenged by Samuel Watts, a National Republican from Norfolk, and two Jacksonians, Peter V. Daniel and James McDowell. On the final vote Tazewell received sixty-two votes, Watts, thirty-seven, and McDowell, twenty-four. All of the McDowell men voted for Philip Barbour for senator, while two-thirds of Tazewell's backers and three-fifths of those who voted for Watts joined to elect Leigh. There were no modern parties directing the affairs of the assembly, and Tazewell himself disdained partisan support.[25]

Historians usually date the Whig party in Virginia from the appearance of the name in spring elections of 1834. Nominations for assembly seats emerged from mass meetings, and national issues intruded into the state politics. What Virginians traditionally had seen as individual elections in each county began to be viewed in concert as a single election to determine a legislative majority that might influence the course of federal politics. Across the state a growing number of candidates stood for election as "Administration" or "Pro-Jackson," and local reports associated them with partisan positions on the Bank and on Rives's resignation. A glimpse of the future could be seen in the Albemarle County election where Gilmer and Valentine Southall faced Thomas Jefferson Randolph and Alexander Rives, the senator's brother. Ritchie treated the election as a referendum on the president's actions and reported the victory of the "friends of Jackson" (Randolph and Rives) as the result of strict "party votes" and the turnout of nearly all of Albemarle's eligible voters.[26]

Clearly, Jackson's removal of the federal deposits from the Bank of the United States did have some significant effects, but Ritchie exaggerated its importance. Few other counties at the time showed the consistency or competitiveness of Albemarle. Many candidates elsewhere were unopposed, and odd numbers ran even where party designations prevailed. In Prince William County, for example, candidates came forth on the deposit issue, but four of the five aspirants for the county's single seat favored removal of the federal deposits from the Bank of the United States and the return of Rives to the Senate. In Mecklenburg County on the Southside, three "Administration" candidates contested against two "Antis" for two seats in the house, while in Accomack County on the Eastern Shore there were four "Antis," one "Jacksonian," and one whom Ritchie's correspondent termed "anything people wish him."[27]

The new Whig coalition captured control of the Virginia House of Delegates in the election with a majority of approximately a dozen seats, but the Jacksonians retained control of the Senate, making any joint votes in the 1834–35 session extremely close. An anti-Junto coalition, however, took the state printing contract away from Ritchie, removed Daniel from the executive council, and returned Leigh to the Senate for a full six-year term. The popular Linn Banks survived as Speaker by a mere two votes. These actions undermined the structural apparatus of the Junto and forced the *Enquirer* to spearhead a struggle to save the Republican party that generated the first extensive preelection campaign for legislative and congressional seats in 1835.[28]

In sharp contrast to the situation in the early years of the decade, these local contests were dominated by partisanship from the day the previous legislative session ended. From early March on, the partisan press editorialized about the importance of the upcoming campaign. The Jacksonian legislators met and issued *An Address to the People of Virginia by the Democratic Party in the General Assembly of 1834–5*. Yet the focus of the press coverage was clearly national, and the leading subject of the address was the question of the senatorial election. The "true issue" before the voters was *"Instructions or no Instructions? Leigh or no Leigh?"* The partisan editors cast this question in the mold of the ancient struggle between the Republicans and the Federalists. Ritchie exhorted the voters "to the Polls," insisting that true Virginians would "court no *union* with Bankmen and Tariffites, with Nullifiers and National Republicans."[29]

Jacksonian papers portrayed Senator Leigh as a "quasi-friend of a National Bank" and an old opponent of Thomas Jefferson. They insisted that the "piebald Whigs" were nothing more than an opportunistic combination of "Federalists and Nullifiers." While all of the candidates for the assembly and Congress (except Henry Wise of Accomack County) were identified with either

Table 5.2. Partisan composition of the House of Delegates, 1834–41

	Democrats	Whigs	% Democratic
1834	62	74	46
1835	72	56	56
1836	77	56	58
1837	85	48	64
1838	61	74	45
1839	61	72	46
1840	62	72	46
1841	66	68	49

Sources: Henry H. Simms, *Rise of the Virginia Whigs, 1824–1840* (Richmond, 1929), 167–92; *Lynchburg Virginian*, May 14, 1840; *Richmond Enquirer*, May 7, 1841. For consistency the *Enquirer* figures are used if available.

the "Administration" or the "Opposition," this indicated little beyond the immediate questions involved in the senatorial seats. "Father" Ritchie, not one to change his ways, called his associates "Republicans," and felt able to list the results of the elections of late March and April 1835 in terms of "Republicans" and "Whigs."[30]

The tenuous Whig hold on the House of Delegates gave way to a comfortable Democratic majority (table 5.2). Jackson's supporters won twenty-eight seats and lost only nine. Two-party contests between Whigs and Democrats took place in three-fourths of the counties—twice as many as in 1833—and in only 15 percent were candidates for the assembly unopposed. This set the scene in the 1835–36 session for conflict between the Jacksonian majority in the legislature and the anti-Jackson governor and senators. The former eventually pushed through resolutions instructing the senators to vote for expunging the censure of Jackson from the Senate's journal and then reelected Rives to the Senate in place of John Tyler, who had resigned rather than follow their instructions.[31]

In kaleidoscopic fashion each new turn had produced a different pattern of popular voting. The Opposition majority in the assembly in 1834 gave way to an administration majority in 1835. In 1836 there was a large turnover, and one-fifth of the seats changed hands from one party to the other, but the Jacksonians maintained control. After the excitement of the fall presidential election, involving slavery and the gag rule, the spring elections in 1837 were relatively calm.

The Democrats gained eight more seats in the House of Delegates. The number of two-party contests fell, and partisan controversy seemed to have abated. The panic of 1837 and the adverse economic conditions that followed occupied the legislature. The assembly chose to come to the aid of Virginia's banks; the only real confrontation came over resolutions on the Van Buren administration's policy.

Rather quietly and with little attention from the partisan press, the Whigs swept the election of 1838, ushering in a new era of party politics in the Old Dominion. They were able to take advantage of the Junto's disarray and public discontent with the Democrats' response to the economic collapse. A modest increase in turnout produced a distinct shift to the Whigs, who gained across the board, winning twenty-eight seats in the House of Delegates while losing only six. The new party then proceeded to win the next three consecutive elections before losing control of the house in 1842. The contest for control of the Virginia legislature that spring produced a significant shift back to the Democrats and bears certain surface characteristics of a classic depression election.[32]

Economic conditions had continued to deteriorate, and prices were down, although they did not bottom out until the following year. Economic issues dominated the public press, and the contrasting policies of the two parties at both the state and the federal level could not have been more clearly articulated. Congressional Whigs had moved to overthrow the laissez-faire policies of the Van Buren administration by repealing the Independent Treasury law and instituting a broad positive economic program, joining a bankruptcy act, the distribution of the proceeds from land sales, a new national bank in some form, and a protective tariff. Resolutions on these policies along with questions of stay laws, new commercial taxes, and banks dominated the state legislative agenda as well. In the 1841–42 session of the Virginia assembly, Democrats demanded immediate resumption and the move to an exclusively metallic currency, but the Whigs, who held a narrow edge in the House of Delegates, were able to defeat these proposals and, with the aid of a small group of Democratic "softs," extended further relief to the banks and passed a small-note bill, provided a charter for a new bank at Scottsville, and set the date by which the banks had to resume specie payments.[33]

Even in the depths of the depression, other matters intruded into the election. One was educational reform. The Whigs were able to push a bill through the house that was then defeated by economy-minded Democrats in the state senate. More important was the slavery issue. Two Virginia Whig congressmen, John Minor Botts and Alexander H. H. Stuart, had voted with their northern colleagues to rescind the gag rule in the special session of 1841. While the pair had only voted to reconsider, their action proved to the Democrats that they were part of an abolitionist plot. The question became further entangled when

Botts accused Abel P. Upshur, Tyler's secretary of the navy, of being a "disunionist." While the *Enquirer* at first let Congressman Wise defend his friend and fellow Tylerite, the Democratic paper kept up a sustained attack on the dangers posed to slavery by the northern Whigs and their local "abolitionist" allies. County meetings that primarily focused upon the Whig economic program also attacked congressional interference with slavery in the District of Columbia and supported the gag on abolitionist petitions.

An *Enquirer* editorial on the eve of the State Rights Democratic Convention pointed to the dangers to slavery posed by northern politicians in league with the British and suggested that only slaveholders could be trusted with power. Throughout March, Democrats agitated the petition question and consistently connected Botts and John Quincy Adams as threats to the South. In their veiled courtship of the Tylerites and Wise, the Democratic papers printed Upshur's defense of his loyalty, favorable comments on Tyler, and even Wise's justification of his role in the deadly duel between congressmen William Graves and Jonathan Cilley in which Wise served as Graves's second. Right before the election Ritchie published a letter signed "Watchman" warning that "the Clay party" endangered southern rights and declaring that the reborn alliance of Clay and Adams presented a spectacle "calculated to strike the South with indignation and disgust." The letter's references to Federalist heresies joined the Whig economic program with support of the abolitionists.[34]

The Virginia voters responded by swinging back toward the party of Jackson. The Democrats gained four seats in 1841, and then in 1842 Ritchie triumphantly reported that the "State Rights Republicans" won twenty-four new seats while losing only six to the "Federal Whigs," giving the Democrats a huge majority. The basic pattern of the second party system held, but small margins in several counties determined a sizable shift in the house (table 5.3). The result, however, constituted a planter's revolt rather than a protest of the poor. Turnout declined, and the Democrats gained seats in the most competitive districts by getting their supporters to the polls. Nearly all of the seats that changed hands were in either the piedmont or the Valley. Two-thirds of those captured by the Democrats were in counties east of the Blue Ridge, and their tax per capita was well above the mean for the state as a whole. The normally Whig constituencies that sent Democrats to Richmond included some of the most commercially oriented counties in the commonwealth: Albemarle, Augusta, Fairfax, Fauquier, Norfolk, Pittsylvania, and Wood.[35]

The Democrats held steady for both the legislative and congressional contests in 1843. While the press gave most of its attention to national economic issues, the Democratic legislature gerrymandered the state's congressional districts, defeated a Whig attempt to pass a stay law, and effectively repudiated the debt by taxing the interest on state bonds. The session was dominated by

Table 5.3. Partisan composition of the House of Delegates, 1842–51

	Democrats	Whigs	% Democratic
1841	66	68	49
1842	84	50	63
1843	75	59	56
1844	61	73	46
1845	78	54	59
1846	72	60	54
1847	71	63	53
1848	75	60	56
1849	76	59	56
1850	76	59	56
1851	89	61	59

Source: *Richmond Enquirer.*

consideration of the new Democratic tax law that lowered rates for planters while taxing stock and artisans' tools and raising license fees of various non-agricultural occupations. The Democrats covered this program in a symbolic appeal to the yeoman farmer, but the redistricting and lowering of taxes most obviously appealed to the German farmers in the Valley and the planters in the eastern half of the state where the Democratic party had made its greatest gains.[36]

Although they had different results, the assembly elections on either side of Polk's election in 1844 correlated closely. The Whigs gained back nine legislative seats in 1843 and actually won a majority of the house seats in the spring of 1844, but the balance quickly tipped back to the Democrats, who controlled the Virginia legislature through the rest of the decade and into the 1850s, holding a wide margin in the malapportioned state senate and a consistent majority of the seats in the House of Delegates. The returns from the spring elections of 1845, however, were very similar to those of the previous fall. The partisan situation remained relatively stable; the seemingly huge swing back to the Democrats resulted again from many small shifts across the board. Whigs lost exactly the same number of seats in the east as they did in the west, and close competition characterized the counties that changed hands. Seventy percent of the counties had two-party contests, and an additional 20 percent had multiple candidates with clear national designations. Only in one-tenth of the Old Dominion's counties were assembly candidates unopposed. Certainly there was yearly fluctuation in the mid-1840s, but throughout the decade between 80 and 90 percent of the seats were contested by candidates representing the two major parties, and the popular press generally identified those who ran unopposed.[37]

Three real changes had taken place by midcentury. In the early 1830s assembly elections drew more voters than presidential elections, but this relationship was reversed in the 1840s. The modern pattern appeared, with the elections held in presidential years drawing more voters than the off-year elections. In 1836 the turnout for the House of Delegates election was three points higher than that for the presidential election. Although participation in the spring assembly contests jumped from 39 percent of the white adult males to 45 percent four years later, turnout for the fall presidential election increased from 35 percent to 55 percent in the counties for which comparable data are available. Even in 1844 turnout for the spring elections edged up slightly, but it still remained below that for the fall presidential election. By 1848, however, the turnout was almost the same in both elections. Although turnout in congressional elections was erratic because of the way the state was districted, popular interest in assembly elections increased steadily and jumped even higher when the electorate was expanded in 1851.

Second, while party labels appeared regularly in the press by the mid-1830s, there continued to be a variety of designations. In 1835 the allegiance of only one-tenth of the candidates was unidentified, but those whose affiliation was stated were called, somewhat randomly, "Republican," "Jackson," "Administration," "Democrat," "Opposition," "Whig," or "White." Ten years later those designated by party were either "Whigs" or "Democrats." What had been county-focused events dominated by the local influentials were increasingly part of a larger statewide endeavor connected to governing not only the commonwealth but also the country as a whole. County politics had taken on a cosmopolitan hue.

There had been little correlation between the behavior of Virginia voters in the spring and fall elections in the early 1830s. Voters sometimes shared joint allegiances to men running for the presidency, but such connections were absent in local elections. Beginning in 1840 partisan responses to the assembly elections in the spring reflected the way Whigs and Democrats would cast their presidential ballots six months later. By the early 1850s, when truly comparable data are available in the form of popular returns from all of the counties for both the gubernatorial and presidential elections, the correlation between partisan preference in the state and federal elections was nearly perfect. Party identification characterized the second party system, and participation reached extraordinary levels.

Both the style and the focus of Virginia politics changed dramatically during these years. The importance of the county courts waned as the legislature assumed a more active role, and partisanship came to dominate the assembly as well as elections to it. In fact, the governors were bending to the influence of party even before the office became elective. In contrast to the independent executives of the 1820s and early 1830s, those who came later in the 1830s and during the 1840s were party men, as illustrated by the differences between the careers of the stubbornly independent John Floyd, governor of the commonwealth at the time of Nat Turner's rebellion, and his partisan son John Buchanan Floyd, who was elected governor as a Democrat in 1849 after a stint in the house and who would later serve as Buchanan's secretary of war.[38]

From the mid-1830s on, candidates for the assembly relied upon recognizable party labels that linked them to national leaders and issues. In his campaign for the House of Delegates in 1845, a typical Southside Democrat, Samuel McDearmond, declared himself "a Polk, Texas, anti-bank, anti-tariff, anti-Distribution Man." There also seems little doubt that aspirants for office in the 1840s courted "the multitude with demagogic arts." Contestants vigorously campaigned and often debated the issues for hours in a carnival-like atmosphere while the partisan press became increasingly vituperative. By 1840 Virginia state politics had become party politics, and the government of the commonwealth, party government.[39]

The "new style" politicians differed significantly in their social status from their Jeffersonian predecessors. Control of the commonwealth shifted from the planter aristocracy who dominated the eighteenth century to the upper middle class of rural nineteenth-century Virginia, farmers holding far fewer slaves and working less land who were forced to share their power with the diverse class of small merchants and businessmen who gravitated to the towns and cities. The Whigs and Democrats who served in the Virginia assembly during these years were contemporaries of Lincoln and Lee, born in the nineteenth century after the Revolution of 1800 and destined to fight the Civil War.

The first quarter of the nineteenth century continued the slow evolutionary change in the class of men elected to the General Assembly. Virginians like John Tyler still left the United States Senate to sit in the governor's chair in Richmond or return to the assembly. Linn Banks happily served twenty consecutive terms as Speaker of the Virginia house and moved "up" to Washington as a member of Congress only after the Whigs deposed him in the 1830s. The "road to power" for the members of the assembly in the early 1820s differed little from that traveled in the eighteenth century, and many of the same sort of men continued to seek office. The makeup of the constitutional convention that met at the end of the decade reflected the political stasis of the Jeffersonian Republican center and the modest transformation that had taken place in the social origins of the Virginia political elite during the era.[40]

Government in the commonwealth emanated from the counties, and it was there that a young Virginian nurtured his political career. Although the power of the county courts waned, they continued to provide the arena in which most future legislators first made their political reputations. Elections were on court days, and justices appointed those who oversaw the procedure. Most of the members of the assembly concurrently served on the county courts. At the beginning of this period, 55 percent of the members of the House of Delegates were justices; near the end 45 percent held that position. Virginia's legislators continued to owe their election to reputation and respectability within the counties they represented.

These commodities were generally purchased with the coin of education, wealth, and family connection. Most Virginia politicians were planters or farmers, and a large proportion owned slaves. Lawyers made up the only other large occupational group in the assembly, but professions in antebellum America were not so distinct as they have become. Men who read law or studied medicine did not always practice. Those who did very often owned slaves and plantations as well. A separate capitalist class of men who invested only in banks, railroads, and manufacturing enterprises did not exist. Local studies reveal the multifaceted nature of local "capitalists'" investments and the readiness of many planters to purchase bank stocks and dabble in manufacturing, although only very few men in the state owned stock in corporations of any kind.[41]

At the time of the formation of the new nation, large planters dominated the Old Dominion's political elite, and only a handful of nonslaveholders held office. By 1850, although the commonwealth continued to be controlled by slaveholders, the number and relative importance of nonslaveholders had increased dramatically (table 5.4). Thirty-six percent of the men who served in the constitutional convention and the General Assembly in 1850–51 had no slaves. The proportion of planters declined to below one-fourth, and only one in twenty of Virginia's political leaders owned over fifty slaves. Obviously planter power deteriorated, and the well-to-do small slaveholders seized control of the commonwealth's political course.[42]

By the 1830s and 1840s, the House of Delegates gradually had grown to mirror the electorate more closely than it had during the previous generation. The typical legislator in 1850 owned far more property of all kinds than the average Virginian and was more likely to be a professional or substantial farmer. Those who owned slaves typically held about twice as many as the average slaveholder in the commonwealth. But the proportion of nonslaveholders in the House of Delegates had grown, and most of the slaveholders owned too few slaves to be

Table 5.4. Slaveholding of the political elite, 1788–1861 (in %)

Slaves	1788–91	1829–31	1850–51	1860–61
None	3	18	36	28
1–9	28	34	24	32
10–19	22	17	18	16
20–49	35	23	17	18
50+	13	8	5	5
$N =$	(276)	(225)	(287)	(363)

Sources: Norman K. Risjord, "Virginians and the Constitution: A Multivariant Analysis," *William and Mary Quarterly* 31 (1974): 618; Alison G. Freehling, *Drift toward Dissolution: The Virginia Slavery Debate of 1831–1832* (Baton Rouge, La., 1982), 272–78; Robert P. Sutton, *From Revolution to Secession: Constitution Making in the Old Dominion* (Charlottesville, Va., 1989), 182–250; Ralph A. Wooster, *Politicians, Planters, and Plain Folk: Courthouse and Statehouse in the Upper South, 1850–1860* (Knoxville, Tenn., 1975), 163; Wooster, *The Secession Conventions of the South* (Princeton, N.J., 1962), 145. The Risjord figures are reported slightly differently for the small slaveholders, using categories of 0–5, 6–12, and 13–24.

considered planters (table 5.5). The legislative leaders were slightly older and wealthier than the average member, and planters were both overrepresented and more powerful than their numbers would dictate, but the men who governed antebellum Virginia were predominately small slaveholders.

Members of the House of Delegates were substantial men, respected in their county communities. As economic historians have pointed out, owning just a single slave made a southern farmer twice as wealthy as his northern counterpart, and the average slaveholder was "more than ten times as wealthy as the average non-slaveholding Southern farmer." While most politicians were not the great planters of the plantation legend, Virginia's antebellum legislators were economically secure and personally interested in the peculiar institution.[43]

From the time of the ratification of the Constitution, two slow evolutionary changes affected the makeup of the Old Dominion's political elite. Both reflected the larger social changes taking place within the commonwealth and constituted an element of the democratization of its government. By mid-century the men who held power in Virginia were more occupationally diverse and more distinctly middle-class than the Founding Fathers. In the late eighteenth century every legislator was connected to the land; by the mid-nineteenth century, while the Old Dominion still had a predominantly agricultural economy, many lawyers and businessmen had joined the political elite. Although the legislators were still predominately slave owners in 1850, far fewer were planters and a larger proportion of nonslaveholders sat in their midst.

The 1830s marked a watershed in the gradual decline in the average wealth of the members. Since slaves were used primarily as agricultural laborers, the increase in the proportion of nonslaveholders serving in the legislature also reflected the diversification of the Virginia economy. Planters and farmers made up from two-thirds to three-quarters of the elite in the late eighteenth century. Although the commonwealth continued to be a major agricultural producer in 1850, only half of the legislators were solely identified with agriculture. Of course, many of the lawyers and "others" served the farmers and planters, but their occupations spoke of a much more complex economy than had existed in the eighteenth century. Half of the members of Virginia's General Assembly designated themselves in the census as lawyers, physicians, and merchants, but there were also "two tavern keepers, one salt maker, one ferryman, one miller, one hotel keeper, one laborer, one carpenter, one saddler, one surveyor, one student, one blacksmith, and one who gave his occupation as 'legislator.'"[44]

Antebellum elections in the Old Dominion were not class struggles pitting candidates drawn from one stratum of wealth against those from another. In each constituency the contestants tended to resemble each other. Neither party ran yeomen farmers for Southside seats or put forth wan, effete planters in the rugged western districts. The losers generally came from the same social status and background as the winners. When Thomas Jefferson Randolph and Alexander Rives defeated Valentine Southall and Thomas W. Gilmer in 1835, it was neither their first encounter nor their last. They traded the Albemarle seats through the 1830s and into the 1840s. Needless to say, their social position and reputations in and around Charlottesville were beyond question.

Reputation was the key to electoral success, but during these years party fidelity replaced family association as a major element of reputation. In contested constituencies the same contenders often competed in a series of elections, sometimes handing the seat back and forth in successive years. While personal character continued to count, partisan commitment became increasingly

Table 5.5. Slaveholding status of members of the House of Delegates, 1788–1860 (in %)

Status	1790s	1831	1850	1860
Nonslaveholder	8	26	35	37
Small-holder	63	57	43	41
Planter	29	18	22	22
N=	(172)	(129)	(135)	(157)

Sources: Richard B. Beeman, *The Old Dominion and the New Nation, 1788–1801* (Lexington, Ky., 1972), 249–67; Freehling, *Drift toward Dissolution*, 272–78; Wooster, *Politicians, Planters, and Plain Folk*, 163.

Table 5.6. Partisan affiliation and social status in the General Assembly, 1850–51 (in %)

	Democrats	Whigs
Occupation		
Planter-farmers	71	34
Lawyers	15	36
Others	13	29
N=	(91)	(58)
Slaves		
Nonslaveholders	22	29
Small-holders	47	52
Planters	31	19
N=	(90)	(63)
Landholding		
None	12	25
Under $5,000	31	35
$5,000–$25,000	50	28
Over $25,000	7	12
N=	(84)	(57)

Source: Wooster, *Politicians, Planters, and Plain Folk*, 147, 154, 163.

important. The modest shifts in county elections for the assembly were correlated with similar shifts in the county's response to congressional and presidential elections. The process began with the political elite seeking consistent support within their own group and rewarding those who played the party game by the new rules; then partisan identification trickled down to the voters who slowly perceived their stake in the game as they were told over and over that their votes mattered.[45]

Although both of the new parties drew their candidates from the socioeconomic elite, the Whig and Democratic leaders differed in crucial ways that characterized the second party system in Virginia. Starkly put, the Democrats tended to be slaveholding planter-farmers while the Whigs epitomized the emerging bourgeoisie (table 5.6). The members of the Old Dominion's antebellum political elite who were only planters or farmers overwhelmingly adhered to the Democratic party. Three-fourths of this group were Democrats. The clustering of Whigs outside of agriculture was most pronounced among the men who represented the eastern half of the Old Dominion dominated by plantation agriculture and slave society. As a consequence, Democratic leaders were much more likely than Whigs to be slaveholders and, if slaveholders, more likely to own large numbers of bondsmen.

A similar pattern held for the Virginia legislators at midcentury and stands in striking contrast to conventional wisdom. Although they were slightly older than their opponents, Whig leaders were less wealthy, possessing less land and fewer slaves than their more agriculturally oriented Democratic opponents. A larger proportion of Democratic legislators owned both land and slaves and thus were implicated in the traditional social order. Three-quarters of the Democratic assemblymen in the Old Dominion in 1850 were planters or farmers while three-fifths of the Whigs were not. A higher proportion of Whigs held no slaves, while planters were much more inclined to be Democrats and assume a greater place in party councils.

Although lawyers played an important role in the politics of Virginia and could be found in both parties, a significantly larger proportion of Whigs than Democrats were lawyers. Only one-fourth of the Democratic legislators practiced before the bar, while 36 percent of the Whigs were lawyers, and these Whig lawyers less often mixed the law with agricultural pursuits and were more likely to be town dwellers. Of the nine lawyer-planters, seven were Democrats. Nearly all of the physicians—seven of eight—were Whigs who were either slaveless or held fewer than five slaves; the one Democratic doctor was also a planter with thirty-seven slaves. Among the merchant legislators, who were often economically tied to the plantation economy, Democrats outnumbered the Whigs five to one.[46]

Society was becoming more complex and the economy more diversified as small towns proliferated, cities grew and a larger nonagricultural sector appeared. The Whigs tended to be "cosmopolitans," who embraced the developing society that was increasingly dependent on the web of expanding market relationships. The party elite included a significant number of men with occupations outside agriculture. Most Democratic legislators were "locals" bound to traditional society: either the backcountry commercial farmers or the market-oriented eastern planters, each in their way profoundly self-sufficient and to a degree psychologically isolated.

The growing influence of parties in the government of Virginia during these years can be seen in the behavior of the members of the House of Delegates. In the early decades of the nineteenth century everyone claimed to be a Republican of some sort, but it is impossible to label precisely most of the members of the House of Delegates in the 1820s and early 1830s. Men did not run for office as members of a party, nor did they vote in a partisan fashion on roll calls. Divisions, when they appeared, were short-lived and reflected regional and local rather than partisan allegiances. The controversies over constitutional reform, slavery and colonization, and nullification were clearly and rather simply sectional. The apportionment of legislative power discriminated against the counties west of the Blue Ridge. The profits and problems associated with slavery and the presence of the quasi-free blacks weighed most heavily on the minds of eastern delegates, who for that reason alone were most jealous of the rights of the states.

The ad hoc, issue-specific behavior of the Virginia legislators was reflected in the session that met in Richmond in December 1831 amid the crisis spawned by Nat Turner's insurrection. The election for the assembly had been nonpartisan and differed little from those that took place in the 1820s. The choice of legislative officers at the opening of the session in no way indicated the existence of partisan conflict. Linn Banks, who had been Speaker since 1818, defeated fellow Jacksonian James H. Gholson by a three-to-one margin. The state printing contract went once again to Thomas Ritchie with only one dissenting vote. The closest contest was for the governor's council between Jacksonian stalwarts Peter V. Daniel and William C. Rives. The house preferred Rives, but a two-to-one majority in the senate elected Daniel.[47]

The roll calls connected directly with the great debate on slavery that occurred in this session showed high levels both of sectional cohesion and of conflict between the east and the west, but the entire array of votes on all questions in the 1831–32 session of the House of Delegates reveals the limitations of a sectional analysis of the governing process at the time. There were not many roll calls—only fifty-one—taken in the session. Most of the members' responses were highly individualistic. A collection of local responses, in which men representing contiguous constituencies voted together, produced the appearance of intrastate sectionalism, but often there were no easily discernible patterns at all. Nine-tenths of the western members of the house voted together on six roll calls relating to slavery, two on internal improvements, and one on education, but on other matters they were less cohesive. The larger, more heterogeneous group of representatives from the east split more often than did the westerners.[48]

The twenty-five delegates from the counties that had voted for Adams in the 1828 presidential election tended to vote together, and not too surprisingly they were generally antislavery, for internal improvements, and in favor of state aid to the counties for education. They had almost exactly the same mean cohesion as the western delegates and the same percentage of roll calls with high cohesion. The two groups clearly overlapped, and the members from the pro-Adams counties were essentially a subset of the western contingent. No such cohesion marked the diverse group of representatives from the numerous counties that had voted for Jackson in 1828. Local considerations and personal connections rather than either sectionalism or partisanship played a major role in determining the way these members voted.

The nullification crisis that flared up the following year divided the House of Delegates into the State-Rights "party" and the Unionists, who reflected once again a rough sectional split between the center and the periphery. Aside from mildly supporting South Carolina and censuring Jackson, the eastern State-Rights majority reelected John Tyler as senator over westerner James McDowell. A letter from the editor of the *Richmond Whig*, John Hampden Pleasants, to Tyler in 1833 reveals the fragmented state of the Virginia assembly at the time. Pleasants mentioned the activities of "State-rights" men, the "Clay party," "Federalists," and "Jackson men," but the editor became more specific in his discussion of the resolutions introduced by William H. Brodnax supporting South Carolina and affirming in principle the right of secession. According to Pleasants: "There are three parties, and some shades of other parties, on the subject in the General Assembly. 1, The honest State-rights men, who are determined to stand up for their principles, though Jackson stands at the door. They go for Brodnax's. 2. The honest Federalists and latitudinarians, who are willing to intervene in the most efficient manner, but are opposed to State rights, and not opposed to the doctrines of the proclamation. 3, The train-bands—the Swiss—the mean dogs who obey the guidance of Ritchie & Co.—who are long professors of the faith, would sacrifice all rather than incur the displeasure of their hero." It is not hard to see where Pleasants stood on the issue, or that he and Ritchie were more than editorial rivals. What is also clear is that Pleasants used the term *party* primarily in an issue-specific fashion that related to only a few roll calls, not in its more modern institutional sense.[49]

The development of partisanship in the Virginia assembly went through two stages. In the mid-1830s when party labels first appeared in the public press, the major areas of conflict involved differences over federal politics as the instruction and election of senators took up the lion's share of the legislature's time. In 1835–36 more than one quarter of the roll calls related to these matters sharply divided the legislature into unified blocs of Democrats and Whigs. The response to the abolitionist threat proved only slightly less contentious and nearly as time-consuming. This fight took place at the same time that Congress was debating proposals that led eventually to the gag rule. But that too was a matter of factions fighting for control of the government rather than partisan policy making. Whigs pushed the issue primarily to embarrass Van Buren.[50]

While the division between Whigs and Democrats on the national level involved the Jacksonian effort to dismantle the American System, questions concerning the economic development of the commonwealth were far less partisan. Jackson's supporters were, in fact, deeply entwined in the commonwealth's conservative banking system. In the mid-1830s the clearest conflict between the Whigs and Democrats came on roll calls related to elections and federal matters such as instructions to the senators to vote for the "expunging" resolution that would remove the previous session's censure of Jackson from the Senate's journal. Fourteen roll calls concerning slavery and black rights—in this case

Table 5.7. Roll-call votes on public policy questions in the House of Delegates, 1835–49

Policy sphere*	Conflict Roll Calls			
	1835–36	1840–41	1845–46	1848–49
Government	28	63	31	22
Fiscal	0	12	12	19
Commerce	28	24	29	55
Social mores	24	16	30	8
Other	1	20	6	23
Total	81	135	108	127**

*The categories follow those in Ballard Campbell, *Representative Democracy: Public Policy and Midwestern Legislatures in the Late Nineteenth Century* (Cambridge, Mass., 1980), 54–78.

** A large number of roll calls (157) on the revision of probate laws and the judicial code were excluded to make the figures comparable.

response to the growth of abolitionism that had been emphasized in Governor Tazewell's message—showed slightly less dissension, but they were clearly partisan. In contrast, the twenty-six votes on banking and internal improvements reflected little party-based disagreement on economic issues.

The depression following the panic of 1837 combined with the institutional development of both parties to alter the situation in the assembly. The late 1830s served as a watershed in public policy as well as electoral behavior in the Old Dominion (table 5.7). In the 1835–36 session indications of the future tendencies of the developing parties lay beneath the surface consensus. The relatively low mean indices of party disagreement resulted from several anomalous votes. In general, the Whigs united in favor of the expansion of credit facilities in the western part of the state, but the majority of the Democrats were much more cautious. The Democrats generally split fairly evenly on internal improvements while over two-thirds of the Whigs consistently favored governmental aid to transportation projects.[51]

Thus, even before the panic Whigs tended to be more eager to expand banking facilities than the Democrats. As economic conditions worsened, anti-bank sentiment within the Democratic party grew, and the probank Conservatives became an increasingly isolated minority eventually forced to join the Whigs. From their sweeping victory in 1838 until their loss in 1842, the Whigs held the House of Delegates, although the common Democratic majorities in the state senate sometimes stymied their initiatives. Voting during the 1840–41 session when Whig power reached its zenith produced more broadly partisan

Table 5.8. Partisan cohesion and conflict on roll-call votes in the House of Delegates, 1835–49

	1835–36	1840–41	1845–46	1848–49
Mean Democratic cohesion	59	54	35	35
Mean Whig cohesion	50	64	44	42
Mean party dissimilarity	48	50	28	28

results than in the mid-1830s (table 5.8). Issues concerning both the federal and state government that directly affected party control continued to be crucial. The sixteen roll calls on the election of a United States senator were complicated by a split in Democratic ranks but featured a high degree of partisanship. Twenty-five contested elections and the nineteen appointments show similar sharp divisions. Banking and currency, however, provided the primary focus of partisan concern over the deteriorating economic situation (table 5.9).[52]

Partisan interpretations of the nation's economic problems revolved around the credit system, and consequently the solutions offered and the symbolism to which politicians appealed centered on banks. Through the twelve roll calls concerning the issue, the Whigs consistently supported state banks, and Democrats opposed them. The influence of party, however, affected nearly all of the assembly's business, and both Democrats and Whigs were associated with fairly clear policy preferences in state affairs and connections with their

Table 5.9. Issue voting and partisan conflict on roll calls in the House of Delegates, 1835–49

	1835–36		1840–41		1845–46		1848–49	
Policy type	No.	IPD*	No.	IPD	No.	IPD	Np.	IPD
Politics**	25	81	64	63	15	58	21	61
Banking	10	36	12	73	1	70	12	60
Transportation	16	24	10	38	23	23	42	14
Taxation			9	32	8	35	13	16
Slavery	17	59	7	34	1	53	5	25
Education	5	12	2	29	26	19	3	31
Constitution					8	17		

*IPD=Index of party dissimilarity.

**Contested elections and resolutions on national questions.

fellow partisans throughout the country. Questions relating to slavery and black rights, fiscal matters, and internal improvements all showed party conflict.[53]

By 1840–41 the polarization over banking and related matters provided the clearest contrast with earlier legislators' behavior. Party differences on these issues stood out as sharply as on the selection of senators. On small notes and the limits of stockholder liability, 95 percent of the Whigs opposed 85 percent of the Democrats. Fiscal proposals separated the parties less starkly, but the Whigs passed a new tax law that relied on land and slaves as a source of revenue, and a slight majority of the Democrats joined them to beat back the planters' attempts to lower rates on both. Internal improvements also produced more party conflict than in the 1830s. Excluding the roll calls on building local roads, there was a fairly high level of party disagreement. Generally Whigs were the prorailroad party while the Democrats split, with the majority opposing their extension.[54]

Matters directly relating to controlling the government—appointments, elections, and instructions—continued to be distinctly partisan and to take up about half of the legislators' time. The Whigs returned Rives to the Senate and chose William S. Archer, a former Jacksonian congressman, to replace the incumbent Democrat, William H. Roane. In both cases the division followed party lines; although the minority Democrats had trouble deciding on a single candidate, none of the Democrats voted for either Rives or Archer. From the organization of the House of Delegates through a string of appointments, Whigs squared off against Democrats and elected their fellow partisans, to the feigned horror of the Democratic press.[55]

The slavery issue invaded the assembly in 1840–41 after New York's Whig governor, William Seward, refused to extradite two black seamen who had attempted to aid a Virginia runaway, leading to a heated exchange with Virginia governor Thomas W. Gilmer, who was ostensibly a Whig. The Democrats were highly unified in supporting a hard line in defense of the constitutional rights of the state. In this they sustained the governor against his own party. The majority of Whigs favored a more conciliatory stance.[56]

The differences between Whigs and Democrats on public education were more subtle than the gross tabulation of roll calls indicates. An 1829 law provided for a "district free-school system," but county courts generally refused to tax themselves to set up school districts, and public education in the Old Dominion remained limited to support of indigent students. The state's high rate of illiteracy became the focus of successive messages at the end of the 1830s by Conservative governor David Campbell, who urged the assembly to reform the system. Outside the legislature education conventions met in 1839 and 1841, reflecting popular concern over education that was particularly strong in the west.[57]

While these conventions were nonpartisan and supported by newspapers from both parties, Whigs took the lead in the movement for reform. At the Lexington education convention in 1841, the Reverend Henry Ruffner put forward a plan to establish a common school system funded by a special tax that would finance a state board of education, establish a system of normal schools, and provide libraries in each new school. In his annual message Whig governor John Rutherford proposed a broad program of development of public and private education at all levels that emphasized a common school system for all white children similar to those in the North. Finally, Senator Rives, acting as a private citizen, presented to the legislature a memorial from the 1842 Richmond convention with his personal appeal for action.

In response the Whig-dominated house voted to devote the monies from the distribution of the surplus revenue from the tariff and the sale of public lands to education and passed a bill to establish a state system along the lines suggested in these various proposals. The vote on the use of federal funds was strictly partisan, but one-third of the Democrats joined in supporting common schools. The *Enquirer* and a few other Democratic papers opposed distribution yet endorsed reform, but the Democrats in the state senate killed the measure.[58]

Whig control of the House of Delegates ended abruptly in 1842, and the party was able to win a majority only once again over the course of the decade. The Democrats consistently held about 55 percent of the seats during these years, but the Whigs functioned as a viable minority, and partisanship continued to structure members' behavior throughout the decade. The election of a senator to replace Rives in 1845 unified the Democrats in favor of westerner Isaac Pennybacker. The only roll call dealing with banking, one on slavery, and two on appointments also displayed clear party conflict. In the mid-1840s, however, these issues were increasingly overwhelmed by roll calls on matters that had traditionally been local or sectional. Internal improvements and education accounted for nearly half of all the roll calls taken in the 1845–46 session when the Democrats regained complete control of the assembly. On both of these issues, and the question of a constitutional convention, the parties were split, and conflict was muted.[59]

In principle, both parties supported school reform, but the relatively low level of party disagreement masks the same divergence over policy seen in earlier sessions. In 1845 an eclectic State Educational Convention met at Richmond and reached a consensus on the need for "a more enlarged, energetic and liberal system of primary schools." The specific recommendations, however, shied away from the Ruffner plan and simply encouraged the assembly to act. The

Democratic legislature then passed a modest reform measure in 1846, far short of the Whig proposals, that allowed any county to establish a free school if two-thirds of the eligible voters supported the idea in a referendum and were willing to tax themselves to pay for it.[60]

In the session of 1848 – 49, this modified partisan pattern continued to prevail, and the degree of party conflict and cohesion changed only slightly. Banking and currency, national resolutions, and appointments and elections still engendered disagreement between Democrats and Whigs. Removing the roll calls on internal improvements would drive the mean partisan difference up to exactly the level of 1835 – 36 and just below that of 1840 – 41. Thus, issues on which clear sectional or local interests were at stake tempered the effects of partisanship while Whigs and Democrats continued to fight bitterly over appointments, policy matters, and the "principles" proclaimed in the party press that had differentiated the two parties for a decade.

With the return of prosperity, it was difficult for Democrats to resist the demands of their constituents. Public interest in internal improvements and the creation of corporations increased dramatically as economic conditions improved. The cleavage roll calls devoted to such matters, which made up one-fifth of the total in the mid-1830s, accounted for nearly 40 percent by the late 1840s. Such proposals split both parties although the Democrats suffered most on these issues. Traditionally the party of Jackson had opposed active government in the Old Dominion as well as the nation. Its members had inherited an antigovernmental tradition from the Old Republicans and exhibited it in the constitutional convention of 1850 – 51 where they attempted to circumscribe legislative power in every way possible. On the other hand, Whigs generally favored internal improvements, and party unity prevailed on roll calls concerning these measures.[61]

From the mid-1830s through the 1840s, partisanship dominated the assembly's activities, although tension often existed between members' allegiance to their constituents' interests and adherence to party regularity. The two parties put forth different partisan agendas and defined the contested issues differently. The number of roll calls devoted to salient cleavage issues was less meaningful than the partisans' understanding of their importance.

Those questions that can be termed party issues in Virginia during these years were the same that distinguished Democrats from Whigs throughout the country. The degree of disputation they engendered and the symbolism in which these issues were enveloped reflected similar concerns. Two of the characteristics that separated the second party system from the first were its penetration into state politics and the uniformity of its policy prescriptions from Maine to Mississippi. Not only did the parameters of party conflict in the Old Dominion resemble those in North Carolina, Kentucky, and Tennessee but also, to a startling degree, those of Illinois, Pennsylvania, New York, and even Massachusetts.[62]

The credit system based on charted banks of issue became the central economic issue in Virginia politics during these years. At several points during the depression years, banks suspended specie payments and sought temporary relief from the assembly. The parties divided into hostile camps on these matters, with the Whigs showing both a willingness to tolerate suspension for limited periods and an overall desire to expand credit facilities to encourage economic activity. The Democrats opposed both and in general took a hard money position. The majority of the party opposed the "special privileges" implied in incorporation of banks and wished to eliminate paper currency other than certificates of deposit or notes in large denominations — over $20.

While the Whigs spoke primarily in terms of economic development, the Democrats attacked the morality of banks, paper money, and soulless corporations. Their antigovernmentalism appealed to republican purity rather than classical economics. The Whigs were generally united, but the Democrats were plagued by factionalism. In 1837 and 1838 the Conservative Democrats joined with the Whigs to oppose the Sub-Treasury in Congress and to support state institutions in the assembly. In the votes on chartering banks or providing them with relief, Whigs were usually far more cohesive than the Democrats, who harbored a small number of "softs" who were ambivalent on the issue in line with the concerns of their constituents. Eventually the soft faction frustrated the Democratic majority, joining with the Whigs to pass a free banking law in 1851 that permitted the general incorporation of banks of issue under state authority without the taint of special privilege that characterized earlier laws.[63]

Most Democrats complained bitterly about the burden of state debt, wishing to dismantle the public works and limit the legislature's power to borrow money for development projects, but local and regional interests played a central role in the legislators' response to internal improvements, muting the effects of party. The general orientations of the Whigs and Democrats reflected those seen on the banking issue. After 1839 there was more clearly partisan conflict on internal improvements, and on occasion roll calls showed impressive Whig unity. Throughout the period Whigs favored the big-ticket items in transportation like turnpikes and railroads. They advocated government action on these matters and the reconstruction of the credit system at both the federal and state level. This developmental perspective also appeared in their advocacy of bankruptcy legislation and stay laws. At the same time the Whigs supported the federal bankruptcy law of 1841, they pushed for a similar state statute. The Democrats closed ranks against both, emphasizing again moral rather than economic arguments in tune with the party's general appeal to agrarian, bucolic symbolism that was used by the planters, like the proslavery argument, to retain the allegiance of the nonslaveholding small farmers.[64]

In its general outlines the call for educational reform was bipartisan. Both Whig and Democratic governors urged the assembly to address the problem, and a coalition of prominent members of both parties presided over the 1845 state convention. The major organs of both parties, the *Whig* and the *Enquirer*, consistently called for change, and the moderate 1846 legislation was pushed through an assembly dominated by the Democrats with the support of both parties. Beneath this surface consensus, however, lay clear differences between the Whigs and the Democrats over the type of system needed by the Old Dominion.

By 1840 a majority of school-age white children lived west of the Blue Ridge where there were half the number of primary and common schools as in the east and only a handful of academies. The planters preferred academy educa-tion for their children and resisted any form of further taxation of their property. As a writer in the *Southern Literary Messenger* pointed out, the old system permitted the county commissioners to use any state money left from the pauper schools for the academies and colleges in the county. "It is clear that our government had done nothing substantial except for the wealthy and the paupers." The eastern planters resisted education on the model of New York and Massachusetts, which was supported mainly by "the middling portion of the community."[65]

The Whigs hoped for federal aid, in the form of the distribution of the surplus revenue, to establish a common school system in the state modeled on those of the North. In 1845 the minority report of the State Education Convention, signed by Whigs Samuel Janney and Daniel N. Edgerton, argued that even with no increase in funds, the system should be changed to remove the "odious distinction between the rich and the poor and establish "equality . . . appropriate to our Republican institutions," to provide for teacher exams and normal schools and to have commissioners select the textbooks. They hoped also that the assembly would reconsider the Ruffner plan and make the school commissioners elective.

Throughout this period it was Whigs in the assembly who continually advocated better teacher-training institutions and were critical of the privileged place of the University of Virginia. As the *Whig* noted at one point, the Democrats liked the traditional system "because it was cheap." A faction in the party wanted to get rid of the Literary Fund altogether. At various times in the midst of debate, William O. Goode and Lewis Harvie both introduced amendments to this effect and received the votes of fifteen to twenty of their Democratic colleagues. In the end the Democrats refused to accept the necessary taxes and the centralization implied in the office of a state superintendent of education.[66]

Common schools formed the basis for both economic development and moral uplift. In their efforts to encourage common schools, the educational reformers directly connected the questions of education and temperance. The *Whig* believed that "the temperance crusade is dependent upon general Education." The antiliquor movement in Virginia had drawn its early leaders from the elite of Jeffersonian society. Many of the same men who were colonizationists were advocates of moderation and members of the American Temperance Society, but by the 1840s as the emphasis shifted from temperance to prohibition, the movement became dominated by Whigs.[67]

The *Enquirer* gave temperance only lukewarm support and bitterly opposed prohibition. Governor McDowell hurt his reputation with his party by presiding over the state temperance convention in 1844, while young Whigs like Waitman Willey and Thomas Galley built their careers on activity in the Sons of Temperance, established to push prohibition in the late 1840s. In 1842 the Whigs forced through the assembly a law prohibiting distillers from retailing ardent spirits; then, when they briefly held control of the house three years later, the Whigs led the fight securing a local option law similar to that of New York. Such connections allowed the Democratic papers, always interested in tarring their opponents with the abolition brush, to call it a Whig "plot" and the outspoken proslavery Democrat Muscoe R. H. Garnett to refer to prohibition as a "bantling of Northern Yankees and Slavery agitators."[68]

The development of partisanship in the Virginia legislature thus followed familiar lines as Whigs and Democrats favored and opposed legislation in a pattern similar to Whigs and Democrats in the other states of the Union. When the major national issues of the day intruded into the assembly, they defined the differences between the parties. The key contrast between the Whigs and the Democrats on state policy involved the Democratic disdain for government activity in general and taxes in particular. The Whigs were the party of "tax and spend" while the Democrats were advocates of "retrenchment and reform." The latter claimed that they wished to spread the burden beyond land and slaves, especially to the symbols of the "money power," such as corporate and public stock. But basically this was a guise to sustain cutting taxes generally; there were just not enough pianofortes or bank shares in Virginia to balance out a substitute for a lower rate on slaves.

The Democrats also opposed building institutions. The Whigs not only wanted schools with certified teachers and an educational bureaucracy but also the geological survey and the expansion of the state lunatic asylum that they consistently supported against the cost-conscious Democrats. More fundamentally the puritanical Whigs encouraged regulating the sale of alcohol and eventually its total prohibition. Middle-class moral reform upheld by the authority of the state appealed much more readily to the bourgeois Whigs than to agrarian Democrats, who advocated personal liberty in moral as well as economic affairs. When it came to public policy, the antebellum Democrats were the party of laissez-faire—limited government and low taxes—while the Whigs were much more eager to channel entrepreneurial energy and restrain individual license.

From the mid-1830s into the 1850s, the main issues defining the parties were national. It was in relation to elections, appointments, and resolutions on federal affairs, including states' rights, that partisanship spread into the state legislature and determined the patterns of voting behavior in the Virginia General Assembly. Year after year federal relations called forth disciplined responses in the legislative party battle that reflected the partisan imperative structuring congressional behavior at the time. Virginia legislators responded as either Whigs or Democrats following the national party line and sharing similar policy perspectives with fellow party members in the other states of the Union.

There can be no doubt that sectionalism had its influences, but this is easy to exaggerate looking back through the prism of the Civil War. The debates over slavery consistently intruded into the assembly, but only on occasion did these discussions take textbook form. In general, the Whigs tended to be more permissive than their Democratic opponents in the area of slave privileges and the rights of free blacks. But most of the legislative discussion of slavery had little to do with either. Whigs and Democrats differed in their response to challenges to the peculiar institution. Most slavery-related roll calls concerned national resolutions, and on these Virginians resembled their fellow partisans in the other states of the upper South.

While these distinctions may strike the modern observer as obtuse, they were clear to contemporaries and differentiated the parties in their adherents' minds. The divergence between Democrats and Whigs involved a collection of both sharp contrasts and more subtle but nonetheless real partisan inclinations about the economic and social course of the commonwealth. This amalgam of policies, symbols, and preferences that spelled out the meaning of being a Whig or a Democrat in the Old Dominion closely resembled the Whig and Democratic persuasions that appeared across antebellum America in the party press and the countless political appeals from the stump.

∾6∾

A Review of
the Slave Question

WHILE PARTY FORMATION in Virginia followed patterns similar to those in the rest of the country, and Whigs and Democrats in the Old Dominion came into conflict on issues similar to those debated elsewhere, they also differed on the slavery issue. The nuances of the slavery debate that could be heard as well in the discourse of the other states of the upper South suggest a lost intellectual world irrevocably altered by the Civil War and nearly beyond contemporary comprehension. In 1861 William Ballard Preston, one of Virginia's best-known Whigs, moved that the commonwealth rescind its ratification of the Constitution and secede from the Union. Thirty years earlier, as a twenty-six-year-old member of the House of Delegates, he initiated the most important southern legislative debate on slavery with a motion that clearly implied his advocacy of the gradual abolition of the peculiar institution from the Old Dominion. Like nearly all Virginians of his day, however, young Preston was unable to conceive of an end to slavery without provision for the removal of the freed blacks.

For three-quarters of a century, the feasibility of colonization lay at the center of the controversy over slavery in the Old Dominion and epitomized the paradoxical position of the commonwealth's planter republicans. In *Notes on the State of Virginia*, Jefferson argued that the peculiar institution debased the slaveholders and stood as an affront to the most fundamental ideals of republicanism. He implored his fellow Virginians to adopt gradual emancipation for their own good. But this forced Jefferson to consider the "physical and moral" differences between the races that dictated the deportation of those freed. "Deep rooted prejudices entertained by whites" and "ten thousand recollections by blacks, of the injuries they have sustained" made colonization necessary, since such sentiments would divide Virginians "into parties and produce convulsions" that would result "in the extermination of one or the other race."[1]

Throughout his life Jefferson continued to emphasize the abhorrent effects of slavery on his fellow whites and to search for a "practicable" plan of gradual

William Ballard Preston. (Courtesy of the Virginia Historical Society)

Nathaniel Beverley Tucker. (Courtesy of the College of William and Mary)

Henry Ruffner. (Courtesy of the Virginia Historical Society)

emancipation and colonization. While he approved of the work of the American Colonization Society (ACS), Jefferson considered that the immense cost of compensation—"thirty-six millions of dollars a year for twenty-five years"—made it "impossible to look at the question a second time." His plan of "emancipating the after born" seemed the only viable alternative. The babies could be given by their owners to the state gratis or in partial payment of their taxes and the expenses for their maintenance and transportation out of the state could come from federal public land revenues. This combination of gradualism and colonization would allow whites to reclaim their "physical and moral characters" at the small price of the "constitutional scruples" of some strict constructionists.[2]

James Madison generally agreed with his friend but was more sanguine about the prospects of the ACS. He became a life member when the society was formed and later served briefly as its president. Madison also assumed that the "existing and probably unalterable prejudices in the U.S." necessitated removal of the freedmen, but he concluded that the cost—Madison's estimate of "600 millions of dollars" was a good deal lower than Jefferson's—could be covered by the sale of one-third of the public lands.[3]

After he received Thomas R. Dew's powerful attack on colonization in 1832, Madison reasserted his earlier arguments in a letter to the young William and Mary political economist, insisting that Virginia's depressed economic condition resulted from the effects of slavery and the state of the market for Virginia's staple products rather than the tariff. "If emancipation was the sole object, the extinguishment of slavery, would be easy, cheap & compleat." The necessity of deportation made ending slavery difficult, but for Madison it remained a great "National object" that must be attempted. Yet as he neared death, Madison despaired over the subject. Colonization floundered because of black resistance, lack of adequate funding, and the advent of immediatism in the North drove public opinion in the Old Dominion toward a "torpid acquiescence" in the perpetual nature of the peculiar institution.[4]

From the 1830s through the Civil War, the ideology of slavery became, in the words of the proslavery conservative Judge Abel P. Upshur, "the great distinguishing characteristic of the Southern states" and the central focus of an emerging sectional self-consciousness. Men like Dew and Upshur shifted the argument away from the impracticality of emancipation and insisted that such a policy would be both unnecessary and unwise. Yet, at the time of Upshur's death in 1844, the argument that slavery was a positive good still represented a minority perspective among Virginia's proslavery writers. Moderate critics of slavery, concerned mainly with "the injuries slavery inflicts on the whites," continued to gain a respectful hearing in the Old Dominion and represented the outlook of the majority west of the Blue Ridge.[5]

Both Whigs and Democrats defended the peculiar institution against abolitionist attacks and attempted to portray their opponents as enemies of the people, but the emphasis on these points of consensus ignores conflicts within the
Old Dominion over the elements that made up the slavery issue—sufficiently
important to lead to the murder of the editor of the *Richmond Whig* by his
Democratic editorial opponent at the *Enquirer* in a duel. Both parties in Virginia played the politics of slavery; in so doing they differed from their northern
counterparts, but they also differed from each other in significant ways. Democrats tended toward the acceptance of the positive good argument, while the
Whigs clustered closer to that portion of the spectrum which accepted conditional emancipation at some undefined distant date and the melioration of the
plight of the slave.[6]

The Old Dominion had the largest free black population of any state in the
Union, and Virginians played a crucial role in the founding of the American
Colonization Society. The idea had been suggested to friends by Virginia congressman Charles Fenton Mercer, who became a tireless worker for colonization and a driving force in the ACS during the 1820s. Supreme Court justice
Bushrod Washington was the first president of the organization, and its initial
vice presidents included Senator John Randolph and the "philosopher of Jeffersonian Democracy," John Taylor. Madison, Monroe, Marshall, John Hartwell
Cocke, and the Reverend William Meade were all life members.[7]

While some men who later favored emancipation joined the ACS, nearly
all of the Old Dominion's best-known colonizationists were "deportationist,
proslavery and anti-Negro." Madison privately connected colonization with
gradual emancipation, but he acknowledged that the goals of the ACS were
"limited to blacks already free." Taylor made colonization a part of his proslavery program for agricultural reform, and Randolph hoped it would strengthen
the peculiar institution in the Old Dominion. The leadership of the ACS repeatedly insisted that the society's sole purpose was the removal of free blacks,
whom its general secretary termed "injurious and dangerous to our social interests." Virginian William H. Fitzhugh, a vice president of the ACS, pushed the
society to declare that it had no intention of interfering with slavery, while Mercer, who detested slavery and was often called an abolitionist, consistently denied any connection between colonization and emancipation.[8]

At the annual meeting of the ACS in 1828, the representative from the
Lynchburg affiliate, Jesse Burton Harrison, connected the racial fears of most
white Virginians with their republican concerns. He believed it was in the interest of both races to remove this "wretched class cursed with ineffectual freedom" in order to approach that "time when we shall be one homogeneous
nation of freemen." In the late 1820s the rhetoric of the commonwealth's colo-

nizationists increasingly expressed open hostility to an inferior race whose integration into the homogeneous community of virtuous and independent citizens demanded by the republican paradigm seemed totally inconceivable.[9]

The ACS had gotten off to an auspicious beginning and quickly enlisted the "most enlightened" men of Virginia. Yet branches committed to its cause were never numerous, and by the end of the decade, colonization in Virginia was languishing, and the ACS was on the verge of bankruptcy. The Virginia constitutional convention of 1829–30, crowded with members of the ACS, ignored the matter, and the reformers repeatedly insisted that they supported slavery's continued existence. Driven by desperation to seek federal funding, Mercer told Congress that the society "recognized the constitutional and legitimate existence of Slavery." But his modest proposal offended proslavery Jacksonians who wished to eliminate the ACS altogether.[10]

At about the same time that Jackson and his supporters in Congress rejected federal support for colonization, the insurrection in Southampton County led by the itinerant preacher Nat Turner prompted the Virginia House of Delegates to consider both emancipation and colonization in January 1832. What was called by both contemporaries and later historians the "great debate" began in earnest when William B. Preston, a young western delegate, moved to amend a committee report on colonization to assert that "it is expedient to adopt some legislative enactment for the abolition of slavery." While it is doubtful that the nondecision that resulted when Preston's amendment was defeated deserves to be considered a watershed in American attitudes toward slavery—the southern equivalent of the emergence of immediatism among northern abolitionists—the heated debate and the votes in the house reflected the nature of the slavery issue and the distribution of attitudes about the peculiar institution in the Old Dominion at the time.

Governor John Floyd's reaction to Turner's revolt reflects the complexity and ambiguity of white Virginians' response to the issue. Born in Jefferson County and educated in Pennsylvania at Dickinson College and the University of Pennsylvania, Floyd practiced medicine in Botetourt County and entered politics. He served in the House of Delegates and then for six terms in Congress before being selected as the first governor under the new state constitution.[11]

During the 1820s his position on slavery vacillated. One of the few men in the Virginia delegation to support the Missouri Compromise, Floyd opposed the Panama Congress called by Simon Bolívar primarily because it raised the specter of a black Haitian ambassador in Washington representing a nation born of a slave revolt. Eventually he joined the coalition of "planters of the South" and "plain republicans of the North" to support Jackson for the presidency, believing that the Old Hero would bring the government back to its first principles, but by 1831 the governor—a westerner who betrayed "an unusual sympathy for the tidewater interests"—had broken with Jackson, supported Calhoun for the presidency, and joined the "ultra States Rights" party in the Old Dominion.[12]

Privately Floyd mulled over various plans for emancipation confiding to his diary that he would "not rest until slavery is abolished in Virginia." Two of the state's leading advocates of gradual emancipation—Preston and James McDowell—were his nephews, and he characterized those who agreed with them as "talented young men." But when he had the chance, Floyd shied away from suggesting emancipation in any form.[13]

Severely shaken by the Southampton uprising, Floyd complained to the governor of South Carolina that "every black preacher in the whole country east of the Blue Ridge was in the secret." He was convinced that "the spirit of insubordination" had been inspired by Yankee peddlers and preachers who told "the blacks God was no respecter of persons" and taught southern women to believe "that it was piety to teach negroes to read and write." Echoing the arguments of the eastern conservatives in the constitutional convention of 1829–30, he decried the subversive nature of abolitionist influence in his annual message. After reciting the events of the Southampton insurrection, he called for harsher laws to subordinate the slave population further and for the appropriation of funds for the immediate removal of Virginia's free blacks, whom he regarded as a dangerous class.[14]

The *Enquirer* and the *Whig* encouraged the commonwealth's lawmakers to consider some plan of emancipation, but both the Richmond papers primarily focused on the problem posed by the growing free black population. Pleasants at the *Whig* believed that it was "the general wish" of the people of Virginia that the assembly address this question, while his rival, Ritchie, worried about the "*concert* and *conspiracy*" between the "Free People of colour" and the slaves and implored the legislature to act: "Something must be done."[15]

Petitions relating to these matters poured into the legislature. White mechanics from Petersburg and Culpeper County called for a prohibition against either free blacks or slaves becoming apprentices in any "trade or art." Thirty-five of the nearly three hundred petitions on all subjects addressed to the General Assembly in 1831–32 dealt with colonization and emancipation. Those from Loudoun and Botetourt called for the removal of both free blacks and slaves. Others spoke specifically of "gradual emancipation." A group of "ladies of Augusta" prayed for the "speedy extirpation of slavery." But no one considered emancipation without colonization. While a petition from Hanover County wished to see no legislation at all on the subject of slavery, most memorials requested that the legislators consider "the speedy adoption of some system for the removal of free negroes from the commonwealth."[16]

The great debate of 1832 that focused the nation's attention on Virginia revived arguments that had been raised earlier in the constitutional convention of 1829–30 and suggested the outlines of the slavery debate for the next three decades. Like the conservatives in the convention, supporters of the status quo portrayed themselves as "practical men" dealing in reality and depicted their opponents as misguided "idealists" whose dangerous proposals emanated from "the ardor of new born zeal." The antislavery men generally advocated gradual emancipation and colonization while their opponents cautioned against precipitous action and feared the social consequences of even debating the issue.[17]

Those who pressed the proposal to consider the expediency of emancipation were impetuous young men and outlanders, rising politicians of the periphery, who resembled in most respects the proponents of democratic reform in the constitutional convention. Aside from McDowell and Preston, they included Philip Bolling, Charles J. Faulkner, Samuel Garland, Samuel McDowell Moore, George W. Summers, and Thomas Jefferson Randolph, the former president's grandson. None was over forty, and the most radical were in their mid-twenties. While these men appealed to natural rights and quoted Jefferson, theirs was basically a moral and economic argument that emphasized the detrimental effects of slavery on "the prosperity and happiness of the whole commonwealth." The advocates of emancipation blamed the peculiar institution for Virginia's economic and political decline. Slavery undermined the "manners, habits and character" of the white population by promoting "miserable notions of self-importance." Summers, the delegate from Kanawha County in the west, insisted that "lisping infancy learns the vocabulary of abusive epithets and struts the embryo tyrant its little domain." Slavery encouraged idleness and disparaged labor "because it is the business of the slave—and when industry is made dishonourable or unfashionable, virtue is attacked in her strongest citadel." Moore, who represented Rockbridge County in the Valley, saw in slavery "the irresistible tendency . . . to undermine and destroy everything like virtue and morality in the community."[18]

The "pernicious influences" of the peculiar institution engendered hostility to enterprise while tolerating widespread illiteracy. At the same time the slaveholding gentry of the east used their disproportionate legislative power to block "a wise and extensive system of internal improvements." Faulkner, also a westerner, combined sectional animosity with class conflict and contrasted the economic interest of the planters with that of the nonslaveholding whites, both the "middle class" and the "mechanics." A similar concern for the economic welfare of the state underlay Preston's appeal to a "higher law" of public necessity to justify the interference with the property rights of the slaveholders involved in any plan for gradual emancipation.[19]

The opponents of slavery also argued that its continued existence posed a danger to the state. Randolph warned the house: "The hour of eradication of the evil is advancing—it must come. Whether it is effected by the energy of our own minds, or by the bloody scenes of Southampton and St. Domingo is a tale for future history!" He proposed a gradual emancipation plan much like that earlier suggested by his illustrious grandfather based upon a *post nati* scheme in which after July 4, 1840, all newborn slaves would "become property of the commonwealth" with the ultimate intent of removing them "beyond the limits of the United States." Even the most ardent antislavery spokesmen in the legislature could not conceive of emancipation without colonization.[20]

The eastern conservatives focused on the removal of the commonwealth's free black population and the threat of outside agitators. They insisted that policy should reflect concrete circumstances rather than abstract principles, and a significant number of these delegates embraced the positive good argument. One Southside planter, Alexander Knox of Mecklenburg County, attacked his opponents as abolitionists who would both undermine states' rights and destroy the economy of the Old Dominion. He denied that slavery was an evil and maintained that "its existence is indispensably requisite in order to preserve the forms of Republican Government." "The cradles of liberty," Greece and Rome, had slavery. England, however, whence the idea of emancipation emerged, contained "a miserable, wretched and degraded peasantry . . . compared to whom our slaves may be regarded as occupying a most enviable condition."

The defenders of slavery maintained that the "peculiar interest" of the east needed protection from the tyranny of the nonslaveholding majority and interpreted any tendency toward emancipation as a threat to the rights of property upon which all civilized government is based. The most outspoken proponent of slavery in the house, William O. Goode, a Mecklenburg County planter who had opposed reform in the constitutional convention, insisted that any emancipation proposal involved confiscation of property and consequently was blatantly unconstitutional on its face.[21]

The proslavery argument shaded very quickly into a defense of the status quo that blamed the "southern decline" on the tariff rather than the peculiar institution. John T. Brown, the delegate from Petersburg, assumed that the continuation of slavery was in the interest of the Old Dominion and that Virginia's slaveholders were practical men. When slavery was no longer profitable, it would wither away. The state's immediate economic problems arose "because she is defrauded in the sale of her produce and the purchase of her supplies from abroad." In theory many eastern conservatives agreed with the prominent Southside colonizationist William H. Brodnax of Dinwiddie County that "*slavery in Virginia is an evil*," but in practice they focused far more attention upon the rights of property and the greater evils attendant upon emancipation.[22]

The protection of slavery was essential to the maintenance of social order. James H. Gholson, a Southside planter, insisted that the antislavery attack on property rights forecast the dissolution of patriarchal relations between "husband and wife, parent and child, master and apprentice, master and servant, governor and governed." Goode taunted his opponents whom he portrayed as dangerous revolutionaries and potential miscegenationists: "When our aged mothers shall call in vain for protection from their slaughtered sons will [you] be found leading or mingling with the black horde?"[23]

Two weeks later further debate on colonization provided additional insight into Virginians' attitudes on slavery and race. Brodnax introduced a proposal to set aside $100,000 a year for colonization; it included the provision that should an insufficient number of free blacks volunteer, specific groups should be forcibly removed. According to this former vice president of the ACS, free blacks had "*legal* rights" in the commonwealth "but no *constitutional* ones." They were not citizens but aliens residing in Virginia illegally and thus subject to deportation at the will of the state. In response the opponents of coercion, such as Thomas Marshall, son of the chief justice, charged that the committee's recommendation was unduly "harsh," an "inhuman" policy that trampled upon the rights of the free blacks and offended the sensibilities of most Virginians. Fiscal conservatives moved various amendments to cut the commonwealth's contribution by as much as half, and Brown sought to discourage manumission by forcing the owners to pay to transport out of the state the slaves they freed.[24]

The House of Delegates split along sectional lines on the slavery issue, and the spectrum of attitudes radiated out from the proslavery center to the antislavery periphery, as can be seen in the origin of the various proposals that came before the house. Early in the session two Southside delegates put forward radical proslavery proposals. Vincent Witcher of Pittsylvania moved that it was inexpedient to enact any abolition law, and Goode introduced a test motion to reject a Quaker petition favoring gradual emancipation and colonization. Archibald Bryce, Jr., from Goochland County in the central piedmont north of the James wrote the moderate proslavery preamble to the report of Brodnax's committee which favored colonization of free blacks but postponed indefinitely consideration of "the removal of slaves." In contrast, Preston, who proposed the amendment to consider emancipation, was a nonslaveholder from Montgomery County at the southern end of the Valley. Finally, John C. Campbell, whose amendment late in the session supported voluntary colonization and sufficient funding for the transportation of those manumitted in the future, was also a nonslaveholder from Brooke County in the "panhandle" north of the Mason-Dixon Line.

The most devout defenders of the peculiar institution concentrated in the state's premier planter counties south of the James River stretching from Isle of Wight west to Pittsylvania: the Southside (map 6.1). Antislavery sentiment

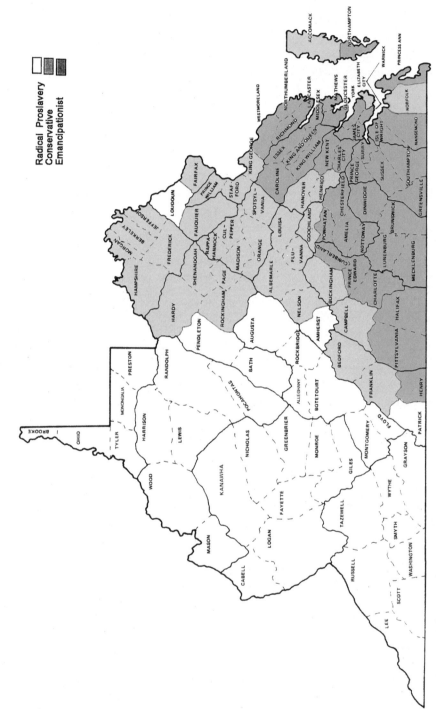

Radical Proslavery
Conservative
Emancipationist

6.1. The great debate on slavery, 1832

increased as one moved away from this center of commitment to tobacco and slaves. Those easterners who deviated from their section's proslavery stance represented what one might loosely term commercial areas around Lynchburg, Norfolk, and Richmond and the northern counties of the piedmont and the tidewater along the Potomac. They were joined in their opposition to the peculiar institution by forty-nine westerners who voted on Preston's amendment.[25]

The house split nearly evenly on the question of entertaining emancipation proposals, but the debates and the roll calls related to emancipation and colonization reveal five voting blocs (Appendix 2) that represent the distribution of Virginia's political elite (and presumably the voters) on the slavery issue. One-quarter of the body—thirty-one delegates—constituted the radical proslavery faction. Nearly all held slaves; two-thirds of them had more than ten (table 6.1). This group included Goode, Gholson, Knox, and Witcher, men who confidently endorsed the positive good argument in the debates and consistently voted against the consideration of any legislation on the matter. All but one were easterners (table 6.2); seventeen came from the Southside. Twenty-nine represented counties that gave over two-thirds of their popular vote to Jackson in 1828.

A slightly smaller group of twenty-five delegates entertained the possibility of ending slavery in Virginia at some undefined distant date but voted to postpone indefinitely any consideration of the matter. This conservative proslavery bloc included John R. Shell of Brunswick County and Brown, who vociferously defended slavery in the debates, but also some men like Brodnax who privately opposed the peculiar institution. They agreed with the proslavery radicals in general but favored colonization and accepted the Quakers' right to petition. Only one of the conservatives represented a constituency west of the Blue Ridge;

Table 6.1. Voting blocs and slaveholding in the House of Delegates, 1832

	Slaves			
	None	1–9	10–19	20+
Radicals	2	10	13	6
Conservatives	3	7	5	10
Moderates	2	9	1	3
Up-Country	15	5	2	0
Progressives	11	20	2	2

Source: Freehling, *Drift toward Dissolution*, 272–78, correcting slightly Joseph Clarke Robert, *The Road from Monticello: A Study of the Virginia Slavery Debate of 1832* (1941; rept. New York, 1970) 113–17.

Table 6.2. Voting blocs and sections in the House of Delegates, 1832

| | East | | West | |
	Tidewater	Piedmont	Valley	Trans-Allegheny
Radicals	8	22	1	0
Conservatives	15	9	1	0
Moderates	9	4	4	0
Up-country	0	0	7	15
Progressives	3	6	11	16

Source: Journal of the House of Delegates . . . 1831 (Richmond, 1832), 29, 109, 110, 134–35, 158.

over half came from the rural tidewater, an area plagued by a declining white population and a massive black presence. Three-quarters of the conservative proslavery delegates had been sent to the house by constituencies that gave huge majorities to General Jackson.

In the middle, between these two proslavery blocs and the antislavery proponents of Preston's proposal, sat seventeen moderates willing to accept the Bryce preamble. This bloc included Bryce himself, Marshall, and John A. Chandler from Norfolk, who spoke out against the evils of slavery that corrupted Virginia society and held back the Old Dominion economically. They were rhetorical gradualists who believed that it was "inexpedient" to act. One of their number, William H. Roane of Hanover County in the upper tidewater, reflected their basic concern and pragmatic approach by proposing the removal of all the free blacks and enough slaves to maintain a balance between the races. This would "give to every *white man* in the State, that *certain* assurance that *this* is *his* country." Only four of the moderates held over ten slaves, and all represented commercial areas. Three-fifths of them came from that small number of counties in the Old Dominion carried by Adams.

Fifty-eight members of the house voted to consider gradual emancipation, but this antislavery element split on what to do about free blacks. A backcountry antislavery bloc, made of westerners from strongly Jacksonian counties, joined the radical proslavery faction in opposition to colonization. Among this group of four frugal Germans from the Valley and eighteen southwestern farmers, only seven men owned slaves. In order to remove the black presence, these delegates considered eliminating slavery where it touched them, west of the Blue Ridge, but they vigorously opposed spending the taxpayers' money on a costly and an unworkable colonization scheme.

The other thirty-six antislavery delegates voted for both the Preston amendment and colonization, which they saw as the first step toward ridding the state of slavery. These progressive emancipationists opposed slavery primarily for economic reasons although they accepted Jefferson's strictures on its moral effects on whites. Two-thirds owned slaves, but only two were planters. All nine easterners in the group and over half of the westerners represented commercial counties. None of them came from the southwest, and a majority represented counties in which Adams made a respectable showing, including thirteen from constituencies that the New Englander carried.

When the house decided to focus on the removal of free blacks and "await a more definite development of public opinion" on emancipation, both the *Whig* and the *Enquirer* expressed disappointment and printed letters continuing the debate. Ritchie sought a middle ground between the "two extreme parties" that could solve "the problem of the multiplying blacks" without interfering with the rights of slaveholders. Pleasants was more favorable to future emancipation than Ritchie but agreed with his editorial opponent that "humanity and policy in the *first* place, demand the removal of the free [blacks], and those who would [in the future] become free." One letter to the *Enquirer*, appropriately signed "Jefferson," defended the antislavery delegates against conservative criticism and called on the "non-slaveholders," the "middle class," and "the mechanics throughout the State" to continue to consider carefully any "*rational and practicable*" proposal to end slavery in the Old Dominion. The *Whig*, however, agreed in the end with the moderates in the house that a consensus existed among the delegates—and probably their constituents—that it was inexpedient "to legislate on abolition."[26]

The events of the early 1830s, including the debate in the Virginia House of Delegates, the end of slavery in the British West Indies, and the rapid spread of immediatism among northern abolitionists, led to the proliferation of proslavery apologetics defending the peculiar institution and the social order it sustained. Two-thirds of all the proslavery pamphlets written in the United States appeared after the Virginia debate, including a fourfold increase in those from the Old Dominion. Religion, literature, economics, political theory, and even the newly invented sociology were all consumed by consideration of slavery as a social institution.[27]

The arguments had been presented before, but they were formalized, infused with a new intensity, and directed toward a broad audience of southern slaveholders and nonslaveholders alike. As William Harper, the chancellor of South Carolina, complained, southerners were being denied a "hearing before the tribunal of the civilized world," and consequently it was necessary that "we the inhabitants of the slaveholding states of America . . . enlighten our minds and fortify our hearts" in defense of slavery in order to protect "the prosperity, character and safety" of the South. While these writers usually synthesized several aspects of the subject, they focused primarily on the morality of the peculiar institution and secondarily on the economic viability of slave society.[28]

In the constitutional convention of 1829–30 and the 1831–32 session of the legislature, the debates on the slavery issue stressed expediency and reflected both political considerations and economic interests. While there was a bloc committed to the positive good argument that included one-quarter of the delegates, there were no unconditional or immediate abolitionists in the Virginia assembly, and the debate took place between these polar extremes. The division on the major roll calls was sharply sectional rather than partisan. Westerners resented the domination of the government at Richmond by the arrogant eastern aristocracy and the planters' studied refusal to provide the Valley and trans-Allegheny with adequate transportation and credit facilities. The opponents of slavery emphasized the effects of the peculiar institution on the nonslaveholding white majority. By degrading work, driving out white artisans, and encouraging the nonproductive pursuits of a leisure class, slavery had caused the economic decline of the Old Dominion.

Sectional hostility also fired the first conservative commentary on the debates to appear in the Virginia press. Benjamin Watkins Leigh, one of the leading opponents of democratic reform during the previous decade, writing under the pseudonym "Appomattox," accused the westerners of violating the "arrangement" in the new state constitution "to secure slave property." Randolph's *post nati* plan, he further argued, would produce more harm than good by raising discontent among the slaves that would result in insurrection, "a general servile war," and ultimately "the destruction of the negro race." Since all schemes of colonization were impracticable, any proposal for emancipation and deportation, no matter how earnestly its supporters protested, would produce in fact "*simple abolition.*"[29]

This, Leigh insisted, was "the end to which all these projects tend" and the secret desire of "many" of the "abolitionists" in the legislature. He quoted Moore, Faulkner, and Summers at length as dangerous radicals infected by the "odd" opinions of Jefferson, the unrealistic rhetoric of "natural rights," and an indecent respect for the sanguinary extremes of the French Revolution. Such subversive views, Leigh believed, were shared by few freeholders. The majority of Virginians well understood that the protection of private property constituted the primary purpose of government, the first priority of the commonwealth, and the basic foundation of all republican liberty. "All of our institutions are founded on the principle that every man's private property is absolutely his own, and that he holds it independently of the power of the legislature and of the will of the majority. When that principle shall be abandoned, republican government must be destroyed with it." In general, Leigh repeated the arguments that he and other conservatives had put forth in the convention against the reformers' attack on the rights of property, but the letters of "Appomattox" also ushered in the final phase in the development of the ideology of slavery in the Old Dominion.

The commonwealth produced the most articulate and most widely read defenders of slavery in antebellum America. Virginia advocates of the positive good argument included the professor of constitutional law Nathaniel Beverley Tucker, the agricultural reformer Edmund Ruffin, the moral historian George Frederick Holmes, the college president Albert Saunders, the evangelical ministers Thornton Stringfellow and Albert Taylor Bledsoe, as well as the man whose work represented the reactionary fulfillment of the proslavery argument, the less-than-successful planter George Fitzhugh. Nearly all of these Virginia defenders of the peculiar institution presented the basic outlines of their position on slavery in the 1830s and 1840s, and all specifically acknowledged the influence of "the masterly essay of Professor Dew." [30]

At the time of the great debate in Virginia, Dew was a young professor of political economy at the College of William and Mary who had published his lectures arguing that free trade would serve as the basis for the revival of Virginia agriculture. In theory he opposed slavery; yet Dew produced an array of utilitarian arguments to show that there was no way to end slavery without a "greater injury to both masters and slaves." He focused his criticism specifically on the views of conservative colonizationist Brodnax and associated his own position with the arguments presented in the debate by proslavery radicals Brown and Goode. The commonwealth simply could not afford the cost of colonization. Emancipation without deportation was unthinkable, because from "*both an economical and moral point of view [Africans] are entirely unfit for a state of freedom.*" [31]

Dew wove various strands of the positive good argument into his proslavery tapestry. He dismissed Jefferson's observations in *Notes on Virginia* and insisted that the slaves constituted the "happiest portion of the society" while their masters were "characterized by noble and elevated sentiments." Dew favorably contrasted "virtuous" southerners to "calculating" northerners and emphasized that authority, rather than hardening men's sensibilities, "humanizes and soften them." The patriarchal bond of master and servant even superseded filial ties: "hundreds of slaves . . . [would] desert parents, wives and husbands, brothers and sisters, to follow a kind master." [32]

Finally, Dew insisted that the South's peculiar institution promoted the interests of the nonslaveholding whites. Only a slave society could be truly republican and free of the class conflict that troubled Europe and the northern states. "Color alone is the badge of distinction, the true mark of aristocracy." "Expedience, morality and religion" dictated the continuation of slavery if the South was to avoid the social chaos represented by "lawless mobs" and the demagogic appeals that northern politicians already addressed to "the indigent and the destitute." "The day will come," Dew predicted confidently, "when the whole confederacy will regard [slavery] as the sheet anchor of our country's liberty."[33]

Dew regularly contributed to the Richmond-based *Southern Literary Messenger*, which shaped the opinions of its elite readers on the slavery question during the 1830s and 1840s and reinforced the romantic and conservative aspects of the political culture of the commonwealth. The magazine also frequently featured Beverley Tucker, Dew's friend and colleague at William and Mary, whose secular conservatism typified the proslavery ideology, drawing upon the precepts of moral philosophy along with "facts and sound reasoning" from history to portray the peculiar institution as a positive good. Southern slavery not only conformed to the essential principles of God's natural law but provided the basis for a more just and harmonious society than had ancient slavery because it recognized the inherent intellectual and moral differences between the races. Tucker insisted that slavery was a peaceful and benevolent institution that had "done more to elevate a degraded race in the scale of humanity . . . and to spread the blessings of christianity among the heathen than all the missionaries that philanthropy and religion have ever set forth."[34]

Slavery formed the basis of the world's greatest civilizations, and the racial form that the ancient institution had taken in the southern states provided the model for the reform of human society in line with God's will. Tucker extended his conception of the paternalistic and hierarchical order of the plantation household to a scheme of "order and freedom" in line with the ideas of Burke. In contrast to the market orientation of the North, the South should strive to build a society "in obedience to the law of Love." Slave society rejected materialistic individualism and reconciled the conflicting demands of liberty and authority by "restoring that beautiful harmony in which Power is gentle and Obedience liberal, and the will of the superior prevails."[35]

Tucker's vision of the ideal government and social order for the Old Dominion resembled that of the reactionaries in the constitutional convention. His views on slavery were shared by his close friend, the outspoken opponent of constitutional reform Judge Upshur, whose 1839 article on "Domestic Slavery" presented a far more explicit defense of the peculiar institution than Dew's essay and expanded the appeal to the nonslaveholder. "We should cherish this institution, not as a necessary evil which we can not shake off, but as a great positive good, to be carefully protected and preserved."[36]

Upshur's argument was solidly based in a classical republican analysis of the relationship between government and society. The "virtue of the people," according to the Eastern Shore judge, formed "the basis of republican government." Government, however, threatened liberty and was at best a necessary evil that must be limited in every way possible. Like Dew and other conservative Virginians, Upshur insisted that slavery in fact had a positive effect "upon the mind and feelings of the master" that prepared "him for the love of freedom and fit him for the enjoyment of it." Slavery also elevated the moral character of the nonslaveholders, engendering in them the "personal independence and self-respect" that formed the "foundation of political liberty."

In one way or another throughout his essay, Upshur returned to this theme. Because its slavery was racial, Virginia's social system contained only two classes: whites and blacks. All whites shared "equally one great and ennobling distinction" that created the kind of stable community most "favorable to republican equality." The differences of status and condition between whites were of minor importance. The judge's sense of "freedom and equality," of course, had nothing in common with what he termed "rude and leveling democracy," which he perceived primarily as a threat to individual liberty.[37]

Although all of these defenders of the peculiar institution contemplated the inevitability of white manhood suffrage, none approved. Had Upshur and Dew lived, they would have joined Tucker in assailing the reformers of 1850–51 and lamenting the descent of the Old Dominion "in the slough of democracy." Both the constitutional conservatives and the proslavery ideologues relied heavily on Burke, emphasizing that "circumstances are what render every political scheme beneficial or noxious to mankind" and denouncing the dangers implicit in innovations of nearly any sort. These Virginians looked to the example of the French Revolution, to Jacobinism and the Terror, to the uprising of the slaves in Saint Domingue for sanguinary examples of the social disorder dictated by the application of abstract principles. The Southampton insurrection brought a new emotional energy to this equation that fueled the outcry against abolitionists.[38]

While these secular conservatives shaped the contours of antebellum cultural life in the Old Dominion through their control of the colleges, their contribution to sectional magazines, and their popular plantation romances, evangelical ministers formed the most important source of the proslavery argument, sustaining the whites' belief in the moral superiority of their society. In such an intensely religious environment, the scriptural defense of slavery touched more Virginians than the bookish arguments of the secular conservatives and had the greatest impact on nonslaveholders. As Dew put it in his *Review*, the New Testament contained not "one single passage calculated . . . to disturb the conscience of an honest slave-holder" and, in fact, "demonstrated that no rule of conscience or law of God can condemn us."[39]

The best-known proponent of the argument from Scripture was Thornton Stringfellow, an evangelical Baptist minister from Culpeper County in the northern piedmont. Although he had a large plantation worked by seventy slaves and he acknowledged the influence of Dew, Stringfellow's defense of the peculiar institution grew out of his desire to serve God in the "moral reform of the world," which also led him to support colonization, temperance, home missions, and the Sunday school movement. In the late 1830s and 1840s, he responded directly to the "inexcusable wickedness" of abolitionists, setting forth numerous examples from the Bible to show that God had sanctioned slavery. Since the Africans were "unprepared for a higher civil state," their condition was presently "better than that of any equal number of laborers on earth and is daily improving."[40]

Virginia Baptist Jeremiah Jeter credited Stringfellow's "plain, logical, and vigorous statement of the scriptural teaching on the subject" with affecting his own understanding. "Up to that time," he wrote in his *Recollections*, "I had believed that slavery in the south was allowable from the necessity of the case, and that its abolition would be fraught with more mischief than good." While he did not go so far as proclaiming slavery a positive good in all cases, Jeter believed that the Bible sanctioned the peculiar institution and under present conditions produced "the best order of society that human or even divine wisdom, can devise." In Virginia it was a "practical question," and the more it was debated, "the more insuperable seemed the obstacles to emancipation of the slaves."[41]

The progression of Jeter's perspectives mirrored that of most Methodist, Baptist, and Presbyterian preachers in the Old Dominion. In the 1820s the "prevalent opinion" had been that slavery was "fraught with many evils" and the slaveholders were weighed down with paternalistic obligations. The three major evangelical denominations had all earlier adopted resolutions against "the great evil" and called for "the complete abolition of slavery as speedily as possible." The aggressive campaigns of the abolitionists forced the evangelicals in the Old Dominion to assert the scriptural argument in the defense of slavery and emphasize the moral superiority of slave society. In effect, ordinary white Virginians were defending their lives as lived and a communal order that they assumed to be both natural and right.[42]

The outpouring of proslavery propaganda during these years sustained white Virginians' faith in the economic and moral soundness of the families and communities into which they were born. Slavery not only served as the source of social stability and guaranteed the security of property but also produced the truest form of republican liberty by fostering equality and common interest among white men. Dew had extended the arguments expressed earlier in both the convention of 1829–30 and the assembly debate, emphasizing the benefits of slavery. The Bible argument removed moral doubts and defined slavery as a secular question of public policy. In the versions of his pamphlet published after 1850, Stringfellow used the census of that year to argue that the people living in the old slave states were better off than those living in New England. Not only was slavery morally sound, but it also provided the basis for a society in which the distribution of resources was as bountiful as it was benevolent, a Cavalier version of the Gospel of Wealth.

During the 1830s and 1840s, as the proslavery appeal expanded to embrace nonslaveholders' aspirations and claim the cover of Christianity, the critics of slavery struggled to be heard in the Old Dominion. Like their opponents, they amplified earlier arguments heard in the house debate. Jesse Burton Harrison, the Harvard-educated lawyer who had represented Lynchburg in the 1828 national meeting of the ACS, responded directly to Dew in an article defending colonization. He insisted that slavery had produced the Old Dominion's economic problems and repeated his earlier argument that the peculiar institution bred inequality among whites and endangered republican society. Harrison agreed with the antislavery delegates in the house debate that slavery retarded economic development, undermined the dignity of labor, and corrupted the morals of the whites. While unsuited by climate and soil to slavery, agriculture in Virginia would flourish if worked by a "homogeneous race of freemen." Colonization combined with gradual emancipation would allow the Old Dominion to "fulfill her destiny" and reclaim its place of primacy in the Union.[43]

Echoing his mentor Madison, Harrison disputed Dew's main contention that colonization was economically impractical and that the fate of those sent to Africa would be disastrous, maintaining both that the public lands provided ample resources to sustain the project and that Liberia was flourishing only eleven short years after its founding. Yet Harrison's commitment to emancipation was distinctly limited. He opposed both Randolph's *post nati* plan and Preston's motion. Had he been in the House of Delegates, Harrison would have voted with the moderates like Bryce and Marshall, whose speech his pamphlet endorsed.[44]

The most widely discussed antislavery tract produced in Virginia during the 1840s, the Reverend Henry Ruffner's *Address to the People of West Virginia*, proposed the abolition of slavery west of the Blue Ridge. In prescribing a combination of gradual emancipation and colonization similar to that proposed by the progressive emancipationists, Ruffner focused upon slavery's detrimental effect upon the whites of western Virginia. The commonwealth lagged behind the northern states in agriculture, manufacturing, and public education because the peculiar institution undermined the virtues of thrift and industry and encouraged illiteracy, "indolent relaxation, false motives of dignity, and refinement, and a taste for fashionable luxuries." White farmers, mechanics, and workingmen would be driven from the land as the "Black Sea of misery" poured over the Blue Ridge from the piedmont.[45]

This moderate attack on slavery grew out of a debate at the Franklin Society and Library Company in Lexington on the subject: "Should the people of

Western Virginia delay any longer taking steps to bring about a division of the State?" Aside from Ruffner, who was president of Washington College, the other participants included Judge John W. Brockenbrough, a former member of the Richmond Junto; Colonel Francis H. Smith, who was also born in the tidewater; John Letcher, editor of the *Valley Star*; and Samuel McDowell Moore, who had been both a reformer in 1829–30 and an outspoken emancipationist in 1832. Westerners Ruffner, Letcher, and Moore favored the division of the state, while the easterners, Smith and Brockenbrough, were opposed. Smith, Moore, and Ruffner were Whigs; Letcher and Brockenbrough, Democrats. Letcher refused to support the pamphlet's publication and vigorously denied his opposition to slavery when he ran as a reform delegate to the convention of 1850–51.[46]

Ruffner remarked that "some" eastern papers "denounced it as abolitionist," but the editors of the Valley were hesitant to publish the pamphlet because they thought it "ill-timed while northern abolitionism was raging." "West of the Alleghenies," where hostility to eastern slaveholders remained strong, his views were "better received." No group in Virginia accepted what Ruffner called "the abolitionist ground that slaveholding is a sin and ought for that reason to be abolished." Rather, Virginia opponents saw slavery as "merely a question of expedience," and those arguing as he did connected emancipation to "the interest of West Virginia."[47]

The only Virginian publicly advocating views remotely resembling those of the northern abolitionists was Samuel Janney, the Hicksite minister and educational reformer in heavily Whig Loudoun County. In his youth he worked with the ACS in Alexandria, and after he moved to Virginia, Janney attacked Stringfellow's scriptural defense of slavery and called for an end to the "enormous evil." But even this less-than-quiet Quaker, who was the brother of one of the commonwealth's leading Whig politicians, emphasized the economic argument comparing the Old Dominion unfavorably to the northern states in economic and cultural development. In several articles that appeared in the *Richmond Whig* in mid-1845, Janney extolled the success of the Yankee farmers in Fairfax County who pointed the way toward the use of advanced agricultural techniques and free labor in Virginia. Although he acknowledged the difficulty of retaining northern laborers in a state where they were "looked down upon by the idle drones who infest all Slave-holding communities," Janney believed that only the elimination of slavery and the reliance upon free labor could bring "improvement"—moral as well as economic—to the Old Dominion.[48]

The public debate on slavery in the Old Dominion during these two decades reveals a spectrum of discourse from radical proslavery to progressive antislavery similar to the arguments presented in the "great debate," but it remains difficult to determine the distribution among Virginia voters of the views expressed by each of these writers. Assuming the legislators reflected public opinion in 1832, the proslavery radicals and progressive emancipationists were of nearly equal strength, with each representing approximately one-quarter of the public and the remaining 50 percent of the white males of the Old Dominion arrayed between them. By 1850 public opinion had tilted toward the proslavery end of the spectrum. In the General Assembly and among the state's congressional delegation, majorities sustained resolutions embodying the positive good argument, but as the Ruffner pamphlet and its reception indicate, the views of the progressive emancipationists still reflected the position of a sizable minority of Virginia voters.[49]

Between the Virginia house debate of 1832 and the congressional debate on the Compromise of 1850, the essential parameters of the slavery issue remained unchanged, but its focus shifted from colonization to the federal territories, and differences on the issue within the commonwealth became increasingly partisan. Response to the issue as it appeared in the 1820s and early 1830s was sectional and set the proslavery center against the antislavery periphery. At the time parties were poorly developed, and Jackson's popularity in the Old Dominion was unchallenged. By the mid-1830s, however, the second party system had appeared in Virginia. Both the Democrats and the Whigs indulged in the "politics of slavery," periodically flaying their opponents on the question and portraying them as threatening the peculiar institution and subverting southern interests. There was a consensus on colonization as a policy, although men came to it for different reasons, and Virginians universally rejected the meddling of northern abolitionists in the domestic affairs of the Old Dominion. But as other aspects of the slavery issue appeared, the parties came into conflict and supported contrasting policies at both the state and federal levels of legislation.

In 1832 the Virginia Colonization Society (VCS) drew its leaders from a cross section of the commonwealth's political elite. When John Tyler became its president that year, the organization's vice presidents included not only William H. Brodnax, Abel P. Upshur, James M. Garnett, and Thomas Massie, Jr., who had been conservative delegates to the convention of 1829–30, but also reformers Philip Doddridge, Charles Fenton Mercer, William H. Fitzhugh, and Lewis Summers. Brodnax had denounced slavery as an evil but voted with the conservative proslavery bloc in the House of Delegates, while James McDowell, also a VCS vice president, was a leader of the antislavery element.

These prominent colonizationists followed the various paths of partisan allegiance in the mid-1830s. Garnett, an Old Republican who took up Jackson, became a Democratic Republican in 1835. Future governors McDowell and David Campbell supported the Van Buren administration. Mercer and Summers advocated the American System and became staunch Whigs. Tyler, Upshur, and Wise had turned against Jackson, were for a time Whigs, then split with that party and became Democrats. In contrast, William C. Rives, who had been an avid Jacksonian senator, became embroiled in the "Conservative revolt" against Van Buren's Independent Treasury proposal and drifted toward the Whigs. In 1844 he campaigned for Clay.[50]

At its 1832 meeting the Virginia Colonization Society reaffirmed its resolve to "confine its operations, to . . . the removal of . . . free people of colour only, with their own consent." After an initial proposal was defeated in the state senate, the assembly consigned nearly $100,000 to the project over the course of the next five years. Ignoring Dew's devastating critique and insisting that private and state support were both sufficient and preferable to federal aid, the society's new president, John Tyler, hailed the assembly's action and assured his audience that "Monrovia will be to Africa what Jamestown and Plymouth have been to America." He contrasted such practical philanthropy with the malignant "spirit of abolition" that had arisen in the North.[51]

Virginians from all points of the political compass also steadfastly opposed the "Northern Fanatics." Governor Campbell wrote privately that he "would not consent that any power on earth should interfere" with Virginians' right to decide how they should treat their property. Tyler insisted that colonization was national in spirit and "equally beneficial" to all of the states. "Nothing sectional enters into it." In contrast, he continued, abolitionism "is sectional, altogether sectional." "Blind" and "stained in blood," the spirit of abolition "invades our hearth, assails our domestic circles, preaches up sedition, and encourages insurrection." At the same gathering Wise proposed a toast: "Slavery—whatever differences of opinion may exist among us Virginians on this vexed subject, we are unanimous on one point, a positive determination that no one shall think or act for us."[52]

A year earlier the assembly had responded to the appearance in Virginia of the black abolitionist David Walker's *Appeal* by making it a crime to circulate inflammatory literature among the slaves in the Old Dominion; and following the "great debate," it enacted further legislation to control free blacks that extended to anyone, regardless of race, "advising persons of color in this commonwealth to commit insurrection or rebellion." In his "Appomattox" letter Leigh, who believed the new laws insufficient, advocated a boycott of newspapers that spoke in favor of emancipation. The senator insisted that Virginians had the perfect right "to suppress to the utmost of our power what we deem inflammatory dangerous, mischievous." This had also been suggested by mass meetings in Mecklenburg, Northampton, and Essex counties decrying the public discussion of the issue and attacking the Richmond papers for publishing the debates of the House of Delegates on this delicate subject.[53]

Hysteria over unrest among the slaves that had briefly abated reappeared in

1835 as rumors of a planned uprising in Mississippi spread and abolition propaganda appeared at the post office at Richmond. A mass meeting was held on August 4 to protest and petition the assembly to restrain "incendiary" publications. There were other antiabolitionist meetings in Amherst, Louisa, Essex, Williamsburg, and Norfolk. In his opening message to the session of 1835–36, Governor Littleton Waller Tazewell called for action against the "fanatics" who were printing and disseminating "seditious and incendiary doctrines." Appealing to international law, the governor argued that just as independent countries "expect from each other courtesy and consideration . . . , the slaveholding states have a perfect right to require of all the others, that they should adopt prompt and efficient means to suppress all such associations existing within their respective limits."[54]

The debate over the commonwealth's response to the threat of abolitionism revealed policy differences that cracked the consensus on colonization and increasingly distinguished the emerging parties. The new 1835 law focused on the activities of outside agitators but also prohibited anyone from circulating abolitionist literature or denying the property rights of masters. The enforcement procedures extended broad powers to postmasters and justices of the peace and encouraged vigilante action by allowing any whites to arrest those they believed were violating the law. The Democratic press, which had been endeavoring to dissociate Van Buren from the abolitionists and to show that he supported the gag rule in Congress, remained silent on the assembly's action; the opposition papers, however, led by the *Richmond Whig*, denounced the new legislation as a threat to freedom of the press and blamed the Democrats who controlled the assembly.[55]

The 1835–36 assembly also passed a series of resolutions directed toward the northern states and the federal government. Thomas W. Gilmer, a Calhounite from Charlottesville, introduced a resolution instructing Governor Tazewell to entreat northern governors to suppress the abolitionists' activities within their states, but this was postponed by Democrats who feared that their opponents intended to exploit the issue. Eventually a two-part resolution, covered by a conciliatory preamble written by a western Democrat, passed, asserting the commonwealth's right to control its domestic institutions and asking the cooperation of northern legislatures in suppressing the abolitionist threat. Then by an overwhelming vote the delegates declared that Congress had no constitutional power to tamper with slavery in the District of Columbia.[56]

The roll-call votes on the related motions and amendments during this session revealed incongruous alignments that reflect the disorganized state of parties at the time. Both the Jacksonians and their opponents harbored discontented elements although they contained contrasting centers of gravity that would affect the parties' positions in the future. The Democratic moderates, most concerned about the upcoming presidential election, tried to compromise on the question of slavery in the District of Columbia by emphasizing the articles of cession and by praising the northern Democrats who spoke out against the abolitionists. These moderates, however, came from the western counties and made up only one-fourth of the administration party in the house.[57]

The majority of the Jacksonians split into two segments based upon their degree of willingness to join the issue. About a third of the members—the remaining westerners and a few easterners from the upper piedmont—counseled caution, but 40 percent of the Democrats in the house were eager to act. Not surprisingly this extreme element represented the planters of the Southside and the tidewater and was led by the radical proslavery members who had participated in the great debate.

The opposition also divided into three groups across the spectrum of antiabolitionism. On the whole the Whigs were more moderate than the Democrats, but at the time the vocal Calhounites made up approximately 25 percent of the coalition in the house. Calhounites, following Gilmer, pressed the Democrats to apply stronger language toward the northern "fanatics." They came exclusively from the eastern half of the state and were centered in the tidewater. The Whig moderates, however, typified by John Minor Botts, comprised half of the members of the party and represented towns and counties either in the upper piedmont and west of the Blue Ridge. Finally, the emerging Whig party included the only members of the Virginia house to accept congressional power over slavery in the District of Columbia. This clique contained one-quarter of the Whig delegates and included three men who had voted with the progressive emancipationists in 1832 and would become party leaders in the next decade.[58]

Eventually the Calhounites in the opposition coalition would rejoin the Democrats and in the process create a clearer contrast between the parties on the slavery issue, but in the mid-1830s the politics of slavery provided the diverse Whigs with a popular platform with which to challenge Jackson's handpicked successor. The presidential election of 1836 pitted the northerner Martin Van Buren against the Tennessee senator Hugh Lawson White. The New Yorker's two-year campaign for the presidency involved his repeated attempts to assure southern voters, especially those in the Old Dominion, that he was truly an advocate of "the planters of the South" as well as "the plain republicans of the North." The Whig attack focused upon the New Yorker's position on slavery, asserting that Van Buren had favored the Missouri restriction, suffrage for free blacks in the New York, and the constitutionality of abolishing slavery in the District of Columbia. The *Richmond Whig* asked Virginia voters: "Can the South be safe at a time like this voting for a President who has successively opposed all her principles?"[59]

Throughout the state the opposition repeated the charges, and Van Buren's ambiguous position on slavery played a primary role in their largely negative campaign. The *Petersburg Intelligencer* connected the vice president to the abolitionists, and the *Lynchburg Virginian* summarized the charges of duplicity. The latter paper also accused the New Yorker of practicing "the knavish art of employing words to conceal ideas." He should stop wasting so much time attacking the Bank of the United States and be frank about his opinions on slavery. Party papers, local county committees, and the "Address of the Whig Central Committee" reiterated the allegation that Van Buren endorsed Congress's right to abolish slavery in the District and refused either to reply to inquiries on the subject or to pledge to veto any bill authorizing emancipation.[60]

The Whigs emphasized the virtues of their candidates. Most eastern Virginians agreed with Senator Tyler that the opposition needed a southern candidate, and White was the perfect choice: a nationally known Jacksonian with impeccable credentials. The Tennessee senator could be depicted as a statesman, a "Republican of the Old School" rather than a party politician; his break with Jackson showed him to be of an independent mind and sound on the other major issues. White was a large slaveholder in whose hands the future of the peculiar institution was safe.[61]

In the western parts of the state a dual ticket allowed electors to choose either White or William Henry Harrison as president. Although living in the North, Harrison was a Virginian by birth, and his vote in Congress in favor of slavery in Missouri showed that the interests of the Old Dominion would be safe in his hands. The *Virginian* assured its readers that like White, Harrison was "a Southern man and a slaveholder" and encouraged them to vote for the "Republican Whig Ticket" of White or Harrison and Tyler, who was supported for the vice-presidency by Virginia Whigs throughout the state.[62]

The Whig strategy put the Old Dominion's Democratic Republicans on the defensive. Not only did they have a northern candidate with a reputation as an unprincipled political manipulator, but also the party convention had rejected Virginia's favorite son, William C. Rives, for the second place on the ticket and nominated instead Richard M. Johnson. Although the Kentuckian was a slaveholder, he had consorted with one of his slaves and, as the opposition press noted, was the "father of a mongrel race." Democrats in the Old Dominion ignored Johnson's existence. Their main task was to convince Virginia's voters that Van Buren merited their support. The vice president's friend and defender Thomas Ritchie scurried to answer the critics point for point by showing that Jackson's chosen heir was a friend of the South and had particular affection for Jefferson's home state.[63]

Van Buren had struggled to reconstruct the Virginia–New York alliance in the 1820s by carefully building his reputation as a Jeffersonian Republican. In

1835 he complained to Rives that he suffered in the North for his "southern partialities" only to be accused in the South of being an abolitionist. He and other Democrats insisted that his opponents were deceitfully creating a false issue. The *Enquirer* charged the "piebald Whigs" with "attempting to convert the abolition question into a party movement" and insisted that one "carried in his pocket the worst pamphlets of the 'fanatics' . . . Smith, Tappan and Co." to frighten Virginia voters "into Whiggery as if they were so many children."[64]

Realizing the gravity of the situation, the Democratic candidate put all else aside in the early spring of 1836 and replied carefully to an inquiry from a group of North Carolinians stating his position and that of his party on the slavery question. In this letter, published in the *Enquirer* and widely circulated throughout the commonwealth, he insisted that Congress could not interfere with slavery in the states and it would be a violation of the spirit of compromise upon which the Constitution was founded to interfere with slavery in the District of Columbia. In uncharacteristically direct language the Red Fox pledged, "I must go into the presidential chair the flexible and uncompromising opponent of any attempt on the part of congress to abolish slavery in the District of Columbia, against the wishes of the slave holding states; and also with the determination *equally decided* to resist the slightest interference with the subject in the states where it exists."[65]

While the *Richmond Whig* continued to attack Van Buren's association with the abolitionists and cast doubt upon his veracity, the vice president was aided by the passage of the Pinckney resolutions including the gag rule. During the campaign Jackson further strengthened Van Buren by appointing Virginian Philip P. Barbour to the Supreme Court. Richard Parker and Peter Daniel assured Van Buren in June that they saw "nothing on the political horizon of a sinister or threatening nature" and that his candidacy was gaining throughout the state. Their efforts along with those of Ritchie and the Junto enabled Van Buren to win handily in the Old Dominion.[66]

During Van Buren's administration most Calhounites rejoined the Democracy as the disposition of antislavery petitions focused the slavery debate in Congress. Twice during the Twenty-fifth Congress (1837–39), the house passed gags similar to Pinckney's third resolution, and in 1837 it refused to accept any petition concerning slaves. Virginia congressman Henry Wise, however, bitterly attacked these as halfway measures that constituted victory for the abolitionists in that even receiving and tabling the petitions implied Congress's constitutional power to grant their prayer. He and his fellow radicals had felt betrayed when Pinckney inserted the phrase "ought not" in his second resolution rather than declare abolition in the District unconstitutional. When a new gag proposed by Virginia Democrat John M. Patton passed the house the following session without this provision, Wise refused to vote.[67]

Hardly a partisan, Wise sometimes worked with the Whigs, but most often acted as "a loner and consulted with no one." The congressman from the Eastern Shore tended to personalize issues and tilt at windmills of his own paranoid construction. Throughout his career this "good southerner" associated the antislavery movement with the British and the return of the redcoats to American shores. He responded to northern criticism of the peculiar institution with taunts about the "white slaves" of the North and the New England origins of slavery in Virginia. In theory Wise accepted gradualism. In practice he opposed any such suggestion as dangerous. "Slavery intertwined with our political institutions is guaranteed by our Constitution and its consequence must be born by our northern brethren as resulting from our system of government, and they cannot attack the institution of slavery without attacking the institutions of our country, our safety, our welfare."[68]

In January 1840 Wise and the other radicals gained something of a victory with the passage of a standing rule stating that no such petitions "shall be received by this House or entertained in any way whatever." The embattled congressional Democrats, who desperately needed to conciliate their Calhounite allies, voted by a two-to-one margin for this extreme antiabolitionist measure, while the optimistic Whigs opposed the restriction by a similar margin. Before the final vote Virginia Democrat Walter Coles attempted to include even stronger wording, but this was rejected by a partisan roll call that set 88 percent of the Whigs in the House against 82 percent of the Democrats. Clearly the southern Whigs had moderated their position and the northern Democrats voted with the proslavery radicals; Virginia's congressmen on both sides of the aisle toed the party line.[69]

The Democrats made these votes a campaign issue in the 1840 presidential election, accusing the southern Whigs of breaking the "compact front of the South" and insisting that the Whigs and the abolitionists in the North were "but one party in Congress." Van Buren once again ran as "the Northern man with Southern principles" on a platform that specifically declared that Congress had no power to interfere with the "domestic institutions" of the states and decried the "dangerous and alarming" consequences of abolitionist activity. The Democratic papers rehashed Van Buren's position on slavery and led the attack upon the abolitionist tendencies of both General Harrison and the northern Whigs. Going beyond his earlier commitments, the president pledged to veto any bill for abolition in the District, and the Democrats in the Old Dominion called upon Harrison to make a similar pledge.[70]

Ignoring the proslavery record of Van Buren's administration, the *Richmond Whig* returned to its previous portrayal of him. Because of the New Yorker's widespread reputation as a political manipulator, the Whigs incorporated his denials and attempts to depict himself as a friend of the South into their portrait of a devious hypocrite whose true principles, if he had any, remained shrouded in mystery. The New Yorker was the mere tool of party dictation, "a cold blooded party despot," and the *Whig* called on the people of the Old Dominion to vote for Harrison and "restore their sons to freedom." Comparing the records of the Whig and Democratic candidates, the *Virginian* asked its readers to judge: "Who is the Abolitionist?"[71]

The Whigs had the advantage on several counts. Harrison had been born and raised in Virginia. Whigs from the western part of the state had shown a preference for Harrison over White in 1836 and had supported Tyler as a friend of Clay and a true Republican. Finally, Harrison was sound on slavery. As governor of the Northwest Territory in 1809, he had proposed loosening the restrictions on slaveholders. He had supported the southern position in 1820 and in the 1830s had spoken out against the abolitionists. To the *Whig*, the candidate's behavior was marked by "the most ardent and devoted attachment to the rights and institutions of the South."[72]

In contrast, Democratic editors throughout the state termed Harrison the "Federal Abolition Candidate" and insisted that those who voted for him not only violated the true principles of the Old Dominion but also were traitors to the best interests of their own people. The "Address of the Democratic Central Committee" defended the incumbent, Van Buren, and put forth the Democracy's rather weak case against the challenger. Harrison had been nominated by a motley crew of advocates of a new national bank, a protective tariff, federally sponsored internal improvements, and the distribution of the surplus. Further, Democrats charged that Harrison was supported by Whigs in Congress who opposed the gag rule and by the leading abolitionists of Ohio and New York. The *Warrenton Jeffersonian* detected in the party's abandonment of Clay a "foul plot" to secure the votes of abolitionists and anti-Masons. "Wake up, freemen of Virginia!" Ritchie implored. "Your altars, your firesides and your liberties are in danger."[73]

The evolution of the politics of slavery in the Old Dominion during these years can be seen in a letter from Ritchie to Pleasants. The editor of the *Whig* had defended himself and Harrison by pointing out that both the *Enquirer* and the Democratic governor, James McDowell, had supported emancipation and colonization in 1832. Ritchie acknowledged the governor's earlier views and admitted that he too at the time had been for "doing something," but he insisted that they had "acted under the impulse of the Southampton Insurrection." McDowell had shown in his recent speeches and his letter to the House of Delegates "that he is an 'Anti-Abolitionist.'" Ritchie also admitted that "the General dealt some hard blows against the Abolitionists" in 1836, but he insisted that Harrison's position on the peculiar institution was most clearly revealed in his earlier "propositions for appropriating the whole surplus of the Federal

Whig

6.2 Whig congressional districts, 1847–49

Treasury to the purchase and colonization of the slaves." This act alone made him both "an affective Abolitionist" and an opponent of strict construction. The voice of the Virginia Democracy concluded, "Certain it is, that I have never gone as far as your Presidential Candidate; nor even as far as your self."[74]

The Whigs continued to be strongest in the central and western portions of the state (map 6.2), and the differences between the Old Dominion's Democrats and Whigs on the slavery issue appeared clearly in Congress where Adams pursued his attempts to rescind the gag rule and became embroiled in a verbal wrestling match with Wise — one that both combatants clearly relished. With the crucial support of a small group of southern Whigs, Adams finally succeeded in removing the offensive Twenty-first Rule. On the vote to reconsider, five Whigs from the slave states, including the Virginians John Minor Botts and Alexander H. H. Stuart, stuck with the Yankee former president and their party's majority.

During the following session, when Wise and Gilmer joined a Democratic attempt to censure Adams for presenting a petition calling for the dissolution of the Union, the regular Virginia Whigs led by Botts took up his cause. The charges of treason gave "Old Man Eloquent" a chance to speak in his own defense, skewering his critics and accusing Upshur, who had just entered Tyler's cabinet, with advocating disunion. Eventually, Botts moved to table the resolution of censure, and Adams was exonerated. This time Botts and Stuart were joined by the four other Virginia Whigs. Showing his contempt, Wise refused to vote; Francis Mallory and Gilmer, along with the six Old Dominion Democrats who voted, opposed the motion. Thus, while the Tylerites decamped, the majority of Virginia's Whigs joined with the northern wing of their party on this touchy issue.[75]

A combination of this position, a general Democratic trend in the off-year elections, and reapportionment sliced the number of Whigs in the Virginia delegation to the new Congress in 1843. Tylerites Wise and Gilmer were returned along with ten Democrats and three Whigs. Among the latter, Calhoun hoped to gain the support of Willoughby Newton from Westmoreland County in the struggle for the annexation of Texas that he and the administration had tied intimately to the defense of slavery. Tyler's policies, however, met a unified Whig opposition and the commonwealth's contingent in Congress opposed both the treaty and the joint resolution.

Throughout the 1840s each party periodically portrayed its opponents as threatening the peculiar institution and subverting southern interests, but generally such charges appeared as part of a partisan appeal, and Virginia's Whigs and Democrats behaved in a consistently partisan fashion. The Whig delegation in Congress was reduced to three by the elections of 1843, but they and the state's two Whig senators, William S. Archer and Rives, opposed the Tyler administration on Texas annexation. In the election of 1844, when both parties ran slaveholders, the Whig press emphasized the stature of their candidate, Henry Clay, and accused the Democrats of trying "to ride the Texas humbug" to victory, while Virginia's Democrats circulated Robert John Walker's pamphlet *The South in Danger* and associated "the Clay party" and sometimes even the candidate himself with the abolitionists. When Polk's actions precipitated war, the Democrats from the Old Dominion supported the administration, but the Virginia Whigs both inside and outside the government joined the opposition. Among this group were not only Botts but also the antislavery westerner George Summers.[76]

The Whigs came close to carrying the commonwealth for the war hero Zachary Taylor, who had been born in Virginia and owned slaves in Louisiana. The editor of the *Whig* smugly proclaimed "Old Zach with his sugar and cotton plantations" preferable to "all compromises" proposed by "trading politicians." The Democrats portrayed the Whigs as advocates of the Wilmot Proviso, quoting northern Whig papers to that effect and pointing to Taylor's pledge not to veto the proviso if it was passed by Congress. The *Enquirer* charged that the Whig party had "two faces" and that the vice-presidential candidate, Millard Fillmore, was an abolitionist. According to the *Petersburg Republican*, "The fight is for liberty, equality and truth." Cass was the only "safe candidate" to protect the rights of the South and preserve the Union. "Democrats you know you are now where you have ever been—with *the people and state rights.*"[77]

While both parties practiced the politics of slavery in their partisan rhetoric, Whigs and Democrats stood in distinctly different places on the spectrum of attitudes and behaviors that constituted the slavery issue. While not all Whigs were critics of slavery, those who publicly attacked the peculiar institution directly or simply criticized it in the course of their discussion of related issues—Burton Harrison, Mercer, Ruffner, Janney, and the political economist George Tucker—were all Whigs. The argument that slavery retarded the state's economic development had its greatest appeal to the Whigs in commercial areas. Mercer connected his lifelong advocacy of colonization to his commitment to Clay's American System. Janney's economic argument in favor of free labor and against slavery was in line with the *Whig's* editorial emphasis on "Improvement in Virginia." The party's commitment to economic diversification and state encouragement of capitalist expansion through aid to banks, internal improvements, manufacturing, and education easily lent itself to an indictment of the peculiar institution.[78]

The best-known and most vocal delegates on the antislavery side in the great debate also moved into the Whig party. Nine of the eleven men who spoke in favor of emancipation were subsequently Whigs. The other two, Randolph and McDowell, who became Democrats, disavowed their youthful indiscretion. On the other hand, eight of ten proslavery speakers who remained in politics were Democrats through the 1840s. One who became a Whig, Vincent Witcher, continued to argue that slavery was not only profitable but the way to wealth for his fellow planters and their state. With adequate access to markets and credit facilities, he said, slavery formed the basis for agricultural prosperity. However, Southside Whig James C. Bruce, who voted with Witcher in 1832, turned against slavery in the late 1840s as he became convinced that the institution deterred economic development.[79]

Virginia's newspapers that opened their pages to the moderate antislavery message, such as the *Alexandria Gazette, Lexington Gazette,* and *Kanawha Republican,* all editorially supported the Whigs. Most important was the position of the party's main organ, the *Richmond Whig.* In the mid-1840s Janney, who believed that "Pleasants . . . was at heart an emancipationist," persuaded the *Whig* editor not only to publish his articles and a few antislavery letters in the party's main organ but also to make public his own misgivings about the peculiar institution and its deleterious effect on the economic development of the Old Dominion. The editor, however, refused to print one of Janney's essays that proposed that the emancipated blacks remain in the state.[80]

Pleasants's tortured venture into antislavery ended tragically. In January 1846 he resigned from the *Whig,* which he no longer controlled and where he found himself "cribbed, cabined and confined." He proposed to found a new paper in Richmond to encourage economic improvement throughout the state. When the *Enquirer* suggested that this new paper was intended to "excite abolitionism," Pleasants hotly responded that he was not an abolitionist and would just as soon see "some of the abolition leaders hanged . . . especially Birney." He aligned his own views with those of "Washington, Jefferson, Henry, George Mason, the two Lees, Madison, Monroe, Wirt and *all* the early statesmen and sages of Virginia WITHOUT EXCEPTION." Pleasants believed with them that slavery was an evil which in time should be eliminated. "I am against it for the *sake of the whites,* my own race!" As long as the commonwealth continued to "carry the burden of the slave," it would be unable to compete economically with its northern neighbors. "We must prepare to contend with equal arms, or consent to be their vassals." When the *Enquirer* continued to repeat its charges of abolitionism, Pleasants challenged Thomas Ritchie, Jr., to a duel in which he was killed.[81]

Finally, the relationship between the emerging second party system and the slavery issue in Virginia can be seen by an examination of the men who served in Congress from 1834 to 1853. As the Democratic and Whig parties came together in the late 1830s and assumed their mature institutional form, the most proslavery elements in the anti-Jackson coalition returned to the Democratic party while the antislavery Jacksonians either modified their positions or became Whigs.

The Calhounites and the small Tylerite clique that Clay called the "corporal's guard" prided themselves on their independence and moved during these years from a loose affiliation with the Whigs into the Democratic party, where R. M. T. Hunter and Henry Wise eventually held formidable positions. Yet these "proslavery Whigs" were geographically isolated party irregulars who account for only a small minority of the anti-Jackson congressmen elected during the life of the Whig party and represented a much smaller proportion of the Whig voters of the Old Dominion.[82]

Twenty-eight of the thirty-three men sent to Congress from Virginia as Whigs were regular party members who supported Clay and the national party's policies throughout the 1840s. These men represented over nine-tenths of the commonwealth's Whigs. The group included a sizable number of men who within the context of the Virginia debate were antislavery. Four had supported the Preston amendment in 1832, and a half dozen others, including the highly visible Mercer and Botts, were regularly called abolitionists by their Democratic opponents. These "antislavery Whigs" came from the congressional districts that constantly turned out the largest numbers of Virginia's Whig voters. They were the party's best-known and most popular leaders, and William B. Preston and Alexander H. H. Stuart were rewarded with cabinet positions reflecting their importance. In the Old Dominion they stood for a position on the slavery issue close to that of Clay and not far from Madison and Jefferson.[83]

In contrast, the Democracy of the Old Dominion had moved away from this position toward a proslavery stance. Of the sixty men who served as Democrats during this period, two had voted for the Preston amendment—James McDowell and Samuel L. Hays, who had been born in Pennsylvania and served only one term from a generally Whig district. The only other Democratic congressman associated with criticism of the peculiar institution was John Letcher, but he vigorously denied any connection with antislavery in order to continue his career as a Democrat. Three Democratic congressmen from these years had voted with the radical proslavery group in 1832. Party orthodoxy on the slavery issue was characterized by the career of the most prominent defender of slavery in the great debate, William O. Goode. He served the Democratic party in the legislature and Congress throughout the antebellum era, was also a leading conservative in both of the constitutional conventions, and later became a prominent southern nationalist.[84]

In the constitutional convention of 1829–30, the relationship between the members' concern about slavery and their positions on democratic reform was one of undisguised self-interest involving property rights and the republican link between taxation and representation. Slavery was defended primarily as a legitimate form of property and attacked as a special privilege. In the subsequent two decades, both sides broadened their purview of the debate, and it became more deeply ideological. Although it was never divorced from self-interest, the nature and scope of that interest were extended, and the connection between Herrenvolk democracy and the peculiar institution, which was always problematic, became even more complex.

The protagonists of the emerging second party system projected opposing orientations summed up in the comment that the Whigs were "less wedded to slavery than the Democrats." The Calhounites in the Old Dominion severed their loose connection with the anti-Jackson coalition and moved into the Democracy, where they joined the conservative planters of the eastern piedmont and tidewater to wield power beyond their numbers. This move further isolated the western Jacksonians, who continued to oppose the peculiar institution from their own racist and economic perspectives as late as the Reform Convention of 1850–51.

While the Whig party was hardly committed to abolition, its leaders included those Virginians who publicly criticized the peculiar institution as late as the early 1850s. Neither the politics of slavery nor evangelical Christianity dictated a unitary position on slavery within the Old Dominion. The economic argument against slavery, the "argument from expediency" in Ruffner's terms, was easily incorporated into the Whig ideology of economic and social diversification and state encouragement of capitalist expansion in the form of aid to banks, internal improvements, manufacturing, and education. Virginia Democrats were among the most proslavery politicians in the country. They tended to accept the positive good argument and to tie their defense of the peculiar institution increasingly to a prosouthern interpretation of states' rights and strict construction.

7

The Doctrines of '98

THE POLITICS of slavery was more pronounced in the Old Dominion because of its intimate connection with the constitutional doctrines of strict construction and states' rights that were sometimes simply referred to as the "Virginia ideas" or the "Doctrines of '98." These concepts presented a potential shield for minority rights but were neither intrinsically nor necessarily democratic, as Madison clearly demonstrated in his argument against South Carolina's nullification. The connection was a historical juncture almost from the first instance. The mystique of the Doctrines of '98 set the tone of the Old Dominion's congressional delegation during these years when it was made up mostly of Democrats and colored the role played by the commonwealth in national politics.

Just as those who publicly disliked slavery were readily portrayed by their opponents as abolitionists endangering home and hearth, so too those who advocated even minimal governmental activism by the Congress were labeled "consolidationists" and "Federalists"—thoroughly un-Virginian in any case. As in the slavery debate, the contrasting positions on states' rights in the antebellum political culture of the Old Dominion were similar to, but essentially different from, those traced out in the twentieth-century defense of segregation.

The term *state rights* entered into the American political lexicon at the end of the 1790s during the debate over the Alien and Sedition Acts. Vice President Jefferson, who considered these measures so dangerous that he proposed secession "rather than give up the rights of self-government," anonymously drew up a protest that led to the Kentucky Resolutions of 1798. These and similar resolves of the Virginia assembly a month later declared that the Union had been formed by a compact of sovereign states and that each of the states had "the right" to judge the constitutionality of federal laws and was "duty bound, to *interpose*" itself between its citizens and any unconstitutional federal legislation. Jefferson's resolutions declared the Sedition and Alien Acts null and "altogether void," and his draft spoke of "nullification" as a proper mode of redress. The

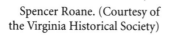

Spencer Roane. (Courtesy of
the Virginia Historical Society)

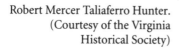

Abel Parker Upshur. (Courtesy of
the Library of Congress)

Robert Mercer Taliaferro Hunter.
(Courtesy of the Virginia
Historical Society)

Virginia and Kentucky resolutions (of both 1798 and 1799) along with Madison's *Report* to the Virginia assembly in 1799–1800 embodied the Doctrines of '98.[1]

While opposition to the sentiments embodied in these resolutions came from nine legislatures north of the Potomac, it also flourished among a substantial minority within the Old Dominion itself. In the assembly debate Federalists insisted that the Constitution emanated directly from the people and taunted the Republicans with the charge that the new federal government was more democratic than the government of Virginia. They successfully opposed a motion, suggested by Jefferson and put forth by John Taylor, declaring the Alien and Sedition Acts "utterly void." On the final vote sixty-three Federalists opposed one hundred Republicans. Thus, in 1798 the Virginia ideas were unacceptable to 40 percent of the state's legislators who represented a larger proportion, perhaps even a majority, of the commonwealth's white population. This minority in the assembly issued a protest written by Richmond delegate John Marshall defending Federalist policy and affirming the right of the federal government representing "the people of united America," to act on "all objects that are general in nature."[2]

Throughout the antebellum period the question of the proper interpretation of the Constitution continued to be the central defining element of the Virginians' political perspectives. The commonwealth generally divided between the advocates of states' rights, who kept alive the antifederalist tradition, and the federalists, who advocated a positive (if limited) role for the national government. While the Doctrines of '98 remained the guiding light on constitutional matters for the majority of the Old Dominion's political elite, there was always a large minority that accepted federalism. The accepted meaning of the Virginia ideas also changed over time as their antifederalist content increasingly asserted itself, first in the form of "particularism" during the states' rights revival after the War of 1812 and then with the emergence of the southern rights movement in the late 1840s.

The collaboration of Jefferson and Madison in creating a Republican opposition in Congress and in asserting and defending the theory of the Union expressed in the Virginia and Kentucky resolutions, as well as their enduring friendship, has obscured the differences between their essential interpretations of the Constitution. Yet this difference was crucial to the continuing debate in the Old Dominion that outlived both Founding Fathers.[3]

After Madison's presidency and particularly after Jefferson's death, the divergence between the two men's ideas became clearer. Jefferson embraced the antifederalist interpretation of the Doctrines of '98 and fought against consolidation, while Madison reasserted his commitment to federalism, eventually accepting the Bank of the United States, defending the tariff, and attacking nullification. As the Whigs and Democrats came on the scene in the 1830s, the contrast between the parties' positions on the Constitution, which assumed a primary place in their belief systems, appropriated these attitudes. The Democrats were advocates of Jefferson's conception of states' rights and strict construction; the Whigs were Madisonian nationalists.

Following the War of 1812, in response to fears of the consolidationist tendencies inherent in John Marshall's judicial nationalism and Henry Clay's American System, Virginia's Old Republicans sparked a states' rights revival that swept over the lower South during the 1820s. Their extreme particularism combined with a growing need to sustain slavery, pushed Virginia states' rights theorists toward John C. Calhoun's "concurrent majority" to protect the property rights of minorities against the dangerous possibility of consolidated government. As John Marshall worried in 1833, "The words 'State Rights,' as expounded in the resolutions of '98 and the report of '99 has charm against which all reasoning is vain. Those resolutions and the report constitute the creed of every politician who hopes to rise in Virginia; and to question them . . . is deemed political sacrilege."[4]

The most important reassertion of states' rights and strict construction emerged from an intramural dispute among Virginians. The Marshall Court forced the issue by deciding a series of cases in a fashion that asserted the appellate jurisdiction of the Supreme Court over not only the acts of Congress and the state legislatures but also the opinions of the state courts. The "first" and "second" conflicts between Virginia and the Supreme Court actually involved an extended controversy within the Old Dominion between the Republican advocates of limited nationalism and the particularism of Judge Spencer Roane, the dominant voice on the Virginia Court of Appeals and, as the head of the Richmond Junto, possibly the most powerful politician in the commonwealth. Three landmark cases handed down by the Marshall Court in 1816, 1819, and 1821—*Martin v. Hunter's Lessee, McCulloch v. Maryland,* and *Cohens v. Virginia*—constituted the essence of judicial nationalism, asserting the power of the Supreme Court over both state legislatures and state courts. The political elite of the Old Dominion rose up against this affront to their republican purity. Following the *Martin* decision in March 1816, the *Enquirer* began immediately and continuously to criticize the Court. Before the month was out, Ritchie printed an attack signed "Amphictyon" written by Judge William Brockenbrough, a member of the Junto. Then in June, Roane contributed four essays under the general title "Rights of 'The States,' and of 'The People,'" signed "Hampden."[5]

Marshall instinctively believed that while the judge entered the lists as "the champion of dismemberment," the evil genius of Jefferson lurked behind these attacks upon the Court. The chief justice was surprised and disappointed to learn that Madison also sided with Roane. He wrote his nationalist Republican colleague Justice Joseph Story, who had been appointed by Madison, "In Virginia the tendency of things verges rapidly to the destruction of the government and the re-establishment of a league of sovereign states." He feared that the "politicians of Virginia" would "grossly misrepresent" the actions of the Court and that the assembly would undoubtedly "pass resolutions not very unlike those which were called forth by the alien & sedition laws of 1799."[6]

Jefferson tried to stay out of the public light, but he privately believed that the tendency of the Court's opinions was "more ominous than any thing which has yet occurred." He wrote Roane on receiving the "Hampden" essays that "I subscribe to every tittle of them. They contain the true principles of the Revolution of 1800 for that was as real a revolution in the principles of our government as that of 1776 was in its form." Yet, the former president complained, "after twenty years . . . we find the judiciary on every occasion still driving us into consolidation." The increasing embrace of particularism that characterized Jefferson's old age was clearly heightened by his reading of John Taylor's various works on agricultural reform and political theory.[7]

The planter politician known as John Taylor of Caroline gained notoriety in the 1790s when he mounted a scathing attack upon the Hamiltonian economic system and partisan corruption. He had taken a hand in the writing of the Kentucky and Virginia resolutions and personally introduced the latter into the assembly. In response to the rulings of the Marshall Court, Taylor put forward his defense of states' rights and strict construction in three books arguing that political authority ultimately resided in the people, who created their state governments by yielding certain powers carefully specified in each state's constitution. The states then entered into a compact that created the Union—Taylor termed it "a league"—by giving up certain of those powers, again clearly enumerated in the federal Constitution. The federal government thus created possessed only those powers specifically delegated to it, and this specified list might be changed only by the concurrence of three-fourths of the states through the cumbersome process of amendment.[8]

A wealthy man, a slaveholder and a planter, Taylor was hardly a democrat seeking to right the iniquities of the commonwealth's constitution, but rather one of those Antifederalists correctly termed "men of little faith." Like so many other Virginian aristocrats of his day, he believed that a society composed of independent gentlemen provided the only basis for a truly republican government. In Taylor's voluminous writings the agrarian argument for states' rights, strict construction, frugality in government, and the need for a landed society to maintain the republic of virtue is combined with the Virginia slaveholding gentry's vision of the Old Dominion as a yeoman society dedicated to the Country ideal.[9]

Nationalism's most immediate opponent in the Old Dominion, however, was neither Taylor, who is sometimes termed "the philosopher of Jeffersonian Democracy," nor Jefferson himself, but Judge Roane, whose antifederalist interpretation of the Doctrines of '98 closely resembled Taylor's. Marshall's Court had been overturning Roane's decisions and challenging the authority of his court. In the "Hampden" essays Roane insisted that the Constitution "conveyed only a limited grant of powers to the general government, and reserved the residuary powers to the government of the states, and to the people," as laid out in the Tenth Amendment.

This "limited grant to congress of certain enumerated powers" included only those *"fairly incidental"* to them, and the "necessary and proper" clause "did not enlarge the powers previously given." Consequently, he reasoned that Congress had exceeded the Constitution in Section 25 of the Judiciary Act of 1789, which extended the power of the Supreme Court to review the decisions of the highest state courts when federal laws were involved, and that the Supreme Court could not review the constitutionality of its own powers.[10]

The judge even more forcefully asserted the Doctrines of '98 in his vitriolic "Algernon Sidney" essays attacking the Court's decision in the *Cohens* case. His slashing arguments were far more politically effective than Taylor's ponderous prose. Jefferson at once affirmed his complete assent, but Madison remained far more circumspect. He praised Roane for combating the "latitudinary" excesses of the Court. Yet the fact remained that Madison disagreed with Roane, Taylor, and Jefferson on the importance of precedent and the necessity for judicial review by the Supreme Court.[11]

The debate entered the political papers of the commonwealth and emerged in various resolutions of the legislature. While the idea of an amendment to the Constitution creating a separate body to handle conflicts between state and federal jurisdiction died, the General Assembly denied the Supreme Court appellate jurisdiction in any case decided by a state court and insisted that the federal court had no right to examine the judgment of "the Commonwealth of Virginia." The roll-call votes on these matters showed a clear conflict between the representatives of the center and those from the periphery. This division, however, did not reflect the ideological differences between Marshall and Roane but something closer to those separating Madison and Jefferson.[12]

In their discussions of constitutional questions, both Roane and Taylor defended slavery and insisted that Marshall's views threatened the peculiar institution. The two perspectives became linked in the minds of most Virginians when in the midst of the battle over the jurisdiction of the Supreme Court, the slavery question broke upon the political scene with Missouri's attempt to enter the Union as a slave state. During the initial consideration of the Missouri bill, New York Republican James Tallmadge introduced an amendment calling upon the prospective state to include in its constitution a prohibition on the further introduction of slaves and a provision for the gradual emancipation of those born in the new state after its admission. Jefferson likened this proposal to "a fire bell in the night" and perceived in its implications "the death knell of the Union." [13]

Henry Clay took the lead in trying to find a peaceful resolution to the problem. In this he cooperated with President Monroe and Virginia senator James Barbour, who savored the role of defender of the Union. It seemed obvious to Barbour that the Missouri matter should be joined with the mundane question of statehood for Maine. This piggyback procedure survived several attempts at further amendment by extremely close votes before one of the senators from Illinois, Jesse Thomas, a southerner by birth and a staunch Republican, suggested as a compromise measure dividing the unsettled portion of the Louisiana lands by extending the southern boundary of the new state and excluding slavery above that line.

The combination of statehood for Maine, Missouri without restriction on slavery, and the extension of the 36° 30' line across the remainder of the Louisiana territory constituted the Missouri Compromise. The situation was complicated when Rufus King, a former Federalist and a senator from New York, launched an attack on slavery. The Virginians and most southern Republican leaders, including President Monroe, took this as a clear sign that the slavery hobby was being ridden to political ends. Although built upon circumstantial evidence and an ignorance of New York politics, the idea of a conspiracy to revive the Federalist party rapidly spread among Virginians. The Republican ascendancy seemed under siege and the Union at risk.

No slave state opposed the Missouri Compromise so adamantly as the Old Dominion. On the crucial votes the House accepted Missouri without restriction by a narrow three-vote margin but passed the Thomas provision overwhelmingly. The first roll call was primarily sectional, although fourteen northerners voted with the southerners. The unanimous Virginia delegation accounted for one-fourth of the proslavery votes. When the southern representatives split their vote on the 36° 30' line with only a slim majority favoring it, the commonwealth's congressmen emphatically rejected compromise. Eighteen Virginians accounted for half of the southern votes against the measure. Only four—John Floyd, Charles Fenton Mercer, Hugh Nelson, and George Strother—condoned congressional power over slavery in the territories. Both Virginia senators opposed the compromise package, although Barbour had played a crucial role in its construction. Nine-tenths of the commonwealth's Jeffersonian elite, through their votes either in Congress or in the assembly, denied the constitutionality of congressional interference with slavery in the territories. [14]

The crisis continued the following year in relation to the status of Missouri's electoral votes and the state's constitutional provision restricting the immigration of free blacks. In both cases the Virginians responded in a petulant fashion, charging the northerners with rank hypocrisy. The entire Virginia delegation agreed with the doyen of the Old Republicans, North Carolina senator Nathaniel Macon, "*There is no place for free blacks in the United States.*" When the final Missouri compromise was struck, giving the new state a free hand in dealing the issue, the congressman from Albemarle County, Hugh Nelson, explained that he "thought it better to make some sacrifice to form than to lose the substance." Eighteen Virginians voted with him to end the two-year-old controversy. In the interest of ideological purity, the keeper of the conscience of the Old Republicans, Randolph of Roanoke, cast the only southern vote against the measure. Two other loyal advocates of the true Virginia Doctrines, Robert Garnett and Severn Parker, refused to vote for what they believed to be a constitutional travesty.[15]

In accepting the Thomas amendment, Monroe had acted against the best advice of his closest colleagues, friends, and family, as well as the private and public expressions of the Virginia legislature. Both Madison and Jefferson rejected the Missouri Compromise. Madison's main concern, like that of Jefferson, Monroe, Clay, and Barbour, was purely political. He believed that the restrictionists sought "to form a new state of parties founded upon local instead of political distinctions thereby dividing the republicans of the North from those of the South." Jefferson, who for once in his life spoke for the Virginia gentry, insisted that morality lay on the side of those who would expand and diffuse slavery. Only unprincipled men would dare to raise such a dangerous question. At the time he expressed his innermost fears concerning slavery and wrote his most conservative commentary on the subject. The author of the Declaration of Independence and the architect of the Northwest Ordinance feared that if the Congress could keep slavery from the territories, it would "declare that the condition of all men with in the United States shall be that of freedom."[16]

Contemporaries noted the degree to which Virginians stuck together and the striking consensus among the commonwealth's elite. In the House debate the most prominent Virginia voice was that of Philip Pendleton Barbour, James's brother. The future Jacksonian appointee to the Supreme Court established the southern position that Missouri constituted a political community equal to the original thirteen states and able to enact its own local legislation. Restriction denied the people of Missouri the essence of self-government: the right to command the disposition of their own property. The purest of the Old Republicans, men such as Macon and Randolph, dismissed the Declaration of Independence and emphasized a narrow interpretation of the Tenth Amendment. Young John Tyler joined them insisting that the Missourians had the same rights as Virginians to "fashion their social environment." Congress possessed no power to forbid slavery in any territory settled or unsettled. Randolph, who always managed an apt phrase to summarize his extreme response, declared, "God has given us the Missouri territory and the devil shall not take it from us." [17]

The *Enquirer* took a particularly strong stand against restriction and assured the Missourians that the Old Dominion supported them completely. While insisting that the essence of the question was states' rights, Ritchie wrote often about the dangers of abolition, published proslavery arguments, and argued repeatedly that the goal of the northerners was "extinction of the slave representation feature in the Congress of the U. States." At various times the editor of the *Enquirer* dismissed the Northwest Ordinance, denied the possibility of the citizenship of free blacks, and talked of disunion. But when he attacked the compromise proposal, Ritchie pictured it as part of a northern plot against Virginia: "No; no, don't encourage them to go on with their demands. . . . They will ride us forever." [18]

None of the Virginians agreed with Tallmadge. What little support the Thomas amendment received came in the form of wavering speeches and hesitant votes from a few representatives whose constituencies lay along the Blue Ridge. Six of the seven congressmen representing the western half of the commonwealth rejected the compromise altogether. The editors of *Niles' Register* received "numerous letters" from northwestern counties of the state opposing Missouri's entry into the Union as a slave state, but Daniel Bryan of Rockingham County in the Valley was the only state senator to vote against the assembly's resolution denying Congress's right to block the entrance of new slave states. When another Valley delegate tried to postpone the vote, his motion was defeated 172 to 9.

With almost complete unanimity the assembly adopted a resolution that the Old Dominion "entered in a common cause with the People of Missouri Territory, and bound to interpose for their defense." One legislator openly predicted civil war "if any restriction is made on our right to hold Slaves and to transport them where we please." Aside from a very few dissenters scattered along the Blue Ridge and in the backcountry, those who represented the Old Dominion rejected overwhelmingly the constitutionality of congressional interference with slavery in any form or fashion. [19]

The two-year debate over the entrance of Missouri forced upon the Virginia gentry the stark realization of their diminishing significance in the political arena that they once had believed to be their own. What is more, their honor had been called into question. The restrictionists posed the possibility that the Old Dominion itself lacked a republican government because it acquiesced in the continuation of the peculiar institution that the Yankees had moved to extinguish. The Tallmadge amendment asked the people of Missouri to accept the restriction on slavery just as Congress had required Louisiana to accept trial by jury and English as the legal language.

The Virginia gentry, rubbed raw by their own economic problems, would not consider such "dictation." Roane portrayed the compromise as Virginia's "own degradation" and an intolerable form of "*voluntary* slavery." The *Norfolk and Portsmouth Herald* considered that "the constitutional guarantee of state rights [had been] set at naught by congressional usurpation." Beverley Tucker, who would become his generation's guide to the Doctrines of '98 as the professor of such things at the College of William and Mary, feared that restriction would make the whole trans-Mississippi area "a Yankee country governed by the sniveling, sanctimonious doctrines in politics and religion which as a Virginian I have learned to abhor."[20]

Jefferson, along with the other advocates of "the revival . . . of State rights," also considered the complex of economic policies that Clay called the "American System" a threat to "government by the people." Even so, a respectable minority of the Old Dominion's representatives had supported the Second Bank, the tariff of 1816, and federally funded internal improvements. The geographic distribution of the vote differed on each issue, with the only clear east/west split coming on internal improvements. All of the commonwealth's congressmen from west of the Blue Ridge supported Calhoun's bonus bill; thirteen of fifteen eastern members opposed it. Under the influence of the Old Republicans in Congress and the Richmond Junto at home, however, Virginians moved quickly to embrace strict construction and states' rights while opposing the emerging American System. During Monroe's first administration they led the fight against the Bank and fought attempts to raise the tariff. In each case they were supported by both the *Enquirer* and the assembly.[21]

The Cumberland Road, the Chesapeake and Ohio Canal, and the general survey bill gained some support from those representing constituencies along the Potomac and in the northwest. Nonetheless, most of the commonwealth's congressmen stood against federal aid to internal improvements on strict constitutional grounds, and the protective tariff proved to be even less popular. James Barbour, who had voted for the tariff of 1816, led the opposition to the Baldwin bill to raise the tariff two years later, and twenty-one of the twenty-two Virginians in Congress opposed protection in 1824. Only three Virginians voted for the "Tariff of Abominations." Most of the members from the Valley and those from the southwest voted with the east. Virginia's proponents of the American System represented pockets of discontent on the periphery in the northwest and the northern piedmont.[22]

The issues mingled in the minds of the Virginia particularists, who in the mid-1820s challenged both the tariff and internal improvements on constitutional grounds. Monroe had vetoed the Cumberland Road bill as an unwarranted invasion of the states' rights, and the *Enquirer* interpreted his action as an expression of the true "principles of Jefferson and Madison in the purest days of the Republican party," echoing "the sense in which the Virginia Convention adopted, and in which the Legislature of '99 interpreted the constitution." In debating the 1824 bill, Philip Barbour extended Taylor's reading of the Doctrines of '98 to deny the constitutionality of the protective tariff as well.[23]

Affirming anew their commitment to "the resolutions of 1798, and the report in support of them of 1799," the members of the House of Delegates by a six-to-one margin endorsed George Dromgoole's resolutions in 1826 that tariff protection was "unconstitutional . . . oppressive and partial," that Congress did not "possess the power under the Constitution, to adopt a general system of internal improvements in the States," and that "the appropriation of money . . . to construct roads and canals in the States is a violation of the Constitution." The following year at the encouragement of the new governor, John Tyler, a more vigorously worded set of resolutions detailing the constitutional case against tariff protection was passed with the support of three-fourths of the delegates and two-thirds of the state senators.

The preamble written by William Branch Giles emphasized that in enumerating certain powers in the Constitution, the states transferred only concurrent, not exclusive, jurisdiction to the federal government. The construction of roads and canals interfered with the state's right to control its own territory, while the tariff both violated the rights of private property and exceeded the constitutional power of Congress. In line with the views Jefferson had expressed privately to him just before his death, Giles insisted that the assumption of such powers could lead directly to either a "Government . . . consolidated in its practice and unlimited in its will" or "the severance of the Union of these States." When Congress ignored the pleas of Virginia and enacted the "Tariff of Abominations," Giles exploded to Tazewell, "Never before were any people subjected to such plunder and degradation."[24]

By the end of the decade, a particularist majority committed to an extreme interpretation of the Doctrines of '98 supported by the *Enquirer* and rhetorically, at least, calculating the value of the Union controlled the Virginia General Assembly. At the end of February 1829, before Jackson's inauguration, the assembly accepted an elaborate report affirming that "each [state] has the right to construe the Compact for itself" and that a protective tariff had not been "authorized by the plain construction, true intent and meaning of the Constitution." The votes in the House of Delegates, however, indicated an increased polarization as well. Between the roll calls of 1827 and those taken two years later, western attendance went up, and as a consequence the size of the majority siding with Giles declined. The lines of battle within the Old Dominion were drawn between the moderate advocates of Madisonian nationalism and the new-model Antifederalists who emphasized state sovereignty.[25]

The geographic distribution of the votes set the nationalist periphery against the center committed to the agrarianism of Taylor, Jefferson, and Giles in a pattern that reflected the vote for Adams and Jackson. Roughly two-thirds of the legislators embraced particularism, and coincidently Jackson received 69 percent of the popular vote. When it took up Adams, the *Richmond Constitutional Whig* shifted its editorial position from condemnation of the tariff as self-defeating and federal aid to internal improvements as unconstitutional to an acceptance of limited nationalism. Pleasants turned his attack upon the advocates of laissez-faire and insisted that the Old Dominion develop a more diversified economy by encouraging its own industries and extending the state's transportation system. Both major Adams papers, the *Constitutional Whig* and the *Lynchburg Virginian*, continually associated their stance with that taken by the patriarch of republicanism, James Madison.[26]

Not only did the majority of the assembly deny his authority as an interpreter of the Constitution, but Giles and the Junto mounted a concerted attack on Madison. Various contributors to the *Enquirer* suggested that Madison had turned "against the whole course of his reasoning for 40 preceding years" and insisted upon their right to determine the meaning of the Doctrines of '98 without his aid. Rives complained about this constant "pecking" at his elderly mentor and the arrogance of "the Richmond party and the southsiders," but most of the Jacksonians agreed with Ritchie.[27]

When Jackson won his landslide victory in 1828, the advocates of particularism and the Doctrines of '98 embraced his candidacy. But the eastern planter aristocracy who supported the Old Hero clearly rejected constitutional reform within the commonwealth and the extension of political democracy to all white men. It was among this group that the states' rights revival and particularism found its greatest support. The contest over the American System, like those over democracy and slavery, set the center against the periphery, tradition against change, the eastern supporters of Jackson against a coalition of western Jacksonians and National Republicans (map 7.1).

Thomas Jefferson's credentials as a democrat are clear, but those who shared his opposition to consolidation usually reviled this aspect of his thought. Those Virginians who advocated the expansion of the suffrage and the white basis of representation and who openly questioned the peculiar institution supported Adams and Clay or tended to follow Madison on federal questions, although his position on local democracy in the convention of 1829–30 was more conservative than theirs.[28]

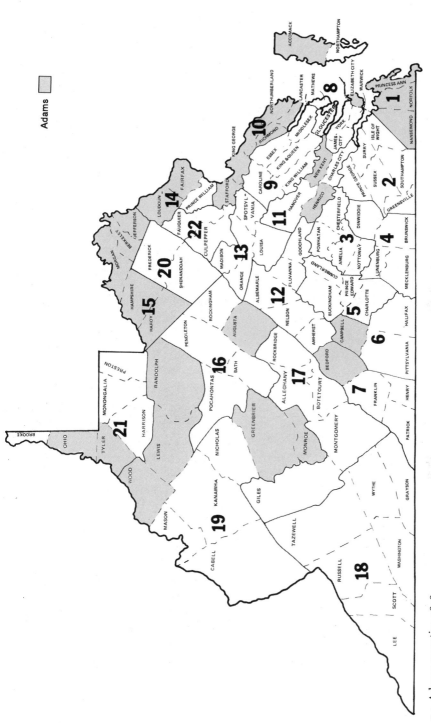

Adams

7.1. Adams counties, 1828

During his first administration Andrew Jackson produced an unblemished record as a champion of the Doctrines of '98 and a protector of southern interests. The removal of the Indians from the southwestern states, a land policy encouraging the rapid sale of federal lands and their cession to the states, and the carefully conceived Maysville Road veto garnered nearly unanimous support from the southern members of Congress. Even in the case of the Bank, the division followed sectional lines. South of the Potomac and east of the Mississippi, only Kentucky favored recharter. Consequently, in 1832 Jackson won two-thirds of the popular vote in the slave states and 90 percent of the southern electoral votes outside of the home states of Clay and Calhoun.

On all of these matters the majority of commonwealth's congressmen and senators supported the administration. Those Virginians who opposed the president's policies came from the northern piedmont and west of the Blue Ridge (map 7.2). While partisan affiliation remained nebulous from 1829 through 1833, eighteen Virginians in Congress consistently supported Jackson. Seven National Republicans, including reformers Philip Doddridge and Charles Fenton Mercer, voted for internal improvements and distribution of federal funds and against quick sale and cession of public lands and Indian removal. They also cast five votes for the tariff of 1832, on which the Virginia Jacksonians split, and all six votes from Virginia in favor of the recharter of the Bank of the United States.[29]

When the assembly met in December following Jackson's overwhelming reelection, the general faced little opposition in the Old Dominion. Governor Floyd called for further moderation of the tariff but concentrated on the "incendiary" activities of the abolitionists. Those in the assembly who had favored Philip Barbour for vice president joined with Van Buren's supporters in elevating to the Senate William C. Rives, Madison's protégé, whom Gilmer described as "anti-bank, anti-tariff, and anti-nullification." The Doctrines of '98 as understood by the editor of the *Enquirer* seemed to be in the ascendancy in Washington as well as Richmond.[30]

Overnight with the publication of the president's "Proclamation to the People of South Carolina," the honeymoon ended. Virginia advocates of states' rights were particularly offended by the passages denying the compact theory and insisting that the federal government acted directly upon the people. It seemed "dangerously national and unorthodox," expressing doctrines "as obnoxious as nullification itself." The states were sovereign and had the inherent right to secede in the face of unconstitutional legislation. Even the *Richmond Whig*, which had backed Clay, insisted, "No government or power has a right to inquire the reasons of her conduct when a state secedes, much less whip her back."[31]

Previous partisan attachments associated with presidential politics evaporated as the legislators split along strict sectional lines. The western Jacksonians

7.2. National Republican congressional seats, 1827–33

received the proclamation "with loud and almost universal applause" and joined the National Republicans in the struggle against nullification. A correspondent to the *Washington Globe* believed that "not 100 men North and west of the Blue Ridge" supported the nullifiers. All of the anti-Jackson meetings denouncing "consolidated despotism" were held in Southside and tidewater counties; the Union meetings were held in the western and northern piedmont, west of the Blue Ridge and in the outlying towns of Lynchburg, Staunton, and Wheeling. In these areas Jackson's former opponents applauded the president's newfound constitutional nationalism.[32]

Jackson's proclamation brought forth hostile responses from the commonwealth's most vociferous conservatives. Those Old Republicans who had never fully embraced Jackson saw in his "new political dogmas" all that they had feared. Senator Tazewell published a series of essays reasserting the compact theory and acknowledging the right of secession. Only if the federal government remained a limited one, acting at all times clearly within the constitutional bounds, could such crises be avoided. Judge Upshur rejected secession and thought that South Carolina had acted rashly, but he defended nullification as a logical extension of the Virginia and Kentucky resolutions. The states could determine the constitutionality of federal legislation that affected them, and it was their duty to interpose themselves against encroachments upon their sovereignty.[33]

The *Whig* found the proclamation a godsend, allowing Pleasants to refocus his attack on the president's personal character. He portrayed Jackson as dangerously dictatorial and arbitrary, awarding friends and punishing enemies like a monarch. His willingness to "array the military power against . . . his 'native state'" raised the specter of a "Consolidated Empire" and dictated the necessity to rally the "friends of state rights." In contrast, the president's position caused consternation at the *Enquirer*. Ritchie had portrayed both Jackson and Van Buren as staunch advocates of states' rights and published a pamphlet entitled *Virginia Doctrines Not Nullification*. The unilateral action of a single state threatened to substitute the minority will for majority rule as Madison had argued. Nullification was "a revolutionary measure . . . an absurd and dangerous heresy" that would never be supported by the Old Dominion, striking as it did "at the very foundation of Republican Government" and threatening "all the horrors of revolution and civil war." Yet the clearly frustrated Ritchie could not accept the proclamation's constitutional argument and urged Jackson to modify his position.[34]

Three days after Jackson's proclamation appeared, Governor Floyd, who clearly supported the nullifiers, submitted it and the South Carolina ordinance nullifying the tariff acts to the assembly, recommending immediate action to "sustain the liberties of our country." A series of legislative maneuvers then rekindled the slavery debate and more explicitly than ever before associated the Doctrines of '98 with the protection of the peculiar institution. The assembly ordered the printing of Madison's *Report of 1800* but then quashed an attempt to print and distribute his recent letter opposing nullification. Gilmer termed the letter "trash." James H. Gholson, a Southside proslavery extremist, pontificated that the Old Dominion would not adopt the words of any man, and the stalwarts of the emerging State-Rights party denounced Madison: "We do not believe that the fabric raised by the youthful Hercules can be thrown down by him in the weakness and decrepitude of old age." [35]

A select committee on federal relations, under the chairmanship of respected Southside conservative William Brodnax, criticized the actions of both the nullifiers and the president but pointedly affirmed the duty of the states to interpose themselves against federal abuse of power and the right of secession as a last resort after "every constitutional effort had been tried and every peaceful experiment exhausted." Thomas Marshall proposed a substitute resolution that merely asked South Carolina to rescind its ordinance until Congress might respond, but William H. Roane, the son of Spencer Roane, moved to replace Marshall's motion with a series of resolutions attacking both nullification and the proclamation. The division on all of the related roll calls was strikingly sectional, with the State-Rights party representing the eastern center and the Union party the western periphery (map 7.3). [36]

After further wrangling, John T. Brown, a proslavery Petersburg Jacksonian, offered another substitute motion that avoided the issue of secession and presented a fourteen-point grab bag of Democratic dogma on states' rights and strict construction similar to the position taken by Ritchie. This motion surprisingly passed by one vote but was replaced the following day with a simple statement that "the doctrines of State sovereignty and State rights as set forth in the Resolutions of 1798, and sustained by the Report thereon of 1799, are the true doctrines of republicanism" and could not be construed to sanction either the South Carolina ordinance or Jackson's proclamation. Finally, William O. Goode of Mecklenburg moved the creation of a select committee to bring forth a new set of resolutions based upon this consensus. The committee presented and the assembly approved a moderate preamble and three resolutions. Thus, the acrimonious debate ended with an innocuous call for the promotion of the "peace and harmony of our common country." Old Republican Benjamin Watkins Leigh was dispatched to Charleston to cool the Carolina hotheads. [37]

The assembly's final action in relation to nullification was to reelect John Tyler as senator. Just before the election by the assembly, he had fought with Rives in the Senate over the force bill. Tyler cast the only Senate vote against it, and in the House his dissent was echoed by seven eastern Virginians. Fourteen of the commonwealth's congressmen followed Rives in supporting the president's

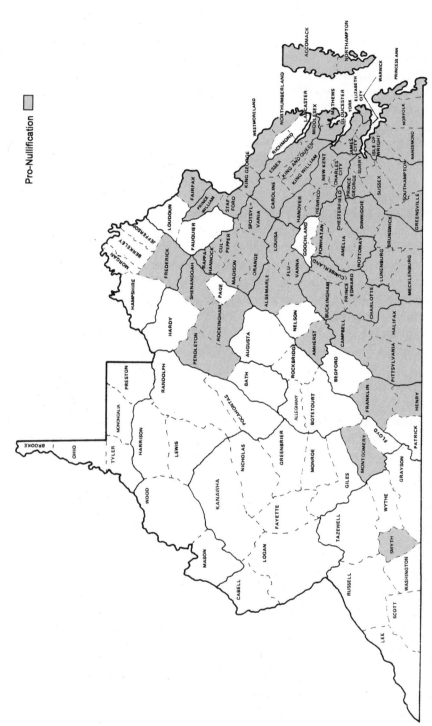

Pro-Nullification ▢

7.3. House of Delegates vote on nullification, 1833

request for legislation to aid in enforcing the tariff laws. In a close vote that again split along sectional lines, the assembly chose Tyler over western Jacksonian James McDowell. The *Lynchburg Virginian* associated Tyler with nullification, and the sixty-three votes he received in the House of Delegates were all cast by members who opposed the proclamation. Roane praised Tyler's independence and fidelity to the true doctrines of the Old Dominion. His support centered in the tidewater and Southside among planter conservatives like Brodnax whom the *Whig* editor termed the "true State-Rights men."[38]

The State-Rights party retained control of the legislature in the spring elections of 1833 and claimed the allegiance of ten of the twenty-one members of the Twenty-third Congress. The new congressional delegation from Virginia included thirteen or fourteen Jacksonians and seven National Republicans. Obviously some voters who had supported the president as a nationalist turned to congressmen who opposed the administration on all other issues. Those affiliated with the State-Rights party were exclusively eastern Jacksonians. Only four of the eleven Unionists supported Jackson. Thus, while all of Virginia's National Republicans accepted the proclamation, nearly three-quarters of the president's own party opposed him on this matter.[39]

The paths followed into the new era of partisanship by those members of the Old Dominion's political elite indicate both the amorphous character of the alignments in the early 1830s and the place states' rights would play in the second party system. In general, the National Republicans became Whigs, and the Jacksonians moved into the Democratic Republican party that supported Van Buren in 1836. The four Jacksonian Unionists—George Loyall, Andrew Stevenson, Edward Lucas, and James M. H. Beale—became Democrats, and the other eight who had been National Republicans—including Charles Fenton Mercer, Samuel McComas, and Samuel McDowell Moore—were later Whigs. Seven of the ten congressmen associated with the State-Rights party had been Jacksonians and continued their careers as Democrats. The three others elected in 1833 were William S. Archer, Henry Wise, and William Fitzhugh Gordon. All had supported Jackson previously and were reelected to their seats but moved into the opposition the following year.[40]

Of these three, only Archer became a regular Whig, and a tenuous one at that. He was an Old Republican who headed the Virginia delegation to the Baltimore convention in 1832 where he favored Barbour for vice president. His break with Jackson came after the removal of the federal deposits from the Bank, and as a consequence he lost his seat in 1835. Six years later he was elected to the Senate by the Whigs. Gordon also turned against Jackson's "strange and incompetent administration," but like Calhoun he never became a Whig. The eccentric Wise slowly drifted into the opposition and was briefly a Whig in his own mind and strictly on his own terms. During Tyler's administration he broke with the party and eventually drifted back to the Democratic fold, emerging as one of its leaders. Similar tangential affiliations with the new party characterized the most outspoken advocates of states' rights—Tazewell, Leigh, Upshur, and Tucker—who all retained a republican hostility toward parties and partisanship. Governor Floyd, who once described himself as "sort of a Clay man," was basically a Calhounite who never became involved with the Whigs.[41]

Among those who served in the House of Delegates in the mid-1830s, the State-Rights party split in half, producing a slightly larger number of Democrats than Whigs, while 60 percent of those supporting the Union party became Whigs. More important, two-thirds of the future Whigs came from the Union party. The Democrats retained most of the legislators sympathetic to nullification. These men, along with the majority of the Jacksonian congressmen who disapproved of the proclamation, molded the Virginia Democratic party in line with their interpretation of the Doctrines of '98 and forced the Unionists to mend their ways or move into the opposition.

The nationalist position prevailed among the proto-Whigs. Moore referred directly to Madison's own interpretation of the Doctrines of '98 to oppose "the new political doctors" and the State-Rights party in the 1832–33 assembly. When Brodnax insisted that men's allegiance should be first to their state and then to the general government, Henry Berry of Jefferson County, who like Moore had opposed Brodnax on slavery during the previous session, contended that the "converse" was true: "allegiance to the general government is primary." Befitting his future role at the Nashville Convention, William O. Goode spoke out in favor of the right of secession with the same enthusiasm that he had displayed defending slavery a year earlier.

Not surprisingly there was a strong relationship between the two issues for men who served in both sessions. Twenty-one of twenty-four Unionists had favored Preston's amendment to consider emancipation in 1832. Thirty-two of the thirty-seven supporters of the State-Rights party had been proslavery. Unionism also closely correlated with advocacy of constitutional reform. Of the congressmen and assemblymen who had also been in the convention of 1829–30, eight of nine Unionists had been reformers, and all nine of the State-Rights men were conservatives acting with Tazewell, Tyler, Leigh, and Upshur.[42]

In preparation for the upcoming presidential election, the Democratic Republicans met in Washington in July 1835 to nominate Martin Van Buren and Richard M. Johnson. They issued a statement of principles that set a middle course between nullification and consolidation. The main thrust of the document was directed at the abolitionists. "Those who would interfere with these reserved and vital rights of the States, cannot be Democrats; and on the other hand those who would weaken the bonds of union . . . cannot be in truth Jeffersonian Republicans." The great economic issues of the day—the Bank, the tariff, and internal improvements—were cast completely in constitutional terms. Headed by the convention chairman Andrew Stevenson, the Old Republican congressman from Virginia, the Democratic Republicans concentrated their criticism on the "consolidationists" and their "latitudinarian construction" of the Constitution.

The Democratic Republican address linked the policies of Jackson to those of Jefferson, whose authority was repeatedly invoked, and portrayed the administration's opponents as men who would "push the authority of the General Government to the most unwarrantable lengths, disregarding State rights and public sentiment (as in the case of the Alien and Sedition Laws.)" Jackson affirmed this commitment in his farewell address, in which he implicitly chastised the South Carolinians but carefully avoided the heresies of his proclamation. Without mentioning the peculiar institution, the Old Hero emphasized that "each state had the unquestioned right to regulate its own internal concerns," warned against the dangers of "consolidated Government," and reasserted his desire "to maintain unimpaired and in full vigor the rights and sovereignty of the States and to confine the action of the General Government strictly to the sphere of its appropriate duties."[43]

As the second party system matured in the late 1830s, the Whigs leaned toward a broad construction of the Constitution that fell somewhere between Marshall and Madison, while the Democrats situated themselves between Jefferson and Calhoun as the defenders of the rights of the states. The Democracy's 1840 platform—the first in American history—committed its candidate, Martin Van Buren, to states' rights, strict construction, and a prohibition upon congressional action against slavery in order to conciliate the Calhounites who had drifted back into the party after 1837. It also included specific economic planks, denying the constitutionality of both a "general system of internal improvements" and a national bank while trimming on the tariff, insisting that "justice and sound policy forbade the federal government to foster one branch of industry to the detriment of another." The followers of President Van Buren were clearly on record as the party of laissez-faire, favoring a "revenue tariff" with only "incidental" protection, the "divorce of bank and state," and a land policy designed to extinguish the federal role within the states as quickly as possible through preemption or outright cession. Yet in all cases these economic policies were wrapped in the cocoon of constitutional orthodoxy and the Doctrines of '98.[44]

The "Democratic Whigs" did not write a platform in 1840, but their economic program represented the acknowledged position of the party and stood as a clear alternative to that offered by the "American Democracy." The parties had been publicly debating these policies for three years. Clay, who consistently claimed to be a Republican follower of Jefferson and an opponent of Federalism, had moderated his position on the tariff to achieve the Compromise of 1833 and in the late 1830s sought to blunt Calhoun's use of the slavery question against him by introducing a series of counterresolutions against the abolitionists that he hoped would appeal to moderates in both sections by avoiding the "black snake" of slavery.[45]

The Whigs looked to gain support in the Old Dominion from the Conservative Democrats, whose grievances primarily concerned the administration's economic policy although they hewed to the Madisonian line on constitutional questions. Calhoun's followers eventually chose Van Buren as the lesser evil, while Upshur and Tucker grudgingly supported Harrison only to rid the country of the Little Magician from New York. The advocates of the Doctrines of '98 in the Old Dominion breathed a sigh of relief when the Whig died a month after taking office and Tyler, a Virginian of the old school, became the eleventh president of the United States. Tyler had a convivial relationship with Clay, but the two men were hardly close, and the popular and headstrong Kentucky senator, who "would rather be right than president," intended to function as his party's leader in Congress.[46]

The common Whig conception of the limited powers of the executive that had given the party its name in the struggle against "King Andrew" dictated a graceful acquiescence in congressional control and the acknowledgment by the acting president that his personal views did not reflect those of the majority of Whigs, even in his own state. While the competition for control of the government between Clay and Tyler involved both the Kentuckian's egotistical attempt at "dictation" and the Virginian's obstinate insistence upon his "independence of party," it also represented further ideological contention between traditional principles of states' rights and the limited economic nationalism associated with the American System.[47]

Clay immediately seized the initiative, sketching the outline of a broad Whig attack on the nation's major economic problems and seeking to reverse previous policy decisions associated with a decade of Democratic rule. Clay called upon Congress "to go forward and re-establish the people in their lost prosperity" by returning to a credit system based upon a new national bank, revising the tariff for added revenue to meet government expenses and spur economic revival, and distributing the revenues of land sales to help the states develop their transportation and education systems. To this agenda the Whigs added their support for a national bankruptcy act that had been introduced in the previous session to provide relief during the depression.[48]

The main fight during the special session in the summer of 1841 involved the question of what sort of "fiscal agent" should replace the hated Independent Treasury. The secretary of the treasury, Thomas Ewing of Ohio, with the advice of Rives, brought forth a plan for the incorporation of a "Fiscal Bank" in the District of Columbia with the power to establish branches in consenting states. The congressional Whigs, however, desired a more muscular national institution, and their revised "Fiscal Bank" bill passed the Senate by three votes and the House by a more comfortable thirty-vote margin. Although only six Whigs voted with ninety-two Democrats against it, the president vetoed the bill on strict constructionist grounds. Whigs in the cabinet and the Congress scurried to respond to his objections. After various consultations that involved John Minor Botts and Alexander H. H. Stuart, Clay supporters from the Old Dominion, the party leaders presented a revised bill for a "Fiscal Corporation." Tyler, who was now referring to "the Whigs" as his opponents, then exercised his veto for the second time in a month, insisting that the new proposal constituted nothing more than "a charter for a national bank." [49]

The frustrated Whigs turned to the tariff when Congress reconvened and passed a stopgap measure termed the "Little Tariff" that Tyler quickly vetoed because it repealed the provision of the land act prohibiting distribution of revenues from land sales if the tariff was increased. Congress then presented the president with a general tariff bill that he rejected, again on traditional constitutional grounds. Finally by the end of August, the modestly protective tariff of 1842, without a provision for distribution, passed by extremely narrow margins in both houses and gained presidential approval. [50]

The behavior of the Twenty-seventh Congress typified the nature of the new politics introduced by the advent of the second party system. The congressional roll calls revealed sharply drawn partisan lines on the array of economic matters before the congress and the country. The debates showed sharply differing positions concerning the constitutional implications of these policies. Latitudinarian Whigs united on one side; strict constructionist Democrats on the other.

Partisanship proved to be far more important than sectionalism as the southern Whigs solidly supported the revival of the American System. Twenty northern Democrats and thirty-five southern Whigs broke party ranks on the final vote on the tariff of 1842, but the original bill with a provision for distribution of public funds had passed as a partisan measure with 99 percent of the Democrats opposed and 90 percent of the Whigs supporting protection. The president's actions led to the resignation of his cabinet, his censure by Congress, and calls for his impeachment. The six Tylerites in the house who opposed their party's banking proposals—those Clay called Tyler's "corporal's guard"—constituted 4 percent of those members elected as Whigs, and three of them were northerners. [51]

The Tylerites were thus very atypical Whigs and focusing upon them distorts the political picture within Virginia. The elections of 1841 had produced a congressional delegation that included ten Whigs, ten Democrats, and one "Independent"—R. M. T. Hunter. The state's two senators, Rives and Archer, were now nominally Whigs. On each of the major questions, most of the members of the delegation from the Old Dominion voted with their party. They had run as party candidates involved in raucous campaigns that often included daylong debates on the issues. The accounts of local meetings depict clear partisan differences on policy matters in nearly all of the counties across the commonwealth. Alexander Stuart from Augusta County, the Whig stronghold in the Valley, who defeated Democrat James McDowell in a hard-fought contest, defined the issues that divided the people and parties of his district: "The Democrats insisted on State banks, a tariff for revenue only, and opposed internal improvements by the general government and the distribution of [revenues from] the public lands under Mr. Clay's bill; while the Whigs favored a United States Bank, a protective tariff, a liberal system of internal improvements by the general government, and the distribution of [revenues from] public lands for educational purposes."[52]

Virginia Democrats in Congress questioned the constitutionality of the entire Whig program and defended the position set forth by Jefferson and Jackson that the executive had the right to review legislation independent of rulings by the Supreme Court. In particular they denied the authority of the decisions in the *McCulloch*, *Dartmouth College*, and *Bank of Augusta* cases, quoting Jefferson's fear of consolidation and referring directly to the Doctrines of '98. "Extra Billy" Smith, the Calhounite congressman from Culpeper County, viewed the bankruptcy act as "much more glaringly unconstitutional and much more immoral than the Alien and Sedition Laws."[53]

When the roll was called, the Democrats from the Old Dominion unanimously opposed the repeal of the Independent Treasury, both bank bills, the distribution act, the bankruptcy law, and a tariff in any form. Hunter voted consistently with the Democrats. His friends and fellow Calhounites Gilmer and Dr. Francis Mallory, from Elizabeth City County in the tidewater, departed from the Whig majority on distribution. Gilmer and Wise voted against both the bank bills. Rives and Archer sustained the president on the "Fiscal Bank" measure, but Archer switched his vote on the revised "Fiscal Corporation" proposal, leaving Rives as the only Whig in the Senate opposed and the only one still speaking to Tyler after the special session. Gilmer and Mallory joined the Democrats on the tariff; Wise abstained and then voted to uphold the president's veto. Within a year Gilmer and Wise had become Democrats, and Mallory had dropped out of politics. Both Rives and Archer turned against Tyler and became active Whigs, opposing Texas annexation and supporting Clay in 1844.[54]

The Whigs of the Old Dominion, like those of the upper South generally, favored distribution of federal funds for internal improvements and public education as well as the other elements of the American System and would accept a protective tariff if their state would profit from the reallocation of tax revenues. Seven of the state's Whigs voted for Clay's version of the tariff that Tyler vetoed. Congressmen Summers, Stuart, Botts, and William L. Goggin epitomized the Virginia Whig party in the 1840s. The party press in the commonwealth supported these men and turned against Tyler. The best-known defections from the party came in the tidewater, but the area remained Whig, and most eastern Whigs stood consistently with Clay. Tyler's old congressional district actually increased its Whig vote between 1840 and 1844. Ironically, this district, which included Richmond, sent to Washington John Minor Botts, the president's most vitriolic opponent, who served as the partisan prosecutor in the Whig move to impeach Tyler. The anti-Tyler *Richmond Whig* affirmed the need for party loyalty and applauded the party's refusal to "reward . . . such characters" as the Tylerites, in order "to render *Cow-boyism* in politics so unprofitable as to be abandoned by universal consent."[55]

The Democrats courted the "Republican faction of the Whig party." They were pleased by the president's vetoes, and Ritchie assured Tyler that he "could rely with perfect confidence on the defense and support of the Republican Party." The *Enquirer* praised Gilmer, Wise, and Upshur as friends of strict construction and true Virginia principles while the paper expressed its frustration with the Whigs in the assembly who supported Clay and the party's leaders in Congress. Ritchie insisted that the Democracy now embodied the Doctrines of '98 and invited all Virginians to join the fight to maintain the Jeffersonian creed against Whig "consolidation."[56]

The Tylerites, however, hesitated to join the party of Van Buren and tried to rally the "moderates of all parties" in support of an administration that adhered to "the old Jeffersonian school." While Tyler's bank vetoes focused upon the specific economic issues, the constitutionality of the Whig proposals was crucial. In all of his letters and messages related to the matter, Tyler began from the idea that Congress could not legitimately "create a national bank to operate *per se* over the Union." He distinguished sharply between the power of Congress "in its character as a national legislature" and its ability to act "as the local legislature of the District." Congress could only incorporate a local bank in the District or appoint as a fiscal agent a bank incorporated by one of the states. The Tylerites' concern with the terms *bank* and *corporation* implied more than mere nit-picking. The various circumlocutions inserted into the bills by Clay and the congressional Whigs confounded the rights of the states in practice and exceeded the specified powers to "collect, keep and disburse public revenue" and only "incidentally to regulate the commerce and exchanges."[57]

Tyler's application of strict construction to the question can further be seen in his own proposal that the Whigs rejected as little more than the Independent

Treasury in another guise. The president favored a state-based scheme sent to him by Beverley Tucker, who proposed a fiscal institution created by a "compact between the States" and governed by an independent bicameral board of directors. Upshur and Dew, who both possessed reputations as political economists, advised him that Tucker's plan was impractical. Rives, who was also something of an expert on the subject, convinced Tyler that an earlier suggestion of Hugh Lawson White met his constitutional criteria. In correspondence with Tazewell the president worked out his final plan described in his message to Congress.

Tyler, who did not know much about banking, stressed the constitutional questions in all his public statements where he constructed an even more vigorous defense of states' rights than the Taney Court. In seeking to avoid "conflict with state jurisdiction" and leave "the banking privileges of the States without interference," the president followed the arguments put forth by Alabama Democrat John McKinley in his dissent in *Bank of Augusta v. Earle* and by the plaintiff's lawyer in that case, Democratic congressman Charles Jared Ingersoll. Commenting on the two Whig proposals that he vetoed, Tyler wrote that they constituted nothing other than "an old-fashioned Bank" and his opponents would tolerate "no appeal to the States." In defending Tyler's veto—which he probably wrote—Wise specifically rejected Madison's argument on the matter and restated the traditional Jeffersonian position.[58]

For the remainder of his administration, John Tyler surrounded himself with a group of men who took distinct pride in their freedom from partisan attachment and commitment to strict constitutional orthodoxy. He replaced Harrison's cabinet with one made up of men more like himself and even offered a post to Calhoun's friend Duff Green before sending him to Europe as his unofficial representative. The "corporal's guard" in Congress were men of principle committed to the Doctrines of '98, opposed to consolidation that threatened to convert the confederacy into a nation governed by "the forbidden idea of a numerical majority of the people." Gilmer consistently portrayed himself as an "honest, independent State-Rights Republican" attached to no faction. In 1838 he noted: "The present position of parties is singular. . . . I am myself not enlisted for the war." As governor he led the fight against New York's refusal to return three fugitive slaves. When the Whig legislature condemned his behavior, Gilmer resigned to run for Congress. Wise was also only loosely attached to the Whigs. Egotistical, "tactless and unduly aggressive," this insecure eccentric from the Eastern Shore gloried in his reputation as the "undoubted dictator" of the Tyler administration.[59]

The Tylerites retained the traditional Republican hostility to parties and emphasized freedom from the bonds of partisanship. Upshur wrote on entering the cabinet, "We came in *against all parties*" with only those friends "our measures would win for us." When these men spoke about creating a new party, they invoked a Burkean concern to establish a harmonious coalition of conservatives whose constitutional scruples produced "*a cohesion of principles.*" The secretary believed that "the people were tired of political intrigue and partisan conflict" and insisted that they would flock to Tyler "from all sides," rejoicing "to find under his auspices some relief from the agitation and strifes of party contest."[60]

Actually, Upshur worried that Tyler himself seemed not "to understand any thing of Sovereignty philosophically viewed." The judge from the Eastern Shore was well known in the Old Dominion for his defense of the conservative planter position in the constitutional convention of 1829–30 and his "Locke" and "Napier" essays defending nullification. In 1840 he published a response to the strong nationalist teachings of Justice Story vindicating the views of Jefferson, Roane, and Taylor that the states were sovereign and the Constitution was a compact formed and ratified by the states, creating a federal rather than a national or a consolidated government. To this he added an extension of his arguments in the convention against numerical majorities, insisting that the sovereignty of the states entitled them to protection from the majority.[61]

As isolated as they were, this small circle of states' rights theorists and proslavery, southern sectionalists gathered around Tyler still controlled executive power and devoted the second half of his administration to the acquisition of Texas. With the addition of Mississippi expansionist Democrat Robert John Walker, who had defended Tyler's vetoes in the Senate, the "Virginia Cabal" became the "Texas Junto." Tyler had been fascinated by the project from the opening days of his presidency. Upshur had a long-standing interest in Texas and launched an extensive propaganda campaign to convert American public opinion to this end. Gilmer joined the call for annexation in a public letter that tied southern security for slavery to the economic benefits of annexation for the northern states and the idea that "our federative Union . . . is capable of indefinite extension." Finally in April 1842 Wise, the loose cannon of the "guard," proposed annexation and welcomed a war with Britain to uphold national honor and protect America's cotton monopoly.[62]

Tyler and the Texas Junto maintained that the British threatened the national interest by plotting to abolitionize Texas and undermine the southern economy. Upshur corresponded with Calhoun, who advised the secretary that it would be necessary to emphasize the economic benefits for the North and join the issues of Texas, California, and Oregon. While the secret negotiations proceeded, Upshur rather cynically filled the Tyler administration organ, the *Madisonian,* with anonymous articles on the systematic and selfish "Designs of the British Government" to deny America's destiny. In line with this general argument, Tyler chastised Mexico and suggested annexation in his annual message in December 1843. An agreement was nearly ready for presentation to the Senate when Upshur and Gilmer were killed in the explosion of a twelve-inch gun on the new navy ship the *Princeton*. Quickly, Tyler, through the intercession of Wise, offered the portfolio at State to Calhoun, who signed an annexation agreement.[63]

In the Senate the treaty's supporters echoed the arguments of the Texas Junto. The speechmaking was almost exclusively partisan. Democrats urged ratification; Whigs opposed the treaty. The key exception was Thomas Hart Benton of Missouri who represented the discontent of the Van Burenites with the whole process. He and six northern Democrats voted with twenty-eight of twenty-nine Whigs to defeat the treaty decisively. Significantly southern Whigs headed up by Virginia senator Archer, who had replaced his colleague Rives as chairman of the Committee on Foreign Relations, led the antiannexation effort. Both of the senators from the Old Dominion voted with their fellow Whigs against Tyler and Texas.[64]

The administration then shifted tactics; the president proposed that Congress annex Texas by passing a joint resolution. Tyler repeated the Jeffersonian argument that the federative nature of the government permitted the infinite extension of the "Empire of Liberty." In his call for a joint resolution of Congress, the president saw no conflict between this and his commitment to strict construction that sustained his June veto of the rivers and harbors bill. During the lame-duck session that lasted nearly to Inauguration Day, Walker maneuvered the president's proposals through Congress.[65]

The final votes on the joint resolution were purely partisan. The Virginians in both houses voted with their parties. Archer and Rives, who had spoken out vigorously against the constitutionality of the joint resolution, opposed it as they had the treaty. The House Democrats from the Old Dominion unanimously favored annexation while three of the four Virginia Whigs opposed it. Willoughby Newton, from Westmoreland County in the tidewater, abstained on the first vote and then accepted the final compromise resolution.[66]

The partisan positions taken in Congress circulated in the party press throughout 1844 and into 1845. The Democratic newspapers led by the *Enquirer* kept up a drumbeat in favor of annexation, continuously playing on the paranoid idea of a British plot and the previous surrender in 1819 of what had been American territory by the "abolitionist" John Quincy Adams. Although the Democrats supported Tyler's actions, they moved to make the issue their own. In contrast, the Whig papers in the Old Dominion backed Clay, attacking both the Tyler administration and the Democrats as land speculators and broken politicians. They insisted that the joint resolution violated the Constitution and endangered the Union. Intraparty conflict over Texas, however, allowed the surging Virginia Democracy to sweep the spring elections. Even the states' rights Whig Willoughby Newton was beaten by the more radical Democrat R. M. T. Hunter.[67]

The annexation of Texas was immensely popular with the Democrats in the Old Dominion, and Tylerites were crucial to Polk's nomination, so the Virginians hoped to play a major role in the new administration. Against the advice of Jackson himself, Polk retained his old college chum Southside Democrat John Y. Mason as attorney general, and Thomas Ritchie agreed to move from Richmond to edit the new administration organ, the *Washington Union*. The most important member of Tyler's inner circle in the new administration was Walker, rewarded for his yeoman service on Polk's behalf with the office of secretary of the treasury. The Old Republican orthodoxy and the Doctrines of '98 clearly dominated the "New Democracy."[68]

In domestic policy the Democrats reinstituted the Independent Treasury on a strict hard money basis and passed the "free trade tariff" proposed by Walker. The divisions on roll calls during the Twenty-ninth Congress followed party lines to a greater degree than in any other pre–Civil War Congress. The only open rebellion against party discipline came when eleven of twelve Pennsylvania Democrats voted against the administration's free trade tariff bill; if they are ignored, 94 percent of the Democrats favored and 97 percent of the Whigs opposed Walker's bill. When the president believed that Congress overstepped its specified powers in the area of internal improvements, he "remorselessly vetoed rivers and harbors bills" with a keen eye to Jeffersonian purity.[69]

While Polk battled consolidation on the domestic front, his foreign policy was constructed upon the doctrine of Manifest Destiny enunciated most clearly by John O'Sullivan in the pages of the *Democratic Review* where he insisted that "our federal system is admirably adopted to the whole continent." The addition of new states acted as a guarantee against dangerous concentration of federal power. In his public statements Polk emphasized his conception of the Union as a confederacy of independent republics whose augmentation enhanced its glory and expanded the area of freedom in the world. By the time Congress met again in December, a new Texas constitution had been written, and the elated president welcomed the twenty-seventh state into the Union.[70]

From the mid-1830s into the 1840s, as the second party system emerged, the Doctrines of '98 came to undergird the entire program of the American Democracy, including the transformation of Jefferson's conception of an Empire of Liberty into the idea of Manifest Destiny. This became fully clear in the entire range of government policies pressed by the Polk administration. Not only were the Old Dominion's Democrats loyal partisans, but so too were the commonwealth's Whigs, whose representatives in Congress consistently voted with their party on nearly every national issue that emerged during the administrations of Tyler and Polk. The constitutional stance that characterized

Virginia Whigs during this decade was that championed by the party's most popular leader, the Virginia-born Henry Clay who, while losing to Polk, retained the loyalty of nearly half of the state's voters.

The annexation of Texas led to the Mexican War, reopening the question of congressional power over slavery in the territories that Congress had closed off with the Missouri Compromise. The war had hardly begun when David Wilmot, a Pennsylvania Democrat, attached to a bill designed to finance the war his proviso prohibiting the expansion of slavery into any territory acquired from Mexico. Most Virginians were alarmed by the sectional appeal of the abstract formula but remained unconcerned until the idea gained the backing of several free-state legislatures. The *Enquirer* worried, "The madmen of the North . . . have, we fear, cast the die and numbered the days of the glorious Union."[71]

The Virginia assembly unanimously denounced the Wilmot Proviso and affirmed that "all territory . . . belongs to the several states of this union as their joint and common property in which each and all have equal rights." The citizens of any of the states had the right to move into them "with their property of whatever description" in accordance with laws of the states from which they came. Anything less tended "directly to subvert the Union itself." The new "Virginia Resolutions" asserted that the Constitution gave Congress "no control, directly or indirectly, mediately or immediately, over the institution of slavery" and that the proviso violated the spirit of the Missouri Compromise.[72]

The assembly's resolutions represented a diluted version of those proposed by eastern Calhounite Lewis Harvie, but they reflected the strength of the southern rights movement among Democrats in the Old Dominion. While most Virginia Democrats still distrusted Calhoun, they increasingly embraced his position and in Congress vigorously supported equal rights for southerners in the territories. The right to control one's property defined the meaning of "equal rights." As the editors of the *Enquirer* put it, "Whatever may be the fate of slavery, our own destiny is united with it and no hands but ours must touch it."[73]

The debate over the Wilmot Proviso within the Old Dominion differed from that in Congress. No Virginian defended the measure. The Whigs found it inexpedient and insulting; the Democrats condemned restriction as unconstitutional. The *Enquirer* repeatedly affirmed that true republicans had always opposed the Missouri Compromise and tried to dissociate Jefferson from the Northwest Ordinance. For good measure, the editors ("Father" Ritchie's sons) added that if Jefferson had supported congressional control of slavery in the territories, his authority should be disregarded: "No man however high shall make us discard the dictates of our own reason."[74]

During the 1848 election the *Whig* referred to the proviso as an "exploded humbug" and played down the issue, looking for a magic solution from General Taylor. Between the election and the inauguration, Congressman William B. Preston proposed the admission of the Mexican cession as one large state, bypassing the controversial territorial stage without forfeiting southern honor. The Virginia Whig, who had been best known for his proposal to consider gradual emancipation in 1832, gained support for his own Whig version of popular sovereignty not only from Robert Toombs, John J. Crittenden, John Bell, and other southern leaders of the party but also from the Whigs in his home state. The leading party papers had favored such a proposal all along, and the sometime Whig patriarch Rives gave his assent. More important, Ritchie approved, as did Preston's moderate western Democratic kinsmen McDowell and John B. Floyd, the former governor's son. Unfortunately this moderate proposal foundered when northern Whigs attempted to saddle it with the Wilmot Proviso and radical southern Democrats denounced its temporizing.[75]

The surreal nature of Preston's position reveals the basic problem faced by the Virginia Whigs. The proviso was an insult that even Clay refused to accept, but it hardly represented just cause for secession and the probable consequences. To men like Botts, a compromise with honor seemed a rather simple matter. They could accept those proposed by the Whig John M. Clayton and the Democrat Stephen A. Douglas, and even Polk's position on extending the Missouri Compromise line that was being supported by his secretary of state, James Buchanan.

The Democracy, deprived of office and facing the possibility of emancipation on their doorstep in the District, embraced Calhoun's position more amorously than ever. At the meeting of southern congressmen and senators called by Calhoun in January 1849, Eastern Shore congressman Thomas H. Bayly presented resolutions to redress southern grievances that eventually led to the Southern Address primarily written by the Carolinian. The response of the Virginians then in Congress reflected the spectrum of opinion on the subject in the Old Dominion. Seven of the eight Democrats in attendance signed Calhoun's address and asserted that it reaffirmed the true Virginia Doctrines of '98. One Virginia Democrat and two Whigs supported a more conciliatory southern appeal written by the aged John M. Berrien of Georgia. The two other Virginia Whigs in attendance refused to endorse either proposal, and two Whigs boycotted the meeting. When the question moved beyond the insulting proviso, the political leaders of the commonwealth divided along partisan rather than sectional lines. None of the Virginia Whigs sustained the extreme position that had become Democratic party policy.[76]

A month-long debate over slavery and state rights in the assembly highlighted these differences. Governor "Extra Billy" Smith met the assembly with the blunt declaration that "the day of compromise has passed." In the House of Delegates, Floyd led the Democrats, insisting upon the unconstitutionality of the proviso. The wavering *Enquirer* endorsed his position as the platform upon which the old Jacksonians and the Calhounites could stand together. The Whigs moved to moderate the Democratic resolutions. Led by Robert Eden Scott from Fauquier County in the northern piedmont, they insisted that the elimination of slavery in the District depended upon the disposition of the people of Maryland who had originally granted the land. Restriction of slavery in a distant and desolate place seemed an unnecessary subject for House debate. Neither measure justified the dissolution of the Union. Some Whigs like Botts preferred a more nationalist position, and the *Alexandria Gazette* criticized Scott's resolutions for going too far in their conciliation of the radicals.[77]

In the congressional elections of 1849, the Virginia Democracy relied upon the question of southern rights to rout the Whigs. Alienated by President Taylor's actions, including his "free soil" speech at Fredericksburg, the majority of the Virginia voters accepted the Democratic interpretation of the Doctrines of '98. Throughout the state Democrats charged their opponents with temporizing and linked northern Whigs to the Wilmot Proviso and the elimination of slavery from the District. Taylor could not be trusted to protect "the constitutional rights of the South." None of the six Whigs who had served in the Thirtieth Congress was returned. The only Whig who won at the regular election was Jeremiah Morton from Orange County in the upper piedmont who ran as an independent advocate of southern rights with the support of the local Democrats against an incumbent Whig, John S. Pendleton. Although incumbents won most of the elections for the assembly where the issue had less force, the usually popular Scott went down to defeat.[78]

In the fateful midcentury session of Congress that began in December 1849 and lasted until the following September, the Old Dominion's delegation included more southern rights radicals than those of either Calhoun's South Carolina or Jefferson Davis's Mississippi. Both of the commonwealth's senators, Hunter and Mason, and half of its fourteen-man congressional delegation supported Calhoun's position. Four of the other five Democrats differed only in degree. Yet the *Enquirer* called for a more resolute response to the antislavery threat. A relatively small shift of voters away from the Whigs produced an extremely unrepresentative delegation. The structure of the electoral system effectively denied a voice to the Virginia Whigs who had made up half of the electorate at the previous presidential election. On top of that, one of the two Whigs was about to switch parties and the other was the precarious product of a special election. The Virginia Democrats were as well positioned as possible to determine the fate of the Union.[79]

The new president, Zachary Taylor, met Congress with his own plan to settle the issue by adopting a version of Preston's proposal. In fact, he had put the Virginian in his cabinet as a representative Whig from the upper South. The general hoped to avoid prolonged debate on the power of Congress over slavery in the territories by calling for the rapid admission of two states. The appearance that Taylor was turning against the interests of the South without a clear understanding of the gravity of the situation led the aging and disaffected Clay to construct a coalition of old moderates in favor of a compromise in which Congress would admit California as a free state, set up territorial governments of Utah and New Mexico without the Wilmot Proviso, trade off a smaller Texas for federal assumption of the republic's debts, curtail the slave trade in the District, and enact a new fugitive slave law along the lines proposed a few days before by James Murray Mason, his Democratic colleague from Virginia.[80]

In the course of the debate on these issues, the dying Calhoun made his final plea for southern rights. His speech, as read by his Virginian disciple Mason, presented the standard statement of the southern Democratic position widely proclaimed in the Old Dominion as a true understanding of the Doctrines of '98. Blaming the crisis upon the "agitation of the subject of slavery" and predicting disunion if his colleagues failed to find "some timely and effective measure" to halt this threat to the Union, Calhoun detailed the assault upon southern rights in the territories and repeated the argument against a tariff first presented in the South Carolina Exposition. In the most important part of his argument, however, Calhoun invoked the fears of conservative Virginians concerning the threats that a "majority of numbers" and federal "consolidation" posed to the continued existence of republican government. Jefferson himself might well have believed that the Federalist wolf was at the door.[81]

A select committee including Mason produced a bill focused upon the territorial question known as the omnibus bill, because it carried several passengers. But what seemed to be reasonable strategy fell apart. Clay's initial effort at compromise failed because of southern opposition led by the Virginia Democrats. In supporting Clay's compromise in Washington, Ritchie had lost what little was left of his credibility at home. Young Democrats now came to believe that the former friend of Jefferson and Madison would sell his soul for a printing contract. Southern rights extremists such as Muscoe R. H. Garnett, Edmund Ruffin, and Beverley Tucker, who had little popular support, mobilized frustration among the commonwealth's eastern conservatives.[82] In its session during the winter of 1849–50, the assembly turned to the idea of a southern convention. Governor John B. Floyd repeated that "the time has already passed" for compromise. The commonwealth should choose its delegates to a convention in Nashville called by the Mississippi legislature to convene in June. Although there was much talk of secession, the argument in the legislature did not involve substance but questions of how the delegates should be selected and their expenses paid. The Democrats supported Floyd's suggestions while the Whigs resisted what they believed was a prelude to secession. The *Enquirer* told its readers that the meeting would organize southern opinion to protect southern rights against the northern fanatics, while the Whigs sought only "a pretext for denying the South and her interests in the hour of Danger."[83]

The Virginia assembly finally agreed to participate in a southern convention, but neither Richmond paper showed much enthusiasm, and the *Lynchburg Virginian* strongly opposed the idea. Meetings held on the Southside and a few tidewater counties selected a dozen delegates to Nashville. In Richmond, where fourteen hundred voters had gone to the polls in the presidential election, a mere three hundred turned out to register a two-to-one margin against sending anyone at all. Only one county west of the Blue Ridge, Senator Mason's home base, Jefferson, chose to address the matter. In those counties that sent delegates, radicals were usually chosen in an informal fashion. Most of the fourteen men selected, including Henry A. Wise and James Lyons, refused to attend. The delegation was thus an odd lot. Beverley Tucker and William Fitzhugh Gordon were Calhounites from the 1830s and close to Hunter. Southside Democratic congressman William O. Goode was the most prominent Virginia politician chosen.[84]

Although the Nashville Convention was basically a failure, the Old Dominion remained deeply divided on the question of southern rights and the votes cast by the state's representatives in Congress revealed the Virginia Democrats' hostility to the Compromise of 1850. Senators Mason and Hunter dictated the party's response. They had opposed every element of Clay's compromise in the spring and voted with Jefferson Davis throughout August and September. They accepted Utah and New Mexico without restriction and, of course, the fugitive slave law that Mason wrote and the Virginia assembly strongly supported, while opposing a diminished Texas, a free California, and a District of Columbia cleansed of slave pens.[85]

Six of the Virginia Democrats in the House supported the extreme position associated with the South Carolinians and Mississippians. In fact, James A. Seddon, Richard K. Meade, and Alexander R. Holladay, all confidants of Hunter, even opposed the Utah bill. These Democratic radicals represented eastern constituencies in the lower portion of the piedmont and the tidewater. Virginia's moderate Democrats came from the Eastern Shore, the northern piedmont, and west of the Blue Ridge. Bayly and four others voted with the majority of southern members to accept Utah, the Texas – New Mexico compromise, and Mason's fugitive slave law. They opposed the admission of a free California and the restriction of the slave trade in the District. One old western Unionist-Jacksonian, James M. H. Beale, broke with his party by accepting the restriction on the slave trade in the District. The only Virginian who voted for all five measures was the Morgantown Whig Thomas Haymond.

In the wake of the compromise, Virginia Whigs supported their party's commitment to "finality," but the Democracy assumed a more aggressively prosouthern stance. A growing number saw salvation of southern rights only in secession. As Senator Mason explained in his defense of the fugitive slave law, "The loss of property is felt; the loss of honor is felt still more." Both the senators from the Old Dominion spoke disparagingly of what Mason called the "pseudo compromise," predicting that it would be "fatal . . . either to the Union . . . or to the institution of slavery." Richmond representative Seddon complained to Hunter, "The Compromise, curse on it, both in inception and accomplishment is perilous ground to every true Southern man."[86]

As the Virginians once again debated the meaning of the Doctrines of '98, the party press divided sharply on the issue of the right of secession. Hunter's nephew, Muscoe R. H. Garnett, the young intellectual protégé of Tucker, attacked the compromise and ably defended the radical position in a widely circulated pamphlet, *The Union: Past, Present, and Future*. The *Enquirer* now termed secession "a conservative principle of our confederacy, which cannot properly be denied and which alone can save us from consolidated tyranny." Father Ritchie's self-righteous son lectured the Whigs on the true meaning of both the Virginia Resolutions and Madison's *Report*. The Democratic papers retraced the argument that the Union was a compact of sovereign states. Secession formed "the basis of, inherent in and inseparable from the idea of compact." The *Whig* rejected this interpretation, reiterating Madison's opposition to nullification, and insisted that "secession, without the assent of other parties to the compact" constituted nothing less that "revolution."[87]

The elections of 1851 in the Old Dominion again pointed to clear partisan differences on the rights of the states and the constitutionality of secession. Both parties ostensibly supported the compromise and waged conservative, negative campaigns, but the Democrats stressed the differences between the parties on the proper construction of the Constitution. Even as the *Enquirer* attacked the Whigs as abolitionists and antisouthern traitors, the Democratic organ cast the argument in the language of strict construction. The fight was the same waged by the "States Rights party" in 1800 against the "consolidation Federal doctrines" that underlay the Alien and Sedition Acts as well as the Bank of the United States, protective tariffs, and federal aid to internal improvements. The Democrats stood on the platform put forth in the assembly's resolutions asserting the constitutionality of secession and raged against the proviso and northern aggression.[88]

The Virginia Whigs insisted that they remained true to Madison and opposed the revival of the Antifederalist heresy. Many Whigs still hoped that the party might win a majority of the seats in the Virginia delegation and control the assembly under the new constitution. They attacked the disunionist "fanatics" within the Democracy and took a strongly unionist position in the congressional election of 1851. Botts was undoubtedly the most outspoken, but all of the Whig candidates were known unionists, economic nationalists, and supporters of the new state constitution that finally provided for white manhood suffrage and reformed representation. Haymond voted to end the slave trade in the District; Philip Bolling and Charles J. Faulkner had advocated gradual abolition in 1832; James F. Strother's father had voted for the Missouri Compromise. In the commonwealth's first popular election for governor, the Whigs nominated westerner George W. Summers, who had been one of the most outspoken champions of gradual emancipation in 1832, an economic nationalist as a congressman in the 1840s, and a liberal reformer in the constitutional convention of 1850–51.[89]

All of the southern rights radicals who had been elected two years earlier were returned except Calhoun's friend Seddon, who "peremptorily" declined to run. The Democrats, however, replaced him with another Calhounite, Judge John Caskie, who defeated Botts in a closely contested race. Radical Thomas S. Bocock beat Bolling in the western piedmont district that included Lynchburg. The moderate Democrats, however, did as well as the radicals. Bayly and Fayette McMullen were returned. John Letcher, after recanting his earlier questioning of slavery, replaced his mentor McDowell, and George W. Thompson regained the seat lost to Haymond in the northwest. The western maverick Democrat Beale also retained his seat. On the other hand, Jeremiah Morton, who became a Democrat, lost to Strother in the northern piedmont, and Faulkner defeated the radical former congressman Henry Bedinger in the northernmost district of the Valley. All of the contested races were quite close. Western Democrat Joseph Johnson, the future Confederate general whom the *Enquirer* described as "sound in States Rights politics," won the gubernatorial race over the "abolitionist" Summers with 53 percent of an expanded electorate, while the Democrats took 60 percent of the seats in the House of Delegates.[90]

The strength of southern rights within the Democracy of the Old Dominion was illustrated early in the next session of Congress. Seven of Virginia's thirteen Democratic congressmen refused to support Henry S. Foote's resolution endorsing the "finality" of the Compromise of 1850, although it passed easily with only a dozen other southerners in opposition. At the party's spring convention, Seddon successfully led the state's Democrats to abandon their previous support of the compromise and to proclaim that in their platform the Doctrines of '98 both justified secession and had always provided the basis of the Democratic party in the commonwealth. Their move from state rights to southern rights was complete. They had long ago left Madison behind and were discarding Jefferson as well. The strongest supporters of southern rights represented the constituencies in the Old Dominion most bitterly opposed to not only abolition but also democratic reform.

8

Political Development
and Political Decay

B Y THE mid-nineteenth century the liberal, democratic political culture of
the commonwealth contrasted sharply with the aristocratic republicanism which had characterized the Old Dominion's Revolutionary center
and produced the Virginia Dynasty. Most of the change had come after Jefferson's death as a much more complex and diverse economy emerged. In practically every way Virginia society had been transformed. The economy was thriving. Jefferson would have been happy with the state of Virginia's agriculture,
and a state agricultural society had been formed to promote the agrarian interest. But also cities had grown up not unlike those of Europe peopled by a motley lot of mechanics, manufacturers large and small, and day laborers; Richmond contained as many people as Manchester had at the time Jefferson
criticized the "mobs of the great cities" in his *Notes*. Fewer than half of the
state's white men were farmers, and the power of planters among the social elite
had declined dramatically.

Political parties had emerged in a modern form that Jefferson never envisioned to dominate the political world of the Old Dominion and structure
both electoral and legislative behavior. Interest group politics controlled the
commonwealth and extended its "corruptions" even to his beloved Albemarle
County. The consensus of the independent gentlemen freeholders had given
way to the conflict between coalitions of communities in which individual citizens had multiple membership. Even the traditional county courts that Jefferson had unsuccessfully tried to reform were affected by partisanship before
they were made elective. In the General Assembly slaveholders retained control, but planters—men with over twenty slaves—held only one quarter of
the seats.

These new parties had managed to contain the conflicts that Jefferson had
found most ominous to the fate of the Union. On slavery, Virginians argued
about how to deal with the effects of the peculiar institution rather than how
to get rid of it. Some, almost always Whigs, contemplated a gradual end in the

John Buchanan Floyd. (Courtesy of the Library of Congress)

John Minor Botts. From John Minor Botts, *The Great Rebellion: Its Secret History, Rise, Progress, and Disastrous Failure* (New York, 1866).

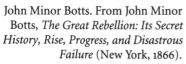

Henry A. Wise. (Courtesy of the Virginia Historical Society)

distant future to a labor system that they believed constituted a drag on the commonwealth's economy, but they were reluctant to force the issue and were as upset with the northern abolitionists as their more traditional colleagues. Others, either Democrats or more often politically marginal men, concocted fanciful schemes to "roll back the Reformation in its political phase," but most elite Virginians simply demanded security for their property rights in human capital, and the mass of whites seemed to concur with them.

By 1850 the party of Jackson had become the party of southern rights, whose essential ideas harked back to the conception of the Union as a compact expressed in the Doctrines of '98 and, particularly, in Jefferson's Kentucky Resolutions. Strict construction, states' rights, and a vigorous opposition to consolidation characterized the Virginia Democracy that led the fight in Congress against the Wilmot Proviso and federal interference with slavery in the territories. A growing element in the party embraced the alternative of secession that Jefferson had only whispered in desperation. Most Democrats in the Old Dominion, however, still believed that southern rights could be achieved within the confines of the Constitution, properly construed, and knew that the Supreme Court and the national Democracy were on their side.

While these issues were debated, the undemocratic nature of Virginia's constitution remained unresolved. The Old Dominion lingered as a genteel republic in the age of the common man. The convention of 1829–30 delayed the inevitable, but Virginia politics had in its limited way democratized without the changes in the fundamental law to support the process. Practically every other state in the Union had embraced the reforms that Jefferson had suggested seventy-five years earlier, but the planter elite of the commonwealth continued to resist until 1850 when the Reform Convention finally convened. As a result, a new constitution brought Herrenvolk democracy to the Old Dominion on the twenty-fifth anniversary of Jefferson's death and three-quarters of a century after the Declaration of Independence.

The traditional view depicting the Democrats as the party of progressive reform and the Whigs as the champions of the conservative order neither accurately depicts the behavior of the delegates nor acknowledges that "reform" was a multifaceted political symbol rather than a single issue. The introduction of white manhood suffrage, the extension of the number of elective offices, the reorganization of the courts, and the reapportionment of representation in the House of Delegates were all outcomes of sectional demands from the counties west of the Blue Ridge, which contained a clear majority of the commonwealth's white population.

Neither party could claim to be the exclusive agent of change, although larger percentages of Whigs than Democrats voted in the assembly to call the convention and in the convention to accept the new constitution. The Democrats were deeply divided between the conservative eastern representatives of the plantation districts and the backcountry reformers from constituencies made up primarily of nonslaveholding farmers, who shared only an aversion to government. In contrast, the Whigs included a sizable moderate element and a clear majority in favor of reapportionment and white manhood suffrage. Delegates from urban/commercial constituencies linked to the outside world and the expanding market tended toward democratic reform and the political economy of positive liberalism.

The sharply drawn economic regions of the state, reinforced by the concentration of the slave population east of the Blue Ridge, gave the debate over democracy in the Old Dominion its truly distinctive character and preordained the ultimate disruption of Virginia. At the same time partisan differences between Whigs and Democrats followed lines similar to those that divided the other states of the Union during the era of the second party system. Virginians confronted the same questions that troubled delegates to the other constitutional conventions across the country and responded in a familiar partisan fashion. Both parties rejected the conservative consensus of 1776 and debated policy prescriptions within the parameters of nineteenth-century liberalism.[1]

Representation remained the main constitutional grievance throughout the 1830s and 1840s as the population of the state grew and settlers filled up the Valley and spread over the mountains onto the trans-Allegheny plateau. Western discontent erupted after 1840 when the legislature refused to respond to the new census that detailed the sizable growth in that region's population. The number of whites west of the Blue Ridge exceeded those living east of the mountains by over two thousand. Western Whigs, frustrated by eastern opposition to state aid for internal improvements and education, led the fight. The Virginia constitution of 1830 had provided for reapportionment, and in 1841 a "Meeting of the Citizens of Kanawha" petitioned the legislature for redress of their grievances.[2]

The reformers associated the supporters of the mixed basis with the seventeenth-century defender of divine right, Sir Robert Filmer, and linked their own cause with that of Filmer's republican opponents, "Locke, Sidney and others." "The white population compose the *people* in whom all power is vested and from whom all delegated power is derived." Similar gatherings that met in Clarksburg, Charleston, and Lewisburg the following year also insisted upon the white basis of representation and assured easterners that this would strengthen rather than harm slavery. The assembly debated the issue in the sessions of 1841–42 and 1842–43 to no avail because of the Democratic domination of the state senate.[3]

By the mid-1840s demands for a new convention appeared regularly in a number of western newspapers that threatened separation of the state if the east continued to oppose reapportionment. In the Valley both the young Democratic editor John Letcher and the old Whig leader Samuel McDowell Moore, who had been a reformer in the convention of 1829–30, publicly deplored the domination of the Old Dominion by eastern planters who stood in the way of the economic development of the western counties. The leading western Whig papers, the *Lexington Gazette* and the *Kanawha Republican* (Charleston), continually called for reform, portraying the situation as one of "Wealth Against Men" in which the westerners were "slaves" of their eastern masters. Governor James McDowell, a western Democrat, called on the assembly to consider a convention in his 1845 message to the legislature, but the eastern planter conservatives staved off reform by again offering concessions to the Valley Democrats, this time elevating a Harrisonburg German, Isaac S. Pennybacker, to the United States Senate.[4]

The Whigs were most active among the western advocates of change and made ominous threats to divide the state, but the movement for reform of the basis of representation continued to be primarily sectional rather than partisan. At the *Richmond Enquirer*, Ritchie had advocated the extension of the suffrage since the early 1840s in the hope of gaining the support of urban workers, and gradually some other eastern Democratic editors followed suit. Eastern Whigs often voted with their section but also saw the political advantages of supporting reform. The *Richmond Whig* favored reform while Pleasants lived, but after his death both the *Whig* and the *Lynchburg Virginian* cast a skeptical eye on the scope of change. By the end of the decade, both parties advocated the extension of the franchise although sectionalism continued to dominate debate over reapportionment. In the fall of 1849, the *Whig* and the *Enquirer* joined the westerners in calling for a convention.[5]

In his speech to the legislature that year, the new governor, western Democrat John B. Floyd, insisted that a convention was "inevitable." "Nothing short of a thorough constitutional reform," he told the assembly, "will satisfy the demands of the people . . . the sooner this is accomplished the better for all the interests of the commonwealth." Finally in mid-February a bill proposing a popular referendum to be held during the regular April elections was passed when a number of eastern Whigs shifted their votes and endorsed the call for a convention. On the final vote a greater proportion of Whigs than Democrats favored reform. The eastern delegates, however, resisted further compromise and insisted that if there was a convention it had to be organized on a mixed basis. When the Valley members accepted this demand, the issue was settled.[6]

While most Americans focused their attention on Washington and the debate over the question of slavery in the territories, the Virginians devoted the summer months of 1850 to the question of constitutional reform. Newspapers discussed suggested changes and took editorial positions that combined various sectional, partisan, ideological, and pragmatic elements. Easterners tended to be conservatives while westerners advocated reform. Partisans could be found on both sides of the debate. As an editorial in the *Whig* noted, "Many Whigs are ultra and many Democrats conservative." Each party tried to cast the issue into its own rhetorical mold, manipulating liberal democratic symbolism to its own ends. Ritchie ridiculed the "aristocratic and anti-republican proclivity" of the Whigs, whose most "fundamental principle," he insisted, was "a deep and fixed distrust of the people." The *Whig* favored "just and moderate reform," disputed the *Enquirer*'s version of the origins of the present parties, and charged the Jacksonians with "monarchism." The Whigs raised the specter of executive power and patronage and mounted a "no party" campaign.[7]

The press listed most candidates for the convention both by party designation and as either "radicals" or "conservatives," but the content of radicalism and the meaning of reform differed from candidate to candidate. While some Whigs simply referred to their previous record and protested the influence of the "caucus" and the spirit of "Vanburenism," most candidates of both parties spoke specifically to the issues in their public statements printed in the party press. A letter to the *Whig* from conservative Richmond lawyer John Meredith typified the miscellany of the candidates' appeals to the voters. He strongly favored a basis of "white population and taxation combined" but would "accept Federal numbers," that is counting the free population and three-fifths of the slaves.

Meredith went on, however, to support "Universal Suffrage" for twenty-one-year-old white males who had been county residents for six months. He also favored popular election of judges at all levels except the Court of Appeals, where he would introduce a mandatory retirement "age of sixty five or seventy." Meredith praised the county courts and wished to retain them with popularly elected but unpaid justices. He also wanted to have the people elect the governor, "Sheriffs and officers of the Court." Like most Whigs, Meredith made a point of removing "all patronage" from the executive.[8]

It was not always easy for the voters to separate the candidates on the issues that supposedly divided them. In seeking seats from the district encompassing Amherst, Nelson and Albemarle, Democratic "radical" Littleberry S. Ligon and "conservative" Whig Valentine W. Southall ran on virtually the same platform. Ligon emphasized his support for the convention and believed that the main issue was the extension of suffrage to "every free white male citizen, 21 years of age" who had resided in the county twelve months and "paid a State or county tax." He would eliminate the executive council, popularly elect "all public officers," and limit the assembly to biennial sessions, but have representation determined by the mixed basis. Running in a district that included two Whig counties, this Democrat seized the "no party" ground, urging voters to show their independence from "party meetings or Conventions" and choose their delegates "without *distinction of party.*"

A month later Southall, a well-known Albemarle County Whig, wrote to the *Virginian* favoring the mixed basis of representation, white manhood suffrage, popular election of the governor, judges, and local officials, and even biennial sessions, which he insisted would "ensure abler men for service." He would limit the governor to one term and hoped to place some restrictions on the legislature to avoid repetition of "the recent course upon the subject of internal improvements." Ligon and Southall were household names in the district, having perviously served in the assembly. In the end both were elected to the Reform Convention and voted for the new constitution.[9]

Elsewhere candidates emphasized economic issues such as banks and internal improvements, as well as the question of public schools. Generally, Democratic candidates called for limitation of the legislature's powers to create corporations and spend the people's money, even for education, which had been pushed by Whigs during the preceding decade. James L. Gordon, a Democratic assemblyman from Louisa, said that he had voted against calling the convention because he "saw a wild spirit of innovation" which he associated with a more activist government. He pledged to uphold the mixed basis and extend the vote to all white adult male militiamen and taxpayers who had resided in the county for twelve months.

Gordon, however, opposed the election of judges and favored retaining the county court system unchanged. He was particularly adamant against taxing the people for a general system of education, which he associated with "agrarianism" and "legislative robbery." Hugh Goodwin, another Louisa Democratic candidate took a similar stance opposing "Free Schools" and state aid to internal improvements. He appealed to localism and antinorthern sentiments, criticizing the education system of New York as too expensive for Virginia while advocating that only "native born citizens" be allowed to vote in order to avoid the "great extremes" of "some of the Northern states" on "so delicate a subject."

On this matter Edmund Ruffin, a candidate from the upper tidewater district including Caroline, Spotsylvania, King William, and Hanover, favored retaining a freehold suffrage but admitted "as it is now extended, no harm would be done by making it nearly universal." The agricultural reformer and southern nationalist, who was nominally an independent Democrat, added that "in regard to persons not born or reared in Virginia (whether natives of foreign countries or of other States of this Union) either much longer residence or a freehold qualification . . . should be required . . . [since] we ought to have some assurance of the immigrant having at least *interest*, if not also *sentiments* and *principles,* in common with those of the natives of Virginia." Ruffin also favored the mixed basis of representation while opposing the election of judges and "the co-partnership of the commonwealth with any bank." His letter included a long passage denouncing the effects of party on the politics of the Old Dominion. In any case Ruffin was defeated.[10]

The compromise in the assembly guaranteed eastern control of the convention, but the conservatives were clearly under pressure from public opinion that favored reform. In contrast to the august body of luminaries that had gathered in the convention of 1829–30, the members of the Reform Convention, as it was commonly called, were by all accounts "a group of obscure men." There were no Madisons, Monroes, or Marshalls, none who had been or would become president or chief justice. Only 6 of the 135 members had participated the earlier convention.

Yet the members of the Reform Convention were no more obscure to their constituents than the men who served in the midcentury constitutional conventions of the other states. Six were at one time or another in the United States Senate, twenty-three were at some time congressmen, and three others later sat in the Confederate Congress. Half of the delegates to the Reform Convention had served or would serve in the assembly; three became governors of the commonwealth in the 1850s. Closer examination of the men in the Virginia conventions of 1829–30 and 1850–51 reveals the larger meaning of the critical conservative commentary concerning the "obscurity" of the delegates to the Reform Convention and the repeated depiction of them as "low politicians" who valued interest over principle.[11]

The two generations of Virginian politicians differed as strikingly as the documents they presented to the voters. The men who held power in 1850 had practically no personal memory of the contests between Federalists and Republicans. They had grown to maturity with the second party system, imbibing its democratic ambiance. They were contemporaries of Lincoln and Douglas rather than Jefferson and John Adams. The most striking characteristic of the members of the Reform Convention was their relative youth. Eighty percent of them were under fifty years of age and thus born after the Revolution of 1800. The largest cohort were in their forties, but over one-third were younger. The men who had served in 1829–30 looked into the political twilight of their careers, while for these new men the sun was rising.[12]

The delegates to the Reform Convention quite clearly constituted a different class of men than their predecessors. The occupational profiles of both groups illustrate the passing of planter hegemony in the politics of the Old Dominion (table 8.1). A startling number of lawyers served in the 1850–51 convention. Not only were men trained in the law predominant, but a significant number of them had no other major source of income. Although some owned

Table 8.1. Occupation of the delegates in two antebellum constitutional conventions (in %)

	1829–30	1850–51
Planters	57.3	28.6
Lawyers	17.7	35.3
Farmers	10.4	18.5
Others	14.6	17.6
N =	(96)	(119)

medium-sized farms, they generally had legal offices in the local market towns where most of them lived. Such men were taking the place of planters in the commonwealth's political elite. Three-fifths of the delegates to the earlier convention had been planters and planter-lawyers, but such men made up fewer than one-third of the members of the Reform Convention.

The growing complexity of the Virginia economy also produced an increase in the proportion of men other than lawyers involved in nonagricultural pursuits, including six physicians and six merchants. Such categories are arbitrary since most members had a variety of interests: William Watts, a Whig from Roanoke County, was a lawyer, small planter, and bank president. Rural doctors and ministers were sometimes planters or millowners as well as "professionals." Rather than belonging to the wealthy planter aristocracy like the majority of their predecessors of 1829–30, the members of the Reform Convention represented the successful middle stratum of midcentury Virginia society.[13]

Although the traditional view of the Old South would suggest otherwise, the commonwealth's political elite on the eve of the Civil War was less personally involved with the peculiar institution than its Jeffersonian forebears and included a smaller percentage of grandees. In the convention of 1829–30, nine-tenths of the delegates owned slaves. Twenty years later the proportion of nonslaveholders had grown dramatically while that of large planters sharply declined. Slaveholders constituted only 60 percent of the delegates in 1850–51. Half of the Jeffersonian elite but only one-fifth of the midcentury Virginia politicians owned twenty or more slaves (table 8.2).

The delegates to the Reform Convention, however, were far from common men. There were only three small farmers and two artisans. The members were much better off and far better educated their constituents: forty-nine had attended college. However, they represented neither the landed opulence nor the old family ties that had characterized the planter Republicans who dominated the politics of the Old Dominion in Jefferson's day. The new men mirrored their

Table 8.2. Slaveholding of the delegates in two antebellum constitutional conventions (in %)

Slaves	1829–30	1850–51
None	7.3	40.0
1–19	42.7	39.2
20–49	33.3 ⎫	15.0 ⎫
50+	16.6 ⎭ 50	5.8 ⎭ 20.8
$N =$	(96)	(119)

own economically and socially diverse society. This is most clearly seen not just in the increased number of lawyers who fulfilled many different roles in the state's complex capitalist economy, but also in the heightened proportion of non-agricultural occupations. The midcentury elite was increasingly bourgeois while the gentry played a declining role in the political arena.[14]

Eastern delegates differed from westerners in both occupation and slave ownership. There were roughly six times as many delegates from the east who were planters or planter-lawyers. Such men made up over 40 percent of those elected from counties east of the Blue Ridge but only 10 percent of those from the west. The west had a much larger percentage of lawyers who were not also planters and nearly twice the proportion of delegates in nonagricultural occupations (table 8.3). Among slaveholders, easterners were three times as likely as

Table 8.3. Occupation, section, and party in the constitutional convention of 1850–51

	Occupation					
	Planter	Planter-lawyer	Farmer	Farmer-lawyer	Lawyer	Other
Eastern						
Democrats	10	11	1	7	5	3
Whigs	1	7	2	2	13	7
Western						
Democrats	1	2	4	2	15	8
Whigs	0	2	0	4	9	3
Total	12	22	7	15	42	21

westerners to hold over a dozen slaves; 92 percent of the planters lived east of the Blue Ridge. Thus, the western counties sent men who reflected a complex nonslave society with a budding capitalist economy not unlike those of their northern and western neighbors.

The members of the Reform Convention represented the new class of political leaders often associated with the "advance of democracy" in yet another way that bothered their detractors: they were partisans—"small lawyers and still smaller politicians"—the product of the modern party politics that appeared in the 1830s. The debates contained the usual antiparty rhetoric, and the Whigs encouraged voters to ignore national party designations in selecting members, but both the Whig and Democratic newspapers identified the candidates by party in reporting the returns of the special election, disagreeing on the affiliation of only one or two of the delegates. Depending on the source, seventy-seven or seventy-eight Democrats and fifty-seven or fifty-eight Whigs sat in the Reform Convention. Members included not only numerous elected officials but also two partisan editors and several professional politicians like Branch J. Worsham, the wheelhorse of the Democracy of Prince Edward County, who had never held office higher than clerk in the circuit court, the position given as his occupation in the census of 1850.[15]

Although there were few differences in wealth and status between Whig and Democratic delegates, the value of slaves meant that the wealthiest members of the Virginia political elite were Democrats and that the Democrats in the convention held more property than the Whigs. There were also clear occupational differences between the party leaders. Democrats were much more agriculturally oriented. Of the twelve planters only one was a Whig. Five times as many Democrats as Whigs were planters or farmers, and most of the farmers in the western Democratic elite were small planters. While Democratic propaganda extolled the noble yeoman, Virginia party leaders were much more likely to be planters than farmers. Of the six doctors, five were Democrats; three-fifths of the remaining delegates whose primary occupations were nonagricultural were Whigs.

The nonagricultural leaning of Whigs can also be seen in the largest occupational group, lawyers. Among the delegates for whom the law provided their primary source of income, Whigs outnumbered Democrats. Most of these men practiced and lived in towns. These tendencies of the Whig leaders to be occupied in nonagricultural pursuits and to be townsmen were more marked in the east than in the west, where the occupational profiles of the two elites were quite similar. Of course, there were Whig planter-lawyers and farmer-lawyers, but they, along with the two yeomen farmers and the single planter who were Whigs, made up only one-third of the party's contingent in the convention. In

Table 8.4. Slaveholding, section, and party in the constitutional convention of 1850–51

	Slaves			
	None	1–19	20–49	50+
Eastern				
Democrats	11	13	10	5
Whigs	17	8	5	2
Western				
Democrats	13	17	1	0
Whigs	7	9	2	0
Total	48	47	18	7

contrast, 55 percent of the Democratic delegates were in these agriculturally oriented occupational categories.

Not only was the Democratic party in 1850 led by men connected to the plantation system but also by men personally involved in the peculiar institution (table 8.4). Five of the six physicians held slaves and treated sick slaves. Two-thirds of the planter delegates and five of the seven with over fifty slaves were Democrats, including the two men who owned over one hundred slaves, Muscoe Russell Hunter Garnett and John R. Edmunds. Only half of the Whigs who sat in the Reform Convention owned slaves.

Although the party elites were far more similar in the western half of the state, even there the delegates who were exclusively planters or farmers were all Democrats and slaveholders. Up-country slaveless yeomen played no role in the leadership of the Virginia Democracy in 1850. The party was led by men who were slaveholders, a majority of whom were planters. The Whig leadership was characterized by economic diversity and a limited devotion to the land and slaves. These differences in the socioeconomic orientation of the Democrats and the Whigs in the Reform Convention interacted with intrastate sectional animosities to produce the new constitution for the commonwealth in 1851.

As in the convention of 1829–30, the easterners were closely wed to slavery and the plantation system while the economic interests of the westerners were far more diverse. The questions before the convention of 1850–51 were much the same as those debated twenty years before: the basis of representation in the assembly; the extent of the suffrage; the mode of election, term of office, and powers of the governor; and the role of the county courts.

During the preceding decade, however, some Democratic reformers also talked about the abolition of the executive council, limitation of the powers of the legislature, biennial sessions, and an expansion of the judiciary. They proposed the creation of a lighter and simpler government for the Old Dominion. Democrats continually warned that the world was too much governed and that legislators, open to the influence of special interests, had acted recklessly in the past and would continue to do so in the future if allowed to pursue their natural course unchecked. These questions were part of a national debate that extended beyond the expansion of suffrage and the equalization of representation and defined the difference between Democrats and Whigs.[16]

While Ritchie's advocacy of reform in the early 1840s suited his immediate political purposes, the *Enquirer's* editorial position mirrored that of dozens of Democratic papers throughout the country and followed the prescriptions of the semiofficial *Democratic Review*. At midcentury most of the American states altered their fundamental law, and both the debates over the calling of conventions and those within the conventions over the provisions of the new constitutions trace the lines of consensus and conflict that characterized the second party system. In principle both Whigs and Democrats accepted white manhood suffrage and equitable apportionment of the state legislatures. Basically they disagreed about the scope of governmental power and particularly the power of legislatures.[17]

These new midcentury constitutions reflected an Americanized version of the model of liberal democracy articulated in the writing of the English utilitarians and philosophical radicals in which the expansion of the suffrage was designed "to protect the governed from the government." American liberals not only constantly referred to government's propensity to abuse power but also cast a suspicious eye on nearly all of the traditional activities associated with its exercise. The midcentury reformers wished to substitute a few general laws and constitutional restrictions for government in the active sense. The Democrats in particular extolled the "withering away of the state" in nearly utopian terms. A writer in the *Democratic Review* envisioned a government in which "the entire apparatus of Presidents, Secretaries, Generals, Post-captains, Foreign Ministers, Members of Congress, and other functionaries with armies, navies, fortifications appropriations, &c. &c. may almost be dispensed with."[18]

The justification for suffrage shifted from the republican idea of a stake in society, which even Jefferson accepted, toward a democratic faith in the people's natural competence to govern themselves. Although they often proclaimed that majorities were not always wise and right, at times even dangerous, the reformers believed that self-government would build character and produce morality. In essence they reversed the terms of the old republican equation and insisted that the practice of democracy would promote civic virtue. Fear of government also implied fear of the tendency of elected officials to abuse their powers. Misgovernment was ascribed to those no longer "fresh from the people" who had lost touch with public opinion.

Actual representation, popular sovereignty, bicameralism, the separation of powers—the entire array of devices that constituted the mechanistic scheme of checks and balances—were all directed toward the end of curtailing the excesses of government to ensure the largest possible extent of personal liberty. The advocates of constitutional revision wished to check corruption and governmental intrusion into individual rights. The target of Democratic agitation was the legislature, which was responsible for the evils of debt, banking, and special privileges. In most states the Democrats favored a strong veto. The executive was the representative of the will of the people, but his function was conceived of as completely negative. This tribune of the common man was to protect the people's rights from violation by the legislature in which the power of money and selfish interest held sway.[19]

Democrats portrayed the state legislatures as centers of corruption, saddling the people with a complex and confusing body of "unnecessary laws" that fostered special privilege. All this was done at tremendous expense to the taxpayers. Consequently these reformers advocated general laws to simplify the process and biennial or even triennial sessions to save money. The Democrats were nothing if not frugal. By substituting general laws for numerous instances of special legislation, equality, simplicity, and economy could be achieved and the need for legislative discretion removed. Constitutions should protect the people from the excesses of legislators, particularly by limiting the size and nature of the public debt and eliminating banks of issue.[20]

While generally on the defensive in the fight over constitutional revision, the Whigs presented their own national program for reform, which was sometimes referred to as conservatism because of its desire to protect the powers of the legislature, which Whigs regarded as representative of the popular will and the agency of public improvement. On the major questions relating to the nature of democratic government, the Whigs agreed with the Democrats. They advocated electing state officials, including judges, by universal white manhood suffrage and also favored basing representation on population since they generally did better in the towns than did their Democratic opponents.

The parties differed most clearly on the scope of governmental support for social reform and economic development. While the political economy of the Democrats emphasized the negative aspects of liberalism, that of the Whigs emphasized its positive potential, what one legal scholar has described as "the release of energy." The Whigs more vigorously pressed demands for publicly supported common schools than their opponents and were less blatantly racist in relation to voting, civil rights, and slavery. In contrast to the Democrats, the

Whigs opposed executive veto power. They saw the legislature as the truly democratic element of the government. Yet they too would curb the state's ability to create debt, substitute general laws for special legislation, and accept biennial sessions to save the taxpayers' money. Although hesitant to return to the free-for-all atmosphere of the thirties, Whigs were more likely to accept the necessity of state aid to internal improvements and oppose the Democrats' antibank, hard money position, advocating instead free banking, which was eventually adopted in most states.[21]

To the agrarian-minded Democrats, the state was dangerous and therefore best limited to a minimum of police functions in order that society might develop "naturally." Government generally should be divorced as much as possible from the affairs of the economy and the society. The more commercial-minded Whigs viewed the legislature as potentially a positive force in structuring the society. They conceived of government as a tool of the people to create the necessary conditions for material as well as moral progress.

Within the context of this national debate over constitutional revision, the continuing strength of the conservative argument in the Old Dominion stands out. Virginia's Reform Convention was dominated by issues that previously had been settled, or quieted by compromise, in nearly all of the other states. The commonwealth's western reformers, aided by their vociferous eastern allies John Minor Botts and Henry Wise, appealed to the idea of natural rights embodied in the Virginia Declaration of 1776. The basis of their argument was that the fundamental principle of democratic government was majority rule. Society had been formed to protect not only property but also life and liberty; the right to own property was a concession from society. The demands for a mixed basis of representation and freehold suffrage were "unrepublican relics" of a former age, and the old constitution formed an "aristocratic, absolute, monarchial union, part French and part English." Although he was a political maverick, Wise spoke like a radical Democrat when he portrayed the fight as one that set "liberty against mammon and the right of the people against the right of money." Most of the reformers' time, however, was taken up with assurances that majority rule would not endanger the economic interests of the planters and rebuttals of the charges laid against them by the eastern conservatives.[22]

The spokesmen of conservatism—Robert G. Scott, John Chambliss, George Purkin, Robert Ridley, Robert Stannard, and James Barbour, Jr.—put forward three general arguments. They began from the proposition that government was designed basically to protect property and consequently representation should reflect a "majority of interest" rather than "the new doctrine that mere numbers are to possess the power of this government." In practical terms this came down to the fact that two-thirds of the state's revenues came from taxes on the eastern gentry's land and slaves. The discussion of property, taxes, and "interests" ultimately revolved around slavery, "the vital, indispensable issue in the eastern argument against democratic change."[23]

In debating these matters the traditionalists held firm and repeated most of the timeworn republican arguments of Old Virginia, while the reformers echoed the liberal democratic sentiments that were heard throughout the country in the midcentury constitutional debates. The representatives of the eastern gentry reviled their opponents as advocates of "French democracy" and predicted that if "their doctrines are carried out, next comes anarchy and finally licentiousness." They insisted that the reformers sought to make Virginia into New York with "the profligacy of her politicians, [and] the moral leprosy of her people."

The fear of tyranny of the majority remained as well. Judge Scott, a Democrat from Richmond, whose father had been a conservative delegate to the earlier convention, asked, "How long is the patience of the good people of this commonwealth to be abused by this eternal demand on the part of western Virginia that we should commit the destinies of this commonwealth to a majority of mere numbers?" He argued that because those without slaves or land did not pay the bulk of the taxes, they should not decide how the money was spent. The conservative eastern delegates continued to insist that some combination of property and population rather than "King numbers" was necessary "to manage this great interest that belongs to us." Scott also revived the eastern fear that the westerners would lay heavy taxes on slaveholders to meet the "boundless wants of the West for internal improvements and the enormous costs necessary for their construction."[24]

Richard L. T. Beale from Westmoreland County in the northern tidewater represented the ideals of Old Virginia on nearly all matters. Although a young man, Beale had been elected as a Democrat to the Thirtieth Congress (1847–49) and later would serve in the state senate and as a brigadier general in the Confederate army. After the war he was returned to Congress for one term from 1879 to 1881 to aid in the "redemption" of his native state. In the convention of 1850–51, Beale attacked the idea of the natural equality of men, urged the protection of the minority from the "plundering propensities" of the masses, associated those who favored a "majority of mere numbers" with those who would "plunder" the state treasury for internal improvements, pronounced railroads as "unnatural" when compared to the "rivers God has placed upon this earth," attacked party politics, defended slavery against the threat from the west, insisted that the first principle of government was the protection of property, and ascribed Virginia's problems to the federal government, which he portrayed as a "vampire" sucking out the lifeblood of the Old Dominion.[25]

The debate over the powers of the governor further revealed the traditional nature of the state's political culture at midcentury. Reformers argued that the governor should not be limited to a single term because that was tantamount to tying "the hands of the people." "I have come here for one," the Whig leader Botts proclaimed, "with the purpose of enlarging the power of the people. I desire to take as far as practicable all power out of the hands of the few and confer it upon the many; or in other words, I am for taking power out of the hands of the politicians and putting it in the hands of the people."

The advocates of restriction, however, were even more fearful of corruption. They often sounded like Antifederalists. William Tredway, a Democratic lawyer from Danville, worried that the governor would "prostitute" the power of his office to secure reelection. "I wish to strip the Executive," he declared, "even of the suspicion of coming down and mingling in the arena of politics."

A succession of delegates grumbled aloud about the possible "abuse of patronage and power." The representative from Goochland, Walter D. Leake, a planter-lawyer Democrat, insisted that "the essence of government is power and power must be lodged in the hands of men, who are ever frail, and power, consequently in their hands is always liable to abuse. . . . The more restraints that you throw around power, the better it is for the rights of all." Others asserted that unlimited eligibility would end in tenure for life. Whig lawyer John A. Meredith of Richmond believed the proposal would make "selfish motives" rather than "patriotism . . . the controlling principle of the executive," undermine the independence of the executive, and lead to a "most despotical tyranny." Clearly the rhetoric and anxieties of eighteenth-century republicanism retained a central role in the political discourse of the Old Dominion.[26]

The questions of reform that related directly to matters of suffrage and representation did not divide the convention along party lines. The parties both split almost equally into eastern and western factions on these aspects of reform. After nearly six months two plans were brought forward by the convention committee: Plan A provided for the mixed basis and Plan B for the "suffrage basis." Even when amended, both failed. The issue was finally settled by a compromise that gave the west a majority in the House of Delegates based on white population and the east an arbitrary ten-seat majority in the Senate. Once the hurdle of representation had been surmounted, the delegates quickly voted to expand the suffrage to all white men without even calling the roll and turned to the business that occupied the conventions of the other states.

It took two more months to complete the constitution of 1851. In the end the reformers carried the day. Representation was made more equitable, suffrage was granted to all white adult males, and the governorship was made an elective office. Perhaps the most radical revision was to allow the people to choose the justices in the county courts. The triumph of democratic liberalism and political individualism, however, was limited; much that was traditional remained.

Many of the revisions that were made came for the most conservative reasons. The convention dealt gingerly with the slavery issue. Wise realized better than any of his contemporaries that antagonism within Virginia was rooted in class as well as sectional interests. He "advocated the white basis and universal suffrage as the only safe protection for slave property." The reform of representation was accompanied by a lowered assessment on slave property, and the assembly was prohibited from entertaining any future schemes of emancipation. Slavery was made perpetual and given a privileged position.[27]

The peculiar institution played a central role in the controversy over representation, but neither the debate nor the crucial roll calls set a proslavery east against an antislavery west. Certainly some of the most conservative easterners attempted to portray the matter in these terms. They remembered the role of the western delegates in the 1832 debate on slavery in the House of Delegates and labeled both the Democrat Letcher and the Whig Moore "abolitionists" because of their recent association with Henry Ruffner's pamphlet proposing gradual emancipation. Conservatives like eastern Whig John Chambliss feared a western desire to "manage this great interest that belongs to us." While Beale professed to believe that the westerners would stand by their eastern brethren if "the storm from the north shall come," he did not trust them to support the continued existence of the institution in the Old Dominion. "Tell me not of constitutional guarantees."[28]

But it was the Eastern Shore eccentric Wise who most fully linked reform to the protection of slavery. In fact, he "believed that protection of slavery, not the liberalizing of Virginia's constitution, was the most significant business before the convention." The unity of the state was necessary to resist northern aggression so that the Old Dominion might exert the influence it once had in national politics. In response to conservative arguments of the gentry, Wise maintained that representation based on the number of voters in a county proffered the best protection of property. If they insisted on making "black slaves . . . the foundation of power" in the government, the planters would "array the free men, the white men of this state" against themselves and threaten the continued existence of the peculiar institution. In exchange for the apportionment of the House of Delegates on the suffrage basis, Wise proposed that the westerners support tax concessions favorable to the eastern slaveholders.[29]

The majority of the convention accepted Wise's arguments. The vote on the provision lowering the tax on slaves was not a matter of partisan dispute. Over three-fourths of both the Democrats and the Whigs sustained the compromise measure. All the easterners voted for the provision, and the only opposition came from a coalition of sixteen up-country Democrats and nine western Whigs who opposed the tax provision as blatantly unfair, valuing whites and

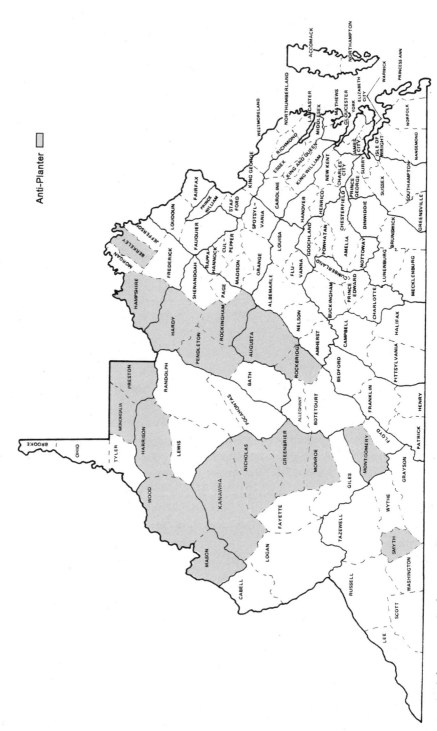

8.1. Antiplanter vote in the convention, 1850–51

slaves equally. Nineteen of these twenty-five dissenting votes were cast by delegates from counties that would become part of West Virginia.[30]

The arguments on apportionment and slavery set interest against interest rather than principle against principle. On the major roll calls related to these questions, from that on November 15, 1850, to adjourn the convention until the new census returns were available through the adoption of the final compromise on May 21, 1851, a consistently predictable pattern emerged, with a handful of delegates perversely extending the process. Party allegiance had no effect on the way delegates voted on apportionment. Instead, delegates from east and west stood fast on the opposite sides of the issue. The final division on representation could have been no less partisan or more sharply sectional (map 8.1). Fifty-five percent of the Democrats and 51 percent of the Whigs favored the provision; 95 percent of the westerners supported it while 81 percent of the easterners were opposed.

The votes on suffrage came rapidly and were anticlimactic. The resolution of this issue displayed both partisan and sectional consensus. The leading newspapers of both parties accepted the need for reform, and the delegates representing both the Democrats and the Whigs gave Herrenvolk democracy their solid support. Thus, with the passage of the new constitution, Virginia moved cautiously and belatedly into the nineteenth century, finally enacting most of the reforms that Jefferson had proposed at the time of the Revolution.[31]

The influence of party emerged on the remaining issues that occupied the convention during the summer months of 1851 as it turned to the provisions concerning the powers of the government. On these matters the members of the Reform convention acted as either Democrats or Whigs, voting the party line exhibited in the constitutional conventions in the other states. Sectionalism affected these issues, but it was far less important than partisanship. The Democrats favored increasing the power of the governor and limiting that of the assembly. Although neither party opposed making the governor an elective office, the Democrats strongly opposed Whig attempts to curtail executive power. The Old Dominion's Democrats, like those in the other states, feared excessive government and emphasized the strict separation of powers to restrain legislative actions, particularly those of the lower house.[32]

The new constitution also included such common Democratic recommendations as biennial sessions with a limit of ninety days and the provision that monetary and tax bills could only pass if a quorum of a majority of those elected was present. Whigs for their part succeeded in sustaining provisions allowing the assembly to make loans to corporations and to increase the public debt, but in both cases these measures passed primarily because the Democrats split and a minority of the party voted with the Whigs. The provision forbidding future legislatures from releasing corporations from their liability for loans produced the most clearly partisan division. This had been a central issue in state politics that defined the difference between Democrats and Whigs throughout the country. Two-thirds of the Democrats voted for restriction; three-quarters of the Whigs opposed it. On these votes on economic issues, Whig cohesion was consistently much higher than that of their opponents. Democrats were divided on money and banking, although the majority of the party took an strong anti-bank stance as the economy recovered they became more ambivalent. The Whigs solidly supported a reformed credit system based on free banking. As a consequence the Democratic proposal to outlaw the suspension of specie payments was defeated. As in other states, the votes of Democratic "softs" enabled the Whigs to frustrate the hard money Democrats.[33]

The final policy issue in the convention that stirred party conflict was education. Western Democrats joined the Whigs in supporting the use of the Literary Fund as a basis for a common school system. These economy-minded Democrats balked, however, when the Whigs proposed that the Land Fund be used to supplement the Literary Fund. Neither party wished to oppose education in principle, but only the Whigs showed a willingness to pay for a public school system. When it came down to roll-call votes, nine-tenths of the Democrats opposed educational reform, and three-fourths of the Whigs favored it. The only similarly divided roll calls were those of a purely partisan nature concerning the control of seats.[34]

Thus, while sectionalism determined the behavior of the delegates on the apportionment issue in 1851, party affiliation proved more important on most of the matters in dispute. Members of Virginia's Reform Convention responded similarly to Whigs and Democrats who cast votes in the conventions held in the other states in the Union. Ironically, the antiparty party, the minority Whigs who urged a nonpartisan convention, showed greater cohesion than the majority Democrats on these roll calls. The final vote on the constitution featured a sectional division with a slight majority of easterners pitted against its passage and a large majority of westerners sustaining it. Majorities of both parties voted for the new constitution, but it received a significantly larger proportion of Whig than Democratic votes.[35]

While it guaranteed the perpetuation of slavery and hoped to relieve the commonwealth of "the free negro population, by removal or otherwise," the constitution of 1851 provided for all of Jefferson's proposed reforms and others that midcentury Democrats favored as well. It did not use the term *wards*, and its authors were deeply hostile to New England ways, but the new document did divide the counties into districts for the election of justices to serve in the county courts and of newly created local officials. On paper it was a revolutionary document, and in fact it created a democratic legal environment as liberal as any in the country. Its most glaring contradiction with the ideal of democracy at that time was its protection of the peculiar institution.

Oddly enough, Virginia's reformed constitution was itself the product of a fairly democratic process, but neither of the political parties could claim the mantle of democratic reform. Both the Whigs and the Democrats were split by sectional interests, and both harbored significant conservative elements who sought to retain the Virginia ideas. On the main matters that can be associated with nineteenth-century liberal democracy—representation, suffrage, and popular elections—the divisions within the convention followed sectional rather than partisan lines. It was on the details of democratic governance that the parties took contrasting positions. In Virginia as elsewhere in the country, Democratic advocates of negative liberalism and severe restraints on legislative power fought with the Whig advocates of positive liberalism and the limited use of legislative power to structure both the society and the economy.

Although Virginia was one of the last states to accept political individualism, the constitution of 1851 brought the Old Dominion belatedly and hesitantly into the nineteenth century. A minority resisted this change and reasserted eighteenth-century principles affirming the necessity of government by gentlemen of property and standing who would resist the tyranny of numbers and the whims of the people. Overnight Virginia's constitution had become nearly as democratic as any in the nation. This revision along with the socioeconomic changes that characterized the 1850s made the new political order seem foreign and potentially dangerous for the Old Dominion's traditional leaders. On the surface at least these changes confirmed the conservative planters' fears that they would lose control of the commonwealth to those with little interest in the peculiar institution.

The tidewater and the tobacco region made up Old Virginia, and these counties clung most tightly to the Doctrines of '98. Yet Old Virginia physically was not even a third of the state, and its planters were vastly outnumbered by the white parvenus of the piedmont and the nonslaveholders west of the Blue Ridge. Herrenvolk democracy came to the Old Dominion because men like Wise believed that it posed no real threat to slavery and the continued control of the commonwealth by the slaveholding class. The eastern squirearchy that had disputed Wise was on the defensive, its dominance threatened by the division within its own ranks.[36]

At the beginning of the 1850s, the Old Dominion could look ahead optimistically toward a new democratic era of peace and prosperity. It is only with hindsight that historians can recognize that the prophets of doom were correct. Yet theirs was a self-fulfilling prophecy. The decade provided nearly a textbook case of increasing social mobilization accompanying institutional decay and ultimately breeding revolution and the horror of civil war that tore apart the commonwealth.[37]

Initially the second party system held together and channeled the first wave of new voters into the expanded electoral arena. The presidential election of 1852 showed a Democratic surge that gave the party a clear majority throughout the decade, but the Whigs retained the loyalty of 44 percent of Virginia's voters and gained two-fifths of the new voters. To a greater extent than their opponents, the Whigs were prone to antipartyism and suffered slow institutional decay, while the Democrats were plagued by factionalism, the disease of majority parties. After 1853, when their national party collapsed and the North entered an era of partisan realignment, the Whigs of the Old Dominion retained their anti-Democratic presence and local organization through a variety of guises although their coherence diminished.[38]

Yet the electorate remained remarkably stable. The gubernatorial election of 1855, when the anti-Catholic, antiradical, and antiparty Know-Nothings ran a former Whig, Thomas S. Flournoy, against Henry Wise, almost cost the Democrats their privileged position, but the elections for the General Assembly in 1855 and 1857 revealed most clearly the unraveling of the second party system. In the latter year the Whig share of seats in the House of Delegates dipped to its lowest point, reminiscent of the Federalists in the first decade of the century. Democrats responded to their constituents' demands for economic development, and only on a handful of roll calls did the old issues come forward to elicit previous partisan sentiments. In 1859, however, the Whigs won sixty-one seats in the House of Delegates (40 percent), and William Goggin, who had earlier served in Congress as a Whig, received 48 percent of the popular vote for governor.[39]

While legislative behavior continued to reflect partisan decomposition, the unionist upturn at the end of the decade did produce the surprising victory of John Bell in Virginia. In 1860 he gained the electoral vote of the Old Dominion with 44 percent of the popular vote. The northern doughface Democrat James Buchanan had won handily in 1856, but unionism, like economic issues involving development, split the Democrats, and the "defection" from the southern Democrat, John C. Breckenridge, to the northerner—and regular party nominee—Stephen A. Douglas gave Virginia's electoral votes to Bell, an old Whig carrying the flag of Henry Clay.[40]

While there was some fluctuation on the anti-Democratic side as the national Whig party disintegrated and its followers drifted first to the Know Nothings and then to Bell's Constitutional Union party, the Virginia electorate showed a relative stability throughout the 1850s. The national Whig party had disappeared, but the old Whig leaders and the fraternity of voters and the anti-

Democratic cadre who had manned the grass-roots party machinery remained to sustain Virginia unionism in its myriad forms. In the course of the entire decade, only a small number of Virginians actually switched allegiance. The changes in the percentage of the vote going to the dominant Democrats in presidential and gubernatorial races involved shifting patterns of abstention and the addition of new voters. Turnout mounted in each presidential election, and in 1860, 71.5 percent of Virginia's white adult males went to the polls. Early in the decade the Democrats held a slight edge among new voters, but toward the end of the 1850s this group favored unionist candidates.[41]

The Old Dominion's traditional eastern planter elite came under increasing pressure from challenges mounted on all sides. From the mid-1840s to the Civil War, the commonwealth's economy expanded at a rapid rate and, like the nation's generally, prospered. Every indicator of economic activity was considerably higher in 1860 than ten years earlier. Virginia's cities were growing; most of the rural areas prospered. The wheat crop increased 17 percent between 1849 and 1859, and the price per bushel went up 32 percent. Because 1849 had not been a good year, tobacco output grew 118 percent during the decade and prices were up 40 percent. Slaveholders did not need to sell their slaves to the Cotton South, but with the increase in slave prices, they could do so at a tidy profit. Virginia's notorious involvement in the interstate slave trade had fallen off in the prosperous years of the 1840s and continued to decline.

The relatively old practice of renting or hiring out slaves spread, and the use of slaves became more diverse. They were being increasingly employed in the state's prospering industrial sector. The total number of people employed in manufacturing jumped 24 percent from 29,000 to 36,000, about twice the rate of population growth in the state. Wages were up, and the value of the product of manufactured articles in Virginia grew from $29.6 million to $50.7 million. One of the arguments put forward by the statesmen of the lower South to lure Virginia into the Confederacy was that the Old Dominion could become the New England of the new nation.[42]

Demographic trends within the Old Dominion, however, threatened the hegemony of the planter elite. The number of planters grew slightly, but the proportion of nonslaveholders increased as the western half of the state outstripped the east in population growth. With each census a declining proportion of white families were intimately entwined with the peculiar institution. The number of slaveholders in the commonwealth fell from 55,000 in 1850 to 52,000 in 1860. Even east of the Blue Ridge, the proportion of nonslaveholders increased significantly. These men had the vote, and the constitution of 1851 provided for future reapportionment that would reflect the fact that a growing majority of the commonwealth's whites lived beyond the Blue Ridge.[43]

In part Virginia's population increase was due to an influx of foreigners of various kinds. The commonwealth's cities drew a considerable immigrant population from Europe. In 1860 there were 35,058 foreign-born immigrants in Virginia. But even more dangerous in the minds of the scions of the First Families was the influx of "Yankees"—anyone from north of the Potomac—as the proportions of people born out of state grew by 45 percent.[44]

Trends that historians have not usually associated with the Old Dominion—immigration, urbanization, and industrialization—were all proceeding at a pace that troubled those trained to rule. Perhaps most startling to the traditional leaders of Old Virginia was the emergence of new men and new families among the commonwealth's social and economic elite. The new structures of democracy placed political power in the hands of these new men and the transformation of the political culture taught their followers to expect their government, however limited, to respond to their demands. The remnants of a paternalistic planter aristocracy were under siege from an emerging bourgeois coalition of businessmen (many of whom held slaves) and commercially oriented small slaveholders.[45]

There was some truth in the fantasies of George Fitzhugh, the Old Dominion's most famous proponent of the proslavery ideology, but few of those struggling to wrest power from the planters actually threatened the peculiar institution. The constitution of 1851 guaranteed that the General Assembly could not "emancipate any slave or the descendant of any slave, either before or after the birth of the descendant." In the short run the greatest threat posed to planter power was not the abolition of slavery but the taxation of their slave property, which had been sheltered by the provisions of the constitution. Constitutions could be changed and had been in their lifetime. Even before the 1865 date set in the constitution of 1851, the secession convention in 1861 was empowered to act on these subjects and westerners like Waitman T. Willey spoke directly to the questions of taxes. But as their behavior ultimately showed, a sizable proportion of the conditional unionists would not even accept the restriction of slavery in the distant and uninviting territories.[46]

The combination of these internal threats to planter power and the external challenge to southern culture and self-esteem posed by the growth of Republicanism in the North eventually led to secession. Between the presidential election of November 1860 and the election of delegates for the state constitutional convention in February 1861, the electoral pattern of the previous decade underwent a radical transformation. While the Democrats had consistently received a higher proportion of slaveholders' votes than the Whigs, slaveholders and non-slaveholders supported both parties and in the presidential election Virginia voters divided along traditional lines. The February election, in contrast, set non-slaveholding unionists against slaveholding secessionists. Four-fifths of those without slaves supported unionist candidates while two-thirds of those owning slaves voted for secessionists.

The startling nature of the electoral realignment can be seen in the unionist coalition that retained a Whig core but received 30 percent of its votes from Democrats (15 percent each from supporters of Breckenridge and of Douglas) and 11 percent from new voters. The secessionist candidates, on the other hand, received 11 percent of their votes from men who had voted for Bell in the presidential election and the remainder from Breckenridge Democrats. Significant segment of both parties had shifted their allegiance, signaling a potential major realignment of the electorate.[47]

The 1861 constitutional convention that ended with a declaration of secession was a product of the new democracy of the 1850s. Although the election for delegates drew a slightly smaller turnout than the presidential election, over three-fifths of Virginia's voters went to the polls. Most of those who stayed home had voted in the presidential election, and thus, their votes can be seen as conscious abstentions. The Virginia voters chose a generally conservative body committed—at least in February—to the preservation of the Union. Slightly fewer than one-third of the 152 delegates were secessionists, but most members were in the middle, conditional unionists of one kind or another.[48]

The secession convention reflected the distribution of the white population, and the socioeconomic background of its members resembled that of the General Assembly. About half of the delegates had served in the legislature, twenty-two had been in the convention of 1850–51, and fourteen had been or were congressmen. No political element in the state was unrepresented. Convention delegates were older and wealthier than the legislators, particularly members of the House of Delegates. A striking characteristic of these men was the large number of lawyers. While lawyers made up about 30 percent of the legislators, they constituted over half of the convention that voted for secession. Most important, however, significantly more of the convention members were slaveholders.[49]

Both former governor Wise and John Tyler, Virginia's only living former president, were delegates. Another member, George Wythe Randolph, was Thomas Jefferson's grandson. About half of the men who sat in Richmond can be clearly identified with the second party system. Two-thirds of these had been Whigs, and they made up the majority of the unionist delegates. Old Democrats like Lewis Harvie, who was closely connected with the Hunter faction in the 1850s, led the "precipitationists," but most of the supporters of secession in the convention were younger Democrats who had not been associated with the party battles of the 1840s. Fourteen of the twenty-three known Democrats from the 1840s voted for secession before the attack on Fort Sumter while twenty voted for it on April 17. Forty-four of forty-seven Whigs opposed secession on the first vote, and only fifteen shifted their position after Lincoln's call for troops to put down the rebellion.[50]

Clearly the vote on April 17 to remove Virginia from the Union of their fathers was far more difficult for the lingering Whigs than for the Old Dominion's Democrats. Nearly all resisted, and in the end three-fifths of the Whig delegates refused to join the *Landsturm* of revolution started by the South Carolinians in December. These die-hard unionists included not only longtime western Whig leaders Alexander H. H. Stuart, Samuel McDowell Moore, George W. Summers, and John Janney, who presided over the convention, but also Peyton Gravely who had voted against considering emancipation in 1832 and defended South Carolina a year later in the nullification crisis. Among the Democrats there was a group of political veterans who hesitated to support secession, but the most "reluctant confederates" were well-known Whigs. Prominent piedmont Whigs Robert Eden Scott and Valentine Southall voted for secession only on April 17.

In that fateful vote they were joined by one of Virginia's foremost Whigs, William Ballard Preston. He had served as a legislator, congressman, and member of Zachary Taylor's cabinet. Lincoln had been one of his colleagues in Congress, and they served together on the corresponding committee supporting Taylor's candidacy in 1848. When Preston accepted the cabinet position, the Illinois congressman entreated his friend on behalf of various office seekers. In early April 1861 the roles were reversed. Along with Stuart and Randolph, Preston visited the president to attain assurances that the administration would not attempt to coerce the Confederate states and would maintain a conciliatory policy. To the conditional unionists, coercion in the form of federal action to collect revenues or retain the forts was unacceptable and in fact an indication of the administration's reckless and illegal behavior. After Lincoln's call for troops to resist the rebellion, Preston was forced to shift his own position. On April 16, in secret session, he introduced the ordinance of secession that was passed the following day. Three decades earlier, as a twenty-seven-year-old member of the House of Delegates, he had proposed that the commonwealth consider some way in which it might emancipate itself from slavery.[51]

Shortly before the delegates voted on Preston's secession resolution, Governor Wise, brandishing a horse pistol, told the convention that he had already set in motion the wheels of revolution and that the armory at Harpers Ferry and the Gosport Navy Yard were or would soon be in the hands of loyal Virginians. The gadfly of the second party system, Wise had been a Jacksonian, State Rights Whig, Tylerite, and Democrat in turn during the 1830s and 1840s although he was always basically his own man, noted for his powerful oratory, eccentricity on the order of a democratically inclined Randolph of Roanoke, and supreme self-confidence.[52]

During the 1850s Wise had led the moderate wing of the Virginia Democracy opposed to Hunter and his followers, but in the 1861 convention he took the reins of the secession movement. While he had showed a certain ambivalence about secession at the beginning of the year and advocated "fighting within the Union," increasingly he served as the spokesman of the secessionists and with his son O. Jennings Wise, the editor of the *Enquirer*, became involved in the machinations of the Virginia fire-eaters who contemplated kidnapping Governor Letcher and seizing the state government.

The secessionists' most public action was to call the "spontaneous" Southern Rights Convention that met in Richmond on April 16. Most of the men involved in this irregular assembly who had been active in the 1830s and 1840s had been Jacksonians, like George Loyall, John Rutherfoord, James M. Mason, and James A. Seddon, but they also included a few of the State Rights Whigs and Calhounites such as William F. Gordon and Willoughby Newton, who had stayed with the party until the mid-1840s. Most interesting, perhaps, was the participation of Thomas Jefferson Randolph, who along with Preston had been one of the advocates of gradual emancipation in 1832. Yet Wise was clearly the dominant voice in the secession movement, and when Letcher refused to act against the federal installations, he forced his hand with a "policy of rashness" even more reckless than the one he had employed earlier against Tyler.[53]

While the general wealth of the members of the convention had little to do with the way they voted on secession, slaveholding certainly did. The secessionists of April 17 included 85 percent of the planters in the convention, while two-thirds of the nonslaveholders opposed Preston's proposal. The piedmont contained the highest proportion of secessionists, but four-fifths of the men from the tidewater joined them. In contrast, 63 percent of the Valley delegates and 83 percent of those from the northwest voted against secession. The anomaly in the vote was the strong support of secession in the southwest, whose representatives were more radical than those of the tidewater.[54]

While party differences had lessened, some traces of former allegiances remained. The handful of delegates from east of the Blue Ridge who opposed secession came from traditional Whig strongholds: Franklin, Henry, Loudoun, and Fairfax in the western and northern piedmont, Henrico and Norfolk in the tidewater, and Accomack on the Eastern Shore. The western representatives who supported secession came from traditional Democratic counties. The breakdown of party influence was a product of a decade of gradual replacement. Most of the Democrats were new men who had not gained office during the heyday of the second party system. The Whigs retained the allegiance of their older voters and gained a proportion of new ones, but they were not recruiting new leaders. As a consequence the members of the convention who had experience as officeholders in the 1830s and 1840s were overwhelmingly Whigs.

While the secession of Virginia was accompanied by conspiracies, bravado tactics, paramilitary activity, and the use of money by special interests like the slave traders in Richmond, the process was an exceedingly democratic one. The crucial vote on April 17 reflected the position of nearly all of the members, although some did change their vote with the tide to give secession even stronger support, 103 to 46. Eventually 143 of the 152 members signed the ordinance, and some unionists even joined in the process of guiding the Old Dominion into the new Confederacy.

In sharp contrast to the Republican interpretation that posited a planter conspiracy, the secession of Virginia was carried out almost scrupulously under democratic procedures—at least procedures as democratic as the mid-nineteenth century's constraints would allow. The convention was elected by free and open elections in which there was widespread participation. All elements of the political nation were represented. In every way secession was a far more democratic process than the original ratification of the Constitution. The convention was exceedingly public, with the proceedings published daily in the *Enquirer.* And the debates were as protracted and serious as those in any similar revolutionary body.[55]

These conservative lawyers rebelled against the administration in Washington because by their lights it was subverting constitutional authority and practicing tyranny. Their logic was impeccable: power came from the people, and the only legitimate and just governments rested on popular authority. Jefferson was their guide. On April 9 the *Enquirer,* urging secession, called upon the convention to be true to the "Virginia platform" expressed in the resolutions of '98 and '99 and the report of 1800: "Jefferson the founder of the Democratic party was elected upon it, and his States rights successors all recognized its orthodoxy. The other anti-Federalist states all followed the states rights lead of Virginia in opposition to the doctrine of consolidated, *coercive* government."[56]

Thus, the Old Dominion seceded from the Union in the name of Thomas Jefferson and the Doctrines of '98 opposing dangerous tendencies toward consolidation and supporting states' rights and strict construction of the Constitution. By reaffirming the ideas associated with the commonwealth at the pinnacle of its power within the new nation, these men and their fellow secessionists hoped to recapture the state's former glory. Among the active secessionists were two of Jefferson's grandsons, George Wythe Randolph and Thomas Jefferson Randolph, as well as former president John Tyler, who always considered himself a true Jeffersonian Republican and a guardian of the rights of the states.

Secessionist sentiment was strongest among Democrats, who had consistently upheld the Doctrines of '98 and by the 1840s had become the party of southern rights. Unionism drew its leaders and most of its supporters from former Whigs who continued to advocate the form of nationalism associated with Henry Clay. The second party system coexisted with slavery and did not immediately threaten the peculiar institution. While the parties differed on the slavery issue, it was not the primary matter that divided the Whigs and the Democrats, and neither could be called the party of the slaveholders or even the party of the slaveholding section of the state. The ownership of slaves had not distinguished the Democrats from either the Whigs or their successors, the Constitutional Unionists.

Between the presidential election of 1860 and the selection of delegates for the Virginia convention in February 1861, the commonwealth witnessed a major political realignment that involved the shift of a small group of eastern Whig slaveholders to the party of disunion and the defection to the ranks of unionism of a more sizable element of the nonslaveholding Democrats, especially in the Valley and the northwest. The realignment of the mid-1850s in the northern states had destroyed the national Whig party although the division between the Democrats and their opponents had remained throughout the fifties in the Old Dominion and other southern states. This transformation in the electorate finally brought an end to the second party system in the Old Dominion.

The conflict over secession pitted a party dominated by slaveholders against one representing men with no direct stake in the peculiar institution and divided the electorate in a sectional fashion that had previously been associated with the question of constitutional reform. Those portions of the state that had opposed democratic reform of representation and the suffrage now advocated secession. Internal class divisions made manifest both by the election of delegates and by the convention debates coincided with external pressures over which the Virginians had little control to heighten fears for the continued existence of the peculiar institution in the Old Dominion. As Wise lectured the delegates, "You talk about slavery in the territories; you talk about slavery in the District of Columbia—when its tenure in Virginia is doubtful. Are we to be submissive to these wrongs? . . . Virginia is brave enough and strong enough distinctly to say to all that rather than be deprived of self-government—rather than be deprived of social safety . . . she will stand erect, sovereign and independent by herself."[57] Slavery had come to dominate the political debate in the Old Dominion. With secession and the rebellion against the Union of the Fathers came the rending of Old Virginia and the division of the commonwealth eighty-five years after its creation.

~

Appendixes
Notes
Index

Appendix 1.
The Augusta County Whig Connection

The new partisan order did not mean that family connections ceased altogether to play a role in politics. In each county there was at least one important connection of cousins and other kin. This was certainly the case in Augusta County, the leading Whig county in the western half of the commonwealth and the county with the second largest number of Whigs in the state. One historian has emphasized the importance of Staunton, its county seat and largest town, in determining both the county's wealth and its extreme Whiggishness. It was at a crossroads—to the east and Richmond through Charlottesville; to the north and south via the Valley Turnpike. Yet Augusta County and Staunton serve better as an example of the continuing importance of family ties among the local elites who controlled the new parties at the county level. A brief and incomplete look at the web of familial relationships that joined the Whig elite of Augusta illustrates a commonplace aspect of the new politics of the Old Dominion that carried over from the eighteenth century.

The most important Whig politician to emerge from the county and gain national recognition during these years was Alexander Hugh Holmes Stuart, who served in the Virginia assembly, in Congress, and as secretary of interior during the administration of Millard Fillmore. He was named for his fraternal and maternal uncles, Alexander Stuart and Judge Hugh Holmes. His uncle Alex married Chapman Johnson's sister and fathered Chapman Johnson Stuart, who in turn married the daughter of Judge Brisco Gerard Baldwin. Johnson and Baldwin were law partners who represented Augusta in the convention of 1829–30 and at various times served in the House of Delegates.

Alexander H. H. Stuart's father was Judge Archibald Stuart, Jr., who represented Patrick County in both the 1829–30 and 1850–51 constitutional conventions; his mother was a Brisco; his wife was another daughter of Judge Baldwin; and his younger brother, Gerard Brisco Stuart, served in the House of Delegates. His brother-in-law John Brown Baldwin was his law partner and also served in the House of Delegates in the 1840s. Baldwin married the daughter of State Senator John H. Peyton (who was directly related to Stuart's grandmother) and thus became the brother-in-law of J. Lewis Peyton, a justice on the county court.

Baldwin was also related by marriage to William Kinney, who served in the House of Delegates. Kinney was related in various ways to other members of the House of Delegates from the county, J. J. Craig and the McCue brothers, Franklin and John, who served on the county court. Aside from the Peytons, the McCues were related to Justice John Cochran, whose brother married one of the daughters of John H. Peyton, which made him the brother-in-law of John Brown Baldwin as well as the brother-in-law of Justice James Crawford who was married to a McCue. Finally most of these Whig politicians were also related in one way or another to the Lewises, the Browns, the Porterfields, and the Moffetts, all important local families.

This incomplete genealogy includes both of Augusta County's representatives to the convention of 1829–30, nine of the eleven members of the House of Delegates from the county between 1828 and 1846, two of the three state senators, seven men who served as justices on the county court, and five mayors of Staunton. Although the Peyton family was originally English and the Baldwins descended from an Englishman who had moved to New England in the early seventeenth century before coming to Virginia, most of the men in this circle were Scotch-Irish descendants of families that migrated south from Pennsylvania in the eighteenth century. These socially prominent, mostly Presbyterian townsfolk were consistent and vocal members of the Whig party.

Source: Peyton, *History of Augusta County, Virginia*, 333–85, provides the genealogical information for this sketch. See also Robertson, *Alexander H. H. Stuart*; Abernethy, "Alexander H. H. Stuart," *DAB*; Freeman H. Hart, "Archibald Stuart," *DAB*; Atcheson L. Hench, "Chapman Johnson," *DAB*.

Appendix 2.
Voting Blocs on Slavery
in the House of Delegates, 1832

Radical Proslavery

1. James C. Bruce, William O. Goode, Peyton Gravely, Samuel Hale, John T. Street, William Swanson, Vincent Witcher, Wyley P. Woods

2. Hezekiah R. Anderson, Richard Booker, Charles S. Carter, William Daniel, Jr., Miers W. Fisher, James H. Gholson, Thomas H. Harvey, Archibald R. Harwood, Houlder Hudgins, Jeremiah T. Land, William A. Patteson, Nicholas J. Poindexter, William Shands, William D. Sims, Thomas Smith, Allen Wilson

3. Edmund Broadus, William Carson, Mark A. Chilton, Thomas Davis*, Alexander G. Knox*, John S. Pendleton, John D. Richardson*

Conservative Proslavery

4. Spencer M. Ball, Linn Banks, William H. Broadnax, John T. Brown, Joseph C. Cabell, Robert Campbell, Robert W. Carter, Jeremiah Cobb, John C. Crump*, Benjamin F. Dabney*, Asa Dupuy, James D. Halyburton, Jesse Hargrave, James C. Jordan, Thomas Miller, Willoughby Newton, Edmund Pate, William N. Patteson, Archibald Ritchie, John E. Shell, Robert Shield, John B. D. Smith*, Thomas Spencer, George Stillman, Richard D. Webb

Moderates

5. James G. Bryce, John S. Gallaher, Southey Grinalds, John Hooe

6. Henry Berry, Archibald Bryce, Jr., John A. Chandler, Miles King, John P. Leigh, Thomas Marshall, Thomas G. Moncure, John Mullen, Robert D. Powell, William M. Rives, William H. Roane, John Rutherfoord, Rice W. Wood

Backcountry Antislavery

7. Samuel Bare, Francis Billingsley, Thomas Carskadon, Joseph Cline, Samuel H. Fitzhugh, John Gilliland, Robert Gillespie, William Good, Lewis Hail, Jacob

Helms, William G. Henry, Harmon Hiner, Archer Jessee*, William Johnson, Hiram Kilgore, John McCoy, Thomas McCulloch, John Persinger, Elias Poston, William Spurlock, John G. Stephenson, William B. Zinn

Progressive Emancipationists

8. James Allen, William Anderson*, Philip A. Bolling, Robert S. Brooke*, Samuel B. T. Caldwell, Andrew W. Cameron, John C. Campbell, Presley Cordell, Charles C. Crockett, John P. Drummond*, Henry Erskine, Charles J. Faulkner, John Garland, Joseph Hart, Samuel L. Hayes, Alexander Jones, John Keller, Anthony Lawson*, Robert A. Mayo*, John McCue, James McDowell, James McIlhaney, William McMahon, Samuel McDowell Moore, Isaac Morris*, John Parriott, William B. Preston, Thomas Jefferson Randolph*, William M. Robertson, Nehemiah Smith, William H. Snidow, George W. Summers, John H. Vawter*, George I. Williams*, George W. Wilson, William Wood

Note: These categories are based on the responses to seven roll calls in the *Journal of the House of Delegates* . . . *1831*, 29, 109, 110, 134–35, 158. Those marked with an asterisk did not vote on all the roll calls and are assumed to fit into the category assigned on the basis of other information. The list of the members and their votes on the most important four of the roll calls are given along with their counties and personal holdings in Robert, *Road from Monticello*, 113–18, and in Freehling, *Drift toward Dissolution*, 273–78.

The "radical proslavery" group includes those in categories 1–3, who differed slightly on the Quakers' petition and colonization but vehemently opposed any discussion of emancipation. Seven individuals spoke in the debate, and two moved major proslavery amendments.

The "conservative proslavery" group in category 4 would allow petitions, favored colonization of free blacks, and opposed any discussion of emancipation. Brodnax was their spokesman although others did echo his views. Brown did not vote on the two roll calls on the colonization bill. John Crump, a planter from Surry County in the lower Tidewater, did not vote on either the colonization bill or the Quaker petition so he may have been more conservative than indicated—adding one more Southside planter to the radical proslavery group. Freehling described John E. Shell and John T. Brown as "intransigent conservatives," although they voted with Brodnax.

She linked Brodnax with Bryce as occupants of the "middle ground," but he and the "conservative proslavery" bloc opposed the Bryce preamble. The "moderates" supporting Bryce include those in categories 5 and 6. The difference between the groups was that four individuals voted for postponement and then voted for the Bryce preamble. None of these four spoke, but seven other moderates did.

The "backcountry antislavery" delegates in category 7 are the most difficult to understand, because none of them spoke in the debate. They were willing to consider emancipation but not using tax money for colonization. Under Virginia law the freed slaves were supposed to leave the state and there were very few free blacks in the counties from which these men came. In contrast, the "progressive emancipationists" in category 8 included all those who spoke in the debates and all of those Governor Floyd termed "talented young men." They favored some form of emancipation and colonization.

Notes

Abbreviations

AHR	*American Historical Review*
DU	Duke University Library, Durham, N.C.
JSH	*Journal of Southern History*
LC	Library of Congress, Washington, D.C.
LV	Library of Virginia, Richmond
UT	University of Texas Library, Austin
UVA	University of Virginia Library, Charlottesville
VHS	Virginia Historical Society, Richmond
VMHR	*Virginia Magazine of History and Biography*
WMQ	*William and Mary Quarterly*
WSHS	Wisconsin State Historical Society, Madison

Introduction. The Partisan Leader

1. William G. Shade, "'Wheels within Wheels': Martin Van Buren and the Election of 1836 in Virginia," *Journal of the Early Republic,* forthcoming; Leonard Richards, *The Life and Times of Congressman John Quincy Adams* (New York, 1986), 89–145; William Freehling, *The Road to Disunion: The Secessionists at Bay* (New York, 1990), 287–352.

2. Eric H. Walther, *The Fire-Eaters* (Baton Rouge, La., 1992), 8; C. Hugh Holman, "Introduction," to Nathaniel Beverley Tucker, *The Partisan Leader: A Tale of the Future* (1836; rept. Chapel Hill, N.C., 1971), xi. See also Robert J. Brugger, *Beverley Tucker: Heart over Head in the Old South* (Baltimore, 1978); Drew Gilpin Faust, *A Sacred Circle: The Dilemma of the Intellectual in the Old South, 1840–1860* (Baltimore, 1977).

3. William W. Freehling, *The Reintegration of American History: Slavery and the Civil War* (New York, 1994), 82–137. See also Michael L. Wallace, "Ideologies of Party in the Antebellum Republic" (Ph.D. diss., Columbia Univ., 1973).

4. Charles Henry Ambler, *Thomas Ritchie: A Study in Virginia Politics* (Richmond, 1913). See also Charles Henry Ambler, *Sectionalism in Virginia from 1776 to 1861* (Chicago, 1910); Henry H. Simms, *The Rise of the Whigs in Virginia, 1824 – 1840* (Richmond, 1929).

5. Tocqueville was aware of Virginia's history and had no doubts that the commonwealth was democratic. Alexis de Tocqueville, *Democracy in America*, ed. J. P. Mayer (Garden City, N.Y., 1969), 110, 381, 715. See also Richard K. Matthews, *The Radical Politics of Thomas Jefferson: A Revisionist View* (Lawrence, Kans., 1984).

6. For the concept of "*Herrenvolk* democracy," see George M. Frederickson, *The Black Image in the White Mind: The Debate on Afro-American Character and Destiny, 1817 – 1914* (New York, 1971), 58 – 70, 90 – 96.

7. See Lyon G. Tyler, *The Letters and Times of the Tylers* 3 vols. (1884, 1885, 1896; rept. New York, 1970); Robert P. Sutton, "Nostalgia, Pessimism, and Malaise: The Doomed Aristocrat in Late-Jeffersonian Virginia," *VMHB* 76 (1968): 41 – 55; Brugger, *Beverley Tucker*; Roland G. Osterweis, *Romanticism and Nationalism in the Old South* (New Haven, 1949); William R. Taylor, *Cavalier and Yankee: The Old South and American National Character* (New York, 1963).

8. On suffrage and representation generally, see Chilton Williamson, *American Suffrage from Property to Democracy, 1760 – 1860* (Princeton, N.J., 1960); J. R. Pole, *Political Representation in England and the Origins of the American Revolution* (London, 1966); Pole, "Historians and the Problem of Early American Democracy," *AHR* 67 (1962): 626 – 46.

9. Michael Chevalier, *Society, Manners, and Politics in the United States* (1839; rept. Ithaca, N.Y., 1961), 99 – 114, noted the difference between Massachusetts and Virginia but saw these as different strains in what it was to be "American."

10. Mid-twentieth-century social scientists, assaying the preconditions of democracy, have emphasized economic development in the form of industrialization, urbanization and the creation of a viable middle class between the extremes of wealth and poverty, and the importance of voluntary associations, communications media, and a generally high level of literacy, all of which facilitate participation in government. See Seymour Martin Lipset, *Political Man: The Social Basis of Politics* (Garden City, N.Y., 1960); T. H. Marshall, *Class, Citizenship, and Social Development* (Garden City, N.Y., 1964); Stein Rokkan, *Citizens, Elections, Parties* (New York, 1970); Robert D. Putnam, *Making Democracy Work: Civic Traditions in Modern Italy* (Princeton, N.J., 1994).

11. Richard Hofstadter, *The Idea of a Party System: The Rise of Legitimate Opposition in the United States, 1780 – 1840* (Berkeley, Calif., 1969); Ralph Ketcham, *Presidents above Party* (Chapel Hill, N.C., 1984); Ronald P. Formisano, "Deferential Participant Politics," *American Political Science Review* 68 (1974): 473 – 87; Lance Banning, *The Jeffersonian Persuasion* (Ithaca, N.Y., 1978); Banning, "Jeffersonian Ideology Revisited: Liberal and Classical Ideas in the New American Republic," *WMQ* 43 (1986): 3 – 19.

12. Gabriel A. Almond and G. Bingham Powell, Jr., *Comparative Politics: A Developmental Approach* (Boston, 1966), 98 – 129.

13. See Maurice Duvergier, *Political Parties* (New York, 1954); V. O. Key, *Politics, Parties, and Pressure Groups* (New York, 1964); Frank Sorauf, *Political Parties in the American System* (Boston, 1964).

14. See Raymond G. Wolfinger and Steven J. Rosenstone, *Who Votes?* (New Haven, 1980); Paul Kleppner, *Who Voted?* (New York, 1982); Paul R. Abramson and John H. Aldrich, "The Decline of Electoral Participation in America," *American Political Science*

Review 76 (1982): 502 – 21; William H. Flanigan and Nancy H. Zingale, *Political Behavior in the American Electorate* (Washington, D.C., 1991); Ruy Teixeira, "The Politics of Turnout," and G. Bingham Powell, Jr., "American Voter Turnout In Comparative Perspective," in *Controversies in Voting Behavior*, ed. Richard G. Niemi and Herbert F. Weisberg (Washington, D.C., 1993); Sidney Verba and Norman H. Nie, *Participation in America* (Cambridge, Mass., 1972). The participation in county committees and the importance of petitions reveal an intimacy of nineteenth-century citizens with their government exhibited in political behavior that is quantitatively and qualitatively different from the mid-twentieth century.

15. William G. Shade, "Political Pluralism and Party Development: The Creation of a Modern Party System, 1815 – 1852," in *The Evolution of American Electoral Systems*, ed. Paul Kleppner et al. (Westport, Conn., 1981), 77 – 112. See also Richard P. McCormick, *The Second American Party System: Party Formation in the Jacksonian Era* (Chapel Hill, N.C., 1966); William Nesbit Chambers and Walter Dean Burnham, eds., *The American Party Systems: Stages of Political Development* (New York, 1967); Walter Dean Burnham, *Critical Elections and the Mainsprings of American Politics* (New York, 1970); Jerome M. Clubb, William H. Flanigan, and Nancy H. Zingale, *Partisan Realignment: Voters, Parties, and Government in American History* (Beverly Hills, Calif., 1980); James L. Sunquist, *Dynamics of the Party System: Alignment and Realignment* (Washington, D.C., 1983); L. Sandy Maisel and William G. Shade, eds., *Parties and Politics in the American Past* (New York, 1994); Warren E. Miller, "Party Identification, Realignment, and Party Voting: Back to the Basics," *American Political Science Review* 85 (1991): 557 – 68; Byron E. Shafer, ed., *The End of Realignment? Interpreting American Electoral Eras* (Madison, Wis., 1991).

16. See Morris P. Fiorina, *Retrospective Voting in American Elections* (New Haven, 1981); Walter Dean Burnham, *The Current Crisis of American Politics* (New York, 1982).

17. Political scientists distinguish "Trustees" whose style is similar to representatives in the eighteenth century from "Delegates" similar to the ideal expressed during the Jacksonian era. Reality at the time was closer to the "Politicos" who "express both orientations either simultaneously or serially." See Heinz Eulau, John C. Wahlke, William Buchanan, and Leroy C. Ferguson, "The Role of the Representative: Some Empirical Observations on the Theory of Edmund Burke," *American Political Science Review* 53 (1959): 742 – 56; Eugene J. Alpert, "The Responsibility of the Representative," in *Encyclopedia of the American Legislative System*, ed. Joel H. Silbey (New York, 1994), 1: 419 – 33.

18. See Ralph Wooster, *The People in Power: Courthouse and Statehouse in the Lower South, 1850 – 1860* (Knoxville, Tenn., 1969); Wooster, *Politicians, Planters, and Plain Folk: Courthouse and Statehouse in the Upper South, 1850 – 1860* (Knoxville, Tenn., 1975); James Oakes, *The Ruling Race: A History of American Slaveholders* (New York, 1982); Bruce Collins, *White Society in the Antebellum South* (London, 1985).

19. See Joel Silbey, "'Delegates Fresh from the People': American Congressional and Legislative Behavior," *Journal of Interdisciplinary History* 13 (1983): 603 – 27; Ballard C. Campbell, "The State Legislature in American History: A Review Essay," *Historical Methods Newsletter* 9 (1976): 185 – 86, 193 – 94; William G. Shade, "State Legislatures in the Nineteenth Century," in Silbey, *Encyclopedia of the American Legislative System* 1: 195 – 214; Ballard C. Campbell, *Representative Democracy: Public Policy and Midwestern Legislatures in the Late Nineteenth Century* (Cambridge, Mass., 1980). Benjamin Ginsberg has suggested a direct connection between the expansion of participation and the

growth of demands on government in *The Captive Public: How Mass Opinion Promotes State Power* (New York, 1986).

20. Ronald P. Formisano, "Federalists and Republicans: Parties, Yes—System, No," in Kleppner, *Evolution of American Electoral Systems*, 33–76. See also Samuel P. Huntington, "Political Development and Decay," *World Politics* 17 (1965): 386–430.

21. James Roger Sharp, *The Jacksonians versus the Banks: Politics in the States after the Panic of 1837* (New York, 1970), 215–46. See also John Jackson, *Constituencies and Leaders in Congress: Their Effects on Senate Voting Behavior* (Cambridge, Mass., 1974); E. E. Schattschneider, *Party Government* (New York, 1942); Julius Turner, *Party and Constituency: Pressures on Congress* (Baltimore, 1951); Aage Clausen, *How Congressmen Decide* (New York, 1973); John W. Kingdon, *Congressmen's Voting Decisions* (New York, 1973); Morris Fiorina, *Representatives, Roll Calls, and Constituencies* (Lexington, Mass., 1974); Joseph Cooper, David W. Brady, and Patricia A. Hurley, "The Electoral Basis of Party Voting," in *The Impact of the Electoral Process*, ed. Louis Maisel and Joseph Cooper (Beverly Hills, Calif., 1977); Glenn R. Parker, ed., *Studies of Congress* (Washington, D.C., 1985); David W. Brady, *Critical Elections and Congressional Policy Making* (Stanford, Calif., 1988); John R. Alford and David W. Brady, "Personal and Partisan Advantage in U.S. Congressional Elections, 1846–1990," in *Congress Reconsidered*, ed. Lawrence C. Dodd and Bruce Oppenheimer (Washington, D.C., 1993); Linda L. Fowler, "Constituencies," in Silbey, *Encyclopedia of American the Legislative System* 1:399–418.

22. John Herbert Claiborne, *Seventy-Five Years in Old Virginia* (New York, 1904), 131. See also Norman Luttbeg, ed., *Public Opinion and Public Policy* (Homewood, Ill., 1974); Peter B. Natchez, *Images of Voting/Visions of Democracy: Voting Behavior and Democratic Theory* (New York, 1985); John H. Aldrich, *Why Parties? The Origin and Transformation of Parties in America* (Chicago, 1995).

23. Simms, *Rise of the Whigs in Virginia*, 163–65; Kathleen Bruce, *Virginia Iron Manufacture in the Slave Era* (New York, l93l), 259–74. See also Sharp, *The Jacksonians Versus the Banks*, 247–73.

24. See Roy C. Macridis, ed., *Political Parties: Contemporary Trends and Ideas* (New York, 1967), 20–21.

25. For applications of the "non-market communal/capitalist liberal" dichotomy to the South and to Virginia, see Harry L. Watson, *Liberty and Power: The Politics of Jacksonian America* (New York, 1990), 231–53; James Oakes, *Slavery and Freedom: An Interpretation of the Old South* (New York, 1990), 119–29; Charles Sellers, *The Market Revolution: Jacksonian America, 1815–1846* (New York, 1991).

26. Lynwood M. Dent, Jr., "The Virginia Democratic Party, 1824–1847" (Ph.D. diss., Louisiana State Univ., 1974), 382. See also Angus Campbell, Philip E. Converse, Warren E. Miller, and Donald Stokes, *The American Voter* (New York, 1960); Norman Nie, Sidney Verba, and John Petrocik, *The Changing American Voter* (Cambridge, Mass., 1976); David Knoke, *Change and Continuity in American Politics: The Social Bases of Political Parties* (Baltimore, 1976); Robert Axelrod, "Where the Votes Come From: An Analysis of Electoral Coalitions, 1952–1968," *American Political Science Review* 66 (1972): 11–20; John Petrocik, *Party Coalitions: Realignments and the Decline of the New Deal Party System* (Chicago, 1981); Eric R. A. N. Smith, *The Unchanging American Voter* (Berkeley, Calif., 1989); Samuel L. Popkin, *The Reasoning Voter: Communication and Persuasion in Presidential Campaigns* (New York, 1991); Harold W. Stanley and Richard G. Niemi, "Partisanship and Group Support over Time," in Maisel and Shade, *Parties and Politics*,

207–25; Gerhard Lenski, *The Religious Factor: A Sociologist's Inquiry* (Garden City, N.Y., 1961); Mark A. Noll, ed., *Religion and American Politics: From the Colonial Period to the 1980s* (New York, 1990); Carol J. Uhlander, "Rational Turnout: The Neglected Role of Groups," *American Journal of Political Science* 33 (1989): 390–422.

27. Charles S. Sydnor, *The Development of Southern Sectionalism, 1819–1848* (Baton Rouge, La., 1946); Clement Eaton, *The Growth of Southern Civilization, 1790–1860* (New York, 1961). The former contains Sydnor's famous characterization of southern politics during these years: "Neither Whigs nor Democrats offered a program that was thoroughly satisfactory to large segments of Southern political thought. Consequently, party conflict south of the Potomac from nullification to the late 1840's, had the hollow sound of a stage duel with tin swords." Clearly he believed that Virginia was a prime example. Lacking industrial development, the Old Dominion "was apathetic toward the class-struggle element of the Whig-Democratic conflict in the North" (p. 316).

28. William J. Cooper, Jr., *The South and the Politics of Slavery, 1828–1856* (Baton Rouge, La., 1978), xi-xv. Cooper directed Dent's dissertation and relies upon it for Virginia, which he believes was one of the states dominated by the "politics of slavery." See also William J. Cooper, Jr., *Liberty and Slavery: Southern Politics to 1860* (New York, 1983).

29. See Joseph C. Robert, *The Road from Monticello: A Study of the Virginia Slavery Debate of 1832* (1941; rept. New York, 1970); Alison Goodyear Freehling, *Drift toward Dissolution: The Virginia Slavery Debate of 1831–1832* (Baton Rouge, La., 1982); Freehling, *Road to Disunion* 1:178–96.

30. Patricia P. Hickin, "Antislavery in Virginia, 1831–1861" (Ph.D. diss., Univ. of Virginia, 1968). See also William Sumner Jenkins, *Pro-Slavery Thought in the Old South* (1935; rept. Gloucester, Mass., 1960); Clement Eaton, *The Freedom-of-Thought Struggle in the Old South*, rev. and enl. ed. (New York, 1964); Carl N. Degler, *The Other South: Southern Dissenters in the Nineteenth Century* (New York, 1974); John McCardell, *The Idea of a Southern Nation: Southern Nationalists and Southern Nationalism, 1830–1860* (New York, 1979); Drew Gilpin Faust, ed., *The Ideology of Slavery: Proslavery Thought in the Antebellum South, 1830–1860* (Baton Rouge, La., 1981); Larry Tise, *Proslavery* (Athens, Ga., 1990).

31. Richard E. Ellis, "The Path Not Taken: Virginia and the Supreme Court, 1789–1821," in *Virginia and the Constitution*, ed. A. E. Dick Howard and Melvin I. Urofsky (Charlottesville, Va., 1992), 49, 50, 51; Ellis, *The Union at Risk: Jacksonian Democracy States' Rights and the Nullification Crisis* (New York, 1987).

32. Ambler, *Sectionalism*, 137–74, 251–72; Fletcher M. Green, *Constitutional Development in the South Atlantic States, 1776–1860: A Study in the Evolution of Democracy* (1930; rept. New York, 1966); Dickson D. Bruce, Jr., *The Rhetoric of Conservatism: The Virginia Convention of 1829–30 and the Conservative Tradition in the South* (San Marino, Calif., 1982); Robert P. Sutton, *Revolution to Secession: Constitution Making in the Old Dominion* (Charlottesville, Va., 1989); and Freehling, *Road to Disunion* 1:162–77.

33. See Ronald P. Formisano, *The Transformation of Political Culture: Massachusetts Parties, 1790s-1840s* (New York, 1983); Paul Kleppner, *Change and Continuity in Electoral Politics, 1893–1828* (New York, 1987); Joel H. Silbey, *The American Political Nation, 1838–1893* (Stanford, Calif., 1991); M. Ostrogorski, *Democracy and the Organization of Political Parties*, 2 vols. (New York, 1902).

1. Notes on the State of Virginia

1. See Joseph Dorfman, "The Economic Philosophy of Thomas Jefferson," *Political Science Quarterly* 55 (1940): 98–121; William D. Grampp, "A Re-examination of Jeffersonian Economics," *Southern Economic Journal* 12 (1946): 263–82; A. Whitney Griswold, *Farming and Democracy* (New York, 1948); Merrill Peterson, *Thomas Jefferson and the New Nation* (New York, 1971); Robert Shalhope, "Thomas Jefferson's Republicanism and Antebellum Southern Thought," *JSH* 42 (1976): 529–52; Matthews, *Radical Politics of Jefferson*; Joyce Appleby, *Capitalism and the New Social Order: The Republican Vision of the 1790s* (New York, 1984).

2. Thomas Jefferson, *Notes on the State of Virginia*, in *The Portable Thomas Jefferson*, ed. Merrill D. Peterson (New York, 1975). The book appeared first in France and then Britain before being published in the United States in 1788. See also Dumas Malone, *Jefferson and His Time*, 6 vols. (Boston, 1948–81), 1:373–89.

3. George Fitzhugh quoted in Louis Hartz, *The Liberal Tradition in America* (New York, 1955), 145; Sutton, "Nostalgia, Pessimism, and Malaise."

4. *Returns of the Whole Number of Persons within the Several Districts of the United States . . . One Thousand Seven Hundred and Ninety-One* (Philadelphia, 1791), 48–51 (hereafter cited *Census of 1790*); J. G. Randall and David Donald, *The Civil War and Reconstruction* (Lexington, Mass., 1969), 68.

5. Richard S. Dunn, "Black Society in the Chesapeake, 1776–1810," and Allan Kulikoff, "Uprooted People: Black Migrants in the Age of the American Revolution," in *Slavery and Freedom in the Age of the Revolution*, ed. Ira Berlin and Ronald Hoffman (Charlottesville, Va., 1983), 49–82, 143–67; Thomas P. Abernethy, *The South in the New Nation* (Baton Rouge, La., 1961), 1–18, 43–73, 414–75; Winthrop D. Jordan, *White over Black: American Attitudes toward the Negro, 1550–1812* (Chapel Hill, N.C., 1968), 101–35, 375–402, 573–82; J. D. B. De Bow, ed., *Statistical View of the United States . . . Being a Compendium of the Seventh Census* (Washington, D.C., 1854), 95. De Bow (p. 108) gives a slightly higher number of plantations—6,015—than planters—5,642—those who owned twenty or more slaves, which is the standard used by most historians.

6. *Return of the Whole Number of Persons within the Several Districts of the United States . . . One Thousand Eight Hundred* (Washington, D.C., 1801); *Fifth Census; or Enumeration of the Inhabitants of the United States 1830 . . .* (Washington, D.C., 1832). In the 1800 census and that of 1820 the Old Dominion is divided into districts at the Allegheny Mountains rather than the Blue Ridge. See also Gerald W. Mullun, *Flight and Rebellion: Slave Resistance in Eighteenth Century Virginia* (New York, 1972); Edmund Morgan, *American Slavery/American Freedom: The Ordeal of Colonial Virginia* (New York, 1975); Mechal Sobel, *The World They Made Together: Slavery and White Values in Eighteenth-Century Virginia* (Princeton, N.J., 1987); Robert McColley, *Slavery and Jeffersonian Virginia* (Urbana, Ill., 1973).

7. *Seventh Census of the United States . . .1850* (Washington, D.C., 1853), 256–57. See also Luther Porter Jackson, *Free Negro Labor and Property Holding in Virginia, 1830–1860* (New York, 1942).

8. *Sixth Census or Enumeration of Inhabitants of the United States . . . 1840* (Washington, D.C., 1841); James Kirke Paulding, *Letters from the South* (New York, 1835), 1:91–92; Henry Howe, *Historical Collections of Virginia . . .* (Charleston, S.C., 1846).

9. "Virginia," in Francis Newton Thorpe, ed., *The Federal and State Constitutions, Colonial Charters, and Other Organic Laws of the States, Territories, and Colonies Now or*

Heretofore Forming the United States of America, 7 vols. (Washington, D.C., 1909), 7:3821–22; Joseph Martin, *A New and Comprehensive Gazetteer of Virginia . . .* (Charlottesville, Va., 1834), 3.

10. See Ambler, *Sectionalism in Virginia*; Henry Shanks, *The Secession Movement in Virginia, 1847–1861* (Richmond, 1934). In the later analysis of voting I will use a "rural Tidewater" in which the cities and their counties are removed from consideration; a larger "upper Piedmont" augmented by Spotsylvania, Stafford, Prince William, and Fairfax counties; and a "Southside" that is essentially the tobacco region south of the James.

11. De Bow, *Statistical View*, 117–18; Frederick Law Olmsted, *The Cotton Kingdom . . .* (1935; rept. New York, 1984). 38.

12. *Mortality Statistics, 1850 . . .* (Washington, D.C., 1855), 279–95; Ira Berlin and Herbert G. Gutman, "Natives and Immigrants, Free Men and Slaves: Urban Workingmen in the Antebellum American South," *AHR* 85 (1983): 1175–1200. The generalizations given here and throughout this book are based on statistical analysis of census data obtained from the Inter-University Consortium for Political and Social Research, Ann Arbor, Mich., and using SPSSX.

13. R. Bennett Bean, *The Peopling of Virginia* (Boston, 1938); Wesley Frank Craven, *Red, White, and Black: Seventeenth-Century Virginia* (Charlottesville, Va., 1971); Bernard Bailyn, *Voyagers to the West* (New York, 1986); David H. Fischer, *Albion's Seed: Four British Folkways in America* (New York, 1989). Cf. Bureau of the Census, *A Century of Population Growth: From the First Census of the United States to the Twelfth, 1790–1900* (Washington, D.C., 1909); American Council of Learned Societies, "Report of Committee on Immigrant and National Stocks in the Population of the United States," *Annual Report of the American Historical Association for the Year 1931* (Washington, D.C., 1932), 1:107–441; Forrest McDonald and Ellen Shapiro McDonald, "The Ethnic Origins of the American People, 1790," *WMQ* 37 (1980): 179–92; "The Population of the United States, 1790: A Symposium," ibid., 41 (1984): 85–135.

14. Bean, *Peopling of Virginia*. See also Herbert Clarence Bradshaw, *History of Prince Edward County, Virginia, from Its Earliest Settlement through Its Establishment in 1934 to Its Bicentennial Year* (Richmond, 1955); Richard R. Beeman, *The Evolution of the Southern Backcountry: A Case Study of Lunenburg County, Virginia, 1746–1832* (Philadelphia, 1984); Robert D. Mitchell, *Commercialism and the Frontier: Perspectives on the Early Shenandoah Valley* (Charlottesville, Va., 1977).

15. John C. Campbell, *The Southern Highlander and His Homeland* (1921; new ed., Lexington, Ky., 1969); Carl Bridenbaugh, *Myths and Realities: Societies of the Colonial South* (1952; rept. New York, 1963); Robert D. Mitchell, ed., *Appalachian Frontiers: Settlement, Society, and Development in the Preindustrial Era* (Lexington, Ky., 1991); Klaus Wust, *The Virginia Germans* (Charlottesville, Va., 1969); John W. Wayland, *German Element in the Shenandoah Valley of Virginia* (Charlottesville, Va., 1908); R. J. Dickson, *Ulster Emigration to Colonial America, 1718–1775* (London, 1966); E. R. R. Green, ed., *Essays in Scotch-Irish History* (London, 1969); James Leyburn, *The Scotch-Irish: A Social History* (Chapel Hill, N.C., 1962); Maldwyn A. Jones, "Scotch-Irish," in *Harvard Encyclopedia of American Ethnic Groups*, ed. Stephan Thernstrom (Cambridge, Mass., 1980), 895–908; Grady McWhiney, *Cracker Culture: Celtic Ways in the Old South* (Tuscaloosa, Ala., 1988).

16. See William Warren Sweet, *Religion in the Development of American Culture, 1765–1840* (New York, 1952); Timothy L. Smith, *Revivalism and Social Reform: American*

Protestantism on the Eve of the Civil War (Nashville, 1967); Sidney E. Ahlstrom, *A Religious History of the American People* (New Haven, 1972); John B. Boles, *The Great Revival, 1787–1805* (Lexington, Ky., 1972); Donald G. Mathews, *Religion in the Old South* (Chicago, 1977); Dickson D. Bruce, Jr., *And They All Sang Hallelujah: Plain-Folk Camp Meeting Religion, 1800–1845* (Knoxville, Tenn., 1974); Deborah Vansau McCauley, *Appalachian Mountain Religion: A History* (Urbana, Ill., 1995).

17. *Seventh Census . . . 1850*, 285–96. See also Richard Beale Davis, *Intellectual Life in Jefferson's Virginia, 1790–1830* (Knoxville, Tenn., 1972), 119–46, 453; Martin, *Gazetteer*; I. Daniel Rupp, ed., *An Original History of Religious Denominations at Present Existing in the United States . . .* (Philadelphia, 1844); Philip Schaff, *America: A Sketch of Its Political, Social, and Religious Character*, ed. Perry Miller (Cambridge, Mass., 1961); Robert Baird, *Religion in America*, ed. Henry Warren Bowden (New York, 1970); Roger Finke and Rodney Stark, *The Churching of America, 1776–1990: Winners and Losers in Our Religious Economy* (New Brunswick, N.J., 1992).

18. Thomas Condit Miller and Hu Maxwell, *West Virginia and Its People* (New York, 1913), 1:164–78, 613–16; Davis, *Intellectual Life in Jefferson's Virginia*, 131–36; Sweet, *Religion in the Development of American Culture*, 59–62, 102–4; Earnest Trice Thompson, *Presbyterians in the South* (Richmond, 1963), 1:80–322; McCauley, *Appalachian Mountain Religion*, 168–200; Anne Royall, *Mrs. Royall's Southern Tour, or, Second Series of the Black Book*, 2 vols (Washington, D.C., 1830–31), 1:118. See also Charles Henry Ambler, *A History of West Virginia* (New York, 1935); Otis Rice, *Allegheny Frontier: West Virginia Beginnings, 1730–1830* (Lexington, Ky., 1970); Rice, *West Virginia: A History* (Lexington, Ky., 1985); William Warren Sweet, *Religion on the American Frontier, 1783–1840*, vol. 2, *The Presbyterians . . .* (Chicago, 1936); William Henry Foote, *Sketches of Virginia Historical and Biographical* (Philadelphia, 1855); Fred J. Hood, *Reformed America: The Middle and Southern States, 1783–1837* (University, Ala., 1980).

19. Martin, *Gazetteer*, 268.

20. *Seventh Census . . . 1850*; Davis, *Intellectual Life in Jefferson's Virginia*, 128–31; Sweet, *Religion and the Development of American Culture*, 14–26, 67–75.

21. Sweet, *Religion in the Development of American Culture*, 104–10; Rhys Isaac, *The Transformation of Virginia, 1740–1790* (Chapel Hill, N.C., 1982). See also W. W. Monross, *The Episcopal Church in the United States, 1800–1840* (New York, 1938); William Meade, *Old Churches, Ministers, and Families in Virginia*, 2 vols. (Philadelphia, 1861).

22. *Seventh Census . . . 1850*; Martin, *Gazetteer*, 76. Martin's estimate for the Methodists fits the figures from the denominational records given in Davis, *Intellectual Life in Jefferson's Virginia*. The Baptist estimate conforms to the recent figures given in Mechal Sobel, *Trablen On: The Afro-Baptist Experience in Virginia* (Princeton, N.J., 1989). See also Albert J. Raboteau, *Slave Religion: The "Invisible" Institution in the Antebellum South* (New York, 1978), 131–36; Jon Butler, *Awash in a Sea of Faith: Christianizing the American People* (Cambridge, Mass., 1990), 129–63.

23. *Seventh Census . . . 1850*; Davis, *Intellectual Life in Jefferson's Virginia*, 136–39; Sweet, *Religion in the Development of American Culture*, 33–36, 56–59. See also William Warren Sweet, *Religion on the American Frontier*, vol. 1, *The Baptists, 1783–1830 . . .* (Chicago, 1931); Robert B. Semple, *A History of the Rise and Progress of the Baptists in Virginia* (Richmond, 1894); Garnett Ryland, *The Baptists of Virginia, 1699–1926* (Richmond, 1955). Church membership does not account for all those who attended and were influenced by each church; I use churchgoers and communicants to refer to the potential number measured by the accommodations listed in the 1850 census. The member-

ship figures given for Virginia in 1854 in Thompson, *Presbyterians in the South*, 420, are 89,929 Baptists, 46,561 Methodists, 12,220 Presbyterians, and 5,842 Episcopalians; he gives in (p. 433) for 1850 in Virginia 151 Presbyterian churches and 11,628 "communicants" while the census gives 240 churches and 103,625 "accommodations." See also Winthrop S. Hudson, *American Protestantism* (Chicago, 1961), 95 – 98; Mathews, *Religion in the Old South*, 46 – 47; Patricia Bonomi and Peter R. Eisenstadt, "Church Adherence in the Eighteenth-Century British American Colonies," *WMQ* 39 (1982): 245 – 86; Roger Finke and Rodney Stark, "Turning Pews into People: Estimating Church Membership in Nineteenth-Century America," *Journal for the Scientific Study of Religion* 25 (1985): 180 – 92; Finke and Stark, "American Religion in 1776: A Statistical Portrait," *Sociological Analysis* 49 (1988): 39 – 51; Butler, *Awash in a Sea of Faith*, 282 – 88.

24. *Seventh Census . . . 1850.*

25. Ahlstrom, *A Religious History*, 327; Davis, *Intellectual Life in Jefferson's Virginia*, 139 – 42; Sweet, *Religion in the Development of American Culture*, 26 – 32, 62 – 66. See also Richard Carwardine, *Transatlantic Revivalism: Popular Evangelicalism in Britain and America, 1790 – 1865* (Westport, Conn., 1978); William Warren Sweet, *Methodism in America* (New York, 1933); Sweet, *Religion on the American Frontier, 1783 – 1840*, vol. 4, *The Methodists . . .* (Chicago, 1946).

26. Sweet, *Religion in the Development of American Culture*, 190 – 233; Thompson, *Presbyterians in the South* 1:144 – 65, 323 – 451; Foote, *Historical Sketches*, 486 – 556; Sweet, *Baptists*, 58 – 101; Ryland, *Baptists of Virginia*, 231 – 42; Ambler, *Sectionalism in Virginia*, 283 – 99; Donald Mathews, *The Methodists and Slavery: A Chapter in American Morality* (Princeton, N.J., 1965).

27. Hudson, *American Protestantism*, 104; James Waddell Alexander in William Cabell Bruce, *John Randolph of Roanoke, 1773 – 1833: A Biography Based Largely on New Material*, 2 vols. (New York, 1922), 2:140; Martin E. Marty, *Pilgrims in Their Own Land: 500 Years of Religion in America* (New York, 1985), 174, 197; T. Eustace to Secretary of the AHMS, in Sweet, *Religion in the Development of American Culture*, 224.

28. Nathan O. Hatch, *Democratization of American Christianity* (New Haven, 1989), 68 – 101. See also Perry Miller, *The Life of the Mind in America from the Revolution to the Civil War* (New York, 1965), 3 – 95; Robert Weibe, *The Opening of American Society: From the Constitution to the Eve of Disunion* (New York, 1984), 157 – 67, 229 – 32, 276 – 83, 303 – 7; John Higham, *The Age of Boundlessness* (Ann Arbor, Mich., 1961).

29. See Charles G. Finney, *Memoir of Charles Grandison Finney* (New York, 1876); Finney, *Lectures on the Revivals of Religion* ed. William G. McLoughlin (Cambridge, Mass., 1961).

30. The following discussion of Virginia's economic development challenges the traditional "decline" hypothesis based on both the commentary of proslavery agricultural reformers like Edmund Ruffin and the antisouthern, antislavery visitors such as Frederick Law Olmsted. Cf. Craven, *Soil Exhaustion*; Craven, *The Coming of the Civil War* (1942; rept. Chicago, 1966); Kathleen Bruce, "Virginia Agricultural Decline to 1860: A Fallacy," *Agricultural History* 6 (1932): 3 – 13.

31. Robert P. Sutton, "Sectionalism and Social Structure: A Case Study of Jeffersonian Democracy," *VMHB* 80 (1972): 70 – 83; William G. Shade, "Society and Politics in Antebellum Virginia's Southside," *JSH* 53 (1987): 163 – 93; Tench Coxe, ed., *A Statement of the Arts and Manufactures of the United States of America . . . 1810* (Washington, D.C., 1811); Craven, *Soil Exhaustion*, 123 – 24; John T. Schlotterbeck, "The 'Social Economy' of an Upper South Community: Orange and Greene Counties, Virginia, 1815 – 1860," in

Class Consensus, and Community, ed. Orville Vernon Burton and Robert McMath (Westport, Conn., 1982), 3.

32. James Madison to the marquis de Lafayette, Nov. 25, 1820, in *Letters and Other Writings of James Madison* (New York, 1884), 3:191; Arthur G. Peterson, *Historical Study of Prices Received by Producers of Farm Products in Virginia* (Blacksburg, Va., 1929); Thomas Senior Berry, *Western Prices before 1861: A Study of the Cincinnati Market* (Cambridge, Mass., 1943).

33. Peterson, *Historical Study of Prices,* 127–28; Schlotterbeck, "'Social Economy' of an Upper South Community," 7. See also John T. Schlotterbeck, "Plantation and Farm: Social and Economic Change in Orange and Greene Counties, Virginia, 1716 to 1860" (Ph.D. diss., The Johns Hopkins Univ., 1980).

34. Jefferson, *Notes,* 217; *Census for 1820* (Washington, D.C., 1821); *Sixth Census . . . 1840,* 210, 216, 475. See also *Aggregate Value and Produce and Number of Persons Employed in Mines, Agriculture, Commerce, Manufactures, etc., . . . 1840* (Washington, D.C., 1841).

35. Jefferson, *Notes,* 185–93; *Sixth Census . . . 1840,* 205, 210.

36. *Statistics of the United States of America . . . Sixth Census . . . 1840* (Washington, D.C., 1841), 228–39; Joseph C. Robert, *The Tobacco Kingdom* (Durham, N.C., 1938), 132–57; Paul W. Gates, *The Farmer's Age: Agriculture, 1815–1860* (New York, 1960). See on wheat and flour: *A Series of Tables of the Several Branches of American Manufacture . . . 1810* (Philadelphia, 1813), 112–14; *Digest of the Accounts of Manufacturing Establishments . . . 1822* (Washington, D.C., 1823), 1922; *Compendium of the Enumeration of the Inhabitants and Statistics of the United States . . . from the Sixth Census* (Washington, D.C., 1841. See also the export statistics in *Historical Statistics of the United States: Colonial Times to 1970* (Washington, D.C., 1976), 238, 247, 251, 256.

37. Robert, *Tobacco Kingdom*; T. H. Breen, *Tobacco Culture: The Mentality of the Great Tidewater Planters on the Eve of the Revolution* (Princeton, N.J., 1985); Allan Kulikoff, *Tobacco and Slaves: The Development of Southern Cultures in the Chesapeake, 1680–1800* (Chapel Hill, N.C., 1986); Lewis Cecil Gray, *History of Agriculture in the Southern States to 1860* (Washington, D.C., 1933), 213–76, 595–617, 752–778; Gates, *Farmer's Age,* 100–115.

38. Robert, *Tobacco Kingdom,* 132–57; Craven, *Soil Exhaustion,* 122–61; De Bow, *Statistical View,* 170–74.

39. *Seventh Census . . . 1850,* 275–78; Gates, *Farmer's Age,* 169–72; Gray, *History of Agriculture in the Southern States,* 811–31; Donald L. Kemmerer, "The Pre–Civil War South's Leading Crop, Corn," *Agricultural History* 23 (1949): 236–39; Sam B. Hilliard, *Hogmeat and Hoecake: The Food Supply of the Old South, 1840–1860* (Carbondale, Ill., 1972).

40. Gates, *Farmer's Age,* 156–69; Gray, *History of Agriculture in the Southern States,* 417–24; Schlotterbeck, "Plantation and Farm," 160–210; James R. Irwin, "Exploring the Affinity of Wheat and Slavery in the Virginia Piedmont," *Explorations in Economic History* 25 (1988): 295–322; *Seventh Census . . . 1850,* 275–76; DeBow, *Statistical View,* 171.

41. De Bow, *Statistical View,* 322–31; Peterson, *Historical Study of Prices,* 129–30, 168; *Eighth Census of the United States, 1860, Agriculture* (Washington, D.C., 1864), 189; Bruce, "Virginia Agricultural Decline," 12.

42. *Seventh Census . . . 1850,* 273–82; Schlotterbeck, "'Social Economy' of an Upper South Community," 6–11.

43. Peterson, *Historical Study of Prices,* 6–16; Craven, *Soil Exhaustion,* 153–54.
44. *Seventh Census . . . 1850,* 273–82; Rice, *Allegheny Frontier,* 309–40.
45. *Aggregate Value and Produce . . . 1840* (Washington, D.C., 1841), 154–77.
46. Olmsted, *Cotton Kingdom,* 64; Manuscript Census Returns, Sixth Census, 1840, Prince Edward County, Virginia, Schedule 1—Free Population, micro. LV; Ronald L. Lewis, *Coal, Iron, and Slaves: Industrial Slavery in Maryland and Virginia, 1715–1865* (Westport, Conn., 1979), 30–31; Charles R. Dew, *Bond of Iron: Master and Slave at Buffalo Forge* (New York, 1994); Sutton, *Revolution to Secession,* 207–30; Wooster, *Politicians, Parties and Plain Folk.*
47. *Seventh Census . . . 1850,* 272; De Bow, *Statistical View,* 128; Schlotterbeck, " 'Social Economy' of an Upper South Community," 15–16; Frederick F. Siegal, *Roots of Southern Distinctiveness: Tobacco and Society in Danville, Virginia, 1780–1865* (Chapel Hill, N.C., 1987), 90. On the definition of "laborers," see also *Eighth Census . . . 1860, Population,* 524–25; Jackson, *Free Negro Labor and Property Holding,* 98–99.
48. Bruce, *Virginia Iron Manufacture,* 80–109; Otis K. Rice, "Coal Mining in the Kanawha Valley to 1861: A View of Industrialization of the Old South," *JSH* 13 (1965): 393–416; Rice, *The Allegheny Frontier,* 315; *Compendium of the Sixth Census . . . 1840* (Washington, D.C., 1841), 155, 167.
49. *Compendium of the Sixth Census . . . 1840,* 154, 166; De Bow, *Statistical View,* 181–82; Bruce, *Virginia Iron Manufacture,* 149–78. See Charles B. Dew, *Ironmaker to the Confederacy: Joseph R. Anderson and the Tredegar Iron Works* (New Haven, 1966).
50. *Compendium of the Sixth Census . . . 1840,* 164; Thomas S. Berry, "The Rise of Flour Milling in Richmond," *VMHB* 78 (1970): 387–408; Charles B. Kuhlman, *Development of the Flour Milling in the United States* (Boston, 1929), 27–54; George Rogers Taylor, *The Transportation Revolution, 1815–1860* (New York, 1951).
51. *Compendium of the Sixth Census . . . 1840,* 176.
52. Robert, *Tobacco Kingdom,* 161–75; *Compendium of the Sixth Census . . . 1840,* 161, 173, 362.
53. Siegel, *Roots of Southern Distinctiveness,* 120–35; Robert, *Tobacco Kingdom,* 175–86; *Manufactures in the Several States and Territories for the Year Ending June 1, 1850 . . .* (Washington, D.C., 1859), 113.
54. Olmsted, *Cotton Kingdom,* 585–92. Webster is quoted in the *Richmond Compiler,* Nov. 16, 1843.
55. Jefferson, *Notes,* 151–52; Olmsted, *Cotton Kingdom,* 31. See also Richard C. Wade, *Slavery in the Cities: The South, 1820–1860* (New York, 1964); Claudia Goldin, *Urban Slavery in the American South, 1820–1860: A Quantitative History* (Chicago, 1976); Leonard Curry, "Urbanization and Urbanism in the Old South: A Comparative View," *JSH* 40 (1974): 43–60; David R. Goldfield, *Urban Growth in the Age of Sectionalism: Virginia, 1847–1861* (Baton Rouge, La., 1977); Goldfield, ""Communities and Regions: The Diverse Cultures of Virginia," *VMHB* 95 (1987): 429–52; Lorraine Eve Holland, "Rise and Fall of the Ante-Bellum Virginia Aristocracy: A Generational Analysis" (Ph.D. diss., Univ. of California, Irvine, 1980), 354–406; Suzanne Lebsock, *The Free Women of Petersburg: Status and Culture in a Southern Town, 1784–1860* (New York, 1986).
56. *Seventh Census . . . 1850,* 258; Bruce, *Virginia Iron Manufacture,* 110–48; De Bow, *Statistical View,* 338–93; *Eighth Census . . . 1860,* 518–20.
57. *Seventh Census . . . 1850,* 258; Siegel, *Roots of Southern Distinctiveness,* 91, 128–33; *Eighth Census . . . 1860,* 526.

58. *Seventh Census . . . 1850*, 258; *Eighth Census . . . 1860*, 518 – 20. The 1850 printed census excluded Staunton and Harrisonburg from the published list although they are in the compendium published in 1854.

59. Robert H. Tomlinson, "The Origins and Editorial Policies of the *Richmond Whig and Public Advertiser, 1824–1865*" (Ph.D. diss., Michigan State Univ., 1971); Ambler, *Ritchie*; Davis, *Intellectual Life in Jefferson's Virginia*, 71–118; *Seventh Census . . . 1850*, 283.

60. Eaton, *Growth of Southern Civilization*, 270; Siegel, *Roots of Southern Distinctiveness*, 25–37; Shade, "Society and Politics in Antebellum Virginia's Southside," 182–83. Cf. George Fitzhugh, *Cannibals All!, or Slaves without Masters*, ed. C. Vann Woodward (Cambridge, Mass., 1960); Eugene D. Genovese, *The World the Slaveholders Made* (New York, 1969), 115–244; Harvey Wish, ed., *Ante-Bellum: Writings of George Fitzhugh and Hinton Rowan Helper on Slavery* (New York, 1960).

61. George T. Starnes, *Sixty Years of Branch Banking in Virginia* (New York, 1931), 18–68; Ambler, *Ritchie*, 66–72; Douglas R. Egerton, *Charles Fenton Mercer and the Trial of National Conservatism* (Jackson, Miss., 1989), 65–79, 100–105. See also William Royall, *A History of Virginia Banks and Banking prior to the Civil War* (New York, 1903).

62. Starnes, *Branch Banking in Virginia*, 68–86; Larry Schweikart, *Banking in the American South from the Age of Jackson to Reconstruction* (Baton Rouge, La., 1987), 120–27; Sharp, *Jacksonians versus the Banks*, 215–46.

63. Starnes, *Branch Banking in Virginia*, 86–109.

64. Caroline E. MacGill et al., *History of Transportation in the United States before 1860* (Washington, D.C., 1917), 264–73; Carter Goodrich, *Government Promotion of American Canals and Railroads, 1800–1890* (New York, 1960), 87–101.

65. "Report of the Committee of Roads and Internal Navigation," Dec. 23, 1815, reprinted in Carter Goodrich, ed., *The Government and the Economy, 1783–1861* (Indianapolis, 1967), 59–77; Egerton, *Mercer*, 100–105; Carter Goodrich, "The Virginia System of Mixed Enterprise: A Study on State Planning of Internal Improvements," *Political Science Quarterly* 64 (1949): 355–87; Robert F. Hunter, "The Turnpike Movement in Virginia, 1816–1860," *VMHB* 59 (1961): 278–89; Wiley Hodges, "Pro-Governmentalism in Virginia, 1789–1836," *Journal of Politics* 33 (1971): 333–60.

66. Goodrich, *Government Promotion*, 92–98; Wayland F. Dunaway, *History of the James River and Kanawha Company* (New York, 1922); Philip M. Rice, "Internal Improvements in Virginia" (Ph.D. diss., Univ. of North Carolina, 1948).

67. Goodrich, *Government Promotion*, 98–101.

68. Gates, *Farmer's Age*, 312–17; Bruce, "Virginia Agricultural Decline," 5–12; Olmsted, *Cotton Kingdom*, 587–90; J. Carlyle Sitterson, "Edmund Ruffin: Agricultural Reformer and Southern Radical," introduction to Edmund Ruffin, *An Essay on Calcareous Manures*, ed. J. Carlyle Sitterson (Cambridge, Mass., 1961), xviii-xxi.

69. Emmitt B. Fields, "The Agricultural Population of Virginia, 1850–1860" (Ph.D. diss., Vanderbilt Univ., 1953), 106; Sitterson, "Edmund Ruffin," xx. Fields computed figures for Westmoreland, Northampton, Prince George, and Norfolk counties from the manuscript census; I have adjusted these figures using the *Seventh Census . . . 1850*, 256–60, and Jackson, *Free Negro Labor and Property Holding*, 102–36, 200–229, for the proportion of free blacks who generally owned neither slaves nor land.

70. See Oakes, *Ruling Race*, and Beeman, *Evolution of the Southern Backcountry*, 212–26, for a distinction between paternalism and the attitudes of the piedmont slaveholders.

71. *Seventh Census . . . 1850*, 258–59; Fields, "Agricultural Population of Virginia,"

112–14, 129, on Amherst, Fauquier, Hanover, Orange, Amelia, and Halifax counties; Schlotterbeck, "Plantation and Farm," on Orange and Greene; Siegel, *Roots of Southern Distinctiveness*, on Pittsylvania; Shade, "Society and Politics in Antebellum Virginia's Southside," on Prince Edward; Sutton, "Sectionalism and Social Structure," on Sussex; and Elaine M. Roubach, "Social Mobility in Henry County, Virginia, from 1850 to 1870" (M.A. thesis, University of Virginia, 1971).

72. Fields, "Agricultural Population of Virginia," 135–50.

73. *Seventh Census . . . 1850*, 29–92, 285–86; Bean, *Peopling Virginia*, has relatively hard data—that is from lists from these years—on forty-three counties.

74. Fields, "Agricultural Population of Virginia," 115, 150, on Bath and Shenandoah counties; Siegel, *Roots of Southern Distinctiveness*, 61–91; *Seventh Census . . . 1850*, 256–57. See also Oren F. Morton, *A History of Rockbridge County, Virginia* (Staunton, Va., 1920); John W. Wayland, *A History of Rockingham County, Virginia* (Dayton, Va., 1912); Wayland, *A History of the Shenandoah Valley of Virginia* (Strasburg, Va., 1927); Lewis Peyton, *History of Augusta County, Virginia* (Staunton, Va., 1882).

75. Bean, *Peopling of Virginia*, 25–27, 177–205, 234–37; Wust, *Virginia Germans*; Herbert A. Keller, "Rockbridge County Virginia, in 1835: A Study of Ante-Bellum Society," in *The Crusades and Other Essays Presented to Dana Munro by His Former Students*, ed. Louis John Paetow (New York, 1928), 321–65; Robert Douthat Stoner, *A Seed-Bed of the Republic: A Study of the Pioneers in the Upper (Southern) Valley of Virginia* (Roanoke, Va., 1962).

76. *Seventh Census . . . 1850*, 285–96.

77. Fields, "Agricultural Population of Virginia," on Floyd County.

78. Ibid., on Washington County; Sutton, "Sectionalism and Social Structure," on Tazewell; *Seventh Census . . . 1850*, 256–57, 270–71. See also Lewis Preston Summers, *History of Southwest Virginia, 1746–1786, Washington County, 1777–1870* (Richmond, Va., 1903).

79. De Bow, *Statistical View*, 320–21.

80. Jackson Turner Main, "The One Hundred," *WMQ* 11 (1958): 354–67; Main, "The Distribution of Property in Post Revolutionary Virginia," *Mississippi Valley Historical Review* 41 (1955): 241–58; Norman K. Risjord, *Chesapeake Politics, 1781–1800* (New York, 1978), 3–68.

81. Holland, "Rise and Fall of the Ante-Bellum Virginia Aristocracy."

82. Ibid., 363.

83. For Herrenvolk democracy, see Pierre L. van den Berghe in *Race and Racism: A Comparative Perspective* (New York, 1967); Frederickson, *Black Image in the White Mind*.

84. De Bow, *Statistical View*, 95, 128. If one assumes that 10 percent of the slaveholders were women, the remaining 50,000 men who owned slaves made up approximately one-quarter of the white adult male population.

85. Bruce, *Virginia Iron Manufacture*, 86.

2. The Constitution of Virginia

1. A. G. Roeber, *Faithful Magistrates and Republican Lawyers: Creators of Virginia Legal Culture, 1680–1810* (Chapel Hill, N.C., 1981); F. Thornton Miller, *Juries and Judges versus the Law: Virginia's Provincial Legal Perspective, 1783–1818* (Charlottesville, Va., 1994). Cf. William E. Nelson, *The Americanization of the Common Law: The Impact of*

Legal Change on Massachusetts Society, 1760–1830 (Cambridge, Mass., 1975); Morton J. Horwitz, *The Transformation of American Law, 1780–1860* (Cambridge, Mass., 1977).

2. Thorpe, *The Federal and State Constitutions* 7:3812–19; Robert A. Rutland, ed., *The Papers of George Mason, 1725–1792*, 3 vols. (Chapel Hill, N.C., 1970), 1:274–91, 295–310; Helen Hill, *George Mason: Constitutionalist* (1938; rept. Gloucester, Mass., 1966), 129–79, 276–79; Jack P. Greene, "Society, Ideology, and Politics: An Analysis of the Political Culture of Mid-Eighteenth-Century Virginia," in *Society, Freedom, and Conscience: The Coming of the Revolution in Virginia, Massachusetts, and New York*, ed. Richard M. Jellison (New York, 1976), 14–76; Charles S. Sydnor, *American Revolutionaries in the Making: Political Practices in Washington's Virginia* (New York, 1962); Sutton, *Revolution to Secession*, 1–51; Pole, *Political Representation*, 129–65, 281–96. See also Gordon Wood, *The Creation of the American Republic, 1776–1787* (Chapel Hill, N.C., 1969), 1–255; Green, *Constitutional Development in the South Atlantic States*, 1–141; Williamson, *American Suffrage from Property to Democracy*, 3–137; Don E. Fehrenbacher, *Constitutions and Constitutionalism in the Slaveholding South* (Athens, Ga., 1989), 1–32.

3. Jefferson, *Notes*, 162–64; Malone, *Jefferson and His Time* 1:235–40. See also Peterson, *Thomas Jefferson and the New Nation*; Matthews, *Radical Politics of Jefferson*.

4. The Republican synthesis is best summarized in Wood, *The Creation of the Republic*, 1–124, and Banning, *The Jeffersonian Persuasion*, 21–90.

5. Jefferson, *Notes*, 164, 176.

6. Jefferson, "Draft Constitution of Virginia," and Jefferson to Edmund Pendleton, August 26, 1776, in Peterson, *Portable Jefferson*, 162–76, 242–50, 355–57; Malone, *Jefferson and His Time* 1:235–40.

7. Madison, "Remarks on Mr. Jefferson's Draught of a Constitution," in Marvin Meyers, ed., *The Mind of the Founder: Sources of the Political Thought of James Madison* (Hanover, N.H., 1981), 34–43.

8. Pole, *Political Representation*, 296–314.

9. Jefferson, *Notes*, 214–15. See also Malone, *Jefferson and His Times* 1:260–69; William Cohen, "Thomas Jefferson and the Problem of Slavery," *Journal of American History* 56 (1969): 503–26; Jordan, *White over Black*, 429–81; John C. Miller, *The Wolf by the Ears* (New York, 1977); Matthews, *Radical Politics of Thomas Jefferson*, 53–75.

10. Edward Shils, "Centre and Periphery," in *The Logic of Personal Knowledge* (London, 1961), 117–30; Shils, *Political Development in New States* (The Hague, 1968); Michael Hechter, *Internal Colonialism: The Celtic Fringe in British National Development* (Berkeley, Calif., 1975). See also Formisano, *The Transformation of Political Culture*; Thomas Jeffery, *State Parties and National Politics: North Carolina, 1815–1861* (Chapel Hill, N.C., 1989).

11. James Mercer Garnett to John Randolph, Oct. 16, 1827, quoted in Sutton, "Nostalgia, Pessimism, and Malaise," 42. See also Taylor, *Cavalier and Yankee*; Davis, *Intellectual Life of Jefferson's Virginia*.

12. John P. Kennedy, ed., *Memoirs of the Life of William Wirt*, 2 vols. (Philadelphia, 1849), 2:304–5; Tucker, *Partisan Leader*.

13. Gordon to Jefferson, Dec. 10, 1825, Jefferson to Gordon, Jan. 1, 1826, in Armistead C. Gordon, *William Fitzhugh Gordon* (New York, 1909), 130–34. See also Malone, *Jefferson and His Time* 6:426–43; Shalhope, "Jefferson's Republicanism and Antebellum Southern Thought."

14. Sutton, "Nostalgia, Pessimism, and Malaise," 46.

15. *Proceedings and Debates of the Virginia Convention of 1829 – 30* (Richmond, 1830), 532 – 33. See also Bruce, *John Randolph of Roanoke* 1:601 – 33; Russell Kirk, *John Randolph of Roanoke: A Study in American Politics with Selected Speeches and Letters* (Indianapolis, 1978), 191 – 227, 287 – 92, 533 – 67.

16. Pole, *Political Representation*, 307; Sutton, *Revolution to Secession*, 60 – 62; Bruce, *Rhetoric of Conservatism*, 16 – 20.

17. James H. Broussard, *The Southern Federalists, 1800 – 1816* (Baton Rouge, La., 1978), 209 – 11; Madison to James Madison, Sr., Dec. 3, 1784, in Robert Rutland et al., eds., *The Papers of James Madison* 8 (Chicago, 1973): 172.

18. *Address* (Harrisonburg, 1815), LV; printed petition from Greenbrier County, in MS Petitions, Greenbrier Co., Dec. 13, 1815, LV.

19. *Niles' Weekly Register* 11 (1816): 17 – 25. See also Sutton, *Revolution to Secession*, 52 – 71.

20. Jefferson to Samuel Kercheval, July 12, 1816, in Merrill D. Peterson, ed., *Jefferson Writings* (New York, 1984), 1377 – 81.

21. Jefferson to Joseph C. Cabell, Feb. 2, 1816, to John Taylor, May 28, 1816, ibid., 1391 – 1403; Matthews, *Radical Politics of Thomas Jefferson*, 77 – 83.

22. Pole, *Political Representation*, 304 – 14; *Proceedings and Debates . . . 1829 – 30*, 257; Stuart to William Wirt, Aug. 25, 1816, WMQ 6 (1926): 340 – 43.

23. *Richmond Enquirer*, June 19 – Sept. 7, 1816, esp. Aug. 23; Stephen W. Brown, *Voice of the New West: John G. Jackson, His Life and Times* (Macon, Ga., 1985), 207 – 22.

24. *Journal of the House of Delegates . . . 1815* (these journals, with slightly varying titles, were published in Richmond shortly after each session and dated with the year in which the session began), 167; *Journal of the House of Delegates . . . 1816*, 28; *Richmond Enquirer*, June 19, Aug. 6, Sept. 7, Oct. 2, 1816, Feb. 8, 1817; *Niles' Weekly Register*, 11 (1817): 399, 15 – 35; Ambler, *Ritchie*, 65 – 68.

25. Harry Ammon, "The Richmond Junto, 1800 – 1824," VMHB 61 (1953): 395 – 418; Joseph H. Harrison, Jr., "Oligarchs and Democrats—The Richmond Junto," ibid., 78 (1970): 184 – 98; F. Thornton Miller, "The Richmond Junto: The Secret All-Powerful Club—or Myth," ibid., 99 (1991): 63 – 80.

26. *Richmond Enquirer*, March 12, 31, April 6, 16, April 30 – May 23, 1824.

27. Jefferson to John Hampden Pleasants, April 19, 1824, *Niles' Weekly Register* 26 (1824): 179, reprinted from the *Richmond Enquirer*, April 27, 1824.

28. *Lynchburg Virginian*, April 15, 1823; *Richmond Whig*, Nov. 22, 1825, Jan. 6, March 21, 1826; *Rockingham Weekly Register* (Harrisonburg), Aug. 11, 1825; *Niles' Weekly Register* 26 (1824): 179, 27 (1825): 17, 33, 49, 66, 97.

29. *Rockingham Weekly Register* (Harrisonburg), Aug. 11, 1825; *Richmond Enquirer*, Aug. 11, 13, 1825.

30. *Richmond Enquirer*, Feb. 10, June 17 – Sept. 26, 1825.

31. Benjamin Watkins Leigh, *Substitute Intended to Be Offered to the Next Meeting of the Citizens of Richmond on the Subject of a Convention* (Richmond, 1824), which first appeared as a series in the *Richmond Enquirer*, April 30 – May 4, 1824. See also Bruce Steiner, "The Prelude to Conservatism, 1781 – 1822: An Account of the Early Life, First Ventures, and Legal Career of Benjamin Watkins Leigh," (M.A. thesis, Univ. of Virginia, 1955). Cf. Norman Risjord's *The Old Republicans: Southern Conservatism in the Age of Jefferson* (New York, 1965), which perpetuates the myth that the Old Republicans were a minority and somewhat eccentric faction of the Virginia Republicans during these years. Yet his evidence shows that his group included all of the leading Republicans in

the state. See also the descriptions of party dinners in the *Richmond Enquirer*, Feb. 22, March 6, 10, 1827.

32. Upshur to Gilmer, July 7, 1825, Francis Walker Gilmer Papers, UVA.

33. *Richmond Enquirer*, April 16, 1824, Feb. 8, 10, 1825; Benjamin Watkins Leigh to Littleton Waller Tazewell, Aug. 22, 1825, Tazewell Papers, LV; Norma Lois Peterson, *Littleton Waller Tazewell* (Charlottesville, Va., 1983), 84–88; Claude Hall, *Abel Parker Upshur: Conservative Virginian, 1790–1844* (Madison, Wis., 1964), 43–44; Egerton, *Mercer*, 218–33. The "Mason" essays by Leigh are in the *Richmond Enquirer*, May 20, 24, June 21, 28, July 5, 19, 1825.

34. *Richmond Enquirer*, June 14, 17, 1825; *National Intelligencer* (Washington, D.C.), June 8, 17, 1825.

35. *Richmond Whig*, March 21, 1826, Jan. 23, Feb. 16, 20, 1828, Jan. 6, 27, 1829; *Richmond Enquirer*, Jan. 25, Feb. 10, 13, 15, 22, 1827; *National Intelligencer* (Washington, D.C.), reprinted in the *Wheeling Gazette*, May 19, 1827; *Wheeling Gazette*, July 7, 1827, Dec. 27, 1828, Jan. 8, March 28, 1829.

36. It is very difficult to tell from the coverage in the *Richmond Enquirer*, April 13 – May 15, 1827, exactly which elections were affected, since none of the elections reported was simply between a conservative and a reformer. The bill did permit a "Neutral" vote as well, but that option was not often used.

37. Ibid., April 11 – May 30, 1828.

38. Ibid., Feb. 10, 12, 1829.

39. *Proceedings and Debates . . . 1829–30*, 160. See also Bruce, *Rhetoric of Conservatism*; Robert Paul Sutton, "The Virginia Constitutional Convention of 1829–30: A Profile Analysis of Late Jeffersonian Virginia" (Ph.D. diss., Univ. of Virginia, 1967); Kathryn Ruth Malone, "The Virginia Doctrines, the Commonwealth, and the Republic: The Role of Fundamental Principles in Virginia Politics, 1798–1833" (Ph.D. diss., Univ. of Pennsylvania, 1981), 299–361; Sutton, *Revolution to Secession*, 73–102; Pole, *Political Representation*, 314–38; Green, *Constitutional Development*, 210–24; Ambler, *Sectionalism*, 137–74; Merrill D. Peterson, ed., *Democracy, Liberty, and Property: The State Constitutional Conventions of the 1820's* (Indianapolis, 1966), 271–86; Freehling, *The Road to Disunion* 1:162–67.

40. *Journal*, 61–62; *Proceedings and Debates . . . 1829–30*, 425, 53–62.

41. *Proceedings and Debates . . . 1829–30*, 66–79. See also Hall, *Upshur*, 30–67; Peterson, *Tazewell*, 165–78; Bruce, *John Randolph of Roanoke* 1:601–33; Bruce, *Rhetoric of Conservatism*, 73–108.

42. *Proceedings and Debates . . . 1829–30*, 160, 789, 363–67.

43. Ibid., 25–31.

44. Ibid., 66–71, 156–62, 316–19.

45. Ibid., 156–57, 366–67; Hall, *Upshur*, 48–49. For antipartyism, see Hofstadter, *Idea of a Party System*; Banning, *The Jeffersonian Persuasion*, 21–90; Ketcham, *Presidents above Party*.

46. *Proceedings and Debates . . . 1829–30*, 156–64, 562.

47. Ibid., 398–99, 158–59. See also C. B. Macpherson, *The Political Theory of Possessive Individualism* (Oxford, 1962).

48. *Proceedings and Debates . . . 1829–30*, 74–75, 316. See also John Randolph to John Brockenbrough, Jan. 12, 1829, in Kirk, *Randolph of Roanoke*, 287–88; John Wickham to Littleton Waller Tazewell, Dec. 21, 1828, Jan. 18, 1829, Hugh Blair Grigsby to John Tazewell, Jan. 10, 17, 1829, Tazewell Papers, LV.

49. *Proceedings and Debates . . . 1829 – 30*, 257; Bruce, *Rhetoric of Conservatism*, 109 – 41.

50. Bruce, *Rhetoric of Conservatism*, 34 – 38; Sutton, *Revolution to Secession*, 182 – 207. I use Bruce's categories with slight revision of names. His cluster analysis does not technically create a "scale" locating individuals on a conservative/reform dimension, which accounts for the seemingly odd placement of Chapman Johnson, Abel P. Upshur, and John R. Cooke; rather it represents groups of men who frequently voted together on forty-six roll calls and shows the complexity of "reform" as an issue. Sutton gives biographies of ninety-eight delegates whom he impressionistically divides into forty-nine "Eastern Conservative Delegates" and forty-nine "Reform Delegates and Their Allies."

51. Sutton, *Revolution to Secession*, 89 – 90; Malone, "Virginia Doctrines, the Commonwealth, and the Republic," 356.

52. Ester C. M. Steele, "Chapman Johnson," *VMHB* 25 (1927): 116 – 74, 246 – 53.

53. The text and table 2.1 are based on a reanalysis of material presented differently in Sutton, *Revolution to Secession*, 74 – 75.

54. Bruce, *Rhetoric of Conservatism*, 39 – 40; Holland, "Rise and Fall of the Ante-Bellum Virginia Aristocracy."

55. See Daniel P. Jordan, *Political Leadership in Jefferson's Virginia* (Charlottesville, Va., 1983).

56. Bruce, *Rhetoric of Conservatism*, 39.

57. Ibid., 41; Sutton, *Revolution to Secession*, 76 – 77.

58. Grigsby quoted in Pole, *Political Representation*, 324; John Campbell to James Campbell, Feb. 1, 1829, Campbell Family Papers, DU. See H. W. Howard Knott, "Philip Doddridge," *DAB*; Waitman T. Willey, *A Sketch of Philip Doddridge* (Morgantown, W.Va., 1875).

59. *Wheeling Gazette*, Jan. 23, Feb. 27, March 6, 20, April 3, 1830; *Richmond Enquirer*, May 4, 1830. See table 3.1 in Peterson, *Democracy, Liberty, and Property*, 444 – 45, which shows that the piedmont and tidewater were overrepresented in relation to the white basis and that the trans-Allegheny was underrepresented.

60. *Wheeling Gazette*, Oct. 25, 1828, Dec. 19, 26, 1829.

61. Sutton, *Revolution to Secession*, 182 – 207; Bruce, *Rhetoric of Conservatism*, esp. 31 – 72; Tyler, *Letters and Times* 2:502 – 5, 710 – 11; Gordon, *William Fitzhugh Gordon*, 191, 237.

62. Frank L. Owsley, "James Murray Mason," *DAB*; Virginia Mason, *The Public Life and Diplomatic Correspondence of James M. Mason, with Some Personal History* (New York, 1906); James Bugg, "The Political Career of James Murray Mason" (Ph.D. diss., Univ. of Virginia, 1950).

63. Cf. William N. Chambers, *Political Parties in a New Nation: The American Experience, 1776 – 1809* (New York, 1962); McCormick, *Second American Party System*; Arthur M. Schlesinger, Jr., *The Age of Jackson* (Boston, 1945); Sydnor, *Development of Southern Sectionalism.*

3. A Candid State of Parties

1. Jefferson, "First Inaugural Address," and Jefferson to John Taylor, June 4, 1798, in Peterson, *Jefferson Writings*, 492 – 96, 1048 – 51.

2. Thad Tate, "The Coming of the Revolution in Virginia: Britain's Challenge to Virginia's Ruling Class, 1763 – 1776," *WMQ* 19 (1962): 323 – 43; Sydnor, *American Revo-*

lutionaries in the Making; Robert E. Brown and Katharine Brown, *Virginia, 1705 – 1786: Democracy or Aristocracy?* (East Lansing, Mich., 1964); David Alan Williams, "Political Alignments in Colonial Virginia Politics, 1698 – 1750" (Ph.D. diss., Northwestern Univ., 1959); Williams, "The Small Farmer in Eighteenth-Century Virginia Politics," *Agricultural History* 43 (1969): 91 – 101; Greene, "Society, Ideology, and Politics"; Mark Engal, "The Origin of the Revolution in Virginia: A Reinterpretation," *WMQ* 37 (1980): 401 – 28; Herbert Sloan and Peter Onuf, "Politics, Culture, and the Revolution in Virginia: A Review of Recent Work," *VMHB* 91 (1983): 259 – 84.

3. See Hofstadter, *Idea of a Party System*; Forrest McDonald, *The Presidency of Thomas Jefferson* (Lawrence, Kans., 1976); Banning, *Jeffersonian Persuasion*; Ketcham, *Presidents above Party*; Noble Cunningham, ed., *The Making of the American Party System, 1789 – 1809* (Englewood Cliffs, N.J., 1965).

4. Jefferson, "Selections from *The Anas*," Jefferson to Abigail Adams, June 13, 1804, to John Adams, June 15, 1813, to Justice William Johnson, Oct. 27, 1822, to William Branch Giles, Dec. 26, 1825, in Peterson, *Jefferson Writings*, 492 – 96, 661 – 90, 1048 – 51, 1144 – 46, 1277 – 80, 1459 – 63, 1509 – 12; Jefferson to William Branch Giles, Dec. 31, 1795, to John Wise, Feb. 12, 1798, to William Short, Nov. 10, 1804, to John Adams, Jan. 17, 1813, in Cunningham, *Making of the American Party System*, 17 – 20; James Madison, "A Candid State of Parties," ibid., 10 – 11; John Taylor, "A Definition of Parties," ibid., 21. See also Robert E. Shalhope, *John Taylor of Caroline: Pastoral Republican* (Columbia, S.C., 1980).

5. McCormick, *Second American Party System*; Shade, "Political Pluralism and Party Development." See also Ambler *Sectionalism*; Ambler, *Ritchie*; Simms, *Rise of the Whigs in Virginia*; Harry Ammon, "The Republican Party in Virginia, 1789 to 1829" (Ph.D. diss., Univ. of Virginia, 1948); Ammon, "The Formation of the Republican Party in Virginia," *JSH* 19 (1953): 283 – 310; Ammon, "The Richmond Junto, 1800 – 1824," *VMHB* 61 (1953): 395 – 418; Ammon, "James Monroe and the Election of 1808 in Virginia," *WMQ* 20 (1963): 33 – 56.

6. On periodization, see Chambers and Burnham, *American Party Systems*; Kleppner et al., *Evolution of American Electoral Systems*; Silbey, *American Political Nation*; Shafer, *End of Realignment?*

7. See Richard R. Beeman, *The Old Dominion and the New Nation, 1789 – 1801* (Lexington, Ky., 1972); Risjord, *Chesapeake Politics*; Risjord, "The Virginia Federalists," *JSH* 33 (1967): 468 – 517; Jordan, *Political Leadership in Jefferson's Virginia*; J. R. Pole, "Representation and Authority in Virginia from the Revolution to Reform," *JSH* 24 (1958): 16 – 50; Noble E. Cunningham, *The Jeffersonian Republicans: The Formation of Party Organization, 1789 – 1801* (Chapel Hill, N.C., 1957); Daniel Sisson, *The American Revolution of 1800* (New York, 1974); Daniel P. Jordan, "Virginia Congressmen, 1801 – 1825" (Ph.D. diss., Univ. of Virginia, 1970).

8. Rex Beach, "Spencer Roane and the Richmond Junto," *WMQ* 22 (1942): 1 – 17; Ollen Lawrence Burnette, Jr., "Peter V. Daniel, Agrarian Justice," *VMHB* 62 (1954): 289 – 305; Ammon, "The Richmond Junto," 395 – 418; Joseph Harrison, "Oligarchs and Democrats"; Dent, "Virginia Democratic Party," 23 – 34.

9. Ambler, *Ritchie*, 53 – 85; Risjord, *Old Republicans*, 174 – 255. Cf. Drew R. McCoy, *The Elusive Republic: Political Economy in Jeffersonian America* (Chapel Hill, N.C., 1980).

10. See Harrison, "Oligarchs and Democrats"; cf. Charles D. Lowrey, *James Barbour: The Biography of a Jeffersonian Republican* (University, Ala., 1984), for an example of the numerous splits within families or among brothers.

11. Miller, "Richmond Junto." Cf. [Alexander McRae], *Letters on the Richmond Party.*

By a Virginian. Originally Published in the Washington Republican (Washington, D.C., 1823); Benjamin Watkins Leigh to Henry Lee, Nov. 29, 1824, in Benjamin Watkins Leigh Papers, VHS. See also Tomlinson, "Origins of *Richmond Whig.*"

12. *Richmond Enquirer,* Jan. 28, May 20, Aug. 26, 1823, Jan. 29, Feb. 12, 19, 21, 24, 25, May 25, 1824; Claiborne W. Gooch to Martin Van Buren, Sept. 14, 1824, Martin Van Buren Papers, LC; Thomas H. Benton to Gooch [?], March 22, 1824, Gooch Family Papers, UVA; John Tyler to Henry Clay, March 27, 1825, in Calvin Colton, ed., *The Private Correspondence of Henry Clay* (New York, 1856), 119–20. On the election generally, see James F. Hopkins, "Election of 1824," in Arthur M. Schlesinger, Jr., and Fred J. Israel, *History of American Presidential Elections: 1789–1968,* 3 vols. (New York, 1971), 1:341–412.

13. The returns are in the Library of Virginia.

14. Risjord, *Old Republicans,* 256–61; John Tyler to Dr. Henry Curtis, March 18, 1828, in Tyler, *Letters and Times* 1:383–86; Jefferson to William Branch Giles, Dec. 26, 1825, in Peterson, *Jefferson Writings,* 1509–12; *Richmond Enquirer,* Dec. 8, 10, 13, 17, 22, 1825; William Branch Giles, *Political Miscellanies* (Richmond, 1830), of which items first appeared in the *Enquirer*; Philip N. Nicholas to Martin Van Buren, Oct. 13, 1826, Van Buren to Nicholas, Nov. ?, 1826, Martin Van Buren Papers, LC; Benjamin Watkins Leigh to Henry Lee, Nov. 29, 1824, Benjamin Watkins Leigh Papers, VHS; Robert V. Remini, *The Election of Andrew Jackson* (Philadelphia, 1963), 11–50; George R. Neilson, "The Indispensable Institution: The Congressional Party during the Era of Good Feelings" (Ph.D. diss., Univ. of Iowa, 1968).

15. Van Buren to Thomas Ritchie, Jan. 13, 1827, Martin Van Buren Papers, LC; *Richmond Enquirer,* May 1, 4, 18, 22, 1827; Herman V. Ames, ed., *State Documents on Federal Relations* (Philadelphia, 1906), 140–43; Giles, *Political Miscellanies*; Merrill D. Peterson, *The Jeffersonian Image in the American Mind* (New York, 1960); Ambler, *Ritchie,* 85–117. See also Dice R. Anderson, *William Branch Giles: A Study in the Politics of Virginia and the Nation, 1790 to 1830* (Menasha, Wis., 1914); Robert V. Remini, *Martin Van Buren and the Making of the Democratic Party* (New York, 1957).

16. Joseph H. Harrison, "Martin Van Buren and His Southern Supporters," *JSH* 22 (1956): 438–58; Richard Brown, "The Missouri Crisis, Slavery, and the Politics of Jacksonianism," *South Atlantic Quarterly* 65 (1966): 55–72; Brown, "Southern Planters and Plain Republicans of the North: Martin Van Buren's Formula for National Politics" (Ph.D. diss., Yale Univ., 1955); Remini, *Election of Jackson,* 51–120.

17. David Campbell to James Campbell, March 19, 1827, John Campbell to David Campbell, Oct. 27, Nov. 3, 1827, John Campbell to James Campbell, Aug. 23, 1827, Campbell Family Papers, DU; Remini, *Election of Jackson,* 104–5; Andrew Jackson to William Branch Giles quoted in ibid., 208 n.1; *Enquirer,* March 1, May 30, June 27, July 8, 29, Aug. 21, Oct., 3, 7, 14, Nov. 18, 1828; Thomas Ritchie to Littleton Waller Tazewell, Feb. 28, 1827, Tazewell Family Papers, LV; Thomas Ritchie to Col. A. Ritchie, n.d., in "Unpublished Letters of Thomas Ritchie," *John P. Branch Historical Papers of Randolph Macon College* 3 (1911): 204–6; Thomas Ritchie to Martin Van Buren, March 11, 1828, Martin Van Buren Papers, LC; Ritchie to William C. Rives, June 1828, William C. Rives Papers, LC; Giles in *Richmond Enquirer,* March 1, 1828; *Virginia Advocate* (Charlottesville), July 26, Aug. 2, 16, Oct. 4, Nov. 1, 1828; Claiborne W. Gooch to George Thompson, Aug. 29, 1828, Gooch Family Papers, UVA.

18. *Richmond Enquirer,* Oct. 26, Nov. 22, 1827; *Lynchburg Virginian* Oct. 10, 1827, April 14, 1828; *Richmond Whig,* Sept. 1, 15, Oct. 3, 6, 21, 1827, Jan. 8, 16, Aug. 2, 9, Nov. 11,

15, 1828; James Barbour to Henry Clay, Jan. 27, 1828, in Colton, *Private Correspondence of Clay*, 190 – 91; Francis Brooke to Clay, Jan. 14, Feb. 7, 1828, Clay to Francis Brooke, Jan. 15, 1828, in Seager, *Papers of Henry Clay* 7:33 – 34, 37 – 38, 83; Samuel L. Southard to Clay, Aug. 8, 1827, in Hargreaves and Hopkins, *Papers of Henry Clay* 5:864 – 65.

19. *Wheeling Gazette*, May 19, June 2, Nov. 1, Dec. 27, 1828; *Richmond Whig*, Jan. 12, 16, Aug. 29, Sept. 6, 10, Nov. 11, 1828. See also Simms, *Rise of the Whigs in Virginia*, 20 – 32; Bruce, *Rhetoric of Conservatism*, 36 – 37.

20. "Address to the People of Virginia, January 17, 1828" in Robert V. Remini, "Election of 1828," in Schlesinger and Israel, *History of Presidential Elections* 1:464 – 75; *Wheeling Gazette*, Dec. 1, 1827, Aug. 23, 30, Sept. 18, Oct. 4, 11, 18, 25, Nov. 1, 1828; *Richmond Whig*, Jan. 12, 16, July 9, Aug. 29, Sept. 6, 10, Oct. 18, Nov. 11, 1828; *Lynchburg Virginian*, April 14, 1828.

21. The returns are from the Library of Virginia, and the turnout figures are presented in Richard P. McCormick, "New Perspectives on Jacksonian Politics," *AHR* 65 (1960): 288 – 301; Pole, *Political Representation*, 562; Jordan, "Virginia Congressmen," app. 2; and Sydnor, *American Revolutionaries in the Making*, apps. 1, 2.

22. Simms, *Rise of the Whigs in Virginia*, 44 – 57; Charles H. Ambler, *Life and Diary of John Floyd* (Richmond, Va., 1918), 100 – 102, 123 – 25, 127 – 28, 130 – 32, 136, 146 – 47; Peterson, *Tazewell*, 178 – 86; John Tyler to John Rutherfoord, March 14, 1830, in Tyler, *Letters and Times* 3:61 – 63; Littleton W. Tazewell to John Tazewell, March 24, 1830, Tazewell Famly Papers, LV; Dent, "Virginia Democratic Party," 90 – 116. On Jackson's first administration, see Robert V. Remini, *Andrew Jackson and the Course of American Freedom, 1822 – 1833* (New York, 1981); Richard Latner, *The Presidency of Andrew Jackson* (Athens, Ga., 1979).

23. Thomas W. Gilmer to Rives, Dec. 3, 1832, Rives to Gilmer, Dec. 8, 10, 1832, Thomas Ritchie to Rives, Dec. 6, 1832, William C. Rives Papers, LC; *Richmond Enquirer*, Dec. 4, 6, 12, 1832.

24. Simms, *Rise of the Whigs in Virginia*, 52 – 86; *Richmond Enquirer*, Jan. 9, Feb. 25, 27, April 1, 18, 1834.

25. *Richmond Enquirer*, April 18, May 13, 1834.

26. On the election of 1836, see Joel Silbey, "The Election of 1836," in Schlesinger and Israel, *History of American Presidential Elections* 1:577 – 642; Dereck Hackett, "The Days of This Republic Will Be Numbered: Abolition, Slavery, and the Presidential Election of 1836," *Louisiana Studies* 15 (1976): 131 – 60.

27. In 1837 the Whigs and Democrats seriously contested only three of the twenty-one seats. R. M. T. Hunter, running as a Republican, won a close victory by a plurality over two other Republican candidates (*Richmond Enquirer*, May 19, 1837).

28. John M. McFaul, *The Politics of Jacksonian Finance* (Ithaca, N.Y., 1972), 107 – 42; George W. Hopkins to David Campbell, June 23, 1836, Campbell Family Papers, DU; Richard H. Parker to Martin Van Buren, June 29, 1836, Martin Van Buren Papers, LC; John C. Calhoun to James H. Hammond, June 19, July 4, 1836, in J. Franklin Jameson, ed., "Correspondence of John C. Calhoun," *Annual Report of the American Historical Association for the Year 1899* (Washington, D.C., 1900), 2:358 – 61, 362; William F. Gordon to Thomas W. Gilmer, Jan. 14, 1834, in "Original Letters," *WMQ* 21 (1912): 2; *Register of Debates*, 23d Cong., 21st sess., 1281 – 88.

29. William C. Rives to Martin Van Buren, June 3, 1837, Silas Wright to Van Buren, June 4, June 22, 1837, John Milton Niles to Van Buren, July 1, 1837, Martin Van Buren Papers, LC; *Daily Madisonian* (Washington, D.C.), Aug. 11, 1837.

30. Van Buren, "Message to the Special Session," in James D. Richardson, *A Compilation of the Messages and Papers of the Presidents, 1789–1897.* 10 vols. (Washington, D.C., 1900), 4:1545–51; *Daily Madisonian* (Washington, D.C.), Aug. 11, Dec. 9, 14, 19, 1837; *United States Magazine and Democratic Review* 2 (1838): 2–15; *Globe* (Washington, D.C.), Oct. 12, 14, 1837; Richard E. Parker to Martin Van Buren, Nov. 14, 1837, Martin Van Buren Papers, LC. See also Raymond Dingledine,"The Political Career of William Cabell Rives" (Ph.D. diss., Univ. of Virginia, 1947); Jean E. Friedman, *The Revolt of the Conservative Democrats: An Essay on American Political Culture and Political Development, 1837–1844* (Ann Arbor, Mich., 1979); Harold D. Moser, "Subtreasury Politics and the Virginia Conservative Democrats, 1835–1844" (Ph.D. diss., Univ. of Wisconsin, 1977). Cf. Schlesinger, *Age of Jackson,* 217–41; Schweikart, *Banking in the American South,* 48–90.

31. Simms, *Rise of the Virginia Whigs,* 118–39; Howard Braverman, "The Economic and Political Background of the Conservative Revolt in Virginia," *VMHB* 60 (1952): 266–87; Sharp, *Jacksonians versus the Banks,* 215–46; Dent, "Virginia Democratic Party," 215–67.

32. Peter Daniel to David Campbell, May 15, 1837, William C. Rives to Campbell, May 22, June 18, 1837, Campbell Family Papers, DU; Richard Parker to Benjamin Butler, May 29, 1837, Martin Van Buren Papers, LC; Campbell to Rives, June 15, 1837, William C. Rives Papers, LC; *Richmond Enquirer,* May 26, June 13, 1837; *Richmond Whig,* May 30, June 13, 1837; Thomas Ritchie to Rives, Sept. 20, 1837?, in "Unpublished Letters of Thomas Ritchie," 225; Claiborne W. Gooch to ?, Nov. 16, 1837, Gooch Family Papers, UVA; Ambler, *Ritchie,* 193–206. See also Andrew Jackson to Francis P. Blair, Sept. 6, 1837, in John Spencer Bassett, ed., *Correspondence of Andrew Jackson,* 7 vols. (Washington, D.C., 1926–35), 5:508.

33. *Richmond Enquirer,* March 21, 1839.

34. Ibid., March 21, 23, 1839.

36. Although the assembly and congressional returns were correlated, the relationship between the Democratic congressional returns of 1839 and the slightly smaller Van Buren vote in 1836 was low ($r = .60$).

37. *United States Magazine and Democratic Review* 7 (1840): 485–87.

38. See Robert G. Gunderson, *The Log Cabin Campaign* (Lexington, Ky., 1957); William N. Chambers, "The Election of 1840," in Schlesinger and Israel, *History of Presidential Elections* 1:643–746; William N. Chambers and Philip C. Davis, "Party Competition and Mass Participation, 1824–1852," in Joel H. Silbey, Allan G. Bogue, and William H. Flannagan, eds., *The History of American Electoral Behavior* (Princeton, N.J., 1978), 174–97.

39. Gunderson, *Log Cabin Campaign,* esp. 162–216. A. B. Norton, ed., *The Great Revolution of 1840* (Mount Vernon, Ohio, 1888), reprints numerous Whig speeches and includes a songbook. Cf. Tyler, *Letters and Times* 1:603–33, 2:1–39, 699–711, 3:71–95.

40. "Democratic Platform," in Chambers, "Election of 1840," 91–92.

41. "Speech of Henry Clay," in Norton, *Great Revolution of 1840,* 187–212.

42. William Henry Harrison to Harmar Denny, Dec. 2, 1838, and speech by Harrison, Dayton, Sept. 10, 1840, in Chambers, "Election of 1840," 695–99, 737–44.

43. Peter Temin pointed out in *The Jacksonian Economy* (New York, 1969), 155–65, that the depression following 1839 differed from the Great Depression of the 1930s in that while prices fell production actually went up. Nineteenth-century editors (and presumably voters) did not see these issues in modern macroeconomic terms, using

language that was mainly moralistic and fraught with symbolism; Whigs were more likely to project the economic impact of policy, but often their arguments were primarily legalistic references to rights of various sorts.

44. *Richmond Enquirer*, Jan. 11, 13, Feb. 5, 8, March 17, April 12, 15, 19, 26, May 20, 1842.

45. Ibid., April 3, May 4, 16, 1841, April 26, May 16, 1843. Ritchie counted former governor Gilmer as a Republican. He ran against regular Whig William L. Goggin, who took his seat when Gilmer resigned to enter Tyler's cabinet as secretary of the navy.

46. See Charles Sellers, "Election of 1844," in Schlesinger and Israel, *History of Presidential Elections* 1:747–861; Charles Henry Ambler, "Virginia and the Presidential Succession, 1840–44," in *Essays in American History Dedicated to Frederick Jackson Turner* (1910; rept. New York, 1951), 165–202; Dent, "Virginia Democratic Party," 310–56.

47. Chaplain W. Morrison, *Democratic Politics and Sectionalism: The Wilmot Proviso Controversy* (Chapel Hill, N.C., 1967), 3–51; Ames, *State Documents on Federal Relations*, 244–47.

48. James Seddon to R. M. T. Hunter, June 16, 1848, in Ambler, ed., "Correspondence of Robert M. T. Hunter," 90–91; Holman Hamilton, "Election of 1848," in Schlesinger and Israel, *History of Presidential Elections* 2:865–920; Shanks, *Secession Movement in Virginia*, 18–24. See also Joseph C. Rayback, *Free Soil: The Election of 1848* (Lexington, Ky., 1970).

49. *Niles' Register* 73 (1848): 277, 74 (July 5, 1848): 8; *Richmond Enquirer*, Feb. 24, 26, March 8, May 12, 1848; *Richmond Whig*, Feb. 24, 26, 1848; *Lynchburg Virginian*, May 10, 1848; John M. Botts to the Editors of the *Whig*, Jan. 29, 1848, *Richmond Enquirer*, Feb. 2, 1848; John M. Botts, *To the Whigs of Virginia* (March 8, 1848); Botts, *To the Whole Whig Party of the United States* (March 30, 1848).

50. *Lynchburg Patriot* reprinted in the *Richmond Enquirer*, Jan. 12, 1849.

51. *Richmond Enquirer*, Jan. 22, March 6, 16, April 3, 25, 1849.

52. William C. Rives to James F. Strother, May 5, 1852, William C. Rives Papers, LC; *Richmond Whig*, April 20, June 22, 1852; Roy and Jeannette Nichols, "Election of 1852," in Schlesinger, and Israel, *History of Presidential Elections* 2:921–1006, which reprints the Whig platform (pp. 956–57).

53. Democratic platform, reprinted in Nichols and Nichols, "Election of 1852," 951–53; *Richmond Enquirer*, March 12, April 9, June 18, Sept. 7, 1852.

54. Alexander Newman was elected from the northwest as a Democrat but died before Congress met, and he was replaced by a Whig Thomas S. Haymond.

55. See "Webster in Virginia," including his speech to the "Ladies in the Log Cabin," in Norton, *Great Revolution*, 328–40, and the numerous references elsewhere in this volume. See also Ronald P. Formisano, "The New Political History and the Election of 1840," *Journal of Interdisciplinary History* 23 (1993): 661–82; Elizabeth R. Varon, "White Women and Politics in Antebellum Virginia" (Ph.D. diss., Yale Univ., 1993).

56. *Historical Statistics*, 1072.

57. Tocqueville's *Democracy in America* is only the most famous of numerous foreign and domestic commentaries. See also Edward Pessen, *Jacksonian America: Society, Personality, and Politics* (Homewood, Ill., 1978), 4–32; Pessen, ed., *Jacksonian Panorama* (Indianapolis, 1976); George E. Probst, ed., *The Happy Republic: A Reader in Tocqueville's America* (New York, 1962); Robert H. Wiebe, *Self-Rule: A Cultural History of American Democracy* (Chicago, 1995), 41–85.

58. The correlation between slaveholding and turnout declined between 1836 and 1840 while farm value and literacy continued to be related to turnout from 1836 through

1852. Although one might raise the possibility of an ecological fallacy in the reasoning from twentieth-century studies and county-level correlations, these relationships are also present in the extant individual data described in Shade, "Society and Politics in Antebellum Virginia's Southside," 175–77.

59. Stability is defined here as fluctuation of less that ten points between the two parties' share of the vote over the course of the remaining elections through 1852, no matter how large the winning party's majority was. It is taken as an indicator of party institutionalization. One of the most striking evidences of partisan influence in the 1840s is that all of the thirteen counties created between 1840 and 1848 showed immediate stability. They were created with citizens already imbued with partisan identities.

60. For example, an ecological regression of the 1851 gubernatorial election on the 1848 presidential election indicates that no voters switched parties. In 1848 more Democrats that Whigs stayed home. The congressional returns are for the 119 counties that have been used here and based on material from the ICPSR. Data for the elections of 1837 and 1841 are missing altogether and those for the other congressional elections are less complete than these for presidential elections. In the assembly election of 1837 held at the same time as the congressional election, there was a turnout of approximately 39 percent, and the Democrats won 63 percent of the seats. In 1841 there was a turnout for the assembly election of 45 percent, and the Democrats took only 49 percent of the seats.

4. Out of the Nature of Things

1. Jefferson to John Adams, Oct. 28, 1813, in Peterson, *Jefferson Writings*, 1304–10; Jefferson to Henry Lee, 1824, to T. Cooper, 1814, in Saul Padover, ed., *Thomas Jefferson on Democracy* (New York, 1939), 85–86.

2. Jefferson to H. G. Spafford, 1814, in Padover, *Jefferson on Democracy*, 84–85; "To Philip Mazzei, April 24, 1796," in Peterson, *Jefferson Writings*, 1035–37.

3. Jefferson, *Notes*, 290–91.

4. Saul Padover, ed., *The Complete Madison* (New York, 1953), 27–29, 32–35, 50–57, 267–69, 276–91.

5. Meyers, *Mind of the Founder*, 181–90.

6. See Ambler, *Sectionalism*, 61–99; Beeman, *The Old Dominion and the New Nation*; Risjord, *Chesapeake Politics*; Risjord, "Virginia Federalists"; Jordan, *Political Leadership in Jefferson's Virginia*.

7. Broussard, *Southern Federalists*, 385, 406; Dunn, "Black Society in the Chesapeake," 60. See also Norman K. Risjord, "How the Common Man Voted in Jefferson's Virginia," in John B. Boles, ed., *America, the Middle Period: Essays in Honor of Bernard Mayo* (Charlottesville, Va., 1973), 36–64.

8. On the Germans, cf. Broussard, *Southern Federalists*, 395–96; Wust, *The Virginia Germans*, 115–18.

9. The four southside districts—the Second, Third, Fourth, and Fifth—contained 15 percent of all of the state's Democrats; if the three contiguous planter, tobacco-producing counties—Isle of Wight, Halifax and Louisa—are included that figure approaches 20 percent. The discussion here is based on the presidential vote in the election of 1840 tabulated for the congressional districts that existed that year. "Clear majority" for either party is defined as 55 percent or more of the vote. Even the northernmost of the counties of the Thirteenth—Rappahannock and Culpeper, just outside the tobacco

region—were Whig like the counties in the Fourteenth District immediately north of them. For maps of the presidential elections, see Ambler, *Sectionalism*; Simms, *Rise of the Whigs in Virginia*; Arthur Charles Cole, *The Whig Party in the South* (1914; rept. Gloucester, Mass., 1962); Frederick Jackson Turner, *The United States, 1830 – 1850: The Nation and Its Sections* (1935; rept. New York, 1965). The analysis of the "Virginia constituencies" in Sharp, *Jacksonians versus the Banks*, 247 – 73, differs from mine primarily in emphasis.

10. Ignoring overwhelmingly Democratic Isle of Wight would add to the list of Whig districts the First, in the southeast corner of the state surrounding Norfolk.

11. There were, of course, more Whigs in some "Democratic" counties than in many "Whig" counties, and vice versa. Pittsylvania and Frederick were in the top ten counties for both parties. Loudoun had the most Whig voters of any county in the commonwealth: 1,269.

12. The seven western congressional districts were organized in a scheme less representative than the legislature itself. Primarily because of the three-fifths clause of the Constitution, the smallest western district turned out 50 percent more voters in 1840 than the largest eastern district, and the largest western district had three times as many voters as the smallest eastern district.

13. The Sixteenth District contained one-fifth more Democrats than the Eighteenth. If one adds two contiguous and heavily German counties—Frederick and Madison—to it, the resulting eight-county area would account for 15 percent of Virginia's Democrats.

14. *Seventh Census . . . 1850*, 258, corrected in De Bow, *Statistical View*, 338 – 93, to include Staunton and Harrisonburg.

15. See Eaton, *Growth of Southern Civilization*, 150 – 76, 247 – 70. To restate the proportions rather more precisely for the election of 1844: 30 percent of the Virginia population lived in counties with towns over 1,000 people; Clay received three fifths of the vote in these counties; and these counties contained 35 percent of all of Virginia's Whigs and only one-fifth of the commonwealth's Democrats.

16. The upper tidewater, north of the James River, resembled Maryland politically, and the conditions and culture of the Eastern Shore of Virginia are related to those of Maryland's Eastern Shore. See Risjord, *Chesapeake Politics*; W. Wayne Smith, *Anti-Jackson Politics along the Chesapeake* (New York, 1989); Smith, "Jacksonian Democracy on the Chesapeake: Class, Kinship, and Politics," *Maryland Historical Magazine* 63 (1968): 55 – 67; Whitman H. Ridgeway, *Community Leadership in Maryland* (Chapel Hill, N.C., 1979); Ridgeway, "The Search for Power: Community Leadership in the Jacksonian Era," in Aubrey C. Land, Lois Green Carr, and Edward C. Papenfuse, eds., *Law, Society, and Politics in Early Maryland* (Baltimore, 1977).

17. These and the following sketches are based on data drawn from *Sixth Census . . . 1840*; *Seventh Census . . . 1850*; Bean, *The Peopling of Virginia*; Martin, *Gazetteer*; Howe, *Historical Collections of Virginia*; Fields, "Agricultural Population of Virginia."

18. Martin, *Gazetteer*, 200 – 201; Alfred Bagly, *King and Queen County, Virginia* (New York, 1908), 92 – 126. I have adjusted the 1850 census figures for the tidewater and the piedmont using the rule of thumb that one-half the Baptists and one-fourth of the Methodists were black.

19. The following draws heavily on Daniel W. Crofts, *Old Southampton: Politics and Society in a Virginia County, 1834 – 1869* (Charlottesville, Va., 1992). See also Thomas C. Parramore, *Southampton County, Virginia* (Charlottesville, Va., 1978); Gregory Bowen, "Political Culture and Political Behavior in a Republican Slave Society: Toward a History

of Voting Behaviour in Southampton County, Virginia, 1850–1860," ANZASA Conference, 1986.

20. See Bridenbaugh, *Myths and Realities,* 1–53; Beeman, *Evolution of the Southern Backcountry;* Darrett B. Rutman and Anita H. Rutman, *A Place in Time: Middlesex County, Virginia, 1650–1750* (New York, 1984); Breen, *Tobacco Culture;* Kulikoff, *Tobacco and Slaves;* Fischer, *Albion's Seed,* 207–418.

21. Gray, *History of Agriculture* 2:19.

22. The politics of the lower piedmont resembled the situation in contiguous North Carolina that has been extensively studied. See Harry L. Watson, *Jacksonian Politics and Community Conflict: The Emergence of the Second Party System in Cumberland County, North Carolina* (Baton Rouge, La., 1981); Marc W. Kruman, *Parties and Politics in North Carolina, 1836–1865* (Baton Rouge, La., 1983); Jeffrey, *State Parties and National Politics;* Robert C. Kinzer, *Kinship and Neighborhood in a Southern Community: Orange County, North Carolina, 1849–1881* (Knoxville, Tenn., 1987); Gary Freeze, "The Ethnocultural Thesis Goes South: Religiocultural Dimensions of Voting in North Carolina's Second Party System," paper presented at the Southern Historical Association Meeting, 1988; Paul D. Escott, "Yeoman Independence and the Market: Social Status and Economic Development in Antebellum North Carolina," *North Carolina Historical Review* 66 (1989): 291–97; Bill Cecil-Fronsman, *Common Whites: Class and Culture in Antebellum North Carolina* (Lexington, Ky., 1992); Charles C. Bolton, *Poor Whites of the Antebellum South: Tenants and Laborers in Central North Carolina and Northeast Mississippi* (Durham, N.C., 1994).

23. Durand de Dauphiné quoted in Fischer, *Albion's Seed,* 416. See also Siegel, *Roots of Southern Distinctiveness;* Maud Carter Clement, *History of Pittsylvania County* (Lynchburg, Va., 1929); W. B. Barbour, *"Halifacts"* (Danville, Va., n.d.).

24. Oakes, *Ruling Race,* in fact, included Halifax County in his sample of ten southern slaveholding counties upon which his statistical generalizations were based.

25. Siegel shows in *The Roots of Southern Distinctiveness* that Pittsylvania's planters invested in enterprises designed to develop the county such as bridges, roads, banks, and ultimately the railroad.

26. Barbour, *"Halifacts,"* 169–85. There is an excellent map of Halifax County in the Library of Virginia. The 1840 census information on population, slavery, employment, and literacy is reported separately for the northern and southern halves of each county; these data combined with the polling place returns sustain the above analysis.

27. Martin, *Gazetteer,* 232–34. Martin's count is higher than the census of 1850, but both leave the same impression of the relative importance of the Methodists and Baptists.

28. Martin, *Gazetteer,* 225.

29. Returns for the polling places are from the *Virginia Advocate* (Charlottesville) and the *Richmond Enquirer.*

30. Edgar Woods, *Albemarle County in Virginia* (Charlottesville, Va., 1901); Martin, *Gazetteer,* 112–26.

31. Schlotterbeck, " 'Social Economy' of an Upper South Community," 15. Cf. Schlotterbeck, "Plantation and Farm"; T. Lloyd Benson, "The Plain Folk of Orange: Land, Work, and Society on the Eve of the Civil War," in *The Edge of the South,* ed. Edward Ayers (Charlottesville, Va., 1990), 56–78, which disputes Schlotterbeck's interpretation of the two counties as typical of the "social economy" of premarket areas by focusing on Orange and emphasizing its commercial development.

32. Bridenbaugh, *Myths and Realities,* 119–96; Maldwyn A. Jones, "The Scotch-Irish

in British America," in *Strangers in the Realm*, ed. Bernard Bailyn and Philip D. Morgan (Chapel Hill, N.C., 1991), 284–313; Fischer, *Albion's Seed*, 605–782.

33. Davis, *Intellectual Life of Jefferson's Virginia*, 122–23, 131–36; Boles, *Great Revival*, 1–11, 83–89; Anne Loveland, *Southern Evangelicals and the Social Order, 1800–1860* (Baton Rouge, La., 1980), 91–129; Hood, *Reformed America*, 168–203.

34. See Wust, *Virginia Germans*. The correlations between German surnames and Democratic voting and between Scotch-Irish surnames and Whig voting are extremely high. While there were obviously many other factors involved in the voters' decisions, historians have properly connected the nonslaveholding Germans of the Valley to the Democratic party; they were not actively antislavery and thus did not come into direct conflict with the planter Democrats of the piedmont.

35. Peyton, *Augusta County*. There was also a high correlation between the presence of Episcopalians and Whigs and a low but positive correlation between the Methodists and the Whig vote. There were relatively few of the former and probably a majority were Whigs, while the latter lived in Whig areas but were probably Democrats.

36. Morton, *Rockbridge County*; Edmund Pendleton Tompkins, *Rockbridge County, Virginia* (Richmond, 1952); Keller, "Rockbridge County."

37. John W. Wayland, *A History of Rockingham County, Virginia* (Dayton, Va., 1912), 243–82.

38. John W. Wayland, *A History of Shenandoah County Virginia* (Strasburg, Va., 1927), 288–89; George W. Featherstonhaugh, *Excursion through the Slave States*, quoted in Wust, *Virginia Germans*, 175. See also Wayland, *German Element*; Harry M. Strikler, *A History of Page County, Virginia* (Richmond, 1952).

39. Millard K. Bushong, *History of Jefferson County* (rept. Boyce, Va., 1972); Martin, *Gazetteer*, 367–73; Merritt Roe Smith, *Harpers Ferry Armory and the New Technology: The Challenge of Change* (Ithaca, N.Y., 1977), 252–304.

40. Roeber, "'Origin of Whatever Is Not English among Us,'" 249.

41. See Richard O. Curry, *A House Divided: A Study of Statehood Politics and the Copperhead Movement in West Virginia* (Pittsburgh, 1964); John Alexander Williams, "The New Dominion and the Old: Ante-Bellum and Statehood Politics as the Background of West Virginia's 'Bourbon Democracy,'" *West Virginia History* 33 (1972): 317–407, which expand on the traditional view of Ambler, *History of West Virginia*. The political situation in this area resembled that in the neighboring states. See Michael F. Holt, *Forging a Majority: The Formation of the Republican Party in Pittsburgh, 1848–1860* (New Haven, 1969); Sharp, *Jacksonians versus the Banks*, 160–89; Stephen C. Fox, *The Group Bases of Ohio Political Behavior, 1803–1848* (Hamden, Conn., 1990); Harry A. Volz III, "Party, State, and Nation: Kentucky and the Coming of the American Civil War" (Ph.D. diss., Univ. of Virginia, 1982).

42. If Kanawha County is removed, the correlation between slaveholding and the Democrats in the trans-Allegheny emerges clearly.

43. See Edward Conrad Smith, *A History of Lewis County West Virginia* (Weston, W.Va., 1920).

44. Martin, *Gazetteer*, 384–86.

45. Howe, *Historical Collections*, 347.

46. Julius A. de Gruyter, *The Kanawha Spectator, I* (Charleston, W.Va., 1953). The Whig *Kanawha Republican* (Charleston), April 30, Nov. 13, Dec. 4, 1844, featured appeals to farmers and workingmen that emphasized the home market idea and praised

Alexander H. H. Stuart's interesting speech to New York workingmen.

47. Martin, *Gazetteer*, 373 – 81; de Gruyter, *Kanawha Spectator*, 353 – 72. The *Seventh Census . . . 1850* and the county histories paint different pictures of the religious makeup of the county. I have generally followed the county historians who probably were referring to whites; the county was 22 percent black and most of them were Methodists and Baptists.

48. See Forrest McDonald and Grady McWhiney, "The Antebellum Southern Herdsman: A Reinterpretation," *JSH* 41 (1975): 147 – 66; McDonald and McWhiney, "The South from Self-Sufficiency to Peonage: An Interpretation," *AHR* 85 (1980): 1095 – 1118.

49. Sutton, "Sectionalism and Social Structure," 71 – 80; Ralph Mann, "Mountains, Land, and Kin Networks: Burkes Garden, Virginia in the 1840s and 1850s," *JSH* 58 (1992): 411 – 34. The Floyds and Holmes were Roman Catholics visited by a priest from Wytheville. Burkes Garden was Democratic in the 1840s by a two-to-one margin. See John C. Inscoe, *Mountain Masters, Slavery and the Sectional Crisis in Western North Carolina* (Knoxville, Tenn., 1989); Martin Crawford, "Political Society in a Southern Mountain Community: Ashe County, North Carolina, 1850 – 1861," *JSH* 55 (1989): 373 – 90; Mary Beth Pudup, "Social Class and Economic Development in Southeast Kentucky, 1820 – 1880," in Mitchell, *Appalachian Frontiers*, 235 – 60.

50. William C. Pendleton, *History of Tazewell County and Southwest Virginia, 1748 – 1920* (Richmond, 1920). Cf. Grady McWhiney, *Cracker Culture*; Rowland Berthoff, "Celtic Mist over the South," *JSH* 52 (1986): 523 – 46.

51. Goodridge Wilson, *Smyth County History and Traditions* (Kingsport, Tenn., 1932); Martin, *Gazetteer*, 452 – 60.

52. The following analysis is based on the poll book data for Allegheny, Caroline, Prince Edward, and Southampton counties presented in Moser, "Subtreasury Politics"; Bourke and DeBats, "Identifiable Voting"; Bowen, "Political Culture and Political Behavior"; Shade, "Society and Politics"; and Crofts, *Old Southampton*, supplemented with material from the poll books, census, and tax records of Mason County.

53. For the strongest statement of the idea that the Democrats were the "planter" party, see Bruce, *Virginia Iron Manufacture*, 259 – 74. The two western counties whose poll books have been examined for this study — Allegheny and Mason — had only two planters, one in each county. Both were Democrats.

54. Timothy Flint, *Recollections of the Last Ten Years* . . . (Boston, 1826), 228 – 29; Frederick Law Olmsted, *A Journey to the Seaboard Slave States in the Years 1853 – 1854* . . . (New York, l856), 356; Bradshaw, *Prince Edward County*, 9 – 11.

55. Lawrence Kohl, *The Politics of Individualism* (New York, 1989), 5 – 6; Marvin Meyers, *The Jacksonian Persuasion* (Stanford, Calif., 1957), vii. See Daniel Walker Howe, *The Political Culture of the American Whigs* (Chicago, 1979); Jean Baker, *Affairs of Party: The Political Culture of the Northern Democrats in the Mid-Nineteenth Century* (New York, 1983), which illustrate the national nature of the symbolic belief systems associated with the major parties.

5. One Hundred and Seventy-Three Despots

1. "Jefferson's Draft Constitution for Virginia," in Peterson, *Jefferson Writings*, 336 – 45; Jefferson, *Notes*, 243 – 55.

2. Jefferson, *Notes*, 245–46; Frank Bourgin, *The Great Challenge: The Myth of Laissez-Faire in the Early Republic* (New York, 1989); Joseph Harrison, "*Sic et Non*: Thomas Jefferson and Internal Improvement," *Journal of the Early Republic* 7 (1987): 335–49.

3. Alexander Hamilton, John Jay, and James Madison, *The Federalist: A Commentary on the Constitution of the United States*, ed. Edward Mead Earle (New York, 1937), 53–61, 332–435.

4. Ibid., 352.

5. Malapportioned districts and staggered elections allowed the Democrats to control of the state senate In 1840–41 there were seventeen Democrats and fifteen Whigs, the closest the Whigs got to a parity; throughout the remainder of the decade the Democrats held two-thirds of the senate seats. On the upper South, see also Kruman, *Parties and Politics in North Carolina*; Jeffery, *State Parties and National Politics*; Paul Bergeron, *Antebellum Politics in Tennessee* (Lexington, Ky., 1982); Jonathan M. Atkins, "'A Combat for Liberty': Politics and Parties in Jackson's Tennessee, 1832–1851," (Ph.D. diss., Univ. of Michigan, 1991); Smith, *Anti-Jacksonian Politics along the Chesapeake*; Volz, "Party, State, and Nation."

6. Except when specifically noted this analysis is based on Ambler, *Sectionalism*, 24–99; Sydnor, *American Revolutionaries in the Making*; Beeman, *Old Dominion and the New Nation*; Jackson Turner Main, *Political Parties before the Constitution* (Chapel Hill, N.C., 1973), 244–67; Risjord, *Chesapeake Politics*; Norman K. Risjord and Gordon DenBoer, "The Evolution of Political Parties in Virginia, 1782–1800," *Journal of American History* 60 (1974): 961–1002.

7. Robert E. Thomas, "The Virginia Convention of 1788: A Criticism of Beard's *An Economic Interpretation of the Constitution*," *JSH* 19 (1953), 63–72; Forrest McDonald, *We the People* (Chicago, 1957), 255–83; Norman K. Risjord, "Virginians and the Constitution: A Multivariant Analysis," *WMQ* 31 (1974): 613–32; Jon Kukla, "Spectrum of Sentiments: Virginia's Federalists, Antifederalists, and 'Federalists Who Are for Amendments,' 1787–1788," *VMHB* 96 (1988): 277–95.

8. Cecelia Kenyon, "Men of Little Faith: The Anti-Federalists on the Nature of Republican Government," *WMQ* 12 (1955): 3–43; Kenyon, ed., *The Antifederalists* (Indianapolis, 1966), which includes both an excellent introduction and several selections from Virginians. See also Richard E. Ellis, "The Persistence of Antifederalism after 1789," in *Beyond Confederation: The Origins of the Constitution and American National Identity*, ed. Richard Beeman, Stephen Botein, and Edward C. Carter II (Chapel Hill, N.C., 1987), 295–314.

9. Risjord and DenBoer, "Evolution of Political Parties," 977; Ambler, *Sectionalism*, 61–65; Thomas J. Farnham, "The Virginia Amendments of 1795: An Episode in the Opposition to Jay's Treaty," *VMHB* 75 (1967): 75–88; Beeman, *Old Dominion and the New Nation*, 119–83. The House of Delegates resolution against assumption passed 75–52. See Ames, *State Documents on Federal Relations*, 2–6.

10. Lisle A. Rose, *Prologue to Democracy: The Federalists in the South, 1789–1800* (Lexington, Ky., 1968), 139–204.

11. Risjord, "Virginia Federalists."

12. Rose, *Prologue to Democracy*, 232–82; Sisson, *American Revolution of 1800*; Cunningham, *Jeffersonian Republicans*.

13. James H. Broussard, "Party and Partisanship in American Legislatures: The South Atlantic States, 1800–1812," *JSH* 43 (1977): 39–58; Broussard, *Southern Federalists*; Risjord, "Virginia Federalists," 506–17; Noble E. Cunningham, Jr., *The Jeffersonian Re-*

publicans in Power: Party Operation, 1801–1809 (Chapel Hill, N.C., 1963). Cf. Robert Shalhope's excellent review essay on Broussard's study, "Southern Federalists and the First Party Syndrome," *Reviews in American History* 8 (1980): 45 – 51.

14. Broussard, "Party and Partisanship in American Legislatures," 48, 50.

15. Broussard, *Southern Federalists*, 199 – 214, 307 – 20; Pole, *Political Representation*, 281 – 333; Sutton, *From Revolution to Secession*, 52 – 102; Bruce, *Rhetoric of Conservatism*.

16. Broussard, *Southern Federalists*, 350 – 62; Goodrich, "Virginia System of Mixed Enterprise"; Dunaway, *James River and Kanawha Company*); Egerton, *Mercer*, 65 – 141; Wiley E. Hodges, "The Theoretical Basis for Anti-Governmentalism in Virginia, 1789 – 1836," *Journal of Politics* 9 (1947): 325 – 54; Hodges, "Pro-Governmentalism in Virginia."

17. *Richmond Enquirer*, April 13, 27, June 9, 1816, July 13, Aug. 25, Oct. 6, 1818; Ambler, *Ritchie*, 66 – 68; Starnes, *Branch Banking in Virginia*, 1 – 71; Broussard, *Southern Federalists*, 332 – 49; Charles E. Wynes, "Banking in Virginia, 1789 – 1820," *Essays in History* 4 (1957): 35 – 50.

18. Broussard, *Southern Federalists*, 313 – 20; Egerton, *Mercer*, 100 – 115, 161 – 76. See also McColley, *Slavery and Jeffersonian Virginia*; David Brion Davis, *The Problem of Slavery in the Age of Revolution, 1776 – 1823* (Ithaca, N.Y., 1975).

19. Edgar Knight, ed., *A Documentary History of Education in the South before 1860*, 5 vols. (Chapel Hill, N.C., 1950), 2:525 – 43, 550 – 60; Rush Welter, ed., *American Writings on Popular Education: The Nineteenth Century* (Indianapolis, 1971), 9 – 14; Malone, *Jefferson and His Times* 6:233 – 82; William A. Maddox, *The Free School Idea in Virginia before the Civil War* (New York, 1918), 42 – 75; David E. Swift, "Thomas Jefferson, John Holt Rice, and Education in Virginia," *Journal of Presbyterian History* 49 (1971): 32 – 58. See also Roy J. Honeywell, *The Educational Work of Thomas Jefferson* (Cambridge, Mass., 1931); Rush Welter, *Popular Education and Democratic Thought* (New York, 1962).

20. *Richmond Enquirer*, Feb. 22, 27, 1817; "Charles Fenton Mercer's Discourse on Popular Education, 1826," in Knight, *Documentary History of Education in the South* 2:297 – 356; Broussard, *Southern Federalists*, 328 – 31; Risjord, "Virginia Federalists," 516 – 17; Egerton, *Mercer*, 116 – 32.

21. *Richmond Enquirer*, May 1, 5, 1829; Sydnor, *Development of Southern Sectionalism*, 52. The *Norfolk Beacon*, April 30, 1829, reprinted in the *Richmond Enquirer*, May 5, 1829, commented that there was a high "degree of *party zeal*" and hoped for a turnout that "exceeded any thing we have ever witnessed."

22. *Richmond Enquirer*, April – May, 1829.

23. Ibid., April 10, 27, May 8, 11, 1832. In the course of the election, candidates in only two counties—Amherst and Westmoreland—were identified with the presidential contestants. Cf. Ambler, *Sectionalism*, 175 – 218.

24. Simms, *Rise of the Whigs in Virginia*, 63 – 89; Ambler, *Life of Floyd*, 235; *Richmond Enquirer*, Dec. 4, 1833; Ames, *State Documents on Federal Relations*, 185 – 89. Nullification failed to draw party lines in the spring elections for both the assembly and the House of Representatives; see *Richmond Enquirer*, April 2 – 30, May 7, 1833; *Lynchburg Virginian*, May 8, 1833. There was a mention of a "Tyler party" in New Kent County, but in the local congressional contest that was supposed to hinge on the issue, "Old Republicans stuck to S [the Jacksonian, Andrew Stevenson] like wax" (*Richmond Enquirer*, April 2, 1833). The *Staunton Spectator*, April 28, 1833, associated Robert Craig, who was running for Congress in the Valley, with the "State-Rights Party" although he remained in the Democratic party through the 1830s.

25. John Wickham to Littleton W. Tazewell, Dec. 10, 29, 1833, Tazewell Family Papers, LV; Tyler to Thomas W. Gilmer, Jan. 7, 1834, in Tyler, *Letters and Times* 1:480–81; *Richmond Enquirer*, Jan. 9, Feb. 25, 27, April 1, 1834.

26. Simms, *Rise of the Whigs in Virginia*, 63–86; Dent, "Virginia Democratic Party," 145–60; McCormick, *Second American Party System*, 178–99; *Richmond Enquirer*, March 28, April 1, 4, 11, 15, 18, 1834; *Winchester Virginian*, March 29, 1834, reprinted in the *Enquirer*, April 8, 1834. The *Richmond Enquirer* reported on April 11 that 1,127 of a potential 1,150 voters had voted Albemarle. At the beginning of the assembly session the returns were challenged and 93 votes were thrown out. *Journal of the House of Delegates . . . 1834*, 184–85.

27. *Richmond Enquirer*, April 15, 29, May 6, 1834.

28. *Richmond Enquirer*, December 2, 4, 9, 11, 1834; Simms, *Rise of the Virginia Whigs*, 88–98.

29. *Richmond Enquirer*, March 7, 12, 14, 17, 27, 28, 1835; the *Petersburg Constellation* reprinted in the *Richmond Enquirer*, March 17, 1834. On the instruction question, see Eaton, *Freedom-of-Thought Struggle in the Old South*, 353–75; Tyler, *Letters and Times* 1:513–38; Peterson, *Tazewell*, 244–49.

30. *Richmond Enquirer*, March 7, April 7, May 12, 19, 1835; *Lynchburg Virginian*, May 7, 1835; *Richmond Whig*, May 5, 22, 1835.

31. *Richmond Enquirer*, Dec. 10, 19, 24, 31, 1835; Jan. 2, 5, 12, 14, 16, 19, Feb. 11, 13, 18, 25, 27, March 1, 5, 8, 10, 15, 17, 21, April 1, 9, 1836; Simms, *Rise of the Whigs in Virginia*, 94–112.

32. Cf. Michael F. Holt, "The Election of 1840, Voter Mobilization, and the Emergence of the Second American Party System: A Reappraisal of Jacksonian Voting Behavior," in *A Masters Due: Essays in Honor of David Herbert Donald*, ed. William J. Cooper, Jr., Michael F. Holt, and John McCardell (Baton Rouge, La., 1985), 16–54.

33. Sharp, *Jacksonians versus the Banks*, 242–46; *Richmond Enquirer*, Dec. 18, 1841, Jan. 20, 22, March 17, 19, 22, 24, 26, 1842; *Lynchburg Virginian*, Jan. 10, 20, 26, Feb. 17, 21, 24, March 8, 14, 17–21, 28, 31, April 28, 1842.

34. *Richmond Enquirer*, Feb. 1, 28, March 1, 3, 5, April 12, 15, 1842; Cole, *Whig Party in the South*, 104–9. While the Whig press supported Botts's charges against Upshur, party papers emphasized economic issues and were optimistic about their chances of winning against the Democratic "panic makers in the legislature." *Lynchburg Virginian*, March 31, April 14, 28, 1842.

35. This analysis of the 1842 assembly elections is based on the partial, although fairly complete, returns in the *Richmond Enquirer*, May 1–10, 1842.

36. Ibid., Feb. 11, March 4, 7, 9, 14, 16, April 4, 7, 11, 14, 18, 1843; *Charlottesville Jeffersonian*, reprinted in *Enquirer*, April 7, 1843; *Fincastle Democrat, Kanawha Banner* (Charleston), and *Warrenton Flag of '98*, reprinted in *Richmond Enquirer*, April 21, 1843; *Petersburg Republican*, reprinted in *Richmond Enquirer*, April 25, 1843; *Lynchburg Republican* in the *Richmond Enquirer*, March 14, 1843; *Lynchburg Virginian*, Jan. 16, 23, March 9, 16, 23, April 3, 6, 10, 1843; *Kanawha Republican* (Charleston), March 25, April 1, 8, 15, 1843.

37. *Richmond Enquirer*, April–May, 1845. The *Richmond Enquirer*, May 7, 1845, tabulated the votes in the 1844 legislative election as a two-party vote in each county along with the presidential vote, which both shows the degree of partisanship at the time and permits an unusual correlation of the results.

38. James Elliott Walmsley, "John Floyd" and "John Buchanan Floyd," *DAB*; Ambler, *Life of Floyd*; John M. Belohlavek, "John B. Floyd as Governor of Virginia, 1849 – 1852," *West Virginia History* 33 (1971): 14 – 26.

39. *Richmond Enquirer*, April 29, 1845; *United States Magazine and Democratic Review* 7 (1840): 485 – 87.

40. Jackson Turner Main, "Government by the People: The American Revolution and the Democratization of Legislatures," *WMQ* 23 (1966): 391 – 417; Anthony Upton, "The Road to Power in Early Virginia," *VMHB* 62 (1954): 259 – 81; Sydnor, *Gentlemen Freeholders*; Sydnor, *Development of Southern Sectionalism*, 33 – 53, 275 – 93; Sutton, *Revolution to Secession*; Jordan, *Political Leadership in Jefferson's Virginia*.

41. Fred Siegel, "The Paternalist Thesis: Virginia a Test Case," *Civil War History* 25 (1979): 246 – 61; Siegel, *Roots of Southern Distinctiveness*; Shade, "Society and Politics in Antebellum Virginia's Southside"; Schweikart, *Banking in the American South*.

42. Main, *Political Parties before the Constitution*, 246 – 47; Risjord, "Virginians and the Constitution," 618 – 19; Beeman, *Old Dominion and the New Nation*, 53 – 67; Robert, *Road from Monticello*, 113 – 18; Freehling, *Drift toward Dissolution*, 272 – 78; Sutton, *Revolution to Secession*, 182 – 230; Wooster, *Politicians, Planters, and Plain Folk*, 163; Wooster, *The Secession Conventions in the Old South* (Princeton, N.J., 1962), 145. Professor Wooster kindly passed his data on to me, and I have reorganized them slightly. The state senators were older and wealthier than their counterparts in the House of Delegates, but the even upper house also included increasing numbers of nonslaveholders and fewer large planters than earlier.

43. Oakes, *Ruling Race*, 136 – 47; Roger Ransom, *Conflict and Compromise: The Political Economy of Slavery, Emancipation, and the American Civil War* (New York, 1989), 41 – 81; Randolph B. Campbell, "Planters and Plain Folks: The Social Structure of the Antebellum South," in *Interpreting Southern History: Historiographical Essays in Honor of Sanford W. Higginbotham*, ed. John B. Boles and Evelyn Thomas Nolan (Baton Rouge, La., 1987), 48 – 77.

44. Wooster, *Politicians, Planters, and Plain Folk*, 147.

45. The *Lynchburg Virginian*, April 28, 1842, is typical telling the often-repeated story of Marcus Morton winning the Massachusetts governorship by a single vote.

46. Wooster, *Politicians, Planters, and Plain Folk*, 42 – 49, 170, 173.

47. *Journal of the House of Delegates . . . 1831*, 3, 17 – 18, 33.

48. See *Richmond Enquirer*, Dec. 1831 – March 1832. This discussion is based on an analysis of all of the roll calls in the House of Delegates for the session of 1831 – 32 given in *Journal of the House of Delegates . . . 1831*. Western mean cohesion on the nine roll calls mentioned was 75, while on all of the roll calls it was 42. The Index of Cohesion requires group identification and is computed as the difference between the percentage of the group on each side of the issue. The mean Index of Cohesion for the eastern members on all roll calls was 40. The mean Index of Disagreement between the sections was 32. The Index of Disagreement is the difference between the percentage of each group voting for the proposal. The usage here follows Campbell, *Representative Democracy*.

49. Ambler, *Sectionalism*, 202 – 18; Tyler, *Letters and Times* 1: 431 – 68; John Hampden Pleasants to John Tyler, Jan. 1, 1833, ibid., 451 – 52. Tyler, who opposed Jackson on the force bill was not considered a partisan but one who followed a "temperate and independent course."

50. The main issue in the Missouri Compromise was the congressional power to ex-

clude slavery from the territories expressed in the Thomas amendment. Only thirteen delegates, all Whigs, would have extended this principle to the District, which had the status of a territory. A small group of eighteen Democrats and two Whigs took the moderate position that Congress could not act because of the deeds of cession from Maryland and Virginia which implied that the states retained a voice in the matter. The remainder of Virginia legislators, the majority of whom were Democrats, believed that any action against slave property was a violation of the Constitution. *Journal of the House of Delegates . . . 1835*, 75 – 76, 81, 87 – 89.

51. The mean Whig Index of Cohesion on internal improvements of all types was 45. This analysis is based on the roll calls given in the *Journal of the House of Delegates* using the ACCUM program given in Lee F. Anderson, Meredith W. Watts, Jr., and Allen R. Wilcox, *Legislative Roll-Call Analysis* (Evanston, Ill., 1966). My own work has been augmented by Robert H. Stanly, "Party Conflict and the Secession Alternative: The Virginia House of Delegates as a Test Case, 1855 – 1861" *Essays in History* 27 (1980): 5 – 27. In interpreting these data the reader must keep in mind what criteria he or she wishes to apply. The classic definition of "party votes" put forth by A. Lawrence Lowell set 90 percent of one party against 90 percent of the other. In that case the IPD would be 80. Yet if 60 percent of each party were in opposition — a difference that probably connotes "party" to most readers — the IPD would fall to 20. Also, the original conception (put forward by Stuart Rice and explained by Anderson, Watts, and Wilcox) was an index of "likeness." It is possible to have majorities of both parties on the same side and have an IDP of 49, nearly the same as if three-fourths of one voted against three-fourths of the other.

52. In the session of 1840 – 41, 90 percent of the Whigs opposed 90 percent of the Democrats on one-third of the roll calls, and on the "average" roll call — that hypothetical entity obtained by taking the means of the indices — three-quarters of one party opposed three-quarters of the other. This shift between the 1830s and the 1840s has been analyzed in other studies designed for different purposes but based on many of the same roll calls: Howard Braverman, "Economic and Political Background of the Conservative Revolt in Virginia"; Sharp, *Jacksonians versus the Banks*, 211 – 73; Herbert Ershkowitz and William G. Shade, "Consensus or Conflict? Political Behavior in the State Legislatures during the Jacksonian Era," *Journal of American History* 58 (1971): 591 – 621; Dent, "Virginia Democratic Party," 215 – 67, 357 – 98; Moser, "Subtreasury Politics."

53. On state legislative behavior, see Shade, "State Legislatures in the Nineteenth Century." See also M. Philip Lucas, "The Development of the Second Party System in Mississippi, 1817 – 1846" (Ph.D. diss., Cornell Univ., 1984); Donald A. DeBats, *Elites and Masses: Political Structure, Communication and Behavior in Ante-Bellum Georgia* (Hamden, Conn., 1991); J. Mills Thornton III, *Power and Politics in a Slave Society: Alabama, 1800 – 1860* (Baton Rouge, La., 1978), 59 – 116; Rodney Davis, "Illinois Legislators and Jacksonian Democracy, 1834 – 1841" (Ph.D. diss., Univ. of Iowa, 1966); Davis, "Partisanship in Jacksonian State Politics: Party Divisions in the Illinois Legislature, 1834 – 1841," in *Quantification in American History: Theory and Research*, ed. Robert P. Swierenga (New York, 1970), 149 – 62; Peter Levine, *The Behavior of State Legislative Parties in the Jacksonian Era: New Jersey, 1829 – 1844* (Rutherford, N.J., 1977); Douglas E. Bowers, "The Pennsylvania Legislature, 1815 – 1860: A Study of Democracy at Work" (Ph.D. diss., Univ. of Chicago, 1974).

54. The votes on small notes and stockholder liability are in *Journal of the House of Delegates . . . 1840*, 107 – 9.

55. Ibid., 83, 169 – 70.

56. Armistead C. Gordon, Jr., "Thomas Walker Gilmer," *DAB*; *Journal of the House of Delegates* . . . *1840*, 177, 183–84, 192, 211–13, 222–24, 226–28, 233; Ames, *State Documents on Federal Relations*, 232–36; Paul Finkelman, "The Protection of Black Rights in Seward's New York," *Civil War History* 34 (1988): 211–34. The Whigs' lack of confidence caused the Calhounite, Gilmer, to resign and run for Congress, where he fought Clay and the congressional Whigs and defended Tyler, who eventually took him into his cabinet.

57. "The School Commissioners . . . Report . . . 1832," and "Governor Campbell Tells the Legislature of Virginia about the Importance of Free Schools in That State," in Knight, *Documentary History of Education in the South* 5:45–79, 85–89. On education in Virginia, see Maddox, *Free School Idea in Virginia*, 96–148; Edgar W. Knight, *Public Education in the South*, 195–215.

58. "Henry Ruffner Suggests a Plan for a School System in Virginia, 1841," in Knight, *Documentary History of Education in the South* 5:92–104; G.E.D., "Education in Virginia," *Southern Literary Messenger* 7 (1841): 631–37; *Journal of the House of Delegates* . . . *1840–41*, 171; James M. Garnett, "Address to the Education Convention," *Southern Literary Messenger* 8 (1942): 114–21; *Lynchburg Virginian*, Nov. 29, Dec. 9, 1841, Jan. 13, 1842; *Kanawha Republican* (Charleston), Dec. 11, 13, 18, 25, 1841, Feb. 26, March 16, 20, 1842; *Richmond Enquirer*, Feb. 22, March 10, 17, 1842.

59. Summary measures of roll-call responses in the mid-1840s indicate an apparent decline in partisan animosity, but this is in large part a statistical artifact resulting from Democratic factionalism. On the "typical" vote three-fourths of the Whigs but only two-thirds of the Democrats voted together. The usual view—derived from Democratic sources—of an ideological polarized Whig party and a unified Democracy does not fit the facts.

60. "Memorial, December 1845," in Knight, *Documentary History of Education in the South* 5:108–9; "Education in the Southern and Western States," *Southern Literary Messenger* 11 (1845): 603–7. Most of the literature on educational reform in Virginia tries too hard to show that the state favored common schools. Maddox, in *Free School Idea in Virginia*, 127, claims: "Virginia moved rapidly towards a state system of free schools. In fact from 1839–49, it may be said to have carried on a campaign, comparable to often exceeding in intensity, the great movements in the other states." See also J. Stephen Knight, Jr., "Discontent, Disunity, and Dissent in the Antebellum South: Virginia as a Test Case, 1844–1846," *VMHB* 81 (1973): 148–69.

61. *Journal of the House of Delegates* . . . *1845*, 101, 119–20, 127, 134, 172, 173–74, 181, 218–20. In the 1845–46 session 70 percent of the Whigs consistently supported internal improvements. The level of party difference fell to a low point in the house in 1846–47 when three-fourths of the roll calls dealt with transportation and corporations.

62. See Gerald R. Grob, "The Political System and Social Policy in the Nineteenth Century: Legacy of the Revolution," *Mid-America* 58 (1976): 5–19; Michael F. Holt, *The Political Crisis of the 1850s* (New York, 1978), 17–38, 101–38; Joel Silbey, *The Partisan Imperative* (New York, 1985), 14–49; Silbey, *American Political Nation*, 176–95; M. Philip Lucas, " 'To Carry Out Great Fundamental Principles': The Antebellum Southern Political Culture," *Journal of Mississippi History* 52 (1991): 1–22; Shade, "State Legislatures in the Nineteenth Century."

63. *Richmond Enquirer*, March 14, 1851; *Richmond Whig*, March 28, 1851; David Campbell to William Campbell, Feb. 20, 1852, Campbell Family Papers, DU; Starnes, *Branch Banking in Virginia*, 102–7; Schweikart, *Banking in the American South*, 120–27.

The press was much less interested in banking than other issues, particularly southern rights. See Hugh Rockoff, *The Free Banking Era: A Re-examination* (New York, 1975); William G. Shade, *Banks or No Banks: The Money Issue in Western Politics, 1832–1865* (Detroit, 1972), 145–74.

64. See L. Ray Gunn, *The Decline of Authority: Public Economic Policy and Political Development in New York, 1800–1860* (Ithaca, N.Y., 1988); Peter Wallenstein, *From Slave South to New South: Public Policy in Nineteenth Century Georgia* (Chapel Hill, N.C., 1987), 1–96.

65. Ambler, *Sectionalism*, 273–82; G.E.D., "Education in Virginia," 633–34.

66. Henry Wise, "Address to His Constituents, 1844," in Welter, *American Writings on Popular Education*, 121–32; *Richmond Whig*, Oct. 25, 1844, Feb. 7, April 1, 15, June 3, 13, July 4, 15, Nov. 14, 25, 1845, Jan. 6, 23, Feb. 6, 10, 1846; *Lynchburg Virginian*, Nov. 6, 1844, April 23, 1846; "Public Education in Virginia," *Southern Literary Messenger* 13 (1847): 685–89; and the correspondence between Virginians H. B. Gooch, Henry Ruffner, John B. Minor, and Horace Mann in Knight, *Documentary History of Education in the South* 5:338–42, 348–50, 354–61.

67. *Kanawha Republican* (Charleston), Nov. 20, 1844; *Richmond Whig*, July 15, 1845; *Lynchburg Virginian*, March 9, 1846. The Whig papers carried many more notices of temperance meetings than the Democratic papers.

68. Lucian Minor, "Temperance Reformation in Virginia," *Southern Literary Messenger* 16 (1850): 426–38; C. C. Pearson and J. Edward Hendricks, *Liquor and Anti-Liquor in Virginia, 1619–1919* (Durham, N.C., 1967), 36–138; Ellen Eslinger, "Antebellum Liquor Reform in Lexington Virginia: The Story of a Small Southern Town," *VMHB* 99 (1991): 163–86. See also James B. Sellers, *The Prohibition Movement in Alabama, 1702 to 1943* (Chapel Hill, N.C., 1943); Ian R. Tyrrill, *Sobering Up: From Temperance to Prohibition in Antebellum America, 1800–1860* (Westport, Conn., 1979); Tyrrill, "Drink and Temperance in the Antebellum South: An Overview and Interpretation," *JSH* 48 (1982): 485–510; W. J. Rorabaugh, "Rising Democratic Spirits: Immigrants, Temperance, and Tammany Hall," *Civil War History* 22 (1978), 138–57; Rorabaugh, "The Sons of Temperance in Antebellum Jasper County," *Georgia Historical Quarterly* 64 (1980): 485–510; Rorabaugh, *The Alcoholic Republic: An American Tradition* (New York, 1979); Douglas Wiley Carlson, "Temperance Reform in the Cotton Kingdom" (Ph.D. diss., Univ. of Illinois, 1982).

6. A Review of the Slave Question

1. Jefferson, *Notes*, 185–93, 214–15. See also Freehling, *Reintegration of American History*, 12–33.

2. Jefferson to Edward Coles, Aug. 25, 1814, to Jared Sparks, Feb. 4, 1824, in Peterson, *Jefferson Writings*, 1343–46, 1484–87; Malone, *Jefferson and His Time* 6:316–27.

3. Madison to Robert J. Evans, June 15, 1819, in Meyers, *Mind of the Founder*, 313–19. On Madison and slavery, see Drew McCoy, *The Last of the Fathers: James Madison and the Republican Legacy* (New York, 1989), 253–322.

4. Madison to Thomas R. Dew, Feb. 23, 1833, in Meyers, *Mind of the Founder*, 332–36.

5. A. P. Upshur, "Domestic Slavery," *Southern Literary Messenger* 5 (1839): 677; John C. Calhoun, "Speech on the Reception of Abolition Petitions," in *Slavery Defended: The Views of the Old South*, ed. Eric L. McKitrick (Englewood Cliffs, N.J., 1963), 12–16;

J. Burton Harrison, "The Slavery Question in Virginia," in *Aris Sonis Focisque: Being a Memoir of An American Family: The Harrisons of Skimino*, ed. Fairfax Harrison (Privately printed, 1910), 342; Degler, *Other South*, 47 – 96.

6. Cf. Cooper, *South and the Politics of Slavery*.

7. P. J. Staudenraus, *The African Colonization Movement, 1816 – 1865* (New York, 1961), 1 – 35; Egerton, *Mercer*, 100 – 115; Early Lee Fox, *The American Colonization Society, 1817 – 1840* (Baltimore, 1919); Philip Slaughter, *The Virginia History of African Colonization* (Richmond, 1855). The actual name of the ACS was the American Society for the Colonization of Free People of Color.

8. Madison to Robert J. Evans, June 15, 1819, in Meyers, *Mind of the Founder*, 314 – 19; John Taylor, *Arator: Being a Series of Agricultural Essays, Practical and Political: In Sixty-four Numbers*, ed. M. E. Bradford (Indianapolis, 1977), 115 – 25, 356 – 58; David W. Steifford, "The American Colonization Society: An Application of Republican Ideology to Early Antebellum Reform," *JSH* 45 (1979), 209; *Richmond Enquirer*, Oct. 11, 25, Nov. 25, Dec. 10, 1825, Jan. 21, Feb. 28, 1826; Staudenraus, *African Colonization Movement*, 169 – 76; Egerton, *Mercer*, 106 – 12.

9. Steifford, "American Colonization Society," 208 – 9; Gordon E. Finnie, "The Antislavery Movement in the Upper South before 1840," *JSH* 35 (1969): 319 – 42; Jordan, *White over Black*, 565 – 69; Davis, *Slavery in the Age of Revolution*, 195 – 212. On the relationship between racism and republicanism, see Morgan, *American Slavery/American Freedom*.

10. Egerton, *Mercer*, 237 – 42; Daniel Feller, *The Public Lands in Jacksonian Politics* (Madison, Wis., 1984), 142 – 71. Jackson vetoed a distribution bill that was designed, in part, to provide support for colonization.

11. Ambler, *Life of Floyd*, 9 – 121. On the Nat Turner rebellion, see Philip Foner, *Nat Turner's Slave Rebellion* (New York, 1966); Stephen B. Oates, *Fires of Jubilee: Nat Turner's Fierce Rebellion* (New York, 1975); Parramore, *Southampton County*; Henry Irving Tragle, ed., *The Southampton Slave Revolt of 1831: A Compilation of Source Material* (New York, 1973).

12. Ambler, *Life of Floyd*, 47, 77 – 78, 86 – 87.

13. Ibid., 170 – 73; John Floyd to James Hamilton, Jr., Nov. 19, 1831, in Tragle, *Southampton Slave Revolt*, 275 – 76; James Elliott Walmsley, "James McDowell," and "William Ballard Preston," *DAB*. Floyd considered emancipation of only the slaves in the western half of the state. Some commentators at the time seem to have considered the possibility of treating emancipation something like "local option" liquor laws. One is reminded of Lincoln's letter to Greeley in which he said he might emancipate some slaves and leave some in chains, as he did in the Emancipation Proclamation.

14. Floyd to James Hamilton, Jr., Nov. 19, 1831, to J. C. Harris, Sept. 27, 1831, in Tragle, *Southampton Slave Revolt*, 276, 274 – 75; *Journal of the House of Delegates . . . 1831*, 9 – 14.

15. *Richmond Whig*, Nov. 17, 1831; *Richmond Enquirer*, Oct. 25, 1831.

16. *Journal of the House of Delegates . . . 1831*, 51, 81, 101, 95, and passim.

17. Quoted in Robert, *Road from Monticello*, 65 – 68. Robert's book represents the traditional view of the debates and their significance while Alison Freehling, *Drift toward Dissolution*, and William Freehling, *Road to Disunion*, 178 – 96, present revisionist statements.

18. Quoted in Robert, *Road from Monticello*, 84 – 87, 62 – 64; James Elliott Walmsley, "Charles James Faulkner," Thomas Perkins Abernethy, "Thomas Jefferson Randolph," and James M. Callahan, "George William Summers," *DAB*.

19. *Richmond Whig*, Feb. 16, 1832; Freehling, *Drift toward Dissolution*, 144–50. Freehling (pp. 122–58) discusses the debates and delineates as abolitionists Bolling, John C. Campbell, Faulkner, Garland, McDowell, James M'Ilheney, Preston, Randolph, and Summers. Speeches of Moore and George I. Williams are printed in Robert, *Road from Monticello*, 62–64, 92–93. *The Speech of Charles Jas. Faulkner (of Berkeley) in the House of Delegates of Virginia, on the Policy of the State with Respect to Her Slave Population* (Richmond, 1832) appeared as a pamphlet.

20. Quoted in Robert, *Road from Monticello*, 65. See also *The Speech of Thomas J. Randolph, in the House of Delegates of Virginia, on the Abolition of Slavery* (Richmond, 1832); Freehling, *Drift toward Dissolution*, 129–35; Abernethy, "Thomas Jefferson Randolph"; Joseph C. Vance, "Thomas Jefferson Randolph" (Ph.D. diss., Univ. of Virginia, 1957).

21. Quoted in Robert, *Road from Monticello*, 61. Brodnax, who like Goode had been a conservative delegate to the constitutional convention of 1829–30, emphasized the fundamental role of property in the maintenance of civilization (ibid., 70–72). See also *The Speech of William H. Brodnax (of Dinwiddie) in the House of Delegates of Virginia on the Policy of the State with Respect to Its Colored Population* (Richmond, 1832).

22. Robert, *Road from Monticello*, 83–84, 70–72, 88–92.

23. Ibid., 61, 65–68, 105–7. In *Drift toward Dissolution*, 122–58, Freehling divided these men into two groups. Her "conservatives" include among those who spoke Brown, Charles S. Carter, Gholson, Goode, Knox, and John Shell. To this group one should add William N. Patteson and William Daniel, Jr., whose speeches are in Robert, *Road from Monticello*, 73–74, 111. Freehling termed her second group the "moderates," exemplified by Brodnax and Archibald Bryce, Jr. She might also have included Willoughby Newton, quoted ibid., 97–98.

24. *Richmond Enquirer*, Feb. 14, 16, 1832. See Freehling, *Drift toward Dissolution*, 177–88; *The Speech of Thomas Marshall, in the House of Delegates of Virginia, on the Abolition of Slavery* (Richmond, 1832).

25. Robert, *Road from Monticello*, 29–34; Freehling, *Drift toward Dissolution*, 160–69; Hickin, "Antislavery in Virginia," 147–53. The four proslavery westerners came from four counties in the Valley that produced three antislavery votes as well. None of these delegates was a large slaveholder.

26. *Richmond Whig*, Jan. 29, Feb. 7, 1832; *Richmond Enquirer*, Feb. 4, 7, 9, 16, 1832.

27. See Jenkins, *Pro-Slavery Thought in the Old South*; McCardell, *Idea of a Southern Nation*; Faust, *Ideology of Slavery*; Bertram Wyatt-Brown, *Yankee Saints and Southern Sinners* (Baton Rouge, La., 1985); Tise, *Proslavery*; Eugene Genovese, *The Slaveholders' Dilemma: Freedom and Progress in Southern Conservative Thought, 1820–1860* (Columbia, S.C., 1992).

28. William Harper, "Memoir on Slavery," *The Pro-Slavery Argument as Maintained by the Most Distinguished Writers of the Southern States . . .* (1852; rept. New York, 1968), 1. See also David Brion Davis, *Slavery and Human Progress* (New York, 1984); and Thomas Bender, ed., *The Antislavery Debate* (New York, 1993).

29. Benjamin Watkins Leigh's "Appomattox" letters appeared in the *Richmond Enquirer*, Feb. 4, 28, 1832, and were published separately as *The Letter of Appomattox to the People of Virginia* (Richmond, 1832). Leigh had acknowledged the "evil" of slavery in the convention debates two years before.

30. Harper, "Memoir on Slavery," 48. See also the other essays in *Proslavery Argu-*

ment; E. N. Elliott, ed., *Cotton Is King; and Proslavery Arguments* . . . (Augusta, Ga., 1860); Wish, *Antebellum*; McKitrick, *Slavery Defended*; Faust, *Ideology of Slavery.*

31. Thomas R. Dew, *Lectures on the Restrictive System* (Richmond, 1829); "Professor Dew on Slavery," *Pro-Slavery Argument*, 451, 381–87, 421–22. On Dew as a political economist, see Joseph Dorfman, *The Economic Mind in American Civilization, 1606–1865* (1946; rept. New York, 1966) 895–909; Allen Kaufman, *Capitalism, Slavery and Republican Values* (Austin, Tex., 1982), 83–120, 165–78; James C. Hite and Ellen J. Hall, "The Reactionary Evolution of Economic Thought in Antebellum Virginia," *VMHB* 80 (1972): 476–88.

32. "Professor Dew on Slavery," 387–90, 354–59. For conflicting interpretations of Dew, see Jenkins, *Proslavery Argument*; Kenneth M. Stampp, "An Analysis of T. R. Dew's 'Review of the Debates in the Virginia Legislature,'" *Journal of Negro History* 27 (1942): 380–87; McCardell, *Idea of a Southern Nation*, 53–60; Bruce, *Rhetoric of Conservatism*, 175–95; Freehling, *Drift toward Dissolution*, 202–8; Tise, *Proslavery*, 70–74, 288–89, 388–89; Eugene D. Genovese, *Western Civilization through Slaveholding Eyes: The Social and Historical Thought of Thomas Roderick Dew* (New Orleans, 1985); Stephen S. Mansfield, "Thomas Roderick Dew: Defender of the Southern Faith" (Ph.D. diss., Univ. of Virginia, 1968).

33. 'Professor Dew on Slavery," 461–62; Thomas R. Dew, "Of the Influence of the Federation, Republican System of Government upon Literature and Development of Character," *Southern Literary Messenger* 2 (1836): 261–82.

34. Brugger, *Beverley Tucker*, 107–13, 145–47, 201–3; Faust, *A Sacred Circle*, 112–31; Dorfman, *Economic Mind in American Civilization* 2:909–20; Nathaniel Beverley Tucker, "Note on Blackstone's Commentaries," *Southern Literary Messenger* 1 (1835): 227–36; Tucker, "An Essay on the Moral and Political Effects of the Relation between the Caucasian Master and the African Slave," *Southern Literary Messenger* 10 (1844): 470–80.

35. Tucker to William Gilmore Simms, Dec. 17, 1851, in William P. Trent, *William Gilmore Simms* (Boston, 1892), 184–88; Faust, *A Sacred Circle*, 116–21; McCardell, *Idea of a Southern Nation*, 207–15.

36. Brugger, *Beverley Tucker*, 146; Upshur, "Domestic Slavery," 687; Hall, *Upshur*, 69–80. See also Freehling, *Reintegration of American History*, 105–37.

37. Upshur, "Domestic Slavery," 677–79.

38. Bruce, *Rhetoric of Conservatism*, 177, 189; "Professor Dew on Slavery," 355; Faust, *A Sacred Circle*, 73–80, 118–19.

39. Oakes, *Ruling Race*, 105; "Professor Dew on Slavery," 451–52. On evangelicals and the proslavery argument, see Mathews, *Religion in the Old South*, 66–88, 136–84; Loveland, *Southern Evangelicals and the Social Order*, 186–218; David Bailey, *Shadow on the Church: Southwestern Evangelical Religion and the Issue of Slavery, 1783–1860* (Ithaca, N.Y., 1985); Elizabeth Fox-Genovese and Eugene Genovese, "The Religious Ideals of Southern Slave Society," *Georgia Historical Quarterly* 70 (1986): 1–16; Robert M. Calhoon, *Evangelicals and Conservatives in the Early South, 1740–1861* (Columbia, S.C., 1988), 163–206; Mitchell Snay, "Southern Thought and Southern Distinctiveness: The Southern Clergy and the Sanctification of Slavery," *Civil War History* 35 (1989): 311–28; Tise, *Proslavery.*

40. Thornton Stringfellow, "The Bible Argument: or, Slavery in the Light of Divine Revelation," in Elliott, *Cotton Is King*, 461–92, in the longest of the four articles by

Stringfellow included in ibid., 461–549. The 1841 essay is reprinted in Faust, *Ideology of Slavery*, 138–67. See also Drew Gilpin Faust, "Evangelicalism and the Meaning of the Proslavery Argument: The Reverend Thornton Stringfellow of Virginia," *VMHB* 85 (1977): 3–17.

41. Jeremiah Jeter, *The Recollections of a Long Life* (Richmond, 1891), 67–76; William H. Allison, "Jeremiah Bell Jeter," *DAB*.

42. Loveland, *Southern Evangelicals and the Social Order*, 192–96. On John Holt Rice and the Presbyterian schism, see Foote, *Sketches of Virginia*, 365–444, 486–556.

43. Harrison, "The Slavery Question in Virginia," which originally appeared in *American Quarterly Review* (Dec. 1832) is reprinted in Harrison, *Aris Sonis Focisque*, 337–400. This volume includes a sketch, "Jesse Burton Harrison of New Orleans," pp. 84–143, and two of his other essays. See also Freehling, *Drift toward Dissolution*, 208–15. On the spectrum of antislavery activity in the Old Dominion, see Hickin, "Antislavery in Virginia"; Eaton, *Freedom-of-Thought Struggle*; Degler, *Other South*; George Ellis Moore, "Slavery as a Factor in the Formation of West Virginia," *West Virginia History* 18 (1956): 5–89.

44. Freehling, *Drift toward Dissolution*, 212. Freehling emphasizes the similarities between the positions of Dew and Harrison to argue that the latter's "antislavery proposal mirrored the Brodnax-Bryce 'middle ground,'" but Brodnax did not vote with Bryce and Marshall. "Jesse Burton Harrison of New Orleans," in Harrison, *Aris Sonis Focisque*, reveals his close relationship to Madison and the fact he was a cousin of Henry Clay.

45. "A Slaveholder of West Virginia" [Henry Ruffner], *Address to the People of West Virginia Showing That Slavery Is Injurious to the Public Welfare, and That It May Be Gradually Abolished without Detriment to the Rights and Interests of the Slaveholders* (1847; rept. Bridgewater, Va., 1933), 37–38. See William Gleason Bean, "The Ruffner Pamphlet of 1847: An Antislavery Aspect of Virginia Sectionalism," *VMHB* 61 (1958): 260–82. This is another example indicating that antebellum Virginians entertained ideas of partial emancipation as well as conditional emancipation.

46. Debate quoted in Ambler, *Sectionalism*, 245; Bean, "Ruffner Pamphlet of 1847," 268–81; F. N. Boney, *John Letcher of Virginia* (University, Ala., 1966), 36–52.

47. *Kanawha Valley Star*, Aug. 3, 1858, quoted in Ambler, *Sectionalism*, 245.

48. *Memoirs of Samuel M. Janney, Late of Lincoln, Loudoun County, Va.* (Philadelphia, 1905), 29–33, 74; Patricia Hickin, "Gentle Agitator: Samuel M. Janney and the Antislavery Movement in Virginia, 1842–1851," *JSH* 38 (1972), 167; Janney to Isaac T. Hoppen, Dec. 15, 1844, *Memoirs*, 87–89; *Richmond Whig*, July 23, 25, Sept. 10, 18, 23, Oct. 18, 23, 24, 27, 1845.

49. Of course this refers exclusively to men. Historians have recently debated the attitudes of southern women toward slavery. Cf. Lebsock, *Free Women of Petersburg*; and Elizabeth Fox-Genovese, *Within the Plantation Household: Black and White Women in the Old South* (Chapel Hill, N.C., 1988).

50. The officers of the Virginia Colonization Society are given in Tyler, *Letters and Times* 1:566–67. Aside from the sources on individuals mentioned elsewhere in these notes, see Avery O. Craven, "James Mercer Garnett," *DAB*.

51. Freehling, *Drift toward Dissolution*, 170–94; Tyler, *Letters and Times* 1:68.

52. Campbell to Arthur P. Hayne, Sept. 3, 1837, in the Campbell Family Papers, DU; Tyler, *Letters and Times* 1:567–69; Barton H. Wise, *The Life of Henry A. Wise of Virginia, 1806–1876* (New York, 1899), 60–61.

53. *Richmond Enquirer*, Jan. 12, Feb. 4, 1832; *Richmond Whig*, Feb. 6, 7, 1832. Both pa-

pers opposed such legislation, and the *Whig* compared Leigh's suggestion to a call for a new version of the Sedition Act. See also Clement Eaton, "A Dangerous Pamphlet in the Old South," *JSH* 2 (1936): 323 – 34.

54. *Lynchburg Virginian*, Aug. 13, 20, 1835; *Richmond Enquirer*, Sept. 25, Oct. 2, 1835; *Journal of the House of Delegates . . . 1835*, 6 – 12.

55. Eaton, *Freedom-of-Thought-Struggle*, 83, 167 – 74, 198 – 99; *Richmond Whig*, March 26, 1836; Hickin, "Antislavery in Virginia," 174 – 80.

56. *Journal of the House of Delegates . . . 1835*, 6 – 12, 23 – 30, 67, 89; Lynchburg *Virginian*, Dec. 24, 1835, Jan. 18, 1836. See also Gordon, "Thomas Walker Gilmer"; Peterson, *Tazewell*, 242 – 54.

57. This is based on ten relevant roll calls given in *Journal of the House of Delegates . . . 1835*, 29 – 30, 75 – 90.

58. The party affiliations are given in Simms, *Rise of the Whigs in Virginia*, 171 – 74. See also Charles H. Ambler, "Robert Mercer Taliaferro Hunter," James Elliott Walmsley, "John Minor Botts," *DAB*; Callahan, "Summers." Future senator R. M. T. Hunter and Senator Leigh's conservative friend Judge Robert Stanard, along with Gilmer, typified the Calhounites. The leader of the antislavery faction, George Summers, had been a progressive emancipationist, was the Whig candidate for governor in the first popular election in 1851, and would be a Unionist opponent of secession in the convention of 1861.

59. Samuel Gwin to Van Buren, May 20, 1834, Martin Van Buren Papers, LC; *Richmond Whig*, April 10, June 27, July 3, Aug. 7, 1835, Jan. 5, 1836; Cooper, *South and the Politics of Slavery*, 43 – 97.

60. *Virginia Free Press* (Charlestown), April 21, 1836; *Lynchburg Virginian*, Aug. 11, 22, Sept. 6, 1836; *Petersburg Intelligencer* reprinted in ibid., Sept. 12; Whig address in ibid., Sept. 1, 1836, and *Richmond Whig*, Aug. 23, 1836.

61. John Tyler to William F. Gordon, Nov. 9, 1834, in Gordon, *William Fitzhugh Gordon*, 293 – 95; *Richmond Whig*, Feb. 13, 1836. See also Thomas Brown, *Politics and Statesmanship: Essays on the American Whig Party* (New York, 1985).

62. *Lynchburg Virginian*, Aug. 8, 22, Sept. 19, Oct. 6, 1836.

63. *Richmond Whig*, March 17, 1836; *Virginia Free Press* (Charlestown), April 21, 1836; *Lynchburg Virginian*, Oct. 20, 1836; *Richmond Enquirer*, April 3, 1835. On the charges against Johnson, see Thomas Brown, "The Miscegenation of Richard Mentor Johnson as an Issue in the National Election Campaign of 1835 – 1836," *Civil War History* 39 (1993): 5 – 30.

64. William C. Rives to Van Buren, April 10, 1835, Joseph Watkins to Silas Wright, Jan. 29, 1835, Ritchie to Silas Wright, March 2, 1835, Peter Daniel to Van Buren, June 7, 1836, Martin Van Buren Papers, LC; Van Buren to William C. Rives, April 1, 1835, B. F. Butler to Rives, May 26, 1835, William Ritchie to Rives, Aug. 23, 1835, William C. Rives Papers, LC; *Richmond Enquirer*, March 20, Aug. 24, Sept. 4, 1835. The Whig politician in question was Vincent Witcher.

65. Van Buren to Junius Amis et al., March 4, 1836, Martin Van Buren Papers, LC. This letter was published as *Opinion of Martin Van Buren, Vice President of the United States, upon the Powers and Duties of Congress in Reference to the Abolition of Slavery Either in the Slave-Holding States or in the District of Columbia* (Washington, D.C., 1836).

66. Richard Parker to Van Buren, June 29, 1836, Peter Daniel to Van Buren, June 7, 1836, Martin Van Buren Papers, LC. Daniel was awarded with an appointment to the Supreme Court. See John P. Frank, *Justice Daniel Dissenting: A Biography of Peter V. Daniel, 1784 – 1860* (Cambridge, Mass., 1964).

67. Craig M. Simpson, *A Good Southerner: The Life of Henry A. Wise of Virginia* (Chapel Hill, N.C., 1985), 29 – 32; Theodore S. Cox, "John Mercer Patton," *DAB*. On the gag rule, see Cole, *Whig Party in the South*, 104 – 34; Turner, *United States, 1830 – 1850*, 430 – 34, 465 – 70; Gilbert Hobbs Barnes, *The Antislavery Impulse, 1830 – 1844* (1933; rept. New York, 1964), 109 – 45; Samuel Flagg Bemis, *John Quincy Adams and the Union* (New York, 1956), 326 – 448; Lee Benson, *Toward the Scientific Study of History: Selected Essays* (Philadelphia, 1972), 319 – 23; George C. Rable, "Slavery, Politics, and the South: The Gag Rule as a Case Study," *Capital Studies* 3 (1975): 69 – 88; Richards, *Life and Times of John Quincy Adams*, 89 – 145; Freehling, *Road to Disunion*, 287 – 352; William Lee Miller, *Arguing about Slavery: The Great Battle in the United States Congress* (New York, 1996).

68. Wise quoted in Ambler, *Sectionalism*, 225. See also Wise, *Henry A. Wise*, 34, 44 – 68; Simpson, *A Good Southerner*, 29 – 44; Henry A. Wise, *Seven Decades of Union . . .* (Philadelphia, 1872), 121 – 28, 167, and passim.

69. *Congressional Globe*, 26th Cong., 1st sess., 89, 93, 122 – 23, 150 – 61.

70. *Richmond Enquirer*, Jan. 7, Feb. 27, Feb. 29, March 3 – 7, March 24, April 17, May 12, Sept. 8, 1840; Richard Williams Smith, "The Career of Martin Van Buren in Connection with the Slavery Controversy" (Ph.D. diss., Ohio State Univ., 1959), 295 – 357; James C. Curtis, *Fox at Bay: Martin Van Buren and the Presidency, 1832 – 1841* (Lexington, Ky., 1970), 189 – 206; Cooper, *South and the Politics of Slavery*, 98 – 148.

71. *Richmond Whig*, June 19, Aug. 3, Sept. 11, March 6, 1840; *Lynchburg Virginian*, April 20, 1840.

72. *Richmond Whig*, March 24, April 20, 1840. See also Cooper, *South and the Politics of Slavery*, 133 – 48; Dorothy Gobel, *William Henry Harrison: A Political Biography* (Indianapolis, 1926), 322 – 65; Gunderson, *Log Cabin Campaign*.

73. Thomas Ritchie to the senior editor of the *Richmond Whig*, February 18, 1840, in "Unpublished Letters of Ritchie," 240 – 45; *Richmond Enquirer*, June 2 – 5, July 3, 10, 24, Aug. 21, 29, 1840; *Warrenton Jeffersonian*, Jan. 15, Feb. 27, March 7, 14, 1840; *Virginia Advocate* (Charlottesville), May 2, 1840.

74. Thomas Ritchie to the senior editor of the *Richmond Whig*, Feb. 18, 1840, in "Unpublished Letters of Ritchie," 240 – 45; *Richmond Whig*, March 1, 1840; *Richmond Enquirer*, March 3, 1840.

75. Richards, *Life and Times of John Quincy Adams*, 139 – 45, 176 – 78; *Congressional Globe*, 26th Cong., 1st sess., 150 – 51; *Washington, D.C., National Intelligencer*, June 9, 1841; Alexander F. Robertson, *Alexander Hugh Holmes Stuart, 1807 – 1901: A Biography* (Richmond, 1925), 26 – 28; Cole, *Whig Party in the South*, 107 – 8.

76. Newton at the last minute switched and voted for the annexation resolution. See Frederick Merk, *Slavery and the Annexation of Texas* (New York, 1970).

77. *Richmond Whig*, June 4, 1844, June 30, Aug. 4, Sept. 8, 1848; *Lynchburg Virginian*, Sept. 2, 16, Nov. 19, 1844, Aug. 10, 24, Oct. 2, 5, 1848; *Richmond Enquirer*, Aug. 2, Oct. 19, 1844, June 6, 30, July 24, Aug. 18, 19, Sept. 1, 2, 15, 1848; *Niles' Weekly Register* 67 (1844): 83; *Spirit of Jefferson* (Charlestown), Nov. 8, 1844; *Norfolk and Portsmouth Herald and Daily Commercial Advertiser*, April 17, 1847; *Petersburg Republican*, Oct. 27, Nov. 1, 6, 1848. The issue was relatively less important for the Whigs than Democrats and far less likely to appear in western papers than eastern. See also Cooper, *South and the Politics of Slavery*, 189 – 219, 259 – 67; Ambler, "Virginia and the Presidential Succession"; Rayback, *Free Soil*, 37 – 42, 231 – 59.

78. Hickin, "Antislavery in Virginia"; George Tucker, *Law of Wages, Profits and Rent Investigated* (Philadelphia, 1837); Tucker, *Progress of the United States in Population and*

Wealth in Fifty Years, as Exhibited in the Decennial Census (Boston, 1843). Cf. Dorfman, *Economic Mind in American Civilization,* 543 – 50; Robert Colin McLean, *George Tucker: Moral Philosopher and Man of Letters* (Chapel Hill, N.C., 1961), 175 – 201; Tipton R. Snavely, *George Tucker as a Political Economist* (Charlottesville, Va., 1964), 134 – 54. See also [Charles F. Mercer], *The Weakness and Inefficiency of the Government of the United States of North America* (n.p., 1845); Hickin, "Antislavery in Virginia," 216 – 19; Charles Francis Adams, Jr., "Charles Fenton Mercer," *DAB*; Egerton, *Mercer,* 304 – 5, 327 – 28.

79. Siegel, *Roots of Southern Distinctiveness,* 21, 55, 111 – 12, 149; Hickin, "Antislavery in Virginia," 214 – 15. See also SamL. M. Wolfe, *Helper's Impending Crisis Dissected* (Philadelphia, 1860), 7 – 57, 204 – 23.

80. Janney, *Memoirs,* 91; *Richmond Whig,* June 27, July 1, 17, 18, 1845. While emphasizing the "Notes Illustrative of the Wrongs of Slavery," kept by Mary Berkeley Minor Blackwell, in *The Other South,* 25, 33 – 36, Carl Degler does not point out that her husband served in both the Harrison-Tyler and the Taylor-Fillmore administrations and edited the influential Whig paper the *Lynchburg Virginian.* See L. Minor Blackwell, *Mine Eyes Have Seen the Glory: The Story of a Virginia Lady, Mary Berkeley Minor Blackwell, 1802 – 1896, Who Taught Her Sons to Hate Slavery and to Love the Union* (Cambridge, Mass., 1954), 49, 92 – 96.

81. *Richmond Whig,* Dec. 12, 1845; Hickin, "Antislavery in Virginia," 356 – 65; Hickin, "Gentle Agitator," 174 – 79; Eaton, *Freedom-of-Thought Struggle,* 119. In his statement Pleasant rankled the Ritchies by equating his position with that of "Father" Ritchie in the early 1830s.

82. Willoughby Newton, one of the "conservative proslavery" delegates in 1832, entered Congress as a Whig in 1843 and moved hesitantly toward Tyler and Texas. By 1850 he was a secessionist representative to the Nashville Convention.

83. Only one regular Whig, John S. Pendleton, had voted with the "radical proslavery" bloc in 1832. He served successive Whig administrations abroad and became a Unionist in the 1850s. Charles J. Faulkner, who had been a "progressive emancipationist" in 1832, remained a Whig until Clay's death and then moved into the Democratic party.

84. Senator William H. Roane had been associated with the ACS in the 1820s and sided with the moderates in 1832, promoting the Bryce preamble. From 1837 to 1841 he consistently supported the Van Buren administration, but he actually represented an earlier day. The proslavery trend of the Virginia Democracy is better represented by the men who occupied the Senate seats from the mid-1840s to the Civil War: R. M. T. Hunter and James Murray Mason.

7. The Doctrines of '98

1. Arthur Bestor, "State Sovereignty and the Civil War: A Reinterpretation of Proslavery Constitutional Doctrines, 1846 – 1860," *Journal of the Illinois State Historical Society* 54 (1961): 145; Peterson, *Jefferson Writings,* 449 – 56; Meyers, *Mind of the Founder,* 229 – 73; David Mattern et al., eds., *The Papers of James Madison* 17 (Charlottesville, Va., 1991): 33 – 351. See also Dumas Malone, *Jefferson and His Time* 3:359 – 424; Adrienne Koch, *Madison and Jefferson: The Great Collaboration* (New York, 1964), 174 – 211. *States' rights* is used here (except in quotations) following the current usage as illustrated in Paul Finkelman, "States' Rights North and South in Antebellum America," in *An Uncertain*

Tradition: Constitutionalism and the History of the South, ed. Kermit L. Hall and James W. Ely, Jr. (Athens, Ga., 1989), 125–58.

2. Ames, State Documents on Federal Relations, 15–26; Henry Lee, Plain Truth (Richmond, 1798); Albert J. Beveridge, The Life of John Marshall, 4 vols. (Boston, 1916), 1:397–405; Beeman, Old Dominion and the New Nation, 194–220; Risjord, Chesapeake, Politics, 534–42; Risjord, "Virginia Federalists."

3. Cf. Richard E. Ellis, The Jeffersonian Crisis: Courts and Politics in the Young Republic (New York, 1971); Ellis, "The Persistence of Antifederalism after 1789"; Ellis, Union at Risk; Matthews, Radical Politics of Jefferson; Matthews, If Men Were Angels: James Madison and the Heartless Republic of Reason (Lawrence, Kans., 1994); Merrill D. Peterson, The Great Triumvirate: Webster, Clay, and Calhoun (New York, 1987); McCoy, Last of the Fathers. Peterson used his conception of Madisonian nationalism interchangeably with the contemporary phrase "the Madisonian Platform" that came from John Pendleton Kennedy's Defense of the Whigs by a Member of the Twenty-seventh Congress (New York, 1844), relevant portions of which are reprinted in The American Whigs, ed. Daniel Walker Howe (New York, 1973), 79–88.

4. Marshall is quoted in Peterson, The Jeffersonian Image in the American Mind, 39. See also Ambler, Ritchie; Anderson, William Branch Giles; Sydnor, Development of Southern Sectionalism; Risjord, Old Republicans; Shalhope, "Jefferson's Republicanism and Antebellum Southern Thought"; Kathryn R. Malone, "The Fate of Revolutionary Republicanism in Early National Virginia," Journal of the Early Republic 7 (1987): 27–51; Malone, "Virginia Doctrines, the Commonwealth, and the Republic."

5. Gerald Gunther, ed., John Marshall's Defense of McCulloch v. Maryland (Stanford, Calif., 1969), 1, identifies Brockenbrough as "Amphictyon" and reprints Marshall's essays and Roane's "Hampden" essay. See also Edwin J. Smith, "Spencer Roane," "Roane on the National Constitution 1. Public Letter of 'Plain Dealer' to Governor Randolph, February 13, 1788," and "Roane Correspondence," John P. Branch Historical Papers of Randolph-Macon College 2 (1906): 4–33, 47–51, 123–42; "Letters of Spencer Roane [to James Monroe], 1788–1822," Bulletin of the New York Public Library 10 (1906): 167–80; William E. Dodd, "Chief Justice Marshall and Virginia, 1813–1821," AHR 12 (1907): 776–87; Beach, "Spencer Roane and the Richmond Junto"; Charles Warren, The Supreme Court in United States History, 2 vols. (Boston, 1922), 1:400–453, 499–540, 2:1–24; Charles Grove Haines, The Role of the Supreme Court in American Government and Politics, 1789–1835 (Berkeley, Calif., 1944), 331–78, 427–62; G. Edward White, The Marshall Court and Cultural Change, 1815–35 (New York, 1987), 485–524; F. Thornton Miller, "John Marshall versus Spencer Roane: A Reevaluation of Martin v. Hunter's Lessee," WMQ 96 (1988): 297–314; Timothy S. Huebner, "The Consolidation of State Judicial Power: Spencer Roane, Virginia Legal Culture, and the Southern Judicial Tradition," VMHB 102 (1994): 46–72.

6. Marshall is quoted in Gunther, John Marshall's Defense, 13–15. See also Beveridge, John Marshall, vol. 4.

7. Jefferson to Spencer Roane, Oct. 12, 1815, Sept. 6, 1819, to Thomas Ritchie, Dec. 25, 1820, to Justice William Johnson, Oct. 27, 1822, to William Branch Giles, Dec. 26, 1825, in Peterson, Jefferson Writings, 1425–28, 1445–47, 1459–63, 1509–12; Thomas Jefferson on Constitutional Issues: Selected Writings, 1787–1825, ed. Noble E. Cunningham, Jr. (Richmond, 1962). See David N. Mayer, The Constitutional Thought of Thomas Jefferson (Charlottesville, Va., 1994).

8. See John Taylor, Definition of Parties; or The Political Effects of the Paper System

Considered (Philadelphia, 1794); Taylor, *Arator*; Taylor, *An Inquiry into the Principles and Policy of the Government of the United States*, ed. Loren Baritz (Indianapolis, 1969); Taylor, *Construction Construed and Constitutions Vindicated* (1820; rept. New York, 1970); Taylor, *Tyranny Unmasked*, ed. F. Thornton Miller (Indianapolis, 1992); Taylor, *New Views of the Constitution* (Washington, D.C., 1823).

9. See Shalhope, *John Taylor of Caroline*; Charles A. Beard, *Economic Origins of Jeffersonian Democracy* (New York, 1915); Benjamin F. Wright, "The Philosopher of Jeffersonian Democracy," *American Political Science Review* 22 (1928): 870 – 92; Henry Simms, *The Life of John Taylor: The Story of a Brilliant Leader in the Early Virginia State Rights School* (Richmond, 1932); Avery O. Craven, "John Taylor and Southern Agriculture," *JSH* 4 (1938): 137 – 47; Bernard Drell, "John Taylor of Caroline and the Preservation of an Old Social Order," *VMHB* 46 (1938): 285 – 98: Eugene Tenbroeck Mudge, *The Social Philosophy of John Taylor of Caroline* (New York, 1939); Manning J. Dauer and Henry Hammond, "John Taylor: Democrat or Aristocrat?" *Journal of Politics* 6 (1944): 381 – 403; William D. Grampp, "John Taylor: Economist of Southern Agrarianism," *Southern Economic Journal* 11 (1945): 255 – 68; Roy Franklin Nichols, "Introduction," to John Taylor, *An Inquiry into the Principles of the Government of the United States* (New Haven, 1950), 7 – 29; William Appleman Williams, *The Contours of American History* (Cleveland, 1961), 227 – 35; Loren Baritz, *City upon a Hill: A History of Ideas and Myths in American History* (New York, 1964), 159 – 203.

10. "Roane's 'Hampden' Essays," in Gunther, *John Marshall's Defense*, 114 – 15.

11. Madison to Roane, Sept. 2, 1819, May 6, June 29, 1821, in Meyers, *Mind of the Founder*, 357 – 69; Madison to Jefferson, June 27, 1823, in Gaillard Hunt, ed., *Writings of Madison*, 9 vols. (New York, 1900 – 1910), 9:141; McCoy, *Last of the Fathers*, 113 – 18; Irving Brant, *James Madison: Commander in Chief, 1812 – 1836*, 432 – 34. For the "Algernon Sidney" essays, see "Virginia Opposition to Chief Justice Marshall — Reprints from Richmond *Enquirer*, 1821," *John P. Branch Historical Papers of Randolph-Macon College* 2 (1906): 78 – 182.

12. Ames, *State Documents On Federal Relations*, 103 – 4.

13. Jefferson to John Holmes, April 22, 1820, in Peterson, *Jefferson Writings*, 1433 – 35. On the Missouri Compromise, see Glover Moore, *The Missouri Controversy, 1819 – 1821* (Lexington, Ky., 1953); George Dangerfield, *The Awakening of American Nationalism, 1815 – 1828* (New York, 1965), 97 – 140.

14. Harry Ammon, *James Monroe: The Quest for National Identity* (1971; rept. Charlottesville, Va., 1990), 449 – 59; Lowrey, *James Barbour*; *Annals of Congress*, 16th Cong., 1st sess., 428, 457, 1587 – 88; Ames, *State Documents on Federal Relations*, 201 – 2.

15. Nelson quoted in Moore, *Missouri Controversy*, 157; *Annals of Congress*, 16th Cong., 2d sess., 1238 – 40.

16. McCoy, *Last of the Founders*, 105 – 15, 260 – 76; Meyers, *Mind of the Founder*, 319 – 27; Jefferson to Albert Gallatin, Dec. 26, 1820, in Peterson, *Jefferson Writings*, 1447 – 50; Jefferson to Adams, Jan. 22, 1821, in Lester Cappon, ed., *The Adams-Jefferson Letters* (1959; rept. New York, 1971), 569 – 70; Davis, *Slavery in the Age of Revolution*, 185.

17. *Annals of Congress*, 15th Cong., 2d sess., 1184 – 91, 1384 – 91, 16th Cong., 1st sess., 164, 1265, 1481, 1495; Tyler, *Letters and Times* 1:308 – 32; Lyon G. Tyler, ed., "Missouri Compromise: Letters to James Barbour, Senator of Virginia in the Congress of the United States," *WMQ* 10 (1901): 5 – 24; Randolph quoted in Moore, *Missouri Controversy*, 93.

18. *Richmond Enquirer*, May 14, 19, July 9, Aug. 18, Dec. 23, 1819, Jan. 27, Feb. 3, 6, 10, 15, 17, 19, 29, March 10, 1820; Ambler, *Ritchie*, 77 – 79.

19. Ames, *State Documents on Federal Relations*, 202; *Niles' Register* 17 (1820): 343 – 44, 363, 416 – 17; Linn Banks to James Barbour, Feb. 26, 1820, in Tyler, "Missouri Compromise," 20 – 22; Moore, *Missouri Controversy*, 231 – 45.

20. Roane to James Monroe, Feb. 16, 1820, in "Letters of Spencer Roane," 174 – 75; *Norfolk and Portsmouth Herald*, Feb. 14, 1820; Brugger, *Beverley Tucker*, 52 – 57.

21. Roane to Jefferson, Feb. 25, 1821, "Roane Correspondence," 138 – 39; *Richmond Enquirer*, June 4, Aug. 13, 17, Oct. 15, Nov. 16, 1919, March 20, April 28, May 2, 1820; Ames, *State Documents on Federal Relations*, 103. See also Abernethy, *South in the New Nation*, 403 – 43.

22. *Congressional Globe*, 18th Cong., 2d sess., 143 – 44, 155 – 57, 192 – 93, 224 – 27, 318 – 21, 20th Cong., 1st sess., 406, 410, 577 – 80, 607 – 9.

23. *Richmond Enquirer*, May 10, 1822; Dew, *Lectures on the Restrictive System*, 126; *Congressional Globe*, 18th Cong., 1st sess., 916 – 45; Merrill D. Peterson, *Olive Branch and the Sword: The Compromise of 1833* (Baton Rouge, La., 1982), 13 – 14; Malone, "Virginia Doctrines, the Commonwealth, and the Republic," 233 – 98; Ames, *State Documents on Federal Relations*, 133 – 63.

24. Ames, *State Documents on Federal Relations*, 140 – 45; Tyler, *Letters and Times* 1:339 – 73; *Journal of the House of Delegates . . . 1826 – 27*, 6 – 18, 191 – 93; *Journal of the House of Delegates . . . 1828 – 29*, 6 – 14, 226 – 29; Giles, *Political Miscellanies*; Malone, "Virginia Doctrines, the Commonwealth, and the Republic," 280 – 84; William B. Giles to Littleton Waller Tazewell, May 21, 1828, Tazewell Family Papers, LV.

25. Ames, *State Documents on Federal Relations*, 156 – 57; *Niles' Register* 33 (1828): 405, 35 (1828): 373 – 74; *Richmond Enquirer* Feb. 24, 1829.

26. *Richmond Whig*, Dec. 13, 1825, July 7, 1831. On the tariff see ibid., Aug. 8, 1827, Oct. 6, 1827, July 18, Oct. 6, 1831. On internal improvements, see ibid., March 15, Aug. 26, 30, 1825, Feb. 11, 1830. On the differences between Madison and the *Whig*, see Brant, *Madison: Commander in Chief*, 470 – 71.

27. William C. Rives to William A. Rives, Jan. 8, 1829, William C. Rives Papers, LC; *Richmond Enquirer*, Dec. 27, 1828, Jan. 7, Feb. 24, March 13, 1829.

28. Madison to Joseph C. Cabell, Sept. 18, Oct. 30, 1828, in Meyers, *Mind of the Founder*, 369 – 89, 417 – 42; Madison to Edward Everett, Aug. 28, 1830, in William W. Freehling, ed., *Nullification Era: A Documentary Record* (New York, 1967), 91 – 95; McCoy, *The Last of the Fathers*.

29. *Register of the Debates* 6:842, 1133, 1135, 1147 – 48; *Register of the Debates* 7:1147, 1296; *Register of the Debates* 9:1920 – 21; *Journal of the House of Representatives*, 22d Cong., 1st sess., 181 – 87, 1023 – 24, 1074. On congressional behavior, see Turner, *United States, 1830 – 1850*, 379 – 432; David J. Russo, "The Major Political Issues of the Jacksonian Period and the Development of Party Loyalty in Congress," *Transactions of the American Philosophical Society* 62 (1972): 3 – 51.

30. *Richmond Whig*, Dec. 5, 1832; *Journal of the House of Delegates . . . 1832 – 33*, 6 – 14, 22; Thomas Ritchie to Rives, Dec. 6, 1832, William C. Rives Papers, LC. See also Ambler, *Sectionalism*, 209 – 18; Simms, *Rise of the Whigs in Virginia*, 63 – 86; Ellis, *Union at Risk*, 122 – 40; Tyler, *Letters and Times* 1:431 – 68; Dingledine, "The Political Career of William Cabell Rives," 63 – 116; James Glen Collier "The Political Career of James McDowell" (Ph.D. diss., Univ. of North Carolina, 1963), 104 – 17; Malone, "Virginia Doctrines, the Commonwealth, and the Republic," 408 – 65.

31. *Richmond Enquirer*, Feb. 2, 1833; John Brockenbrough to Rives, Jan. 11, 1833, Thomas Mann Randolph to Rives, Feb. 21, 1833, William C. Rives Papers, LC; *Richmond*

Whig, Dec. 18, 1832, Jan. 4, Feb. 8, 1833.

32. *Washington, D.C., Globe*, Jan. 23, 1833. There were nearly forty meetings in all; see practically every issue of the *Richmond Enquirer* and the *Richmond Whig*, for January and February 1833.

33. Kirk, *Randolph of Roanoke*, 119 – 21; Hall, *Upshur*, 86 – 94; *Address of Abel P. Upshur to the People of Northampton County* (Richmond, 1833); [Abel Parker Upshur], *The Essays of Napier originally Published in the Jeffersonian and Virginia Times* (Norfolk, 1833); "Locke" [Abel P. Upshur], *An Exposition of the Resolutions of 1798* . . . (Philadelphia, 1833); "A Virginian" [Littleton W. Tazewell], *A Review of the Proclamation of President Jackson* . . . (Norfolk, 1833); Ambler, *Life of Floyd*, 103 – 17, 199; Peterson, *Tazewell*, 220 – 23.

34. *Richmond Whig*, Dec. 14, 18, 21, 1832, Jan. 15, 18, Feb. 15, 28, 1833; *Richmond Enquirer*, Aug. 17, Sept. 15, Oct. 25, 26, Nov. 30, Dec. 13, 1832, Jan. 1, 3, 5, 8, 17, 18, 24, 26, 31, Feb. 2, 8, 1833; C. W. Gooch to William S. Archer, Dec. 27, 1832, Gooch Family Papers, UVA; C. W. Gooch to Rives, Feb. 16, 1833, Ritchie to Rives, Jan. 6, 18, Feb. 2, 1833, William C. Rives Papers, LC; Ambler, *Ritchie*, 148 – 52. The *Whig* had moderated its position on states' rights earlier in support of Adams and Clay.

35. *Journal of the House of Delegates . . . 1832 – 33*, 30 – 31; Ambler, *Life of Floyd*, 202 – 4; John Floyd to Littleton Waller Tazewell, Dec. 23, 1832, Tazewell Family Papers, LV; *Richmond Enquirer*, Dec. 22, 1832, Jan. 5, 29, Feb. 12, 1833.

36. *Journal of the House of Delegates . . . 1832 – 33*, 79 – 80; *Richmond Enquirer*, Jan. 1, 3, 5, 12, 17, 1833; *Richmond Whig*, Jan. 1, 4, 8, 11, 15; John Wickam to Littleton Waller Tazewell, Jan. 8, 1833, Tazewell Family Papers, LV; R. Wallace to William C. Rives, Jan. 9, 1833, William C. Rives Papers, LC. The sons of the great judicial opponents had both voted in a moderate fashion on slavery in the previous session.

37. *Richmond Enquirer*, Jan. 20, 21, 25, 27, Feb. 28, 1833; *Richmond Whig*, Jan. 18, 22, 1833; John Murdaugh to Littleton Waller Tazewell, Jan. 12, 16, 1833, Tazewell Family Papers, LV; Lawrence Dale to William C. Rives, Jan. 12, 1833, John Brown to Rives, Jan. 16, 1833, William C. Rives Papers, LC; Ambler, *Life of Floyd*, 207 – 12.

38. *Journal of the House of Delegates . . . 1832*, 184; *Richmond Enquirer*, Feb. 16, 1833; *Lynchburg Virginian*, Feb. 21, 1833; John Hampden Pleasants to Tyler, Jan. 1, 1833, and ? to Tyler, Jan. 29, 1833, in Tyler, *Letters and Times* 1:451 – 55.

39. *Richmond Enquirer*, April 9, 12, 16, 19, 23, 26, 30, May 7, 1833. The problematical congressman was William Penn Taylor, John Taylor's son, who served one term and was defeated by a Democrat John Roane; Taylor was a Calhounite and a friend of Hunter, but hardly a Whig. Most states' rights Jacksonians who opposed the proclamation remained supporters of the administration and became Democrats in the course of the 1830s. Throughout this chapter the material on political leaders is primarily drawn from *The Biographical Directory of the American Congress* and the *DAB*.

40. Ambler's discussion of the 1833 congressional elections in *Sectionalism*, 218 (which has been followed by Francis Fay Wayland, *Andrew Stevenson: Democrat and Diplomat, 1785 – 1857* [Philadelphia, 1949], 95, and Ellis, *Union at Risk*, 139) overemphasizes the importance of states' rights and the difference between the *Richmond Enquirer* and the *Richmond Whig* on the issue. The National Republicans who won defeated Unionist Democrats. Loyall, a Unionist Jacksonian defeated a States-Rights Jacksonian, King, not the National Republican, Newton, who had held the seat in the district around Norfolk. Stevenson won in a district generally unfavorable to nullification although anti-Jackson. John Robertson was defeated by Stevenson but later took his seat and then

was reelected as a Whig. He was called a "Nullifier" by Ritchie but actually was in line with Pleasants and the *Richmond Whig*.

41. Mary Newton Stanard, "William Segar Archer," *DAB*; William F. Gordon to Littleton Waller Tazewell, May 14, 1834, Tazewell Family Papers, LV; John C. Wyllie, "William Fitzhugh Gordon," *DAB*; Walmsley, "John Floyd." See also Gordon, *William Fitzhugh Gordon*; Peterson, *Tazewell*; Hall, *Upshur*; Brugger, *Beverley Tucker*; Ambler, *Life of Floyd*; Simpson, *A Good Southerner*; Wise, *Henry A. Wise*; Wayland, *Stevenson*; Egerton, *Mercer*.

42. *Richmond Enquirer*, Jan. 3, 10, 17, Feb. 14, 16, 28, March 2, 5, 1833. Cf. Cooper, *South and the Politics of Slavery*, 54, which repeats the traditional view that the nationalists were "silent and minority partners" in the original Virginia Whig party. While some vocal opponents of the proclamation and supporters of South Carolina broke with Jackson and joined the emerging Whig opposition, they constituted a minority of opposition leaders and represented an even smaller minority of opposition voters.

43. "Statement by the Democratic Republicans of the United States, Washington, July 31, 1835," in Schlesinger and Israel, *History of Presidential Elections* 1:616–38; Wayland, *Andrew Stevenson*, 103–11; Richardson, *Messages and Papers* 3:292–300. At the same time that Jackson put Philip Barbour on the Supreme Court, he named Stevenson to be ambassador to England where he served the interests of Virginia and the Van Buren administration.

44. "Introduction," *United States Magazine and Democratic Review* 1 (1837): 1–15; "Democracy," ibid., 7 (1840): 215–29.

45. Henry Clay to Francis Brooke, Jan. 13, 1838, Harrison Gray Otis to Clay, Jan. 11, 1839, in Colton, *Private Correspondence of Henry Clay*, 423–24, 437–38. See also Peterson, *Great Triumvirate*, 281–91; Seager, *Papers of Clay* 9:117–298.

46. See Gunderson, *Log Cabin Campaign*; Chambers, "The Election of 1840."

47. On the Tyler administration, see Turner, *United States from 1830–1850*, 488–534, George Rawlings Poage, *Henry Clay and the Whig Party* (1936; rept. Gloucester, Mass., 1965); Oscar Doane Lambert, *Presidential Politics in the United States, 1841–1844* (Durham, N.C., 1936); Oliver P. Chitwood, *John Tyler: Statesman of the Old South* (New York, 1939); Robert J. Morgan, *A Whig Embattled: The Presidency under John Tyler* (Lincoln, Nebr., 1954); Robert Seager II, *And Tyler Too: A Biography of John and Julia Tyler* (New York, 1963); William Brock, *Parties and Political Consensus* (Millwood, N.Y., 1979); Norma L. Peterson, *The Presidencies of William Henry Harrison and John Tyler* (Lawrence, Kans., 1989); Robert V. Remini, *Henry Clay: Statesman for the Union* (New York, 1991).

48. Calvin Colton, *The Life and Times of Henry Clay*, 2 vols. (New York, 1846), 2:355–403. See also Seager, *Papers of Clay* 9:470–903.

49. *Congressional Globe*, 27th Cong., 1st sess., 256, 260, 303, 372, 423, app. 351–54, 385–89; Richardson, *Messages and Papers* 4:36–51, 63–72; "The Diary of Thomas Ewing," *AHR* 18 (1912): 97–112; Tyler, *Letters and Times* 2:1–134; Peterson, *Presidencies of Harrison and Tyler*, 57–75; Chitwood, *Tyler*, 219–48; Sidney Nathans, *Daniel Webster and Jacksonian Democracy* (Baltimore, 1973), 148–214.

50. *Congressional Globe*, 27th Cong., 2d sess., 367, 717, 762, 852; Richardson, *Messages and Papers* 4:180–89; Tyler, *Letters and Times* 2:160–89, 553; Stanwood, *Tariff Controversies* 2:1–37; Brock, *Parties and Political Consensus*, 102–6, 234; Peterson, *Harrison and Tyler*, 101–8.

51. Peterson, *Harrison and Tyler*, 77–93.

52. Robertson, *Alexander H. H. Stuart*, 26. On the campaign, see Collier, "James McDowell," 198–230, and the various county party notices in late August and September, such as those from the Democrats of Westmoreland in the *Richmond Enquirer*, Sept. 18, 1840.

53. *Congressional Globe*, 27th Cong., 2d sess., app., 355, 382; Warren, *Supreme Court in United States History* 2:366–75; James Elliott Walmsley, "William Smith," *DAB*.

54. Dingledine, "William C. Rives," 378–481; William C. Rives to Judith Rives, June 17, 27, 1841, William C. Rives Papers, LC; Stanard, "William Segar Archer," *DAB*; William S. Archer to Richard T. Archer, Jan. 10, May 23, 1844, Feb. 7, 1845, Richard Thompson Archer Family Papers, UT.

55. *Niles' Register* 61 (1842): 35–36, 62 (1842): 389, 395–97, 64 (1843): 331–32; *Lynchburg Virginian*, March 14, 17, 21, 31, 1842, *Kanawha Republican* (Charleston), July 16, 30, Aug. 6, 20, 21, 1842, March 16, 20, 1843; *Richmond Whig*, July 22, 1843. See also Callahan, "George William Summers"; Thomas Perkins Abernethy, "Alexander Hugh Holmes Stuart," *DAB*; Walmsley, "John Minor Botts"; Lonnie E. Haness and Richard D. Chesteen, "The First Attempt at Presidential Impeachment: Partisan Politics and Intra-Party Conflict at Loose," *Presidential Studies Quarterly* 10 (1980): 51–62.

56. *Richmond Enquirer*, late summer and fall 1842.

57. Friedman, *Revolt of the Conservative Democrats*, 101–26; Tyler to Clay, Sept. 18, 1839, April 30, 1841, in Tyler, *Letters and Times* 3:75–76; 92–94; Richardson, *Messages and Papers* 4:63–72.

58. Richardson, *Messages and Papers* 4:63–72; Tyler to Beverley Tucker, April 9, May 25, 1841, June 16, 1842, Henry A. Wise to Tucker, May 29, June 5, 18, Aug. 29, 1841, Tyler to Abel P. Upshur, June 14, 1842, James Lyons to Tyler, Aug. 28, 1841, Tyler to Littleton Waller Tazewell, Oct. 11, Nov. 2, 1841, in Tyler, *Letters and Times* 2:33, 34, 37–38, 46–47, 90–91, 117–18, 129, 168–69; Wise's speech in ibid., 60–64; Chitwood, *Tyler*, 271–72; Rives to Tyler, May 4, 15, 1841, Tyler to Rives, May 8, 1841, Rives to Judith Rives, May 30, June 1, 17, 27, 1841, William C. Rives Papers, LC. See also Charles Grove Haines and Foster H. Sherwood, *The Role of the Supreme Court in American Government and Politics, 1835–1864* (Berkeley, Calif., 1957), 193–200. Tyler, *Letters and Times* 2:79, interprets the case as one "emphatically treating the States as sovereign communities."

59. Hall, *Upshur*, 106–19; Ames, *State Documents on Federal Relations*, 232–33; Francis Mallory to R. M. T. Hunter, Jan. 12, 1840, Thomas W. Gilmer to Hunter, March 11, 1840, in Ambler, "Correspondence of Hunter," 31–34; Thomas W. Gilmer to John Slater et al., April 12, 1841, Thomas W. Gilmer to George R. Gilmer, Dec. 18, 1838, Thomas W. Gilmer to Franklin Minor, Feb. 12, Dec. 30, 1840, Aug. 7, 1841, in Tyler, *Letters and Times* 1:610–11, 2:699–709; Gordon, "Thomas Walker Gilmer"; Wise, *Henry A. Wise*, 90–101; Simpson, *A Good Southerner*, 52–55.

60. Tyler to Littleton Waller Tazewell, Feb. 11, 1835, Oct. 24, 1842, Abel P. Upshur to Beverley Tucker, Dec. 12, 1841, and n.d., in Tyler, *Letters and Times* 2:247–49; *Daily Madisonian* (Washington, D.C.), April 27, May 7, June 15, 17, 29, 1842. See also Littleton W. Tazewell to John Tazewell, Oct. 24, 1842, Aug. 15, 1843, Tazewell Family Papers, LV; Friedman, *Revolt of the Conservative Democrats*, 101–20.

61. Hall, *Upshur*, 96–102; Haines and Sherwood, *Role of the Supreme Court, 1835–1864*, 16–23; [Abel P. Upshur], *A Brief Enquiry into the True Nature and Character of Our Federal Government, Being a Review of Judge Story's Commentaries on the Consti-*

tution of the United States (1840; rept. Philadelphia, 1863); Brugger, *Beverley Tucker,* 101 – 6, 138. Ruffin was also a correspondent of the president.

62. Merk, *Slavery and the Annexation of Texas,* 3 – 33, 185 – 204, 213 – 17. See also Simpson, *A Good Southerner,* 45 – 60; Hall, *Upshur,* 194 – 213; James P. Shenton, *Robert John Walker: A Politician from Jackson to Lincoln* (New York, 1961), 23 – 55; Frederick Merk, *Fruits of Propaganda in the Tyler Administration* (Cambridge, Mass., 1971).

63. Merk, *Slavery and the Annexation of Texas,* 33 – 44; *Daily Madisonian* (Washington, D.C.), Oct. 30, 31, Nov. 15, 16, 27, 1843; David Pletcher, *The Diplomacy of Annexation* (Columbia, Mo., 1973), 113 – 38; Tyler, *Letters and Times* 2 : 269 – 302.

64. Merk, *Slavery and the Annexation of Texas,* 44 – 83; Pletcher, *Diplomacy of Annexation,* 139 – 71; *Congressional Globe,* 28th Cong., 1st sess., 393 – 96.

65. Merk, *Slavery and the Annexation of Texas,* 101 – 20; Pletcher, *Diplomacy of Annexation,* 172 – 208; Richardson, *Messages and Papers* 4 : 307 – 13, 330 – 52.

66. *Congressional Globe,* 28th Cong., 2d sess., 362, 372.

67. *Richmond Enquirer,* April 29, May 6, 1845; *Lynchburg Virginian,* Feb. 3, 17, 24, March 6, 10, April 14, May 1, 5, 1845; *Richmond Whig,* Feb. 25, May 2, 1845; Norborne E. Sutton to William C. Rives, Jan. 31, 1845, James F. Strother to Rives, Feb. 2, 13, 1845, James Lyons to Rives, Feb. 3, 1845, in William C. Rives Papers, LC; Robert G. Scott to Calhoun, April 27, 1845, in Jameson, "Correspondence of Calhoun," 1032 – 35; Dixon Lewis to Hunter, Feb. 1, 1845, in Ambler, "Correspondence of Hunter," 74. There were a few vocal pro-Texas Whigs, other than the Tylerites, but historians have exaggerated their importance.

68. On the Polk administration, see Charles Sellers, *James K. Polk: Continentalist, 1843 – 1846* (Princeton, N.J., 1966); Paul H. Bergeron, *Presidency of James K. Polk* (Lawrence, Kans., 1988).

69. See also Shenton, *Robert John Walker,* 70 – 87; Joel H. Silbey, *The Shrine of Party: Congressional Voting Behavior, 1841 – 1852* (Pittsburgh, 1967), 49 – 97; Alexander, *Sectional Stress and Party Strength,* 51 – 69; Turner, *United States, 1830 – 1850,* 535 – 73; Brock, *Parties and Political Consensus,* 114 – 83.

70. Frederick Merk, *Manifest Destiny and Mission in American History* (New York, 1963), 26 – 60; Major L. Wilson, *Space, Time, and Freedom: The Quest for Nationality and the Irrepressible Conflict* (Westport, Conn. 1974), 94 – 119. For a collection of documents, see Norman Graebner, ed., *Manifest Destiny* (Indianapolis, 1968).

71. *Richmond Enquirer,* Feb. 19, 1847. On the Wilmot Proviso, see Morrison, *Democratic Politics and Sectionalism;* Eric Foner, "The Wilmot Proviso Revisited," *Journal of American History* 46 (1969): 262 – 79; David Potter, *The Irrepressible Conflict* (New York, 1974), 18 – 89; Don Fehrenbacher, *The South and Three Sectional Crises* (Baton Rouge, La., 1980), 25 – 45.

72. Ames, *State Documents on Federal Relations,* 244 – 47.

73. David Campbell to William E. Campbell, March 4, 1847, Campbell Family Papers, DU; R. K. Crallé to John C. Calhoun, April 18, 1847, in Jameson, "Correspondence of Calhoun," 1112 – 16; *Richmond Enquirer,* Feb. 20, Feb. 17, 18, March 9, 26, 29, April 7, 1847; *Congressional Globe,* 29th Cong., 2d sess., 453 – 55, app., 76 – 80, 86.

74. *Richmond Whig,* Feb. 19, 1847; *Richmond Enquirer,* Aug. 27, 1847.

75. *Richmond Whig,* Nov. 24, 1848; Shanks, *Secession Movement in Virginia,* 18 – 27; Walmsley, "William Ballard Preston"; Poage, *Clay and the Whig Party,* 183 – 96; William J. Cooper, Jr., " 'The Only Door': The Territorial Issue, the Preston Bill, and the South-

ern Whigs," in Cooper, Holt, and McCardell, *A Master's Due*, 59 – 86; Louis T. Wigfall to John C. Calhoun, Jan 4, 1849, in Chauncey S. Boucher and Robert P. Brooks, eds., "Correspondence Addressed to John C. Calhoun, 1837 – 1844," *Annual Report of the American Historical Association for the Year 1929* (Washington, D.C., 1930), 493 – 95; *Richmond Whig*, Dec. 22, 1848; *Washington, D.C., Union*, Dec. 9, 10, 1848, Jan. 13, 16, 20, 21, 27, 28, Feb. 4, 8, 16, 1849; *Congressional Globe*, 30th Cong., 2d sess., 477 – 80.

76. *Niles' Register* 75 (1849): 45 – 46, 84 – 88, 100 – 104; *Richmond Enquirer*, Jan. 23, 26, 30, Feb. 2, 1849.

77. *Journal of the House of Delegates . . . 1848*, 148 – 49; *Richmond Enquirer*, Dec. 25, 1848, Jan. 2, 30, 1849; Belohlavek, "Floyd as Governor of Virginia"; *Richmond Whig*, Jan. 2, 1849; *Alexandria Gazette* reprinted in the *Richmond Enquirer*, Jan. 9, 1849; Ames, *State Documents on Federal Relations*, 249 – 52; *Niles' Register* 75 (1849): 73; John C. Calhoun to Mrs. T. G. Clemson, Jan. 24, 1849, in Jameson, "Correspondence of Calhoun," 761 – 62. The *Richmond Enquirer* praised the resolutions, and in Congress both Hunter and Mason supported them. Even the Whigs felt the northern personal liberty laws "a deliberate insult" and saw the need for a fugitive slave law. C. J. Faulkner to Calhoun, July 15, 1847, in Boucher and Brooks, "Letters to Calhoun," 385 – 87.

78. *Richmond Enquirer*, May 4, 15, 1849, Nov. 23, 1849. The other Whig in the Virginia delegation to the Thirty-first Congress that debated the compromise measures of 1850, Thomas S. Haymond, was a lawyer from Morgantown in the northwest corner of the state who was chosen in a special election to replace an elected Democrat, Alexander Newman, who died in September.

79. *Richmond Enquirer*, March 1, April 26, Sept. 10, 17, 1850; *Richmond Whig*, March 21, May 17, 31, June 21, Sept. 17, 1850; *Lynchburg Virginian*, May 12, 16, June 24, Aug. 15, Sept. 9, 1850. On the Compromise of 1850, see Holman Hamilton, *Prologue to Conflict: The Crisis and Compromise of 1850* (Lexington, Ky., 1964); Robert W. Johannsen, *Stephen A. Douglas* (New York, 1923), 235 – 303; Allan Nevins, *Ordeal of Union: Fruits of Manifest Destiny, 1847 – 1852* (New York, 1947), 219 – 345; Avery O. Craven, *Growth of Southern Nationalism, 1848 – 1861* (Baton Rouge, La., 1953), 57 – 115; David M. Potter, *The Impending Crisis, 1848 – 1861* (New York, 1976), 90 – 120; Peterson, *Great Triumvirate*, 415 – 93; Freehling, *Road to Disunion*, 487 – 510; Peter B. Knupfer, *The Union as It Is: Constitutional Unionism and Sectional Compromise, 1787 – 1861* (Chapel Hill, N.C., 1991); Shanks, *Secession Movement in Virginia*, 18 – 46.

80. Richardson, *Messages and Papers* 5:9 – 24; Poage, *Clay and the Whig Party*, 197 – 264.

81. "Speech on the Admission of California — and the General State of the Union," in Ross M. Lence, ed., *Union and Liberty: The Political Philosophy of John C. Calhoun* (Indianapolis, 1992), 571 – 601; Mason, *James Murray Mason*, 72 – 85; Charles M. Wiltse, *John C. Calhoun: Sectionalist, 1839 – 1850* (Indianapolis, 1951), 458 – 65.

82. Shanks, *Secession Movement in Virginia*, 39 – 41; Henry A. Wise to R. M. T. Hunter, Feb. 1851, in Ambler, "Correspondence of Hunter," 124.

83. *Richmond Enquirer*, Jan. 10, March 26, April 16, 17, 1850.

84. Ibid., Oct. 16, 1849; *Richmond Whig*, April 9, 1850; Shanks, *Secession Movement in Virginia*, 29 – 35. See Thelma Jennings, *The Nashville Convention: Southern Movement for Unity, 1848 – 1851* (Memphis, 1980). Willoughby Newton was a Calhounite Whig. Thomas S. Gholson is called by Jennings a "states' rights Whig." Although he had been a Barbour delegate to the 1832 Jacksonian convention and showed sympathy for South

Carolina in the assembly in 1833, Gholson did not serve in the assembly again. Both men prided themselves on their republican independence and were moderates in Nashville.

85. Hamilton, *Prologue*, 191–200; Ambler, "Correspondence of Hunter," 104–19.

86. *Richmond Whig*, Nov. 22, 29, 1850; John Minor Botts, *The Great Rebellion: Its Secret History, Rise, Progress, and Disastrous Failure* (New York, 1866), 97–101; *Congressional Globe*, 36th Cong., 2d sess., 56; Mason, *James Murray Mason*, 85; James A. Seddon to R. M. T. Hunter, Jan. 18, 1852, in Ambler, "Correspondence of Hunter," 131–32.

87. *Richmond Enquirer*, Nov. 12, 19, 1850; *Richmond Whig*, Nov. 29, 1850; Ames, *State Documents on Federal Relations*, 268–70, 75–76; *Proceedings and Address of the Central Southern Rights Association to the Citizens of Virginia, Adopted January 10, 1851* (Richmond, 1851); "A Citizen of Virginia" [Muscoe R. H. Garnett], *The Union Past and Future: How It Works and How to Save It* (Charleston, S.C., 1850); James Mercer Garnett, "Biographical Sketch of Hon. Muscoe Russell Hunter Garnett of Essex County, Virginia (1821–1864)," *WMQ* 17 (1909–10): 17–37, 71–89.

88. *Richmond Enquirer*, June 23, Aug. 6, Sept. 2, Oct. 17, 21, 1851. The *Richmond Enquirer*, May 8, 1851, denied that Jefferson ever opposed slavery.

89. Shanks, *Secession Movement in Virginia*, 42–45; *Richmond Times* reprinted in *Richmond Enquirer*, Aug. 6, 1851; John Minor Botts to Alexander H. H. Stuart, Nov. 30, 1851, Alexander H. H. Stuart Papers, UVA.

90. On Caskie, see the *Richmond Enquirer*, Nov. 19, 26, 1850. Letcher privately questioned McDowell's commitment to southern rights, and Faulkner, who as a representative of a district in the northernmost part of the Valley was particularly concerned by the fugitive slave issue, later went over to the Democrats after Clay's death. The *Enquirer*, the *South Side Democrat* (Farmville), and the *Fredericksburg Recorder*, all reprinted Summers's speech from 1832 and attacked his abolitionist tendencies along with his commitment to the Bank, tariffs, and internal improvements. Johnson, they pointedly noted, had no connection with the "abolitionists" of 1832. *Richmond Enquirer*, Nov. 3, 4, 8, 21. While the Democrats did much better among the nonvoters of 1848, the Whigs who voted then voted Whig in 1852 and the Democrats of 1848 voted Democratic.

	1848 Pres.	1851 Gov.
Democrat	46,739	65,527
Whig	45,265	57,040

An estimate based on ecological regression confirms that there was no movement from one party to the other between 1848 and 1851.

	1848 Dem.	1848 Whig	1848 Nonvoters
1851 Democrat	25	0	8
1851 Whig	24	25	8
1851 Nonvoter	3	23	39

8. Political Development and Political Decay

1. See Hartz, *Liberal Tradition in America*; Hartz, *Economic Policy and Democratic Thought: Pennsylvania, 1776–1860* (Cambridge, Mass., 1948); Hartz, *The Founding of New Societies* (New York, 1964); Asher Horowitz and Gad Horowitz, "*Everywhere They*

Are in Chains": Political Theory from Rousseau to Marx (Scarborough, Ontario, 1988); David E. Ingersoll and Richard K. Matthews, *The Philosophical Roots of Modern Ideology: Liberalism, Communism, Fascism* (Englewood Cliffs, N.J., 1986). See also Merle Curti, "The Great Mr. Locke: America's Philosopher, 1783–1861," *Huntington Library Bulletin*, no. 11 (April 1937): 107–51; Isaac Kramnick, "Republican Revisionism Revisited," *AHR* 87 (1982): 629–64; John Patrick Diggins, *The Lost Soul of American Politics: Virtue, Self-Interest, and the Foundations of Liberalism* (New York, 1985); Steven M. Dworetz, *The Unvarnished Doctrine: Locke, Liberalism, and the American Revolution* (Durham, N.C., 1990).

2. The 1841 meeting was chaired by western Whig Lewis Summers, who had championed reform in the convention of 1829–30 and was the brother of Whig congressman George Summers.

3. *Memorial to the Legislature of the Commonwealth of Virginia Adopted at Full Meeting of the Citizens of Kanawha, August 9, 1841* (n.p., n.d.); *Kanawha Republican* (Charleston), Dec. 18, 1841, Jan. 15, March 19, May 7, July 9, Aug. 6, 1842. See also Francis Pendleton Gaines, Jr., "The Virginia Constitutional Convention of 1850–51: A Study in Sectionalism" (Ph.D. diss., Univ. of Virginia, 1950), 1–91; Sutton, *Revolution to Secession*, 103–21.

4. *Valley Star* (Charleston), July 17, 1845, Feb. 5, 1846; *Lexington Gazette*, June 26, Aug. 13, Sept. 4, Nov. 13, 20, 1845, Feb. 12, 1846; *Journal of the House of Delegates . . . 1845*, 14–15. Eventually these demands for reform led to the publication of Ruffner's *Address to the People of West Virginia*, which is treated in chapter 6 as part of the opposition to slavery but emphasized the constitutional grievances of the west.

5. Green, *Constitutional Development*, 288; Sutton, *Revolution to Secession*, 111–15; *Richmond Enquirer*, Jan. 27, 1842, Nov. 29, 1845, June 6, Aug. 28, 29, Sept. 1, 1846, Dec. 4, 14, 21, 28, 1849; *Lynchburg Virginian*, Dec. 3, 1849; *Richmond Whig*, Feb. 8, March 19, April 5, 1850.

6. *Journal of the House of Delegates . . . 1849*, 9–12, 261; Sutton, *Revolution to Secession*, 114–17; Belohlavek, "Floyd as Governor of Virginia," 18–19.

7. *Richmond Whig*, Feb. 8, March 19, June 28, July 16, 24, Aug. 23, 1850; *Richmond Enquirer*, April 5, 12, 1850; *Lynchburg Virginian*, June 12, July 22, 24, Aug. 3, 15, Sept. 2, 1850.

8. *Richmond Whig*, July 23, 1850.

9. *Lynchburg Virginian*, Aug. 8, 14, 1850. Ligon's statement was dated July 2, 1850. The designations "radical" and "conservative" are from the *Richmond Whig*, Sept. 3, 1850.

10. *Richmond Whig*, July 19, Aug. 3, 1850. See also *Lynchburg Virginian*, July 24, Aug. 1, 3, 8, 1850.

11. For contemporary conservative criticism, see Beverley Tucker to William Gilmore Simms, March 17, 1851, in Trent, *William Gilmore Simms*, 184–88; Alexander Rives to William C. Rives, Nov. 15, 1850, William C. Rives Papers, LC; John P. Little, *History of Richmond* (rept. Richmond, 1933), 253–96. The antidemocratic "New South" myth-makers ridiculed the constitution at the end of the century. See Julian A. C. Chandler, *A History of Suffrage in Virginia* (Baltimore, 1901); David L. Pulliam, *The Constitutional Conventions of Virginia from the Foundation of the Commonwealth to the Present Time* (Richmond, 1901), 89–90.

12. This analysis is based upon the material collected in Sutton, *Revolution to Secession*, with modest corrections and additions from a variety of other sources.

13. John Harley Warner, "The Idea of Southern Medical Distinctiveness: Medical Knowledge and Practice in the Old South" and "Southern Medical Reform: The Mean-

ing of the Antebellum Argument for Southern Medical Education," in *Science and Medicine in the Old South*, ed. Ronald L. Numbers and Todd L. Savitt (Baton Rouge, La., 1989), 179–225; Todd L. Savitt, *Medicine and Slavery: The Diseases and Health Care of Blacks in Antebellum Virginia* (Urbana, Ill., 1978).

14. See Holland, "Antebellum Virginia Aristocracy."

15. *Richmond Enquirer*, Aug. 29, 1850; *Richmond Whig*, Aug. 30. 1850; *Lynchburg Virginian*, Aug. 29, Sept. 5, 1850; Little, *History of Richmond*, 254, 258; Bradshaw, *History of Prince Edward County*, 174–237; Sutton, *Revolution to Secession*, 120–21.

16. *Richmond Enquirer*, Jan. 27, 1842.

17. *Democratic Review* 29 (1851): 3.

18. C. B. Macpherson, *The Life and Times of Liberal Democracy* (New York, 1977), 23–43; John D. Freeman quoted in Rush Welter, *The Mind of America, 1820–1860* (New York, 1975), 166; *Democratic Review* 1 (1838): 148. See also Welter, *Mind of America*, 165–249, 415–30; Bayrd Still, "An Interpretation of the Statehood Process, 1800 to 1850," *Mississippi Valley Historical Review* 23 (1936): 189–204; Still, "State Constitutional Development in the United States, 1829–1851" (Ph.D. diss., Univ. of Wisconsin, 1933).

19. See Meyers, *Jacksonian Persuasion*; John Higham, *From Boundlessness to Consolidation: The Transformation of American Culture, 1848–1860* (Ann Arbor, Mich., 1961); John William Ward, "Jacksonian Democratic Thought: 'A Natural Charter of Privilege,'" in *The Development of an American Culture*, ed. Stanley Coben and Lorman Ratner (Englewood Cliffs, N.J., 1970), 44–63; Joel H. Silbey, *A Respectable Minority: The Democratic Party in the Civil War Era, 1860–1868* (New York, 1977), 3–29; Baker, *Affairs of Party*; Kohl, *Politics of Individualism*.

20. Shade, *Banks or No Banks*, 112–44.

21. James Willard Hurst, *Law and the Condition of Freedom in the Nineteenth-Century United States* (Madison, Wis., 1956), 3–32; Lee Benson, *The Concept of Jacksonian Democracy: New York as a Test Case* (Princeton, N.J., 1961), 216–53; Glyndon G. Van Deusen, "Some Aspects of Whig Thought and Theory in the Jacksonian Period," *AHR* 63 (1958): 305–22; Elliott R. Barkan, "The Emergence of the Whig Persuasion: Conservatism, Democratism and the New York State Whigs," *New York History* 52 (Oct. 1971): 367–95; Barkan, *Portrait of a Party: The Origins and Development of the Whig Persuasion in New York State* (New York, 1987); Howe, *Political Culture of the American Whigs*; Wilson, *Space, Time, and Freedom*; Phyllis F. Field, *The Politics of Race in New York: The Struggle for Black Suffrage in the Civil War Era* (Ithaca, N.Y., 1982), 19–114; Brown, *Politics and Statesmanship*; J. David Greenstone, *The Lincoln Persuasion: Remaking American Liberalism* (Princeton, N.J., 1993).

22. Gaines, "The Virginia Constitutional Convention of 1850–51," 143–62; William G. Bishop, reporter, *Register of the Debates and Proceedings of the Va. Reform Convention* (Richmond, 1851), 299, 333, 373; Simpson, *A Good Southerner*, 78–86.

23. Gaines, "The Virginia Constitutional Convention of 1850–51," 128–42; *Richmond Enquirer Supplement*, March 3, 7, 1851; Sutton, *Revolution to Secession*, 130.

24. *Debates and Proceedings from Reform Convention*, 114, 116, 315, 292–93, 283–84.

25. Ibid., 311–16.

26. Ibid., 88–91, 105–19.

27. Sutton, *Revolution to Secession*, 139–40.

28. *Debates and Proceedings of Reform Convention*, 302, 313.

29. Ibid., 284, 293–316; Craig Simpson, "Political Compromise and the Protection of Slavery: Henry A. Wise and the Virginia Constitutional Convention of 1850–51," *VMHB*

83 (1975): 387 – 405; Sutton, *Revolution to Secession*, 128 – 132, 136 – 37, 139 – 40; Gaines, "Virginia Constitutional Convention of 1850 – 51," 140 – 41, 158 – 62, 263 – 66.

30. *Journal, Acts, and Proceedings of a General Convention of the State of Virginia . . .* (Richmond, Va., 1850), 331. For comments on western hostility to lowering the tax on slaves, see Letcher in the debates and an undated fragment from this time in the Campbell Family Papers, DU.

31. Little, *History of Richmond*, 258; Gaines, "Virginia Constitutional Convention of 1850 – 51," 169 – 213; *Journal, Acts, and Proceedings*, 75, 190 – 92, 240, 310 – 11, 313, 315 – 16. The Whigs split on a poll tax sponsored by eastern Democrats, but partisanship was far less important than sectional affiliation. See Stephen J. White, "The Partisan Political Elements in the Virginia Constitutional Convention of 1850 – 51," seminar paper done for Michael F. Holt, Univ. of Virginia.

32. *Journal, Acts, and Proceedings*, 283 – 85.

33. Thorpe, *Federal and State Constitutions* 7 : 3829 – 52; *Journal, Acts and Proceedings*, 337 – 38, 347, 352. Cf. Shade, *Banks or No Banks*; Sharp, *Jacksonians versus the Banks*.

34. *Journal, Acts, and Proceedings*, 351, 381 – 82, 391 – 92, 401 – 3.

35. Ibid., 419. The president of the convention, John Y. Mason, had been an opponent of reform in the convention of 1829 – 30. He served as a Jacksonian congressman, was appointed to the federal bench by Martin Van Buren, then served in the cabinets of Tyler and Polk. Mason was a vigorous exponent of Manifest Destiny, and when Franklin Pierce sent him to be minister to France, he helped draft the Ostend Manifesto. Mason voted against the reform constitution.

36. Cf. Simpson, "Political Compromise and the Protection of Slavery," and Freehling, *Road to Disunion*, 511 – 15, who see the constitution as a victory for the conservatives because of the apportionment of the upper house and the clause concerning slave taxation.

37. Samuel P. Huntington, *Political Order in Changing Societies* (New Haven, 1968).

38. Holt, *Political Crisis of the 1850s*, 219 – 59; Joseph F. Rishel, "West Virginia: Analysis of the Secession Referendum, May 23, 1861," *West Virginia History* 32 (1970): 49 – 53.

39. Ambler, *Sectionalism*, 300 – 38; Shanks, *Secession Movement in Virginia*, 18 – 120; Stanley, "Party Conflict and the Secessionist Alternative"; Clement Eaton, "Henry Wise: A Study in Virginia Leadership, 1850 – 1861," *West Virginia History* 3 (1942): 187 – 204; Philip M. Rice, "The Know-Nothing Party in Virginia, 1854 – 56," *VMHB* 55 (1947): 51 – 75, 159 – 67; Simpson, *A Good Southerner*, 106 – 56; Clement Eaton, "Henry A. Wise and the Virginia Fire Eaters of 1856," *Mississippi Valley Historical Review* 21 (1935): 495 – 512; F. N. Boney, *John Letcher of Virginia: The Story of Virginia's Civil War Governor* (University, Ala., 1966); William G. Bean, "John Letcher and the Slavery Issue in Virginia Gubernatorial Contest of 1858 – 59," *JSH* 20 (1954): 22 – 49.

40. Douglas received 15 percent of the 1856 Buchanan vote and 5 percent of the American vote. He was strongest in the Valley and the northwest, but he did get votes — probably from ex-Whigs — in the more commercially developed eastern counties. Lincoln got 1.5 percent of the vote, entirely in northern counties along the Potomac and Ohio rivers. On Virginia politics in the 1850s, see Daniel Crofts, *Reluctant Confederates: Upper South Unionists in the Secession Crisis* (Chapel Hill, N.C., 1989); David R. Goldfield, "The Triumph of Politics over Society: Virginia, 1851 – 61," (Ph.D. diss., Univ. of Maryland, 1970); Patricia Hicken, "John C. Underwood and the Anti-Slavery Movement in Virginia, 1847 – 1860," *VMHB* 73 (1965): 156 – 68; Richard Lowe, "The Republican Party in Antebellum Virginia, 1856 – 1860," *VMHB* 81 (1973): 259 – 79.

41. This is based on Crofts, *Reluctant Confederates*, and the results of his ecological regressions on all of the elections from 1851 to 1861. The interelections correlations (pp. 55–57) are fairly high but below those for the previous decade. Crofts turnout rates, like those of McCormick for the earlier period, are a bit lower than those presented by Burnham (which I have used to maintain consistency). Some of this material was supplied to me by Crofts and is not displayed in his book.

42. *Eighth Census . . . 1860, Population,* 518–20; Gates, *Farmer's Age,* 109, 160; Peterson, *Historical Study of Virginia Prices,* 188–92; Robert, *Tobacco Kingdom,* 143–57; Lynda J. Morgan, *Emancipation in Virginia's Tobacco Belt, 1850–1870* (Athens, Ga., 1992), 33–76; *A Compendium of the Ninth Census . . . 1870* (Washington, D.C., 1872), 798–99.

43. *Eighth Census . . . 1860, Population,* 599; *Eighth Census . . . 1860, Agriculture,* 247–48.

44. Olmsted, *The Cotton Kingdom,* 38; *Eighth Census . . . 1860, Population,* 522, 598–99, 619, 623. The foreign-born population grew by 64 percent. See Goldfield, *Urban Growth in the Age of Sectionalism*; Berlin and Gutman, "Natives and Immigrants, Free Men and Slaves: Urban Workingmen in the Antebellum South"; George W. Smith, "Antebellum Attempts of Northern Business Interests to 'Redeem' the Upper South," *JSH* 11 (1945): 177–213; Richard H. Abbott, "Yankee Farmers of Northern Virginia, 1840–1860," *VMHB* 76 (1968): 56–66.

45. See Holland, "Rise and Fall of the Ante-Bellum Virginia Aristocracy."

46. George Reese, ed., *Proceedings of the Virginia State Convention of 1861, February 13–May 1,* 4 vols. (Richmond, 1965), 1:766, 2:10–25. Of course, many slaveholders complained that higher taxes would drive them out of business. In *Speculators and Slaves: Masters, Traders, and Slaves in the Old South* (Madison, Wis., 1989), 12, Michael Tadman estimates that in the decade Virginia slave owners sold 82,000 slaves out of the state.

47. Crofts, *Reluctant Confederates,* 55, 189. This analysis is based on that of Crofts, pp. 164–94. The correlation between the Constitutional Unionist vote and that of the Whigs in 1852 was .75, but that between the 1852 Whig vote and the unionist vote in February was only .24.

48. This analysis is from material supplied by Crofts, who analyzed the election in detail in *Reluctant Confederates,* 164–94. Estimates of the number of secessionists vary from thirty to fifty: see Shanks, *Secession Movement in Virginia,* 153; Wooster, *Secession Conventions,* 142; Simpson, *A Good Southerner,* 240; and Crofts, *Reluctant Confederates,* 140. On the limits of Virginia unionism, see Dean A. Arnold, "The Ultimatum of Virginia Unionists: 'Security for Slavery or Disunion,'" *Journal of Negro History* 48 (1963): 115–29; William S. Hitchcock, "Southern Moderates and Secession: Senator Robert M. T. Hunter's Call for Union," *Journal of American History* 59 (1973): 871–84; Hitchcock, "The Limits of Southern Unionism: Virginia's Conservatives and the Gubernatorial Election of 1859," *JSH* 47 (1981): 57–72; Shearer Davis Bowman, "Conditional Unionism and Slavery in Virginia, 1860–61: The Case of Dr. Richard Eppes," *VMHB* 96 (1988): 31–54.

49. Wooster, *Secession Conventions,* 239–54; Wooster, *Politicians, Planters, and Plain Folk,* 133, 154, 170, 147.

50. William H. Gaines, Jr., *Biographical Register of Members Virginia State Convention of 1861, First Session* (Richmond, 1969). Wise, Tyler, and Randolph were consistent advocates of secession. The political affiliations are from the *Richmond Enquirer's* lists of legislators, congressmen, and constitutional convention members from 1835 to 1852. See

also Anne Sarah Rubin, "Between Union and Chaos: The Political Life of John Janney," *VMHB* 102 (1994): 383 – 416.

51. "Reply to a Committee from the Virginia Convention" and "Proclamation Calling Militia and Convening Congress," in Roy P. Basler, ed., *The Collected Works of Abraham Lincoln* (New Brunswick, N.J., 1953), 4:329 – 332; *Richmond Enquirer,* April 15, 1861; Shanks, *Secession Movement in Virginia,* 191 – 213; Crofts, *Reluctant Confederates,* 308 – 33.

52. Wise, *Seven Decades of Union,* 221 – 25; Simpson, *A Good Southerner,* 57 – 58. Wise claimed that he had made Calhoun secretary of state after the *Princeton* disaster in 1844 by presenting President Tyler with a fait accompli.

53. James B. Dorman to Davidson, April 16, 1861, James D. Davidson Papers, WSHS; *Richmond Enquirer,* April 15, 17, 18, 22, 1861; Wise, *Seven Decades of Union,* 223, 276 – 79; Simpson, *A Good Southerner,* 239 – 51; Shanks, *Secession Movement in Virginia,* 202 – 7; Crofts, *Reluctant Confederates,* 308 – 41; William K. Scarborough, ed., *Diary of Edmund Ruffin,* 2 vols. (Baton Rouge, La., 1976), 2:568 – 71; John Sherman Long, "The Gosport Affair," *JSH* 23 (1957): 155 – 72; Boney, *John Letcher,* 112 – 16; Wise, *Henry A. Wise,* 274 – 80.

54. Wooster, *Secession Conventions,* 149; Shanks, *Secession Movement in Virginia,* 204 – 7.

55. This does not mean that the process was without intimidation of various forms. See Crofts, *Reluctant Confederates,* 340 – 47.

56. *Richmond Enquirer* April 9, 1861.

57. Reese, *Proceedings of the Virginia State Convention of 1861* 1:44 – 45.

Index